THE PASTOR

THE PASTORAL THEOLOGY OF WILHELM LOEHE

The Pastor

J. K. Wilhelm Loehe

Edited by Charles P. Schaum
Translated by Wolf Dietrich Knappe
and Charles P. Schaum

CONCORDIA PUBLISHING HOUSE • SAINT LOUIS

Der evangelische Geistliche

Offered to the next generation of evangelical pastors.
1852/1858

Copyright © 2015 by Concordia Publishing House
3558 S. Jefferson Ave., St. Louis, MO 63118-3968
1-800-325-3040 • www.cph.org

Manufactured in the United States of America

Library of Congress Cataloging-in-Publication Data

Loehe, Wilhelm, 1808–1872.

[Evangelische Geistliche. English]

The pastor / J.K. Wilhelm Loehe ; edited by Charles P. Schaum ; translated by Wolf Dietrich Knappe and Charles P. Schaum.

pages cm

Includes bibliographical references and index.

ISBN 978-0-7586-5027-6

1. Pastoral theology—Lutheran Church. I. Title.

BV4011.3.L6413 2015

253--dc23 2015012206

4 5 6 7 8 9 10 29 28 27 26 25

Contents

Editor's Notes

Johann Konrad Wilhelm Loehe intended this work to be a practical resource for Protestant clergy written from a Lutheran standpoint. He used *evangelisch* and other words often in the broader Protestant context.[1] He also used Roman Catholic theological vocabulary in a way that caused controversy in his day as he sought to be ecumenical and Lutheran. This work highlights the general Christian history and practice of pastoral care. This study edition for church professionals facilitates practical use. It is not a critical edition.

A Short Treatise on How to Preach Aright and How to Expound and Apply the Sacred Text is included as Appendix C. It was penned by Andreas Adam Hochstetter (1668–1717), who received a master's degree in 1683 and held contacts with theologians in Germany, Holland, and England. Like his father, he was a professor in Tübingen, among other high church offices.

Translating this book involves the art of discerning the intent of the author and his setting. For example, here *Methodismus* is not "Methodism" but "methodology." *Länder* usually refers to the states and territories in Germany. *Geistlich* refers to pastoral matters and is translated as "pastoral." Other examples abound.

Loehe included Greek and Latin sources without translation because mastery of Greek and Latin was required for most Lutheran clergy for centuries after the Reformation. Sadly that is less so today. Greek and Latin texts here are translated in the body text with the original texts in the footnotes. Some errors in Loehe's text have been corrected without comment. Substantive changes are discussed in the footnotes. Scripture passages either conform to the ESV or are translated from the German as indicated. Greek texts come from Loehe, the SBL Greek New Testament, and other named sources that may vary at times from Loehe's sources.

Enumeration of footnotes begins with 1 for each chapter and appendix. Footnotes from the original text begin with [Loehe:]. Other footnotes are editorial changes, annotations, and additions. Where it is necessary for editorial comments to appear in Loehe's footnotes, they are indicated by [Editor's note:].

Originally, chapter titles were enumerated with A, B, C, etc. The first booklet used Roman numerals for section headings while the second used Arabic numerals. The first booklet enumerated various paragraphs while the second did not. For consistency and readability we have chosen a system based on *Pastoral Theology* by John H. C. Fritz (St. Louis: Concordia, 1945).

---

[1] This is in keeping with G. C. Adolf von Harless (Harleß, 1806–79), who brokered a resolution to conflict between Lutherans and Reformed in the Bavarian Territorial Church. The Reformed and Lutherans each got their own synod.

We retain the topic numbering in the first booklet, but we have created new paragraphs where Loehe explores subtopics. This makes the text more readable, less of a "run-on," in English. We have adapted a more readable style of English that does not attempt to correspond word-for-word with the original.

Words appearing with emphasis (*Sperrdruck* in the original) are rendered in **boldface** here. Non-English words within English text are in *italic*. Em-dashes in the German that only show a pause have been changed to paragraph breaks or removed.[2]

Some material is absent here. That includes a chapter-length poem, "The Good Life of a Virtuous Servant of God," by Johann Valentin Andreä (1586–1654), sometime court preacher in Württemberg, among other high offices. The challenges of translating seventeenth-century German rhyme, meter, and dialect into suitable English verse exceed the scope of this publication.

The lengthy documentary commentaries (*Erläuterungen*) from the complete edition of Loehe's works[3] are not translated here. They include an introduction and a brief sketch of Loehe's work on pastoral theology, a lengthy appendix on the medical interplay between body and soul, and a detailed study of textual variants, remarks, and related texts from the 1844 "Pastoral Theology" manuscripts, Loehe's diary, letters, and other sources. Such material is suited for a scholarly critical edition and would comprise a volume in itself.

---

[2] Through the nineteenth century and into the early twentieth it was common practice to indicate a dramatic pause, as it were, with either an em-dash or the so-called "dog's bollocks" (:—).

[3] Wilhelm Loehe, *Gesammelte Werke*, herausgegeben im Auftrage der Gesellschaft für Innere und Äussere Mission im Sinne der Lutherischen Kirche e.V. von Klaus Ganzert (Neuendettelsau: Freimund-Verlag, 1951–86).

Booklet One

FOREWORD

The following pages are a reworking of the article "Contributions to Pastoral Theology" that was submitted in the years 1847–48 to the Erlangen University journal, *Zeitschrift für Protestantismus und Kirche* [*Journal for Protestantism and Church*]. The appendix for pastors' wives first was printed in Brandt's *Die Christliche Jungfrau im Brautstande* [*The Christian Virgin in the Bridal Estate*] (Frankfurt am Main: Schmerber, 1838). For the newly arranged printing [of 1852], based on multiple requests, the excellent poem of Valentin Andreä, "Concerning the Good Life of a Virtuous Servant of God" [was] included.[1] For that, one hardly needs any apology.

This entire booklet deals especially with the personal affairs of a pastor. If it finds favor with the intended public for whom the author is writing, a second booklet will follow, in which viewpoints and experiences concerning the various areas of work of the evangelical pastor (sermon, catechesis, liturgy, specific points of pastoral care) will be conveyed.

The standpoint from which I am writing is primarily that of a **country pastor** in the **territorial church** (***Landeskirche***).

In this volume, the confessional questions of the day move to the periphery, as is intended. For that same reason, the title has been chosen as to look outward. A title such as *The Lutheran Pastor* might have promised to offer something that was not intended, even apart from the fact that when one tried to use it, one would sense quite strongly how ill-suited the name of [the] man [Luther] is to the nomenclature of the Holy Office. Yet it should remain self-evident that the author does not therefore betray his confessional convictions.

May this little book serve those for whom it is intended, and may they so heartily receive and approve of it as it is offered to them! God bless the reader and the writer! Amen.

On the Visitation of Mary, 2 July 1852

---

[1] For the materials not included in this edition see the editor's notes above.

Chapter One

Preliminary Matters

A. Some Remarks about Preparation for the Pastoral Office

1. Among us the specific preparation for the pastoral office begins first at the university level. As long as the future servants of the Church are studying at the *Gymnasium*,[1] they are in no way different from the other students, unless they plan ahead and learn Hebrew. Other than that, they enjoy the same common training as all the others that are being prepared at the universities for some specific calling in life.[2]

So, to be fair, one has to admit that this general preparation could also be accomplished in some other way. But first it should be asked: Is it necessary at all for a pastor? It is, for without it the position of a pastor in public life would be completely different. His horizon would be much narrower. Today, from a servant of the Church, one requires knowledge and an overview of all human conditions. This is only fair. For this very reason he needs a certain level of general education. Based on this he will be equal to all levels of society and can claim admittance to even the highest circles. Therefore, this general **preparatory education** is necessary for the pastor, so much more since one cannot trust the *Gymnasium* student at his tender age to choose his life profession sincerely and without regret.[3]

---

[1] The German *Gymnasium* (seed-bed) is a six-year preparatory school between primary school and university. The focus is on a classical humanist education, including high proficiency in Latin and Greek.

[2] In Germany there are specific career tracks that begin at middle school. Exams evaluate students, who are guided either toward college preparation and the *Abitur* final exams or toward more general career and vocational technology paths.

[3] In many European countries, the stratification of society codified by Roman law during the fourth and fifth centuries AD only began to be lifted broadly in the nineteenth century. Many cultures still have a more stratified society, including the Far East's debt to Confucianism's celestial mandate.

True, there is a certain inner calling from God for the pastoral office,[4] which often is manifested in early youth by an unconquerable love and inclination toward this office. But this inclination will not be eliminated or lessened by postponing the final decision to the end of the *Gymnasium* years. On the contrary, if it is genuine, it will be proven, clarified, and strengthened, so that one can walk toward this goal with greater certainty and confidence. In fact, one would have to be suspicious of even the most pronounced inclination if it could not endure the proper preparation and acquire the fruits thereof.

2. There have been complaints at times (see, e.g., Fecht 10)[5] that in the Protestant Church not many truly clever people are turning to the study of theology. If this were true, one would have to feel sorry, both for the clever people and for the study of theology. But in no case could one blame theology itself. Theology and the pastoral office that it is supposed to empower make the greatest demands on a person's strength. Theology rises to the highest heights and descends to the deepest depths; it has the widest scope of knowledge and all other areas of human knowledge border it on all sides. Those areas of knowledge receive light, life, and meaning from theology.

Of all human professions, the pastoral office demands the greatest mental power of production. He who has to give daily must have a rich source from which he can draw. If not, he will sink into a torturous, painful poverty. One therefore should think that especially the richest minds would be drawn toward theology, like iron to a magnet. If this does not happen, as said above, the fault does not lie with theology.

Often a young man cannot choose as he wants to. Some are prevented from recognizing the existing gift and the driving force of the Holy Spirit by the sinful machinations of an evil heart. Among the so-called upper classes, who do not always produce better heads than the lower ones, often riches and worldliness suffocate the desire that is deep in the heart, desire for a study and a profession of which the visible part is insignificant and small, but the invisible is great, and which causes a restless conscience and an inborn desire that inflames the longing for that which is permanent.

---

[4] [Loehe:] The inner call of God (*vocatio Dei interior*). This is what our theologians call the inner, almost innate inclination toward the sacred office. This is rightly so, for God also gives such inclinations. But one must examine the circumstances that can turn such an inclination into something bad. For example, there cannot be a true inner call if, with all the enthusiasm, there is no real gift. Compare [Paul] Tarnov, *De ministerio*, p. 63, Johannes Fecht *Instructio pastoralis*, second edition, Rostock 1729, p. 10ff; Mayer, *Museum ministri ecclesiae* 1708, p. 7.

[5] All references to Fecht are to the edition of *Instructio pastoralis* mentioned above. Johannes Fecht (1636–1716) was a historian and theologian who defended against radical pietism, yet also sought to reform and defend orthodoxy. Johann Friedrich Mayer (1650–1712) was a pastor, church leader, and professor in Leipzig, Wittenberg, Kiel, and Greifswald. He approved piety but opposed conventicles.

3. This is another question, one that the point given above does not negate in any way: Might one not even use mediocre and small gifts in a blessed manner in the Church under certain circumstances? This is not difficult to answer. We spoke of high requirements only in order to defend against the criticism that theology and the pastoral office would not be worthy of better heads.

On the other hand, no one will deny the fact that theology and the pastoral office are two different things. One can perform the office without being a theologian who made much progress in scholarly knowledge. The strength to produce, which is needed by the pastor, by no means depends solely on learned insight. Often it shows itself in the richest and most fruitful way when it is a matter of taking common knowledge available to everyone and applying it to the various conditions of private and public life.[6]

Here often a drop of water turns into a spring gushing up into eternal life. Otherwise, how could it happen that so many pastors with but a few gifts produce the most blessed successes, while on the other hand, often highly gifted and learned men stand in their congregations like tall but fruitless trees?

The truth is that in God's kingdom there are different gifts, and none should be unused. Many gifts are needed for the building of Zion. Each one can find work and its blessing, if only one does not let it shrivel up through one's own fault or through haughty and crippling envy of the gifts and successes of others.

4. Once the future servant of the Church has finished the *Gymnasium* and moves to the university, he is required to dedicate part of his time to the study of the general disciplines.[7] One cannot object to this requirement since one must admit that it is useful and necessary for a pastor to have some general education, which the *Gymnasium* could not give to the fullest extent.

But why not give the young man a certain amount of freedom when it comes to satisfying this requirement? Why not at least give consideration to his individual talent and also to his choice of profession? If only a general education is achieved, then in the end it will make no difference how much time this or that young man might use for it, whether as a full time student all at once or as a part-timer in successive periods. There is a preference for

---

[6] Loehe writes of *inneres und äußeres Leben*, which denotes two spheres. Internal life, a rough synonym for "private," begins with one's thoughts and extends to the home, the most immediate place where those thoughts are expressed and acted on by a person. External life, a rough synonym for "public," begins where home life, such as marriage, vocation, church life, and other responsibilities engage the greater public sphere with their legal and moral aspects and obligations.

[7] German *Wissenschaft* denotes more than just science over against the humanities. It has also the broader meaning of a scholarly discipline, a systematic branch of knowledge that goes beyond individual opinion or tastes to engage factual human knowledge within a broader social context.

letting the general studies precede the professional study, and certainly some of them, like logic and similar subjects, are well suited for the threshold between the *Gymnasium* and academic studies. But would this be true of all general studies? Could it perhaps often be the case that the progress from the specific to the general, from professional study to general study, be just as natural as the progress of love, from brotherly love, which comes first, to the general love [for mankind] that follows?[8] Are not some subjects of study too far removed for many heads, too high, and also requiring mature thinking?

Perhaps there would be a good deal less arguing among students, if they did not have the idea that they **had to be** educated **especially** philosophically according to the newer German thinking. They have no trouble learning the philosophical **terminology**. In a wanton youthful way they apply it to everything, even their teachers, especially those who are to introduce them to their professional studies, and there is no end to their hubris (ὕβρις) until it looks like the portals of an examination hall shall appear in their near future. Then indeed one can say: "Be philosophers, but with few words, for it is altogether harmful."[9]

5. Regarding the specific study of theology, it would be greatly desirable if what is useful in the pastoral office were taught and learned first. True, there is some advantage to a certain carefree learning with free movement in the wide-open spaces of scholarship. But it is always most beneficial to learn what is most necessary. Even if there are limits, most students will have enough freedom of movement.

What good is it if the teacher teaches only what excites and moves him, the teacher, the man of scholarship in his scholarly calling, instead of what will be proven good and blessed in the future vocation? What good is it to elevate the student to the standpoint of a scholarly theologian and introduce him to research that his immature spirit cannot appreciate? What good is it to soar in lofty spheres of scholarly undertakings—or really, to be carried there on the wings of the teacher—when soon one will plunge down to the sober land of one's vocation as a foreigner to it?

Neither teacher nor student thus does justice to their calling. The teacher [errs] in regard to the present, which should be used primarily for equipping

---

[8] Compare C. S. Lewis, *The Four Loves* (New York: Harcourt, Brace, 1960).

[9] *Philosophandum est, sed paucis, nam omnino nocet.* The LCMS strongly criticized nineteenth-century German educators like J. H. Pestalozzi and others. The synod also rejected American progressive models for education, including those of William T. Harris in St. Louis. With the LCMS, other German educators also criticized utilitarian and social Darwinist education methods by Herbert Spencer and other Englishmen. Yet by the 1920s, progressive models from the University of Chicago and the University of Michigan began to make inroads into the synod. In the early 1950s, Edward L. Schapsmeier of Illinois State University guided Concordia Teachers College, River Forest, Illinois to adopt progressive education methods of John Dewey. See also Thomas Korcok, *Lutheran Education: From Wittenberg to the Future* (St. Louis: Concordia, 2011).

future pastors. The student [errs] in regard to the future pastoral office. With this kind of learning one really must pity the many mediocre and not very gifted students—who, by the way, constitute the majority of students—since in this manner they are not helped toward their goal, but become mixed up and incapable! Certainly, in order to avoid laziness of the spirit, daydreams, deceptions, and many detrimental wrong turns, one should remind the students again and again that what awaits most of them is not the lectern of their teachers, but the modest lot of a country pulpit.

A young man, guided by the hand of his teacher of philosophy, had flown into the limitless space of scholarship. He was surprised to find that he had become estranged from the teacher and father of his youth. Since he was not looking for the cause of this in himself, he asked the teacher and received this answer:

> You are a student, while I am a pastor. Your way goes here, there, and everywhere, while mine is small and narrow, the way of the determined profession. You see broad vistas, while I am like a mountain climber who sees only the bit of the way before my feet. Once your wideness becomes narrow again and you steer toward your calling, you will be close to me again, in the manner of a child.

That happened, and it happens often. But often the transition is so difficult, and many a man remains so caught in the ropes of his university years, that he will never be able to adjust to a serious professional life. Some have to pay so dearly for their little bit of pseudo-knowledge that they enter the pastoral office completely useless. For that very reason, they remain unhappy for the rest of their lives. Then they have to say a [lament of] *perdidi* (I have wasted them) with regard to their academic period of four or five years without being able to undo the damage.

6. Clearly, having said all this, there is no shame attached to learning and true scholarship, and I say so expressly. It would be foolish to criticize learning and scholarship indiscriminately, since truly they are found seldom enough. Only, one ought to study the right things, and those things [he should study] quite seriously. One should pay close attention only to faithful academic teachers. More is to be learned from them and better than from any book. There is a more lively and blessed way from mouth to ear than from book to eye. Jerome, in [his treatise] *ad Paulinum*, says: "The living voice has [more] hidden energy [than] I could know, and it is expressed more strongly when going directly from the mouth of the author to the ears of the disciple."[10] One ought to gather knowledge and store it. A. H. Francke says:

---

[10] *Habet nescio quid latentis energiae viva vox et in aures discipuli de ore autoris transfusa forties sonat.* This also was the method used by C. F. W. Walther and others at Concordia Seminary in St. Louis. The student association also printed the professors' class notes.

> If one simply learns a lot, [and what he learns, he learns] well, nothing will be too insignificant. At the right time he will be able to use it. Given the mixed-up conditions of the Church, sometimes even useless things can come to good use, so that one can serve others with them.[11]

Without hesitation, one can say with Theophylact: "Doctrine is the strength and the character of the bishop."[12] With Hilary, [one can say]: "The sum of all the virtues of a bishop is wisdom and doctrine."[13]

Everything that should have been said above can be summed up in these words: "Learn for the pastoral office and let yourself be taught as much as possible with the office in mind." We cannot say it better than with the words of our first teacher of pastoral theology, [Johann Ludwig] Hartmann:

> With a patient, a doctor can talk a lot about the body in an erudite way concerning the differences, the qualities, the causes, and even the healing of sicknesses. He can show to his listeners, and prove and assert experiences. But for the sick person, nothing else will be helpful except the medicine that [the doctor] applies to his present evil. The most potent thing that the doctor says is not about what is the latest and most subtle in medicine, nor, due to the shortness of time, should he talk to the sick person about what he recently read or thought of, but he should only speak to that which can remove the present sickness, and give information and comfort to the sick person. Thus the pastor of the church, who is the doctor of the most precious souls for quite some time, should not seek to make long speeches (of which the listeners often grow tired), which he thought out as they came to him, though they might be erudite and pleasing

---

Jerome (Eusebius Sophronius Hieronymus, c. 347–420) was a priest, confessor, theologian, and historian known best for his translation of the Bible into Latin (the Vulgate), as well as many commentaries, letters, and other works. He was named a Doctor of the Church.

[11] August Hermann Francke (1663–1727) was a pastor, professor, and a pietist leader, a protégé of Philipp Jakob Spener. He became a professor at Halle in 1692, developed a school for the poor, among other mercy efforts, and was the center of the Danish Halle mission that pioneered Lutheran foreign mission efforts.

[12] *Doctrina est virtus et character episcopi.* Theophylact (c. 1050–c. 1108) was the archbishop of Bulgaria from 1090 to his death. He wrote numerous Bible commentaries using the work of Theoderet, John Chrysostom, and others.

[13] *Summa omnium virtutum episcopalium est scientia et doctrina.* Hilary, bishop of Poitiers (c. 315–67), opposed the Arian heresy. After exile to Phrygia in Asia Minor (356–60) he cleared Gaul of Arianism.

to him. But he should be anxious to say what for most of his listeners will bring improvement, information and comfort; see Acts 20:19.[14]

7. If at times things are in bad shape with the program of study that is [designed] to prepare [one] for the Holy Office, this would still be tolerable, except that so many things depend on this one thing. Luther is completely right when he says that prayer, study, and struggle shape a theologian (*oratio, meditatio, tentatio faciunt theologum*). This expression in all its brevity includes everything that is necessary to train [a man] for the Holy Office. But who today says this to himself and to others in all seriousness? Who today seriously emphasizes *oratio* and *tentatio* to the same extent as the *meditatio*?

Some think it might hinder the scientific development of a student if he would occupy himself as much with prayer and struggle as with his studies. Yet what [Johann] Eberlin von Günzburg says is true: "There are two things that should take precedence over all studying: Spiritual devotion and the need of your brother." Another teacher (Johannes Fecht), often maligned yet worthy of respect, is right in warning: "If it is not immediately connected to them at the beginning of one's studies, for many, piety often remains frigid for one's entire life!"[15]

And yet the temptations of students are so great that they should constantly be praying in order to escape them with their soul intact. Think only of the dangers that always are connected with academic studies, but especially in our days! Only a praying spirit is able to experience, suffer, and

---

[14] *Medicus corporis coram aegroto multa erudite de discrimine, qualitate, de causis item et medela morborum disserens suam audientibus ostentare et verbis depraedicare atque adserere potest peritiam: infirm autem aliter prodesse non poterit, quam si pharmaca sua praesenti malo adplicet et ea dicat potissimum, non quae in arte medica sunt acutissima et subtilissima, aut quae ad fallendum tempus dicis causa aegroto narranda nuper legit et excogitavit, sed quae unice faciunt ad praesentis morbid depulsionem et aegroti informationem et consolationem. Ita pastor ecclesiae, qui longe pretiosissimarum animarum est medicus, non quam multa (quibus non raro obtunduntur aiditores) et quam erudite excogitate sibique arridentia et occurentia, sed quam accomodata et pro plerorumque captu maximeque ad auditorium suorum emendationem, informationem et consolationem facientia dicere queat, sollicitam navabit operam. V. Act 20, 19.* J. L. Hartmann (d. 1684) wrote the first Lutheran systematic treatment of pastoral theology. His *Pastorale Evangelicum* (1678), cited here, was used with A. H. Francke's *Collegium Pastorale* (1745), the latter as a commentary on the former. Walther drew on Hartmann periodically in the journal *Lehre und Wehre* and he incorporated its ideas into his *Amerikanisch-Lutherische Pastoraltheologie*. Walther also used Hartmann's *ministerium in abstracto* and *ministerium in concreto* in his own work on the relationship between the Church and the pastoral office. See also Walther, *The Church and The Office of The Ministry*, edited by Matthew C. Harrison (St. Louis: Concordia, 2012). All references to Hartmann are to *Pastorale Evangelicum*.

[15] *Frigida est plerumque per totam vitam pietas, quae non statim cum ipsa studiorum origine conjuncta fuit!* Johann Eberlin von Günzburg (c. 1470–1533) printed many reformist flysheets (*Flugschriften*) and pamphlets.

conquer temptations. Only praying students can notice and avoid the snares and nets that Satan lays for those that occupy themselves mainly with works of reason! Unfortunately, it is precisely the inculcation of prayer and struggle that remains almost completely overlooked and neglected at the universities. Because of this, most university graduates are inexperienced and inept in prayer and temptation, and impractical and timid in the work of the Holy Office. One can only marvel that they attempt it anyway. Being neophytes themselves, they often experiment with other souls who have been bought at a price and can easily be ruined, since they do not know their worth or lack of worth from their own experience. Yes, there are many souls who trust young pastors and are led astray, or at least are no longer rescued from trouble and despair, because those who are now shepherds of their souls wasted their time of preparation between book and mug.

One cannot offer praise if A. H. Francke and others with the best intention did some damage to the true study of theology by means of their popular lectures because they made their good intentions an excuse for shallowness when they were thorough. But there is a true, deep, all-inclusive learning (just think of Thomas Aquinas, Luther, Johann Gerhard, etc.) that never becomes an end in itself, never boasts, and for that very reason works in a more powerful and salutary way. At the same time, [this learning] is more effective and salutary. There is a scholarship that powerfully prepares for life and does not falter in Francke's direction. In temptation it can carry the torch and give the praying spirit cleansing and confidence. This is what the Church needs, and it is not just one school of thought: all students ought to strive for it. "Tell me why you are here"[16] should be written over the study door of every young student, and none should forget that he is striving for a profession which is to save himself and all his listeners. In the final analysis, the Holy Office should accomplish nothing except to enlighten the way to eternal life in this valley of deadly life and living death, and to lead the soul with a strong hand on that way to life. What else should this time of preparation be, if not to enable this in every possible way?

B. Testing Fitness for the Holy Office: Examination

8. From ancient times onward, the final examination tests one for the fitness without which no one should receive a call or ordination. Due to the close connection between the final examination on the one hand and the call and ordination on the other, formerly the examination was placed between

[16] *Dic cur hic.* [Loehe:] Any student of theology should have this memorable sentence of Paul inscribed in his book of poems: "Godliness is of value in every way" (1 Timothy 4:8 [ESV]) and that one from Psalms: "The way of the wicked will perish" (Psalm 1:6 [ESV]). [*Cuiuslibet theologiae studiosi museo inscripta esse debet memorabilis Pauli sententia: "Pietas ad omnia utilis est" 1. Tim. 4, 8 et illa Psaltis: "Impiorum via peribit!" Ps. 1* (Fecht p. 16)].

call and ordination. Without a call there seemed to be no reason for an examination. Yet this placement of the examination began to produce some awkward results that were felt with ever-increasing keenness. By admitting only those with a call to the examination, sometimes pastors with a call had to be declared unworthy or incapable. Thus, standing just in front of the door of the pastoral office—and through it, the means of making a living—they were refused entrance. Of course, the bad lot of pastors that were thus examined also put the examiners into an embarrassing situation. Indeed, in the case where incompetence was proven even before the end of the examination, a certain embarrassment and injustice could arise, one that would be quite easy to bring to an end, if one gave the matter some consideration.

It would be far more bearable for the one being rejected and easier for the one rejecting him if it could be done without being tied up with a regular call. For that reason, already in days gone by, it was considered advisable to examine the candidates before they received a call. This advice was followed here and there, e.g., in the formerly Swedish duchy of Bremen.[17] Our present custom to grant the *examen pro ministerio* right after completing the studies would at least avoid the inconvenience of the examinations mentioned above.

9. An examination for the ministry is not only justified in the Word of God, it is demanded. In 1 Timothy 3:10, the apostle commands: "The deacons should first be **tested**; then, if they prove themselves blameless, let them serve." And in 1 Timothy 5:22, it says: "Do not lay hands on anyone **hastily**." Both passages not only order an examination (δοκιμασία) of those aspiring to church offices, but a strict δοκιμασία.[18] In the first passage, one could find only the establishment of an examination for the diaconate. But the diaconate in this case appears to be the entrance to the pastoral office. First Timothy 3:10 certainly includes the examination of the elders (presbyters), especially since the qualifications for both deacons and presbyters in 1 Timothy 3 cannot be determined without examination.

10. In general, the **subject of the examination** is the **fitness** (ἱκανότης) for the teaching office (2 Timothy 2:2 "What you have heard from me through many witnesses entrust to **faithful people who will be able to teach others as well**." Cf. 2 Corinthians 2:16; 3:5). Based on Holy Scripture, our fathers rightfully account to this fitness the following:

---

[17] [Loehe:] See J. Gerhard's Locus XXIV S. XIII p. 171; Hartmann p. 116 V; Fecht p. 49. [Editor's note: Sweden controlled the Duchy of Bremen and Verden from 1648 to 1712 as a trophy of the Thirty Years War until Denmark held it for three years. From 1715 to 1823 the territory was controlled respectively by the Kingdom of Hannover and Great Britain. The territory lies to the north of the Free City of Bremen, originally having been two prince-bishoprics from 1180.]

[18] LCMS president C. F. W. Walther also referred to this in Thesis III of his Law and Gospel lectures. See Walther, *Law and Gospel: How to Read and Apply the Bible* (St. Louis: Concordia, 2010), p. 59, n. 14.

Confessionis sinceritatem, **purity of the confession**;[19]

docendi dexteritatem, **ability to teach**;

morum integritatem, **moral purity**.

11. Of the three requirements, the **first** and **third** equally have to be demanded from all those aspiring to the pastoral office. Each of these two is as necessary as the other; both are indispensable. Both together should form the *character indelebilis* of the evangelical pastor.[20] But in recent times these two requirements have not been checked as closely as they should have been. Wholehearted faithfulness to the confession especially has been looked at with suspicion, even considered as a disastrous narrowness.

On the other hand, without any justification, the examination for the ministry was made into a mainly "scientific" examination. Since the Church had been diminished to a school, nothing higher was considered than the easily attainable and very misleading praise of a scholarly method. It is right to state with Theophylact, "Doctrine is the strength and the character of the bishop," and with Hilary, "The sum of all the virtues of a bishop is wisdom and doctrine." There is good reason to push the students and the candidates toward learning. But on the other hand, Theophylact and Hilary are not glorifying that which is praised as scholarship today. In any case, it is wrong and harmful to lift up the second requirement over the first and third, especially the way it is done in some places, when excellent scholarship can cover up even the most blatant lack in the other two.

12. Completely right, but with too little internal agreement, Hüffell says:

> The apostles already made a great effort to safeguard **agreement in pure doctrine** (Acts 15:22, 29; Romans 14:20; 2 Timothy 2:15; Titus 3:10; 1 Corinthians 5:1–5); they warned of false doctrine and feared writings that were introduced spuriously (2 Thessalonians 2:2). **Orthodoxy, therefore, was the center of all virtues of the new Church, and Origen could judge the one who had fallen away**

---

[19] Confession (*Bekenntnis*) refers here to the public doctrine of the Church.

[20] The indelible character (*character indelebilis*) is a Roman Catholic theological concept that emerged from ideas in the papal reform movement from the eleventh through thirteenth centuries and was represented by statements in the Council of Trent (1545–63). They say the pope, as Vicar of Christ, has the power to impart a holy seal by means of the Sacraments, which only the pope and magisterium control and impart. This is used to explain valid sacraments, except for emergency Baptism. Martin Luther, Philip Melanchthon, and Martin Chemnitz flatly rejected this term and stated in AC V and elsewhere that the Word of God is the sole basis by which the Holy Spirit creates faith through valid sacraments as through instruments, and the Word also constitutes the ministry of teaching the Gospel and administering the Sacraments. Loehe probably does not mean to endorse the Roman Catholic concept, yet he tends to experiment with an ill-defined "evangelical catholic" vocabulary.

from the main teachings of the Church harder than the one who had committed a bad deed.[21]

Certainly Origen was right in this matter, just as were Irenaeus, Tertullian, Cyprian, and Lactantius in similar passages. One can say that the apostles and the Fathers were wrong only if one denies that holy thoughts are the cause of all holy life, and that lack in these thoughts will cause lack in life, or at least will cause some sort of consequences. The disciple of love does not even want to be host to those who bring a different doctrine, and does not greet them, 2 John 10–11. That is how sure he was himself, so confident was his high opinion of the value of completely pure doctrine!

Pure "orthodoxy" that does not produce any kind of effect [in terms of moral life] is an evil that offers [only] the appearance of holiness, from which one cannot draw any conclusion regarding true orthodoxy. One ought to demand nothing less than orthodoxy, one that agrees exactly with the confession of the Church! The more serious and strict this demand is, the more that the hypocrisy [of false orthodoxy] will be recognizable.

13. In his pastoral aphorisms, A. H. Francke already complains about the neglect of life and conduct in the δοκιμασία of the candidates. And yet the demands of the holy apostles are apparent especially in these areas (1 Timothy 3:2ff. and Titus 1:7ff.).

A teacher must be above reproach, the husband of one wife, temperate, sensible, respectable, hospitable, not a drunkard, not violent or greedy for gain. He must manage his own household well, keeping his children submissive and respectful in every way, honest, not double-tongued, having the mystery of the faith in a pure conscience, and summing it up: A teacher, priest or preacher, bishop or chaplain should be a person who has a good testimonial from those outside, so that he would not fall into shame or the attacks of the slanderer.

This is how [Leonhard] **Hutter** sums up the apostolic requirements, and certainly every candidate should be judged by this measure, as far as it can be applied, given the youthful age of most candidates.[22] And even more so, there

[21] Johann Jakob Ludwig Hüffell (1784–1856), known as Ludwig, was born into a pastor's family. He studied philosophy at Marburg and theology at Giessen, where he eventually became a professor. In 1826 he became a leader of the territorial church in Baden and in 1829, its president until 1850. It is not clear what writing is being cited by Loehe. Origen (184/85–253/54) was a scholar, catechist, and biblical commentator who blended Hellenistic metaphysics with biblical doctrine. Some of his teachings later were condemned, yet he did champion many orthodox teachings in his lifetime, which was shortened by the severe Decian persecution (250–52).

[22] Leonhard Hutter (1563–1616) was at Jena (1594–96) and Wittenberg (1596–1616), serving also four terms as rector. He is known chiefly for his *Compendium locorum theologicorum*. He also wrote *Concordia concors* in defense of the Formula of Concord and

is a higher command, one that includes all others, from which flow all others, namely the love **of Christ**. When the Lord wanted to confirm the fallen disciple anew in his apostolate, wanted to entrust his lambs and sheep anew to him, he asked him three times about his love: "Peter, do you love me; if you love me, pasture my sheep."[23]

The pastoral teachers of our Church call attention to this high requirement for the Holy Office (e.g., Balduin, *Instit. Past.* p. 65),[24] and a great shepherd of the ancient time, John Chrysostom, says in reference to the love for Christ (Περὶ ἱεροσύνης ed. Tauchn. Λογ. II Κεφ. II 93): "Let those be brought forward who by measure are greater than all, and are so much superior in the virtue of their soul as Saul was greater in body than all Hebrews, but also much more."[25] However, it is not given to us poor humans to look into the heart. We depend on the known fruits, and therefore we must not take as truth any kind of apparent love or charm of a candidate, if he is not proven by the measure of 1 Timothy 3 and Titus 1.

14. Finally, concerning the **ability to teach**, the apostle insists upon it using the [Greek] word for teaching ability, διδακτικός, in 1 Timothy 3:2. One includes with that here, according to Luke 21:15, word and wisdom, i.e., ability to interpret and spiritual understanding.[26] The latter includes all scholarly knowledge that one can rightly demand of a servant of the Word; the first includes the practical skill of speaking, teaching, and social intercourse. Hutter sums it up beautifully when he says, based on Holy Scripture (1 Timothy 4:13; 2 Timothy 2:2, 15; 3:14, 16; 4:1, 2, 5; Titus 1:9):

> Lutheran (*evangelische*) preachers must have these qualities: 1) they have studied and learned useful knowledge and [biblical and classical] languages, 2) are well read in the Scriptures, 3) understand well the articles of the Christian religion from the Word of God and are able to refute all kinds of error, 4) so that, having been endowed with

---

several tracts against Calvinists attempting to unite Lutheranism and Calvinism by trying to bypass the deep Christological divide between the two.

[23] Loehe writes: Πέτρε, φιλεῖς με; Εἰ φιλεῖς με, ποίμανε τὰ πρόβατά μου. This combines separate elements in John 21:15–19, along with the change from Simon to Peter, to create a kind of patchwork Greek paraphrase.

[24] Perhaps Loehe means *Institutiones Prudentiae Pastoralis* by Salomo Deyling (1677–1755), a Saxon church official, pastor, and professor at the university in Leipzig. Deyling became the center of opposition against the encroaching rationalism of Christian Wolff. Friedrich Balduin (1575–1627) was known for his commentary on the Pauline epistles, polemical addresses, and *Tractatus de casibus conscientiae*. Loehe may instead be referring to Balduin's *Tractatus*. Both Loehe and C. F. W. Walther made use of Deyling and Balduin in their writings.

[25] Ἀγέσθωσαν εἰς μέσον οἱ πολλῷ τῷ μέτρῳ πλεονεκτοῦντες ἁπάντων, καὶ τοσοῦτον ὑψηλότεροι τῶν ἄλλων κατὰ τὴν τῆς ψυχῆς ὄντες ἀρετήν, ὅσον τοῦ παντὸς ἔθνους Ἑβραίων κατὰ τὸ τοῦ σώματος μέγεθος ὁ Σαοῦλ, μᾶλλον δὲ καὶ πολλῷ πλέον.

[26] στόμα καὶ σοφίαν, i.e., δύναμιν ἑρμενευτικὴν and σύνεσιν πνευματικήν.

such gifts by God, they may be able to teach and instruct others in what they have studied and learned.

15. While the first and third requirements with regard to teaching ability must be seriously directed equally to all candidates, clearly not every parish will demand the same degree of training. Thus also in the examination one does not have to make the same demands. The whole system of grading, which today is often misused to secularize the Church, nevertheless deserves to be appreciated. For it recognizes that people with different talents, and in different degrees, can find a place in the Holy Office. (See section 3 above.) "There are certain degrees of spiritual [or mental] understanding as well as of hermeneutical power, but the highest degree of gifts should be attributed to the one who is promoted to some lowly office in the church."[27] So says one from whom we can trust to have a judgment having superior competence, Johann Gerhard.

16. During recent examinations of candidates it became readily apparent that too much mental synthesis and understanding (σύνεσις πνευματική), rather than too little, was being required of those being examined. This was a byproduct of the entirely perverted, exaggeratedly scholarly direction taken by Protestant theology. And yet one can hear from Roman Catholic laypeople that even more is required from their clergy. We often hear this from Roman authors, especially from the Jesuit party. They loved to blame Lutherans in former times, claiming that:

> They call and install as preachers those who are common idiots and lay people. They do not know or understand anything, probably can neither read nor write. They are butchers, weavers, cooks, cobblers, tailors, etc., and after they have preached for a while they no longer want to continue and return again to their trade and business.[28]

One can reply easily to these accusations of the Romans by pointing to the required minimum, which one can find in the *Pontificum Romanum*:

---

[27] *Tum συνέσιως πνευματικῆς, tum δυνάμεως ἑρμενευτικῆς,—sunt certi gradus, nec sumus illorum donorum gradus exigendus ab eo, qui ad inferius aliquod ecclesiae ministerium promovetur.*

[28] [Loehe:] The fact that this cannot always be criticized is proven by the following fact in America: The first person sent to America from Neuendettelsau was formerly a cobbler. In America he became a pastor. A throat affliction forced him to give up his office. After that he became a council person under another pastor and made a living from his old trade. When his suffering was overcome, the congregation again elected him as their pastor. Far be it to let a dark shadow fall on the man or the congregation. This case should rather honor both. [Editor's note: Loehe refers to Pastor Adam Ernst (1815–95), whose indefatigable work blessed both The Lutheran Church—Missouri Synod and, perhaps more so, the Lutheran Church—Canada, originally a district-synod of the LCMS.]

> Sufficient grammatical knowledge, an examination of one's birth, in order that no illegitimate man will be ordained, exploration of bodily members, so there be no debility, deformity, or impotence in them, wherefore one should touch and number the face, eyes, ears, nose, hands, fingers, and feet of the one to be ordained, if necessary without shoes, lest [the feet] be made of wood.[29]

However, we can give them an even better answer. When the Romans thus accused us, they had in mind the time of the Reformation. It is true that, here and there, less educated preachers stepped into the pulpit. Today they could make the same accusations in regard to many of our messengers to the heathen, and many Lutheran preachers in North America. To this we could answer them with Hutter:

> Granted that there might be a lack of learned people and properly called preachers during a time of persecution or other unavoidable emergency. Then one or several lay people or artisans would be installed as teachers. As a result, our enemies would report this to us and ask whether this ought to be reckoned as sin. Should that be considered as being such a great evil? Would it not be much better and beneficial under these conditions to hear **something** of the Word of God than to be deprived of all instruction and comfort? And one could hardly regret it if, in former days, during the darkest papacy, such common people would have appeared and publicly taught in places where the pope and his mass-babbling priests (*Meßpfaffen*) not only failed to teach [the Word], but also in many ways persecuted it and endeavored to completely obscure it. And certainly one ought to listen here to what Christ answered the scribes and Pharisees when they wanted to forbid the people and the children [to shout] Hosanna: "I tell you, if these are silent, the very stones will cry out."—God can prepare praise for Himself out of the mouths of young children and babes, even out of the mouth of common lay people, and through such people He can build His Church, especially if the so-called pastors have turned into wolves and tyrants and persecute good and pure teachers and remove them from their midst.

Besides that, it would show great narrowness if one would consider only those who have gone through our normal training process as being qualified for the office. There are many uneducated preachers in North America who, when it comes to capability and blessing, stand in no way behind their

---

[29] *Sufficiens litteratura grammatica, examen natalium, ne ordinentur illegitimi, exploratio membrorum corporis, ne sit in eis debilitas, deformitas vel impotentia, quam ob causam palpare et numerare iubent ordinandi faciem, oculos, aures, nasum, manus, digitos, pedes, si opus fuerit discalceatos, ne forte sint lignei.*

educated colleagues. One could bring forth similar proofs from different times of the Church. In his ***Christian State*** (e.g., chapter 7, section 5) Seckendorf brings a conclusive and beautiful comparison between the first years of the Reformation and the early years of the Church after Christ.[30] He shows that one should not judge everything according to the circumstances of one's own time and situation. St. Paul did not find many noble or many wise [men] who would have given themselves to Christ. He had laid his hands on ordinary citizens and common workers and made them into presbyters and said of them emphatically: "The Holy Spirit made them overseers and bishops to shepherd the congregation of God" (Acts 20:28, Loehe's paraphrase).

These then not only became "the very best bishops and teachers, but they also instructed their sons for the same office, and sometimes there were many members following each other in presiding over a congregation" (p. 430). Seckendorf does not say this to downgrade scholarship, but only in order "that no one should be so deceived as if the kind of studying, of the academic life, the *graduum* and the like (still used today **and not rejected**) would be an **essential work** for the training of preachers and teachers."[31]

Johann Gerhard also agrees with Seckendorf (Loc. XXIV Cap. III, p. 1 sect. LXXIV, Tom. XII, p. 70f.). He points out that in the view of the ancient days, among the **pagans**, when the Church and the preaching office were not yet **in order**, and the **teachers** had turned into **wolves**, every Christian had the duty to take care of his fellow human beings through teaching. He points at the activity of the Christian young men Frumentius and Edesius among the Abyssinians, at the activity of imprisoned Christian women among the gentiles and confirms these old examples through the judgments of Origen and Ambrose.[32] The latter comments on Ephesians 4: "In order for the people to grow and multiply, in the beginning it was granted to all to evangelize

---

[30] Veit Ludwig von Seckendorf (1626–92) held judicial offices in Saxony and Zeitz from 1652 to 1681. His works include *Teutscher Fürstenstaat* (1656 and 1678), *Der Christen-Stat* (1685), and *Commentarius Historicus et apologeticus de Lutheranismo sive de Reformatione* (3 vols., Leipzig, 1692).

[31] The *graduum* is the tiered system of academic degrees known also in the U.S.

[32] Frumentius (d. 383) was the first Christian bishop in the Kingdom of Aksum, located in Ethiopia (Abyssinia). He and his brother Edesius were captured as boys and made slaves of the King of Aksum. Frumentius was freed and became the tutor of the king's heir. He was appointed as bishop by Athanasius of Alexandria and is credited as the source of the Ge'ez script and the Ethiopian translation of the NT. Ambrose (Aurelius Ambrosius, c. 340–97) served as consular prefect of Liguria and Emilia before he was acclaimed Bishop of Milan in 374. He became a noted opponent of Arianism, an influence on Augustine of Hippo, and one of the original four "Doctors of the Church."

and baptize, and to explain Scripture in the church."[33] In perfect agreement with Ambrose, Luther also says:

> Indeed, how is that so? If a Christian is not called to do it, therefore is he not allowed to preach? Answer: Here you must put a Christian into two kinds of places. First: If he is in a place where there are no Christians, he does not need any other call, except being a Christian, and is inwardly called and anointed by God; there is his duty to preach to the erring gentiles and non-Christians and to teach the Gospel out of brotherly love, even if no one has called him. For **necessity breaks all laws and has no law**. But if he is in a place where there are other Christians who have the same power and right, he should not put himself forward, but let himself be called and brought forth so that he might preach and teach for the others and at their behest. (See vol. II. Jena German ed., fol. 244.)

17. Since the first and third requirements of the examination of the candidates are completely indispensable and have to be expected of all with equal strictness, yet with the second requirement there are several grades, this second one becomes a place of vain and haughty efforts. If one does not see that, one unconsciously **looses something in the third requirement**, as soon as one gives in to arrogance in regard to the second. By dreaming of a high flight, one becomes unfit and sinks very low. For it is true that humility and sanctity of life are more significant for the inner fitness of a pastor than are talent and scholarship.

One should also learn from those who are not well-disposed toward us. May it be permitted therefore to quote a few strong pronouncements for the necessity of a pure life from the excellent *Remarks Concerning Pastoral Care, Especially in Rural Areas* by Father Aegidius Jais, fifth ed., 1843:[34]

> P. 65: "The life of the cleric is the Gospel of the people."[35]
>
> P. 63: "The one who is not loved well will not be heard well," says Gregory the Great.[36] But the word *diligo* wants to say more than

---

[33] *Ut cresceret plebs et multiplicaretur, omnibus inter initia concessum est et evangelizare et baptizare, et scripturas in ecclesia explanare.*

[34] *Bemerkung über die Seelsorge besonders auf dem Lande.* Aegidius Jais (1750–1822) was a Bavarian Benedictine monk and priest. In 1803 he became a professor of theology at Salzburg, where in 1805 he was elevated to *Rector magnificus.* He became the private tutor of Electoral Prince Ferdinand of Salzburg, which led him to Würzburg and Florence, before his return to Germany and death. He was a popular author whose works attained many editions. Jais, Martin Boos (see later), and other Roman Catholic figures helped form for Loehe the basis of an "evangelical catholic" position reminiscent of the Oxford Movement, albeit with a Lutheran approach.

[35] *Vita clerici evangelium est populi.*

[36] *Non bene auditor, qui non bene diligitur.*

amo. Tullius wrote to his friend, "I not only like you, I truly also love you."[37]

P. 17: "The Gospel to worldly people is the **life of the priests, of which they are witnesses**." Massillon.

P. 65: "The best preparation, the most beautiful beginning of a sermon is the pious conduct of the preacher."

C. THE CANDIDACY YEARS

18. Once a student has left the university and has passed the examination successfully, he usually has to wait a good many years before a pastorate is given to him.[38] So the question is how best to spend this time of waiting. In any case, the better or bigger piece of bread should not be decisive in answering this question. Without any doubt, anyone who is becoming or is already a servant of the Church should constantly keep in mind the word of the prophet (Jeremiah 17:16): "I have not desired days among [certain] people; you know that."[39] The glory of the Holy Office should fill every candidate so completely and all his wishes should point to this end that he wants to be ever more mature and fit for it. Therefore, he should use all his time to further the fulfillment of his innermost and greatest wish and not become the cause of being cheated out of his life's work.

19. Many candidates spend this time of waiting as teachers at schools of higher education, as private tutors in individual families, or as vicars.[40] Some will enter public seminaries for preachers. The question is now: What is the value of these various ways of spending the time of waiting for the future calling and what would be the wisest choice?

20. As far as teaching in **schools** and in individual families goes, one cannot deny a certain benefit. Time at the university does not offer an opportunity to get to know life in a school or to acquire experience in teaching through practice. If the period of waiting also does not help in this regard, it is hard to tell how one can rightly take on the [pastoral doctrinal] inspection of a school in the future. It is indeed often that even very gifted pastors cannot gain any influence in schools and among teachers because of their inexperience and incompetence [in teaching]. Rather, they give their teachers

---

[37] *Non tantum te amo, verum etiam diligo.*

[38] This section engages the reality of pastors in the territorial churches at Loehe's time. It yet may be worthy of some consideration in those cases where one sees more candidates than calls.

[39] The wording is from the pre-1912 Luther Bible editions. Luther's explanation to this passage reads: "That means, to live among and spend ones days among people who have misery and naught else for their reputation, and to have a good reputation among them." Later editions speak of "evil days," similar to English editions.

[40] In the German tradition, a vicar is a pastoral intern, not parish clergy.

reason for haughty self-elevation and disobedience. Even if one might not take Luther's advice that one should tend school for ten years before taking over a pastorate, at least it is good advice during the waiting period to become acquainted with school matters and how to tend a school, and to learn by teaching.

Therefore, the time certainly is not lost when a candidate spends it as a teacher in public or private schools. And it will be most beneficial for his future office if, as a teacher, he enters a **rather normal** school in the city or in the country. In God's name, let him teach the elements of all knowledge to the youth. If only God would make it so that there were not just a few congregations here and there where the candidate could take over the position of pastor and teacher; rather, that candidates of theology would be used **regularly** in the school for a while. School matters should be given more attention, even at the universities. It would be beneficial for the schools as well as for the candidates, and finally there would be both a humbling and an elevating effect upon the ordinary schoolteachers who are not university trained. Not to mention that this would also be a means for closer cooperation between school and church.

21. Filling the waiting period by **private tutoring** is less recommendable than tending a school. First, in the houses of the upper class, the candidate easily can get used to certain needs and a lifestyle that later on he has to do without—this never happens without pain and aggravation. But also, he easily can get used to a tenor of life and behavior unsuitable for a future father of his parishioners. Nor does private tutoring of one or several children of the nobility produce what is desired for the future office, despite all the trouble, training, and temptation that it can give to a young man. His experiences regarding the subjects of teaching are too manifold; regarding his students, they are too uniform. He cannot learn for school, Sunday school, and office what he could have learned by tending a school.[41] Of course, joy and talent have to be taken into account.

22. If you ask what more a young candidate could do specifically in order to prepare himself for the pastoral office, there is the choice between preach-

---

[41] Here *Kinderlehre* is translated as Sunday school, but that is only a poor rendition in order to engage modern readers. The tradition of specific *Kinderlehre*, or general *Christenlehre* involved lengthy catechetical sermons in addition to the church services. The LCMS fathers brought this tradition with them from Germany. Sunday school came in two varieties. One occurred at church on Sunday, arising from the English church tradition in the 1780s to teach religion and literacy to the poor. It was into this tradition that the LCMS transitioned. The other comes from Scandinavia, where Sunday school often was a self-contained activity of mission societies. That went along with the lengthy summer Bible school tradition of the Scandinavians, which helped to form the vacation Bible school concept in the LCMS.

ing seminaries (*Predigerseminarien*) and vicarage internships.[42] Perhaps no single preaching seminary is of a quality that it could introduce the candidate to the sacred office. What good is it to write ever so many sermons, as long as these sermons are not related to a congregation, as long as they are only exercises, where one has to imagine conditions in a congregation? In the end, one can know a context only by being involved in the active life of a congregation. Just like a painter cannot learn to make portraits by painting pictures from his own imagination, one does not become a preacher by writing imaginary sermons. Just as preaching here and there in various congregations—even as a student—cannot be very useful, in the end the writing and memorizing of such sermons cannot be very useful either.[43]

The same goes for catechetical instruction. Even if one brings in children from the schools so the candidates can practice in front of them, such exercises are nothing but catechetical entertainment for the children. The children deny the catechist their heart, which has to be involved. In a word: Whether he preaches or catechizes, the young man lacks the **official position** that changes everything.[44]

One could hardly imagine that a candidate could engage in any other practical matters besides preaching and catechizing, unless a preaching seminary would be used to serve a congregation. But in that case it would need a rector and *moderator studiorum*, so that the candidates do not experiment without knowing their goal. Then the rector would have to be a pastor and there could not be too many seminarians. In the end, that would mean the same thing as what we are going to say presently.

23. We believe that **vicarages** offer by far the best opportunity to introduce a candidate to the Holy Office. But you must understand us well here. We are not talking about a vicarage with some old pastors who are at the end of their lives and are becoming childish again. Those situations require practiced, experienced candidates. Nor are we talking about vicarages with over-

[42] Concordia Theological Seminary in Fort Wayne, Indiana started as a *Predigerseminar* and became a fully-accredited seminary. A preaching seminary is a practical vocational institution that focuses on homiletics and other pastoral tasks, making theological candidates fit to serve the Church. The term *Vikariat* in German usually refers to a pastoral internship, although Loehe also refers to a kind of ordained vicar. In the LCMS, *vicarage* is used for such an internship. Many Protestants, on the other hand, understand a *vicarage* to be analogous to a parsonage.

[43] [Loehe:] This does not deny the fact that even exercises of this kind can be profitable for the raw beginner as an exercise in form.

[44] [Loehe:] Experience has taught us that American emergency helpers (*Nothelfer*) have achieved great things in both [categories] in North America. [This was] as soon as they **came into the office,** even though in Germany one did not expect much skill from them for either sermons or catechesis. There is that much difference between education and life, and certainly life [experience] has the greater significance. [Editor's note: Walther discusses a similar point regarding experience; see *Law and Gospel: How to Read and Apply the Bible*, 49–67.]

burdened pastors, or serving exceptionally large congregations. In general, we are not even talking about vicarages in a city church.

In the first scenario, there would be little instruction. In the latter two, something would be lacking—we would call it something like a **compendium**—that is very conducive to a general orientation and understanding of the Holy Office. In particular, city churches do not offer a clear view of a congregation and congregational conditions. Even the pastor is not as easily recognizable in his true character and position as in the country.

We are talking here of vicarages under an able country pastor. He is old enough to have experience, young enough to bear the trouble of teaching and instructing, scholarly enough to be able to pass on his experiences, and sufficiently lacking in envy so he can grant a rising star the necessary space in his congregation. In this way, the candidate can become at home in the congregation, in congregational life, and in the office. Of course one can say that such country pastors who are still strong and are serving congregations that are easy to oversee do not take on vicars. And it is correct that they **ought not to take** any, meaning that they should have no reason to take on vicars at their own expense. But what could prevent one from using the money that is used for some useless institution to support candidates who would like to spend two years with an experienced pastor, or should do so?[45] Even if the candidates had to tighten their belts significantly with respect to material things, what would it matter? Should they not be allowed to practice what awaits them once they enter the office and marriage—namely, a life of slender means? Do not the office and the Church grant them enough nobility to comfort them in their temporal poverty?

Now, on the one hand, one would have to leave to the candidate the choice of the pastor who will show the vicar the transition from theory to practice; for trust in the teacher is necessary, especially in this kind of a teacher. On the other hand, one would have to be careful that a false choice would not be made. What good would it do, and what blessing could one hope for, if **so-called** experienced pastors would be chosen who have learned to practice their office with the greatest ease, like a trade, but have forgotten and lost the higher idea and the higher goal of the Church and of the office? Candidates would have to be entrusted to men highly gifted in spirit and disposition. Such a pastor could be entrusted with not just one, but with several candidates. The congregations of such country pastors could be the noblest greenhouses of the Church, true seminaries, and such country pastors also would be most qualified for the office of seminary rector.

24. **Ordination would not be required** for such a biennium. On the one hand, those matters that require ordination belong to the pastors and therefore cannot be done by anyone else. On the other hand, they can be learned

---

[45] In Germany, even in the present, vicarages tend to last two years. In the U.S. this period often has lasted only for one year, except during the Great Depression.

well by watching and taking part.[46] The lack of ordination would demonstrate to the congregation a very wholesome difference between the pastor and the candidate.[47]

D. VICARAGES

25. We already talked about vicarages that candidates should seek with able pastors who are full of life, in order to be introduced by them to the affairs of the Holy Office. This position with a pastor should not even be called a vicarage, because the candidate is not really a vicar or substitute, and he occupies this position not for the sake of the pastor, but for his own sake. He has sought it and accepted it as a kindness.

A proper vicarage is totally different. A candidate occupies it not in order to be introduced to the office, but because it has become necessary to support an overburdened, or sick, or old pastor. In this case, he is truly *pastor vicarius*, a substitute for the pastor. In this case, ordination is required.[48] One can say that by entering into this kind of vicarage the candidate's time of waiting has come to an end. From this time on he has all the spiritual rights and privileges of the office, and anything an ordained vicar cannot or should do is not part of the Holy Office. The greater income and the licenses, duties, and rights that a pastor has over a vicar will bring a change to the pastoral office of one ordained, just as much as if he would enter into matrimony. Still, an ordained vicar is not a pastor, and it is mainly the difference between the two that we now want to discuss.

26. The natural relationship between a vicar and his pastor is mainly that of **subordination**. The pastor, whom the circumstances forced to accept a vicar, does not stop being a pastor. He retains all his duties, all his rights, all

---

[46] [Loehe:] Preaching should be allowed to those not ordained, if it is done for the sake of practice. But administering the Sacraments, hearing people make confession, and similar things should only belong to the ordained ministry. **For those things practice is not required** (Balduin, p. 77f.). [*Conscionari quidem licet non ordinatis, si fiat exerciti causa; sacramenta vero administrare, confessiones audire et similia debenture ordinario ministro: in his enim exercitio non est opus.*] Even so, to participate in pastoral care outside of the confessional should be permitted to the young candidate under the supervision and responsibility of the pastor. There are even cases when the pastor may well be able to use the help of an intermediary, and it can be a great blessing.

[47] [Loehe:] Such an introduction to the office would agree very well with the position of a candidate who took over the school of a pastor. A candidate could take the school as a vicar. If the candidates would have to proceed through the school to the office, this would be the best opportunity for a preliminary training. It would also be very useful if they would fill the job of a cantor and deacon for a while.

[48] In the U.S., one encounters specialized paths to ordination as well as multiple kinds of internship. The "vicarage" concept, as it exists in the LCMS, can be an internship with the intent of being called elsewhere, or it can be intended as an on-the-job prelude to a call at the same location, and with greater or lesser restrictions.

his honor, all his responsibility. He is also responsible for his vicar, as long as he himself is still of a sound mind. The vicar, on the other hand, is and remains only an assistant pastor, a substitute, and only for those affairs in which the pastor needs and desires a representative. The pastor has the privilege to keep certain areas for himself. One cannot blame him when he transfers certain pastoral acts, those that properly make him the pastor, like confession and the administration of the Sacraments, to the vicar only with difficulty, and slowly. It is possible that certain acts he does not do as well as his vicar; he might do a great favor to his congregation if he would transfer all his pastoral acts to his vicar. But if he does not do it, if he fights the turning over of any business, any right as if he was fighting death itself, who can force him, unless he has been pronounced unworthy or incapable of the office by an official declaration? He always does or does not do only that which is his right, no matter what he does or whether he omits doing.

Any vicar has to agree from the start with this kind of relationship. Let him obey, serve, and do what he is ordered to do. He also will be old someday and it can happen that he will need a vicar. Let him see himself in his old pastor and be easy on him. It is only respect for his own future if he truly understands the difference between pastor and vicar and observes it. There is nothing nobler and more beautiful in a young man than modesty in the old sense of the word, and being content with the situation in which one is and ought to be. No vicar is more charming and more beloved than the one who moves gladly, joyfully, and eagerly within his borders. And certainly one will trust him more and more as time goes on.

27. A young man, even if he is smart about the office, nevertheless cannot have much **experience in the office.** Thus, upon entering an ordained vicarage it is easy for him to make mistakes. Therefore, he should be happy if he is not burdened, right from the start, with much responsibility. Even if he already completed a vicarage of the first kind, a practical biennium under a capable pastor, he should not put too much trust in his maturity.[49] Nor should he lightheartedly step up to greater independence. He should rather seek and accept the guidance of his pastor whenever he can. He should gladly be his amanuensis and disciple as much as possible, since this can be done without any sacrifice of independence and originality. Rather it is a sign of proficient mastery over one's own heart and powers.

And yet this very thing is so difficult for most vicars. The youthful joy of independence and of not being bound makes it so difficult for them. If the pastor, as is often the case, wants to hang on to his rights and does not hide this, the vicar is unhappy and soon starts to see all of his pastor's actions and inactions in the worst light.

---

[49] In Germany one encounters a two-year vicarage internship period, followed by what one might call a probationary pastoral period (*Pfarrvikariat*) that has some commonalities with Loehe's ordained vicarage.

Perhaps finally it happens that the pastor, who maybe also once had a time of greater energy, greater activity, and recognition, remembers those days and overestimates his present achievements, especially when he is confronted with the achievements of his vicar. At such a time, if he devalues the successes of his vicar, the approval that the vicar gets, the strength that the vicar develops; if perhaps he sees through the pride, the vanity, and the selfishness of the vicar—or if envy and jealousy eat up the heart of the "old man"—then good night, pastor, good night, peace, and joy! The relationship of such a young man to such a man or senile person is then just as difficult as the one of a bad daughter-in-law to a bad mother-in-law, and for similar reasons. But who can help such people in this case?

28. How wonderful it would be if **pastors** who need a vicar would show them the kind of **humility** that adorns old disciples so beautifully and wins respect and honor for them from the young. How miserable it is when the old ones do not want to be old or weak, do not want to quit or step back, do not want to die and through this very attitude prove that they have not learned the lesson that they should learn during their long life.

Their grey hair and their weak body should scare them mightily and remind them that now is the time to be humble and to complete their life's task in humility. The longer their life is, the heavier is the burden of sins, the more humiliating is the recognition of old sins and frailties, [and] the fewer are the demands. Yet one all the more finds grace sufficient; one longs more for transfiguration and eternal completion; one has more mildness toward everybody; one has more hope for the next generation; one has more of a willing and complete acknowledging of youthful activity and ability; one has more forbearance toward youthful vanity and bravado!

That is how it should be! And one ought to recognize that it should be that way. And if one finds himself resistant to such knowledge and such conduct, one should be frightened by one's own arrogance and cry so much louder from the depth of the soul for humility, for light and grace, so that one can find in the relationship to the vicar a school of daily dying and rising again, and joyfully and confidently walk into it and its good instruction. Oh, how many old people overlook the fact that, in their relationship with the young, they are offered their last chance and a school for the most beautiful completion before their passing away! Oh, how many old pastors behave toward their vicars in such a way that the best thing the vicars can learn from the pastors—if they are pious young men—is this lesson and this decision: "You are not going to be that way once you are old." May God grant to his Church and her clergy (*Lehrstand*) such humble old men!

29. But on the other side also: How much, **how much do the vicars transgress**! How good it would be if they would take to heart what is written: "It is a precious thing to be patient and wait on the help of the Lord. It is a precious thing to him that he should bear the yoke in his youth!" (Lamentations 3:26–27, Luther). How good it would be if they would courageously

take up the yoke of submission and experience the fact that it is not hard, but soft. As often as I think of the relationship between Deacon Lawrence and his bishop Sixtus, and of the wonderful talk they both had when the bishop went to his death—which so beautifully expressed both childlike and fatherly love[50]—I also think of the relationship between vicar and pastor and I wish for nothing more than that there could be a similar talk of heart and lips between them. Lawrence called to the bishop who was going to his death:

> Where are you going without your son, father? Where do you hasten, holy priest, without a deacon? Do not leave me, holy father, for I have already spent the treasures you passed on to me. Where do you go? You never used to offer sacrifice without a deacon. What is it in me that displeased your fatherhood? Did you find me degenerate? Test whether you have chosen an able deacon whom you have entrusted with the dispensation of the Lord's blood.[51]

Such intimate childlike love for the old man found a glorious echo from the heart of the bishop.

> I do not desert you, my son, nor leave you behind, but greater battles for the sake of the faith in Christ are due you. We receive the course of a lighter struggle as old men. But for you, a young man, there remains a more glorious triumph over a tyrant. After three days, oh deacon, you will follow me, the priest![52]

Oh, how often the banter among pastors and vicars sounds quite different! There is no respect for old age in the heart, no giving of honor, no tenderness, no consideration or forbearance, no kindness, no friendliness, no childlike behavior of the vicars. Nowhere are they as bored as in the company

---

[50] Saint Lawrence (Laurentius, c. 225–58) was one of the seven deacons in ancient Rome during the papacy of Sixtus II (r. 257–58). Lawrence was born in Spain and became close to Sixtus. Both went to Rome in 257, where Sixtus repaired relations between the Latin churches, which did not call for rebaptism after lapsing, and some African and Eastern churches that had broken fellowship over the question. Sixtus II was beheaded in the persecution under Emperor Valerian on August 6. Lawrence was martyred three days later.

[51] *Quo progrederis sine filio pater? Quo, sacerdos sancte, sine ministro properas? Noli me derelinquere, pater sancte, quia thesaurus tuos jam expendi, quos tradidisti mihi. Quo progrederis? Tu nunquam sine ministro sacrificium offerre consueveras. Quid in me displicuit paternitati tuae? Numquid degenerem me probasti? Esperire, utrum idoneum ministrum elegeris, cui commisisti dominici sanguinis dispensationem, etc.* This text exists in various forms. Ambrose of Milan is the earliest source for the traditional story of Lawrence's martyrdom. This translation reflects traditional Roman Catholic usage in English.

[52] *Non ego te desero, fili, neque derelinquo, sed majora tibi debenture pro Christi fide certamina. Nos quasi sense levioris pugnae cursum recipimus: te autem quasi juvenem manet gloriosior de tyranno triumphus. Post triduum me sequeris sacerdotem, Levita!* On referring to deacons as Levites, see Caspar Ziegler, *The Diaconate of the Ancient and Medieval Church* (St. Louis: Concordia, 2014).

of the pastor. Talkative at other times, they become silent here. Despite all manner of reflection, no subject of conversation is found; every spoken word is painful.

It is significant if, gradually, one introduces an obligatory politeness and cold formality. Often even this does not happen. Often ill will, disgust, and estrangement take place between the two. And as it happens in the house, so it happens in the office. The vicar often forgets that he is a vicar. He talks as if the congregation were **his** congregation, as if **he** were its father, as if **he** were officiating in his own, and not in another's realm. He talks as if he were the originator of all faith in the congregation, the only, the first evangelist. In all areas he tries to see much farther than his "old man." He finds in the latter only a roadblock to all progress, and he would do everything differently and better if he would only be allowed, if he would not always be stopped.

How often one can find proofs for this description in life! How much injustice and sin, connected with being a vicar, do many young men heap upon themselves! How much injustice often is done to the old ones! Oh, what seeds of retribution youth sows for its own old age! Unfortunately the immodest, unreasonable bravado of the vicar often is applauded by the congregation and by those loud-mouths who always turn toward the rising constellation! Oh, there is so much darkness, so much that is saddening in life, and yet it could be so much more beautiful if everybody would recognize his calling and within its limits would simply want to prove and confirm his Christianity. The vicar or pastor who does not desire to live in harmony with his **neighbor** from the bottom of his heart is no Christian, let alone a servant of God! May God give us **true Christians** for the Holy Office, Christians as pastors and vicars!

E. INTERIM PASTORS

30. In many German states vacant congregations are served by neighboring pastors until there is a new pastor. Without a doubt, a vacant congregation can be served only poorly in this way. At the same time the congregation that is supposed to share its pastor with the vacant one is also short-changed.

In other German states vacant congregations are served by specially-appointed **interim pastors**.[53] It makes sense to pick such interim pastors from the more mobile class of clergy, namely from the candidates. One cannot deny the fact that specially appointed interim pastors will bring more blessing to a congregation than regular neighboring pastors who have enough work to do in their own congregations. But it is also certain that an

[53] The usual LCMS parlance includes *vacancy pastor* and *interim pastor*. English texts during Loehe's lifetime used "clergy in residence" for *Pfarrverweser*, which term one can still find today. A pastor (*parochius*, *Pfarrer*) is assigned with tenure to a geographical parish, whereas clergy in residence are temporary and mobile.

interim pastor cannot replace a pastor. Both the age of the interim pastor and the short duration of the interim, as well as the very term "clergy in residence," raise serious objections against greatly favoring the interim as an institution.[54]

31. If an interim pastor is a strong young man, especially if he is a lively and pleasant preacher, he usually finds more, disproportionately more **favor** and **approval** than an equally strong and gifted pastor.[55] In city churches a gifted young preacher attracts the female youth and women in general in such a manner that offends propriety, so that occasionally one must blush. In country churches he usually wins over the majority of the population, indeed, more often for bad reasons and causes than for good ones.

The farmer, as a rule, pays the pastor his due with a certain envy (*invidia*). That does not happen with an interim pastor. Indeed the latter can insist on the payment of dues without causing ill will because he does not collect them for himself but has to give an account. And the low salary of the young man invites a person to bring him gifts.

If one gives to someone voluntarily, one will also protect him. One becomes party to the person to whom one rendered "honor." The more one gives, the more one is attached to the man (see Micah's priest, Judges 17:7–13).

In the case of the pastor, he stays longer and there is less chance for a change. He comes into much closer contact with the congregation, gets to know people, conditions, hurts, and sins much more closely. He is less likely to be fooled and easier to be disappointed. His more exact knowledge of things makes him less inclined to praise and gives his preaching of repentance more the appearance of intentionality: His whole behavior hits home more, cuts faster and deeper into the secret wounds, causes more pain, etc.

It is totally different with a clergyman in residence. He never settles down. He is a guest, and the more his talents appear in innocent youthful charm, the more his eagerness is accepted gracefully. The time of his stay and the lack of judgment and experience prevent him from getting to know the people, their conditions, their wounds, and their sins.

He is not feared like the pastor, because he has not been initiated into the secret frailties and sins of the congregation and he cannot penetrate there. Even with his best will, because of lack of time, he cannot start anything that

---

[54] Some pastors serve in the LCMS as intentional interim pastors. They often are retired or mobile and have skill sets that aid the restoration of parishes that have experienced significant problems.

[55] [Loehe:] Concerning lively and pleasant preachers, compare here Dr. Heinrich Müller's *Geistliche Erquickstunden* [*Spiritual Hours of Refreshment*] No. 197, [Editor's note: Heinrich Müller (1631–75) earned a doctorate from Helmstedt in 1654 and was a pastor and church official in Rostock, as well as a university professor. He was known as a superior preacher and prolific author.]

would upset the congregation or would endanger any wrongfully claimed rights or goods. It is easier to question him about pastoral relationships. He can easily become involved in interests that are against the former, perhaps also the following pastor. While he is in office it might be easy to do things that serve only the self-interest of the congregation. He is less interested in being careful toward the congregation.

In short: The effectiveness of a substitute pastor, even if it makes deep impressions, cannot go as deep as that of a permanent shepherd. As encouraging, refreshing, uplifting, and arousing the life and work of a substitute pastor may be, as highly as it may be appreciated, there is always a certain superficiality connected with it. And that is exactly why many, often the worst congregations, are often so happy with their substitutes. If the substitute pastor also has a good voice, a pleasant delivery, lively, concrete and penetrating thoughts, a winning personal conduct, a congregation can easily "fall in love" with such a young pastor. All passions are aroused in favor of the beloved and one hates to see the time of his parting coming. One wishes to keep him instead of the designated pastor. There is no lack of petitions to the consistories or the patrons to get him as pastor.[56]

And if all this fails, one tries to satisfy oneself in all possible ways. One showers the young man with gifts and promises, with praising speeches and signs of love. And it is self-understood that a newspaper notice cannot be missing. A newspaper is a public place for all kinds of rendezvous that one wants to have noticed.

Thus there will be a hard beginning for the new pastor, who often cannot find a better comfort in his fate than justice, for he also had prepared the same kind of suffering when he was a substitute—perhaps quite innocently—and now it serves him right to suffer the same. However, there remains **yet another** (bad) comfort for the newly arrived pastor. If in receiving him, his congregation gives him the cold shoulder, he enjoys so much [more] the hearty welcome of his neighboring colleagues, for whom the young, strong substitute was a test of patience, especially if he had the misfortune to excel over them with his shiny gifts. This has the effect of throwing fireworks into a crowd of people.

32. As far as the **clergy in residence** is concerned, the interim position **also has two sides for them**. One side: It cannot be denied that interim positions give many opportunities to gather experience. Young men who work first in a school, then in a biennium as described above, and finally in a proper vicarage could not find a more appropriate step for further education than being an interim.

---

[56] A consistory is a governing church administration that oversees either a region or an entire church body. Patrons are nobles or heads of trusts that fund the operation of one or more parishes.

Not infrequently, young men in interim situations celebrate a blossoming of their spiritual life and work. And the learning that they undergo is so pleasant due to the independence that is lacking in other learning situations. It is training in which one can prove himself. And right at this point lies all the danger. An interim pastor has the same rights and duties of the office that the pastor himself has, only not for such a long time. True, he is lacking the experience of life and of office. But since an interim pastor seldom gets into the difficult and cumbersome aspects of the office, the little he has is usually enough, as long as he has other gifts. His lack of experience is usually not so noticeable that it should cause him qualms of conscience.

The other side: An interim pastor usually enjoys the earthly benefits and temporal success of the office, but also walks under the strong temptation to become arrogant. Many a young clergyman has laid the foundation to a self-centered life and sulky arrogance while serving as an interim pastor. This made him later incapable and at the same time unhappy, once he heard the applause go silent and could not find the reason in himself.

33. Therefore one can give no better advice to interim pastors than to **be satisfied** with what their calling involves, and not to cross over any barriers that their office or their youth may put up. They are filling in a gap between a predecessor and a successor, but are never called successors of a pastor. Part of the essence of an interim is to **limit oneself to the necessary things.** [Those include] working in Word and doctrine in whatever **manner** the congregation is used to, refraining from undertakings that will have **many consequences**, etc.

The holy respect that an interim pastor has for the intimate relationship of the called shepherd with his flock should show in all that he does or omits. This should include a sacred piety toward the former pastor and toward the successor. To carry this piety in his heart and to impress it on the congregation is his duty. In addition to pure doctrine, it is the best fruit he can and should bring, unless there are more important reasons and considerations that require him to do otherwise. Therefore an interim pastor must make exact inquiries concerning everything connected with the office, how the last pastor handled things. Unless it is against the Word and the oath of his office, he should do everything the same way.

In any case, he should mistrust his own opinion and speak very carefully about the former or the future pastor and consider it a virtue to honor their way of fulfilling their office. It is not proper for an interim pastor to bring up new things. **If at all possible, he should leave everything the way it was.** If it is not possible, he should only make such plans that do not offend the new pastor, do not limit him, unless he could talk over things that fall under the competence of a pastor with the newly designated pastor. No matter how blessed he is in his office, he should never forget that his proper glory and task is to work as a guest, a person who is hastening away and cannot become a permanent citizen, and that he should turn over the congregation and its

hearts to the new pastor in the best possible condition. If the humility of a vicar is that of a son toward his father, the **humility** of an interim pastor is that of **John the Baptist**, and its motto is: "I must decrease." Doing this, he erects the most beautiful monument for himself.

F. ON THE KIND OF PASTORAL POSITION TO WHICH ONE SHOULD APPLY[57]

34. Gregory the Great says in his *Regula Pastoralis* (Book I, Chapter 7):[58]

> Moses trembles when the Lord calls him. Being weak, perceiving the burden of honor, he gasps. Whoever is strongly urged toward a case away from his own will gladly submit his shoulder to oppressive, strange burdens. What he is in need of, he cannot carry and the burden gets heavier.[59]

Many others, even in the Protestant Church, have made the same complaint. And how much would one have to complain, especially currently, if one would start complaining! The way applications are handled is tremendously irresponsible.[60]

---

[57] In the LCMS a placement process exists in which the seminaries and the Placement Subcommittee of the Council of Presidents work together to match a candidate with a first call.

[58] Gregory I (Gregorius, c. 540–604) was pope from 590 to his death. He was a prolific author, a major figure in the shaping of Christian liturgy, and the first pope to come from a monastic background. He converted his villa into a monastery and was chosen to be the papal ambassador to Byzantium under Pope Pelagius II. His papacy was known for mission work in England (Augustine of Canterbury), greater influence in the locally-dominated Gallican church, liturgical reforms, and the largest volume of papal writings to that time. His works shaped the medieval Western Church. He argued that the resurrected body would be glorified, yet real flesh and blood, contrary to Patriarch Eutychius, who favored an incorporeal body.

[59] *Moyses suadente domino trepidat, et infirmus quisque, ut honoris onus percipat, anhelat; et qui ad casum valde urgetur ex propriis, humerum libenter opprimendus ponderibus submittit alienis; quae egit ferre non valet, et auget, quod portat.*

[60] [Loehe:] Without any doubt, one of the saddest pages in our Lutheran *Landeskirchen* is the system of employing the applicants according to their age. This is easy and comfortable, but a source of unspeakable evil! This is a strong statement, but one could write books full of proofs for this claim. Let these buildings collapse!

According to ancient understanding the pastor is the groom, the congregation the bride, and the installation is the wedding when the bride is given to the groom. But one changes the marriage and the wife so often, and for such comparably small reasons, and there is so little manly love and faithfulness, that it is no wonder when the congregations also have not much left of feminine, faithful love. Whoever leaves his wife so easily and so often cannot be very effective, not only because of the shortness of time, but also because of a changeable attitude. O that God would grant repentance to the shepherds—in all things—especially in this one!—Go ahead and apply, but do not forget that the Head Shepherd will demand an account.

Yet this does not do away with the right use of applications, grounded in 1 Timothy 3:1, especially at a time when there are so many applications that one hardly receives a call any more without having applied for it. To write *De clerico renitente* [*Concerning the Resistance of the Pastors*] is fairly superfluous for our conditions. Dr. Ziegler wrote about this.[61] Nevertheless, it would be good if the eagerness to apply for a parish position (*Pfarrei*), or for a different one if one already has a position, would be a little more restrained and cooled off by the words "to be without fault" (ἀνεπίλημπτον εἶναι) that follow the words "to desire something" (ὀρέγεσθαι) in 1 Timothy 3:1. See the chapter in Gregory's *Regula* that fits well here. In any case, we have no desire to praise the misuse of applications here, even if we are presently trying to solve some questions regarding pastoral placements for which one can apply.

35. Should one apply for a position where one is not alone in the office, but has **colleagues**? True, colleagues in the office should always be the best colleagues. If anywhere on earth, brotherly love should flourish among them and bear fruits. However, things are not what they should be, and Psalm 133 is seldom sung by colleagues in fellowship. If there is to be peace, love has to come from **two** sides, and how seldom one finds a two-sided love! (It is a shame that one has to say this.) Therefore, a wise man will ensure that his love is not tested too much and a smart man does not trust himself too much.

Whoever wants to apply for a position where he will have colleagues, should first of all not only inquire about the character of the colleagues, but also be sure whether the rights and duties of colleagues are clearly defined or not. If that is not the case, it would not be good to accept such a position. Uncertainty concerning rights often leads to arguments and can kill off love. But if the mutual rights and duties are well defined, or one can be sure that everything can be ordered peacefully before one starts in the new position, a man who is conscious of his love and peacefulness, who humbly is ready to bear another's burden, may well dare to become a colleague.

The Lord is able to preserve him from the evil and misfortune of discord that robs so many noble souls of all joy and cheerfulness, making them old and grumpy before their time. And He can do more than that: He can give true brotherly love and deep peace and complete harmony. We read in Proverbs 16:7, "When someone's ways please the Lord, He causes even his enemies to be at peace with him." Why should the Lord not make colleagues, who walk the right way, content with each other?

36. "Should one apply for a position **in the city or in the country**?" This is not an unimportant question either. Whoever prefers to work in a city

---

[61] Caspar Ziegler (1621–90) was from a wealthy Leipzig family that suffered in the Thirty Years' War. He became a law professor and rector of the university in Wittenberg, writing about canon law and its relation to Lutheranism. Loehe refers here to Caspar Ziegler, *De Clerico Renitente, Sive Muneris Ecclesiastici Fuga, Dissertatio Justinianea* (Wittenberg: Henckel, 1684).

usually has to take colleagues "as part of the deal" and has to be prepared to stand the pain of that kind of rivalry that we already hinted at. For that reason alone, some people are afraid of "city positions." But this is not the only reason for fear. One also usually considers work in the city as being more difficult than in the country. While the life of a country pastor is painted as almost idyllic, one sees the task of a city pastor as especially difficult and full of trouble. And yet it is a real question whose task is more difficult. In the end, will not the little needle of the scale turn toward the side of the country pastor? Whoever has tried both, to serve in the city and in the country, will agree.

One can dare to assert this even if others should be of the opposite opinion, even if they quote Goethe and Rousseau, as does Hüffell, for example.[62] A lazy pastor, or one with a sunny disposition who likes to see everything through rose-colored lenses, who allows himself to be torn away from the dream of youthful enthusiasm only with the greatest resistance, may well live quietly and comfortably for a summer in the country. But winter will come, and if that does not cure him of his idyllic views of the life of a country pastor, people will sooner or later cure him, once they get the idea to present themselves as they truly are. In general, things in the country are the way Pestalozzi described them in the first part of *Lienhard und Gertrud*.[63] One can also see the same in the older little book by Andreas Hartmann, the little practical theology book for country pastors.[64] Compare A. Hartmann's *Gespräch vom Landleben*.

---

[62] Johann Wolfgang von Goethe (1749–1832) and Jean Jacques Rousseau (1712–78) were influential respectively in the formation of the *Sturm und Drang* (seething and longing) movement and romanticism (with the French revolution). These general movements stressed the emotions and human existence itself as factors additional to reason in shaping truth and accepted norms. Noted aspects included heroism, nationalism, anti-naturalism, and the tension between the individual and society.

[63] Johann Heinrich Pestalozzi (1746–1827) was a Swiss educator whose methods have been very influential, yet strongly shaped by romanticism. Educated as clergy, he nevertheless changed careers due to the influence of Rousseau and poor performance. His *Lienhard und Gertrud* volumes (1781–87) depicted country life. He was strongly influenced by Herder, Goethe, and Fichte. His philosophy included breaking a subject into small component parts, understanding the role of language, understanding the respective roles of home and family, state and nation, individual and vocational self-determination, and a basic human goodness. He believed that education promoted inner peace and greater faith in God. His ideas were opposed strongly in the early LCMS because they saw in his approach a rejection of original sin and a religiosity dominated by individual feeling instead of Scripture.

[64] [Loehe gives the reference, here translated with the original title:] *An Unprejudiced—Simple—and Well-Meaning Sketch of How a Village Pastor May Guide the Congregation Entrusted to Him in an Edifying Way, to the Acclamation, Honor, and Praise of Jesus Christ, the Arch-shepherd of Our Souls, and to Be of Profit and Service in the Fear of the Lord for the Righteous Under-Shepherds; Written Previously, but Now Published by Magister Andreas Hartmann, Serving in the Territory of the Most Serene Duke of Würt-*

Whoever starts a **pastorate in the city** first has to conquer his entire position; nothing is ready-made. He comes, he preaches, one listens to him, his public forms and gathers itself completely freely, his confessional is sought or avoided according to what this one or that one wants. Every pastor is worth as much as he is capable, and things can get pretty sad and depressing if he finds no approval, or only very little.

Yet it is always easier to find one's way in a small circle of parishioners and to blend in, rather than to be father confessor of unwilling, contrary people and enemies. But that is the case in the country and cannot very well be different. The new country pastor has to accept so many previously unknown members and confessors, and they have to accept him, whether they like him or not, whether they trust him or not. That means a hard task on both sides, becoming accustomed against one's inclination. Much time must pass to solve this, and many an unkind word spoken, many mean steps taken on both sides.

The miserable enticing and tempting away of confessing members that a young city pastor can experience from his colleagues, and all the pain and aggravation that he gets to enjoy, together with all other city burdens, could be of little consequence in comparison with the difficulty to win the trust of a congregation that is composed of so many different elements.

Whoever takes on a **pastorate in the city** has to understand city customs and know how to deal with the people. However, it is easier to adapt to city customs, which are pretty much the same everywhere, or at least similar. A candidate grew up at the *Gymnasium* and at the university. Even if he grew up in the country, he does not first learn about the city as something new by the time he takes over a city church. The **country person**, on the other hand, also has his customs and traditions. They can be very stubborn and very different in different areas. How can a pastor who was not reared in the parish either know or get to know the customs and traditions of his congregation? Customs and traditions often seek to be invisible before him. The farmer often withdraws bashfully from the pastor, does not explain himself, and often does not know how. Often he does not know why he is not being understood by the pastor, since from his youth on he was always understood by his own, even without talking or explaining. It certainly is not easy even to understand the dialect of the farmer, or the way he talks. It is even more difficult to get accustomed to the whole being and life of a country congregation, to understand it and—very important!—to make oneself to be under-

---

temberg, Pastor at Truchtelfingen (Ulm: Georg Wilhelm Kühns, 1710). [*Unvorgreiflich—einfältig—und wohlgemeinter Entwurf, wie ein Dorfpfarrer seiner anvertrauten Gemeinde erbaulich vorsehen moge, Christo Jesu, dem Erzhirten unserer Seelen zu Lob, Ehr und Preiß, und redlichen Unterhirten zu Nutz und Dienst in der Furcht des Herrn, ehemals verfasset, anjetzo aber ans Licht gegeben von M. Andreas Hartmann, hochfürstl. württenb. Pfarrer zu Truchtelfingen*].

stood, without giving up the tone and the way it is proper for a pastor to act toward a congregation. Thus shepherd and flock face each other as strangers and many troubles stem from this relationship.

If one were to believe certain people, the education of the city person would be an obstacle, the simplicity of the **country person** an advantage for the Holy Office. However, education, of which the city person has more than the farmer, is a formal means to the opposite [conclusion], because it helps the pastor's language and expression to be more understandable. The farmer especially lacks this in comparison to the city dweller—so there is an advantage.

And by the way, the farmer is extensively familiar with his surroundings. He is smart and cunning. By cleverly guarding his advantages, he is equal to many city people. He stubbornly does not want to understand whatever he does not understand, is not easily fooled, and behaves toward city people something like a Jew behaves toward a Christian, namely, daring and often convinced in his self-interest. It is hard to say how much the farmer knows of the vulgar regions of life and is a master of them, how he knows how to use everything, how little he cares in general whether he heaps sin and guilt upon himself or not. Cheating, stealing, lying, swearing falsely—oh, what other gross sin would one have to omit here? You will find that the farmer can cleverly or not so cleverly hide it. Wily and cunning so that he does not get caught, he goes the path of his father, and his whole simplicity is usually only **superficial**, with a few comforting exceptions.

And [for a pastor] to penetrate through this, penetrate with a public that did not choose the pastor, received him with suspicion and watches him with a sharp eye and a listening ear—truly, that is a difficult and great task. To solve it, great spiritual and emotional gifts are needed, which one would have to call impossible without the powers of the world that is to come. It seems so much easier for a narrowly gifted man to reach his goal in a city, rather than in the country. There it is easier to win true, unfeigned recognition. It may be that there one needs a little more outward skill in speech and behavior, but skills of the spirit, certainty of purpose and means, consequence and endurance, strength, patience and forbearance, in short, all manly virtues—the country pastor needs these to an exceptional degree. In addition, even for his own sake, he needs much joy and desire for holy studies. Constantly working among coarse people necessarily requires a strong antidote if one is not to learn from them subconsciously and accept what is not decent.

Surely one could say much more about the **difficult position of a country pastor**, but let this suffice, and an intelligent person might learn from it what he does and chooses if he applies for a country pastorate. All in all, whatever position one might choose, one should consider and weigh everything. Often there remains a great difference among pastorates of the same kind. Each one should question **himself** above all, whether he would be a good fit for the pastorate for which he wants to apply. Will he be capable enough for the circumstances? Could he not become miserable and make others miserable? For everybody must ensure that every position will receive the right man, and every man the right position. Gregory the Great says in *Regula Pastoralis*, Book 1, Chapter 1:

> No one presumes to teach an art till he has first, with intent meditation, learned it. What rashness is it, then, for the unskillful to assume pastoral authority, since the government of souls is the art of arts! For who can be ignorant that the sores of the thoughts of men are more occult than the sores of the bowels? And yet how often do men who have no knowledge whatever of spiritual precepts fearlessly profess themselves physicians of the heart, though those who are ignorant of the effect of drugs blush to appear as physicians of the flesh![65]

[65] *Nulla ars doceri praesumitur, nisi intent prius meditatione discatur. Ab imperitis ergo pastorale magisterium qua temeritate suscipitur, quando ars est atrium regimen animarum? Quis autem cogitationum vulnera occultiora esse nesciat vulneribus viscerum? Et tamen saepe qui nequaquam spiritalia praecepta cognoverunt, cordis se medicos profiteri non metuunt; dum qui pigmentorum vim nesciunt, videri medici carnis erubescunt, etc.* Translated by James Barmby from Philip Schaff and Henry Wace, eds. *Nicene and Post-Nicene Fathers, Second Series* (New York: Christian Literature Company, 1896–1900) 12:2b.

Chapter Two

STARTING OUT IN THE OFFICE

A. BELONG TO ALL YOUR PARISHIONERS

37. Today's congregations are composed of many contradictory parts. If one were to classify them, one could perhaps divide them into two main groups: The first would be those who respect religion and church, the other would be its despisers and enemies. Each group still has many subdivisions. But as many parties as may be found in a congregation, it is the duty of a pastor who has the courage to take over such a congregation **to recognize all of them as his parishioners**. His eye should see every group, if possible each individual soul; his heart, his undivided love, and his great diligence belong to all. Just as a shepherd counts both goats and sheep, mother sheep and little lambs, sick and fragile sheep as belonging to his flock and turns his shepherd love toward them all, the shepherd of souls should turn his eye and heart toward all the different members of his congregation.

His sacred intention, which he should pursue with greatest responsibility, should be the salvation of all. With each sheep he has this purpose—each should be treated according to its need, and all of them should be treated with the same kind of love. The Lord, the arch-shepherd, leaves the ninety-nine that have been found and seeks the one that is lost. He loves not only the loveable ones, but also the poor sinners that are lying in the dust by the road. Every pious shepherd of souls should love and act as He does. Nothing can turn his love away from anyone, as long as God's Word itself does not order otherwise.

No offense will make him angry; it only will awaken his love and his pity anew. One should be able to say about him: "If you offend him, he will love you so much the more." An unconquerable love must fill and drive him. One could object here that such behavior would be contrary to the separation between brotherly love and general love, which is founded in Holy Scripture; that indifferent people and enemies of Christ are not brothers, that one should use discipline and strictness with them. But all that does not do away what has just been said. We did not say that one should love the enemies of Christ as brothers, that one should mix brotherly love and general love, or that one should omit discipline and strictness where they are needed. On the contrary, we believe that discipline and severity themselves are only forms of love, that the increasing of discipline through grades of admonition should also be considered an increase of love, that one should love everybody, but each according to his need for salvation, just as all should be saved, even if salvation comes to different people via different ways.[1]

The majority of congregations today do not know any discipline. They do not know yet of the sacred duty of punishing love, disciplining love, and through those two, saving love. The wonderful passages in Matthew 18 and 1 Corinthians 5, etc., as much as they speak clearly and plainly, yet they remain hidden and dark to their eyes. They count everyone a Christian who calls himself that.

If there is to be any discrimination, if disciplining, saving, educating love should happen, it first has to be striven for by the pastors through word and deed. It is up to the new pastor to bring about better days through the gracious help of the Holy Spirit. But this again can happen only slowly. The pastor comes into the congregation that has been newly assigned to him. He does not know the individuals. He does not know yet where he should exercise general love, where brotherly love, and where discipline. **But this much he knows: All** individuals are assigned to him. Thus he includes them all in his love, until the love becomes clarified into certain and manifold expressions of love. He has been called for all. He has accepted the call. As his call is, so is his will, his intention. He stands in the congregation in order to save all, if possible; if not all, then at least as many as possible. Toward this end is directed all his strength, all his faithfulness, his desire, his love. And thus for him there is no contradiction when he tells himself: "You belong to all your parishioners."

38. As soon as the new pastor has started working in his congregation, his people will approach him. There comes the pious simplicity that loves the office of the shepherd and opens its heart to every new pastor in love and in hope. Therefore a new pastor should take care not to give offense.

But there also appear among the first those who, being of the pietistic party, are pretentious enough to expect to be noticed first by every pastor, to be preferred and drawn close to his heart. Among them there are people who

---

[1] Here Loehe refers to people's sensibilities and their likelihood to respond to Christian discipline, not to different means of salvation. Both Loehe and Walther showed sensitivity to this point, but Walther was more reticent than Loehe to explore the interplay between personal traits and divine truth. Walther preferred to state biblical truth as self-sufficient and deal with human reactions to that as subsequent casuistry. Part of that was the LCMS reaction to the role of emotion and reason seen to mediate religion in romanticism. See Walther's *Amerikanisch-Lutherische Pastoraltheologie* and *Law and Gospel: How to Read and Apply the Bible*, 343–52.

must be purified, turned, changed, but it would not be right to give up hope. Therefore they also must find a friendly eye and a resounding fatherly heart. But among them there sometimes are also those one cannot stand: desperate, impossible people. They become more unpleasant as time goes on. They embarrass the pastor who trusts them, love to play the role of confidante, take his side as long as he does the same for them, and sting with poison once he no longer can do that.

For their sake the new pastor should season his friendliness and love toward those approaching him with the dignified seriousness of an upright and open reserve. I say an "upright and open reserve" because in the end, one can reveal the reason of this reserve in the friendliest and most open way.—Sometimes the very best parishioners are the last to approach the pastor. This is not right. The "best" are missing here, but that is how it is. Despite their reticence, they have to be taken into consideration by the pastor, even before he knows them. And because it will upset them if the pastor joins those well known professional pietists that we mentioned before, for their sake he has to go slow in bestowing personal trust. Besides those "best" we mentioned, at last the worst also will come. They are that bad because they know that there is nothing to the Christianity of the party people. If the pastor turns toward the latter, the former lose their personal confidence in him right away, since they have never had any confidence in his office. Therefore, even for the sake of the worst, the pastor should go slow with his trust.

Perhaps one could sum up the principal points of correct behavior in these words: Do not easily have fellowship or even camaraderie with a parishioner, least of all right in the beginning. Do not forget in your private life either that you are supposed to be a shepherd of **all** your sheep. You are as human as others, you need personal love and you will find it, be sure of that. You will find it most surely and most sweet, the less you chase after it, the more totally you are a pastor. As a rule, approach others only in an official way, when the office requires it, with the mercies of the office. All personal love should be poured into your official coming, so that you appear as the best friend when you come in the business of Jesus and of souls. Stand as bishop, shepherd, guardian, and watchman over all, and do not give up your standpoint, so that you can come to everybody at his time and can be everything to all. Conduct yourself in such a way that no one will get angry with you because you preferred this one or the other, and would close his heart toward you in times of trouble. Conduct yourself in such a way that everybody can believe in your love, your loving wisdom, your loving, wise, and strong manliness and dignity of a shepherd.

39. From these general rules comes all the wisdom for the new pastor behaving in specific cases. Whoever observes them also will find the right behavior toward the rich and the poor, which is so often lacking. Accepting the "needy" and the poor is uncomfortable and unpleasant for a pastor (oh, also for the new and especially for the young pastor) who himself would like

to enjoy the peacefulness and the rest of a fortunate life. On the other hand, to be close to the rich and fortunate feels good for the one who would like to be fortunate himself. And for the sake of the pleasant and comfortable feeling that goes with the fortunate, one also considers him as possessing inner fortune, the peace of a just spirit.

A young pastor should guard against this, especially at the beginning when all impressions are simply overwhelming. Go slow with your trust in the rich and in the poor!—The same goes for the behavior of a pastor toward those who are **preceded by a good report of true piety, just as much toward gross sinners**. No one should be received as a saint or as perfect. Everyone should hear the call "forward!" and be challenged to chase after the goal that has not yet been reached. Friendly and brotherly respect goes well with this. Appreciation and the call to a holy "forward" can go together well; both, spoken together, will easily be understood in their connection by one who is absorbed in the apostolic word "I press on."

The pastor should likewise be oriented the same way in his behavior toward gross sinners and enemies. A pastor sees every person that comes to him as a candidate for eternal life. There is no difference between such a one and a saint except for the wonderful hour when things start to get better. But this hour can still come for anyone still living. Since a pastor knows this, he treats every sinner that comes to him with the fullness of that love that does not approve, justify, or excuse any sin, but hopes and prays for every sinner. Unexpected silence where one expected a severe rebuke, an unexpected friendly reception from the one from whom one had expected severity, goodness of a man in whose entire life and action one is inclined to see an embodied sermon, has often had an effect on those for whom one had given up hope. This is true in general. It is doubly true for the early days of a pastor, during which time one can gain much, which later cannot be won.

40. It feels good to people and is encouraging if the new pastor shows in word and action that **he takes it for granted that no parishioner despises the good and the right way**; that it was not ill will, but other, less culpable causes that have held up any progress so far. It is depressing and negative, if from the start mistrust seems to **rule**. Of course, enough ill will can be found everywhere. But since one does not know who has it, and a brief encounter is not enough to recognize it, it is not a sham, but human truth and wisdom to treat **everybody** with hope, until one has more experience, which perhaps is contradictory. For trust is needed for the beginning of all work, and the verse "Love hopes all things" has its most natural place at the beginning of one's career. Of course, it is understood that this hoping is not stupid, not indiscriminate, not naive, not built on human factors, but it builds on the grace of God. This hoping will succeed quite well with the expectation of one who knows human nature, even in the new congregation where one finds many who walk on the wide road. The more mature the pastor is, the more peacefully and easily hope and fear, trust and mistrust can abide together.

B. GET READY TO STAY A LONG TIME

41. All human conditions are imperfect, and nothing is more visible in new conditions than imperfections. Because new pastors have not prepared themselves for this, they often are very surprised and depressed by the imperfections and deficiencies of the new parish, the congregation, the house, and the income. It happens before they even take time to become inwardly reconciled with their situation and to overcome disappointment. It happens while they feel overcome by homesickness for their former life, so that they have not yet been acclimatized. In one word: right at the very beginning, already they run out of patience.

Then they assert—which sounds so ridiculous to the more experienced ones—**that they do not want to stay for very long in the new position**. They do not even realize that their coming and going is not in their own power, or else they would leave immediately. They do not consider that with their improbable talk nothing is changed, just as no one can jump out of his own skin, even if he would like to do so. It is unmanly and childish to want everything good, which shows that one does not want what one ought—that one does not comprehend the exalted love of a shepherd—that one has sought oneself, not the office and the kingdom of God, if one sighs and moans with homesickness for an earthly home.

One ought to resist this misery by recognizing one's sinfulness and ask God, and also quietly the congregation, to forgive the lack of love of such longing. Doubtlessly it would depress the congregation and hinder the effectiveness of such a shepherd if it came out how dissatisfied and unhappy he is with the new position.

42. Instead of contemplating the existing deficiencies and nuisances, one should rather consider the unhappiness resulting from them as a vexing **temptation**. Once one has overcome this, one will have strength for the task that one has taken on. But in order to overcome it, one must vividly believe that one is not put on earth to have everything good on earth, but in order to serve the Lord and His kingdom. Remember that there is no other calling in which one can do this to such a high degree as in the spiritual one. One should not forget what the congregations are, what is owed to them, and what should become of them, and that they should become everything through the service of the shepherd. May the exalted calling and the heavy responsibility wake them out of the torturing dream of selfish misery and spur them on to the work in the office, which makes one forget oneself! One ought to be clear in what one is to do. One should decide faithfully and patiently to press on toward the clearly envisaged goal. **One should only be concerned about achieving what one ought to accomplish, and not torture oneself in figuring out how much time that will take.** Under no circumstances should one promise to stay only a certain number of years. But one should not refuse that promise because one wants to leave again. The time

should be of no importance. As long as it is God's will, one should quietly and faithfully do what God wills. One should recognize God's will in the call and joyfully sacrifice his own will, dedicating all strength to God. Our time is in His hands. He knows when it is evening for us, wherever we are. He gives patience until the evening comes.

C. Do the Work that Lies Before You; Let Everything Else Come to You

43. Nothing is more common than having new pastors want to attack and improve, if not everything, then at least too much. Once the despair of the beginning is past, many pastors may find the **vigor, truly indeed, the arrogance of the beginner**. Because one considers the task easy and overestimates one's own strength, one gets ready to take the place by storm. One attacks too hard, and as a consequence, one tires quickly and has to scale down. One does too many things at the same time and soon one has to leave a heap of things that had been started just lying there. One did too many things before, now one does too little.

This causes an inwardly crippling and shaming feeling of impotence. In the congregation the fair judgment will arise, which nevertheless is very damaging, that the pastor is a beginner and does not yet know his job. That is a heavy price to pay for the urge to do great things. The laurels that one already thought to possess are withered before they could ripen. The best thing in this case is the fact that the vanity, which ought to die, has received a mortal blow.

44. **Whoever does not want to give the impression of being a beginner—let him be a beginner**. Even though one may have the burning desire to reach the goal, one should not forget that the best long-distance hikers start a journey with short daily treks and go slow. In this manner, little by little, strength for greater efforts and endurance will increase. A wise person therefore will plan things in such a way that he can gradually do more and more, rather than having to quit too soon. The people will soon recognize and honor such a beginning and trust that such a beginner is skilled and a master and they will not be mistaken in their judgment.

45. According to these principles, at the beginning a new pastor will do only what is necessary, and he will use all diligence to do it right and completely, as the circumstances require it. Only once he has mastered what is necessary, he will also start something else. The work that he does, he conquers. But he will be sought by it, rather than seeking it. He lets it come by itself. By going slow he can better learn his terrain, and while he goes forward step by step, his walk is right and certain and he does not have the immediate need to take a step back. He will conquer one evil after another and win one victory after another. The more everything goes unnoticed and the more the progress is natural and appropriate, the less it appears forced and the more it

will proceed undisturbed. The people then will gradually recognize the master by his work. Even before enemies' resistance has found an opportunity, one is recognized as experienced. Those who know how much this kind of experience helps praise it highly.

46. One can observe this careful but blessed procedure especially in the area of **pastoral care**. By no means should one believe that there is some way, right at the beginning, to get to know the congregations surely and quickly. Methodical visitation challenges the people also to find a method.[2] If you try to get to know them in a methodical way, they will also know how to hide and cover up methodically. They will easily achieve their goal, and you will have it so much harder. Therefore, avoid any methods, and from the beginning keep to the principle that any spiritual care is **case-by-case**. Wait for the opportunities and use them. Of course people will not reveal themselves in these either. But the opportunities during which a pastor can approach his parishioners in his office usually are of the kind that opens the heart more than at other times. In addition to this, a pastor can learn a lot through simple watching and observing of the general conditions of his congregation, and gradually he can become acquainted with his field of labor and its characteristics. Without much running around, during which he seldom gets much done, in this way soon enough he will get to know his congregation and the individual members. Soon enough, he will have some kind of a relationship with all of them. Soon enough, he will be the spiritual center of his people. And in all quietness the relationships will become more frequent and more personal; the bonds will connect more numerously and more personally. It will become apparent that no person will work more quietly and in a general way, no one more secretly and yet publicly, than a pastor who stays within the limits of his profession.

47. This kind and manner of working also includes the fact that in **sermons** one will not immediately speak with the intent of curing souls or about

---

[2] [Loehe:] S. J. Baumgarten does a good job setting limits for **house-calls** in *Kurzgefaßte casuistische Pastoraltheologie* (Halle: Bauer, 1752), 847ff. He states them under "**Consideration of the education of children, arranging home services, caring for the souls of the domestics, considering social life, also how to gain the confidence of listeners in a permissible way.**" He disapproves of methodical house calls as being indecent and a disadvantage. There is "no call for them; **nor can one achieve even a minimum of preparation of the listeners.**" [Editor's note: Siegmund Jakob Baumgarten (1706–57) became a pastor in 1728, assistant professor at Halle in 1730, and professor there from 1734 to his death. He served as rector and was prolific as an author and translator. He was influenced by Christian Wolff (1679–1754), whose rationalism struck a center-right political note and helped usher in the rationalist German Enlightenment. Baumgarten's work was continued by his assistant, Joachim Salomo Semler (1725–91), who differed from the radical approach of Baruch Spinoza (1632–77), nevertheless undermined religious piety in Halle. Baumgarten and Semler helped usher in historical-critical exegesis, yet Baumgarten's pastoral theology was read widely in Germany. The German-era LCMS avoided Baumgarten's works.]

specific cases.[3] Ignorance about conditions in the beginning is a **privilege** that the pastor may use with the best knowledge and a good conscience. He has no opinion about this congregation, cannot have one and does not want to form a poor judgment. Therefore, as long as possible, he treats all people in the way one ought to view and treat all people, even the unknown, according to Holy Scripture, namely, as souls that have been bought for a price and are in need of the office of a shepherd. Therefore, he preaches repentance and redemption in a general way. He stands by the verses that say that God orders all people everywhere to repent, that he wants all people to be helped, etc. With time, there will arise counsel and enough occasions to become more casuistic and specific.

Of course, there are occasions right at the beginning where one sees clearly and feels forced to give a witness, despite the fact that one has just come into the congregation. And the understanding people will view the exception as justified and the judgment of the others does not count. But in secret, the one who becomes casuistic and specific too early will lose respect and effectiveness for later times. Of course, he was **not able** to hit the mark. He became **ridiculous**, and that spoils things for everybody for a long time.

Of course, it is true that sermons only become very interesting and appealing and successful if they are made for the specific conditions of the congregation. But the fact is that one **is not able** to preach that way right from the start. Let one save the good wine for later and be happy if in the long run more water is changed into wine, and not wine into water!

48. There is a way to get at least an outward knowledge of the congregation, right at the beginning. One should not overestimate its importance, but nevertheless it is worth noticing and paying attention to, so it should be mentioned here. It consists of the study or writing of an accurate **family register**. A family register contains names, birthdays, dates of Baptism, confirmation, marriage and death, also the other main events in the public and moral life of a family and its members. It is arranged according to towns and house numbers, and once it is done, one can also add to it the register of confessions, also according to families, so that it can serve as a supplement to the family register.

For the one who is not the shepherd of the congregation such registers are worthless. But the pastor will learn very much to appreciate them. Not only does one get to know the congregation to a certain extent when reading or starting the registers, but they are also a big help for memory and for the time when the pastor recalls his members in prayer, not to mention the advantages one enjoys when issuing certificates of birth, confirmation, marriage, and death. If it is necessary to start such registers from scratch—and

---

[3] [Loehe:] The best beginner in pastoral care is the one who tries his best to win souls through sermons, catechesis, and the liturgy. To win [souls] through general and objective lectures is better than anything else in the beginning.

there are indeed many congregations where this is necessary—this admittedly laborious, but subsequently very fruitful work offers an excellent opportunity to call upon the fathers of the families, and with them to review their families, their names, etc. That is the simplest way to get acquainted with members of the congregation. May the author be permitted to reproduce a few pages from a family and confessional register of this kind in the appendix.[4] Perhaps many a young pastor who follows this advice to start a family register and a confessional register that is based on it later will bless this apparently unimportant paragraph from the bottom of his heart.

49. **Trust** from the congregation is necessary for a shepherd, yes, very necessary! But because one can trust only the person who has proven himself, it is natural that one cannot demand or expect this trust until one has proven himself. But this happens if one does honestly and simply what needs doing, and proves in all situations that one does not desire anything except to do the right thing for the salvation of the congregation.

Trust can never be achieved immediately, only gradually. The means for this are works, works of love—faithful, patient works of love. Yet trust is not the immediate goal; rather, it is the kingdom of God and its righteousness. Trust **comes to the one** who seeks the kingdom of God and its righteousness. It is therefore an undignified whoring if a new pastor seeks to win trust at any cost. Men of God wish for trust and they do what they can to awaken trust, but they do not run after it; rather, they wait for it. In this way it usually comes sooner and remains longer, once it has arrived. Here also one can say: "Work at what is at hand. Let everything else come to you."

50. Every pastor will and ought to wish to accomplish as much as possible in his congregation. But he knows that he himself is only one factor in this product. He does not know whether the other factors will be found. He does not know whether God will use and bless him the way he wishes. He knows that his primary goal is his own salvation, and he does not know whether much success would not be harmful for his soul. Because he knows all this, he does not promise himself what he wishes, but he simply works in such a way that he meets what needs to be done in his place, so that he will do his best in order to accomplish what he wishes. Everything else he submits in prayer and supplication to the One who is and remains Love, even in his

[4] [Loehe:] See the appendix at the end. [Editor's note: The excerpts from the registers are in Appendix B. Note that confessional registers became mere formalisms in the face of numerical growth (almost 200% between 1930 and 1962) and corresponding spiritual decline in the LCMS as a result of changes in the postwar U.S. From levels of over 80% across-the-board involvement in worship and Christian education in 1916, adult education dropped to 10% by 1950, with Lutheran school attendance at 25%, regular Communion at about 33%, and regular Sunday worship at 40%. Confession and announcement to commune gave way to advance Communion notices, then Communion cards, and now little if any formal preparation. See also J. E. Herrmann, *The Chief Steward* (St. Louis: Concordia, 1951), 4.]

hidden counsels and guidance in the dark. "He does what is at hand; everything else he lets come to him."

D. Spare Your Predecessor and Your Successor[5]

51. Whoever has had the opportunity to deal with newly arrived pastors will know how they usually do not have a good feeling about their predecessors. He did not do much. He made many mistakes. He must be at fault for every evil in the congregation. Any kind of allegiance that may be shown here and there to the predecessor, even timidly and softly, he must have gained through performing his office wrongfully, just pleasing people. He deserved any ill will directed toward him. And the internal inclination of the heart is so plagued with antipathy that the new pastor has to talk about it at every occasion. It can also happen that there is no occasion, so he produces it forcefully. And then it does not matter to whom one speaks, whether to trusted friends or to parishioners, who should really show some kind of piety toward their former shepherd.

Of course it is true that many a pastor has a predecessor whom it would be a sin to praise, whose esteem by the congregation is founded on sinful premises. Only the equally unrepentant sinner can show him any kind of piety and favor. Yet often the predecessor was an honest man, but not perfect. One should spare such a person.

And often it is only envy of the predecessor's decisive and overwhelming excellence and his open recognition that fills one's heart and mouth with complaints. At that point one should have the courage to eradicate the envy with love, for there is no better remedy against envy than love. (This is a paradox, but a true one.) One therefore should embrace the one who caused suffering for his successor with nothing but gift and virtue.

Oh, it throws such a bad light on the new pastor if it seems from his words that the better time started when he first came, that before him only darkness covered the congregation. On the other hand, an unaffected, honest recognition of the predecessor is beautiful and will win the hearts! It seems to indicate a noble and fair heart if from a pastor's lips flow easily and without effort words of praise and recognition of his predecessor. If many a new pastor would only know how much farther he can get through recognition of the good, rather than through disapproving the faults of the predecessor, he would fight the envious arrogance of his soul quite differently, and the Lord would also come to his aid and deliver him from sin and dirty consequences. Spare your predecessor; you will save your conscience by doing so, also your

[5] [Loehe:] To that, one should add **spare your colleagues**. How often it is that especially younger pastors overlook this rule! Through thoughtlessness, e.g., by methodical and unannounced house visits, they invite upon themselves the suspicions of adultery and of greed.

congregation's respect, and your effectiveness! Let this be the unforgettable rule for a new pastor.

52. If the first half of the heading of this paragraph, "Spare your predecessor" is easy to recognize, it is different with the second one. "Spare your successor" does not seem to make any sense. But it only seems that way. Even if one does not know the successor by name and cannot see any of his work, nevertheless, by pushing things without any regard, one can limit and confine one's successor, no matter who he is. Much lies in the power of a pastor for the practice of which the consideration of his successor should lead him to the word of the apostle: "All things are lawful for me, but not all things are beneficial." If anyone, e.g., can achieve more in one area than someone else, perhaps his successor, he should consider whether it would not be more beneficial for the congregation if they can see their pastors acting in unison, rather than having to watch how the predecessor surpasses the successor.

If a lesser amount of work is done with different gifts and in a different way, but with equal dedication and equal seriousness, there is more blessing to be gained on the whole than if someone wants to outdo the other. A different gift nevertheless has its effect, **without bothering the other**; otherwise the congregation is misled to choose. It will be human preference of the one over the other, which usually involves passions. In order to give an example: Let us assume a pastor has much physical strength, which would enable him to preach six times a week. Strength gives him the desire, and thus he starts out doing this, without asking whether his successor would be able to do the same or not. Would one not have to criticize such behavior?—Of course it would be different if certain circumstances would require daily sermons for a while. This would be justified by the circumstances. And if these circumstances would extend to the time of the successor, one could not blame the predecessor.

There are many such cases. An upright man, therefore, will act in such a way that, as far as he is concerned, he will not give an offence, whether he is present or absent. He is concerned with the true salvation of the congregation and does not want in any way to elevate **himself**. He always thinks himself as a link in a chain, as one that is between others, as is usually the case. His intention is to continue the work of the predecessor, and to prepare things for the successor as best he can. Just as he is happy if his predecessor has left him some points of contact, he also seeks to make it easy for his successor to follow in his footsteps. As for himself, he works toward the goal that he personally will be missed as little as possible. He wishes his good deeds to remain hidden because of the connection between predecessors and successors. He does not want them to become public. It is enough that the Lord sees them.

If things would go according to his wishes, no transfer, no death of a pastor would leave an empty space. It would lead to the point where the members of his church would have to say: "From time immemorial one could tell here that the office has changed hands only by someone moving in or out, or by death."

This we mention here only because beginners are the ones who sin against it the most. And yet, at their age, they have no more assurance than in other circumstances that they would not soon have a successor.

E. As with All Other Things, Put Public Life in Order from the Start

53. In our time, a pastor, right at the beginning of his office, takes on quite a number of outward rights and duties. He knows that. Therefore, it is good if, right at the beginning, he acquires the most complete and exact knowledge of them.

It is something uncomfortable, feeling almost indecent, if one has to ask right at the start what the limits are and what the extent of one's rights and duties is. And yet it is only natural that in taking over the office, if possible even before then, one would get to know these things as exactly as possible.[6] Also, as uncomfortable and oppressing as they may be, making exact inquiries is more fitting at the beginning. To inquire into certain cases after one has started in the office will give the impression of thoughtlessness and inconsideration when applying for the office. And yet it is a sign that a man is master of his profession, which one cannot be without knowing the limits.

It can easily happen that a close inquiry into rights and duties can lead to many an unpleasant investigation, many complications, much friction, offense, and aggravation. But if there is to be aggravation, it is always more advisable to have it right at the beginning, because then there is probably more time to forget and to come to an agreement, rather than saving the unpleasant for later. Even if at first there was a disagreement, and this one or that one distanced themselves, they usually come back again once it becomes apparent that the pastor nevertheless remains in the quietness and innocence of a good conscience and will not be interrupted in the practice of love, not even by those who think they were offended. Yes, whoever has the courage to have a disagreement right at the beginning in order to keep an undisturbed peace later on will in the long run be acknowledged for the uprightness of his attitude. Of course, the upright attitude has to be there first, the driving motivation cannot be ambition and greed, for the sake of which one would interfere with the interests of others from the start.

54. In connection with what has been said, one ought to be clear from the beginning what **written reports** for secular authorities are required of

---

[6] [Loehe:] A well-meaning advice concerning **moving expenses**: Do not think that you can trust the liberality of the congregation, but have the whole matter of cost fixed even before the move. If you neglect this, you will regret it, and the joy over the new position will soon be watered down.

pastors, or have been found necessary to submit to the church government.[7] An exact **calendar** listing the periodically recurring requirements and a timely naming of the **due dates** when they have to be submitted should be hanging in a place where one often sees it. Just because these things usually leave a bad taste and are unpleasant, and although any secretary easily could do them as well or even better than the pastor, yet one should familiarize oneself with them in order to take care of them as soon as possible.[8] It is easy and very advisable to imitate *Eulenspiegel* who would run uphill to the top and then look down on those who follow.[9]

Right from the beginning, one should learn completely the right way of this so-called "administration" so that one gets it behind him. If one fails to do this, one can cause for oneself unnecessary trouble, much grief, and aggravation. Experience teaches that these things are more difficult if one does not know them well. Many a skilled worker has accomplished the same thing in half an hour that can eat up half a day or even whole days if one does not go about it the right way. Once there is a mistake, it will vex the sloppy worker in a miserable way. Just like the teasing of an evil spirit, these things can persecute a pastor all his life because he did not learn from the start to do them easily and happily.

It is very advisable for a beginning pastor to get to know his **registers** and, if necessary, to put them in order. It is a tremendous job to put even modest registers in order. Many a day will be wasted in ordering files, writing summaries, indexes and alphabetical registers of the individual files. But one goes through this trouble only once and then enjoys it for the rest of one's ministry. For it is no trouble to continue an ordered register and to use it. On the other hand, to continue a disorderly one and to use it is a displeasing pain. Nothing saves more time than, for once and all, to know one's register exactly and to have mastered it.

55. Some written jobs, e.g., bills for the poor chest, memorial funds, schools, etc., are not the direct duty of the pastor, but it is good he occupies himself with them. Inexperienced pastors, who cannot get enough of the means by which the Holy Office influences people—all because they do not know them—believe that if they take over these jobs they can secure

---

[7] Examples of this in the LCMS include submission of statistical reports; prompt, correct processing of marriage licenses; and careful recording of official acts.

[8] [Loehe:] But do not lightly settle accounts just to be rid of them and thereby to **forget about** them. Occasional forgetfulness could find its revenge in the necessity of being occupied with them ever more frequently. Finish them quickly, but also respect them and remember them well!

[9] Till Eulenspiegel (owl's mirror) is a German folk character who lives the life of a vagrant and, through miscommunication and tricks, he exposes vice, greed, folly, and hypocrisy. These humorous and scatological tales from the Middle Ages use comedic wit for entertainment, social commentary, and critical reflection.

influence over the congregation.[10] And yet this influence, even if it is achieved, is not great, does not last, and does not bring any thanks.

The schoolteacher may accomplish these jobs just as well as the pastor. If the pastor does the work, the benefit for the congregation is very little. But the loss of time for the Holy Office is very great. It cannot even be estimated how often he will come in touch with the secular government. They often enjoy letting the pastor who submitted this work feel their superiority. They reject and criticize, often causing the pastor to rub them the wrong way and thereby also put him into an undignified, passionate excitement. Even in order to spare himself such sinful excitement, the pastor should leave such work to those whose job it is, and keep himself as independent on secular business as is possible. A pastor should do his office. Other offices he should leave to others, and he should not hunger for praise, as if he were a good businessman.[11] For this praise is small. It requires no studying of theology, no ordination, no spiritual gift. It really does not concern the Church and its servants. It is fitting that it belongs to them who have been appointed to such in the world. How beautifully Balduin says at this point:

> Every office has its own place, like a circle in which it is contained. Its accounts should not be vague, but should be useful to a certain group of people.
>
> The servants of the Word should stay within the limits of their job! The Lord prohibits getting mixed up with another bishop! Luke 22:25. If the servants of the Word should stay within the house of the Lord, which is the Church, they must not spend time in public affairs or in the political realm, having one foot on the political platform, the other in the courts. They should not dictate forensic laws to the magistrate, nor promote political assemblies, nor promote wars. They should not govern whole kingdoms and provinces.
>
> They can render judgment in general criminal matters, e.g., what should be declared murder, the punishment for a stubborn free person, and the doing away with adultery. And this is not outside of the pastoral office, since the Word of God extends to everything that happens under the sun, and therefore in former times was expressly prescribed for the priest, Deuteronomy 17:8. But they should **commit to the deserving magistrate** both the examination of the present fact and the judgment to be applied. **But to litigate in court,**

---

[10] [Loehe:] However, there are also some very skilled pastors who have a good mind for figures, etc., finish them quickly, and lose less time when they do it themselves than when they supervise others. For them a different sort of advice would apply.

[11] [Loehe:] Does it mean more fame if a pastor is a good **parliamentarian**? "Let those who have the time attend the territorial congress," said a poor sick woman to a pastor who wanted to leave the care of the sick to others to go to the parliament.

> even in matters of transferring ecclesiastical goods, is something foreign to the pastoral office. Thus one should commit this to the prefects of the treasury, **lest the ministers be called away from their sacred labor and think about stirring up hateful things for others.** Therefore in the imperial laws clerics are also exempt from public actions in the courts and it is said that **it would be absurd, even scandalous, if they would want to show themselves as experienced in forensic debates,** etc.[12]

If a pastor follows such principles from the start, the congregation soon will get used to it, and later will find much that is good in this. Even if the predecessor followed another practice, one does not have to follow him, because one will not cause him, or the successor who might act differently, any displeasure. And the people will for once learn by this example that their pastor has more to do than to act as a secretary, and that they do not have to measure or appreciate him based on this. A pastor should supervise such work, but he should not do it.

56. Part of putting things in order at the beginning is also that the pastor should realize **who is under him, who is equal to him, and who is above him,** and how far his authority goes in all directions. As soon as he knows that, he should also behave accordingly. He should not be a buddy either to his superiors or to those that are under him. To the former he should be obedient in humble simplicity, as far as the Word of the Lord permits this. To the others he should be a friendly and mild superior. To those who are under him he should be the way he wishes his superiors to be toward him.

---

[12] *Omne ministerium suum habet locum et quasi circulum, intra quem continetur, ne vagae sint eius expeditiones, sed certo hominum generi prosint.—Intra cancellos muneris sui se contineant ministerii verbi!*

Ἀλλοτριεπισκοπήν *prohibuit Dominus! Luke 22:25. Si ministri verbi in domo domini, quae est ecclesia, versari debent, non versentur in republica, seu in foro politico, alterum pedem in suggestu, alterum in curia habentes; non dictent magistratui leges forenses, non cudant consilia politica, non procurent bella, non gubernent tota regna et provincias.—In genere et in thesi de causis quoque criminalibus iudicium ferre possunt, ut quod homicidae sint occidendi, immorigeri liberi puniendi, adulteri tollendi; idque non fit praeter officium ministri, cum verbum Dei ad omnia, quae sub sole fieri possunt, se extendat, ideoque olim sacerdotibus in specie praeceptum fuit Deuteronomy 17:8. Sed facti praesentis examinationem et theseos ad hypothesin applicationem* ***merito committunt magistratui.*** *Sic litigare in foro etiam ob alienationem bonorum ecclesiasticorum a ministrorum officio alienum est; ideo praefectis aerarii committi debet,* ***ne ministri a laboribus sacris avocentur et aliorum in se concitare odia cogantur.*** *Idcirco legibus Imperatorum etiam clerici ab actionibus publicis in curia exemti sunt* ***et absurdum esse dicitur clericis, immo etiam opprobriosum, si peritos se velint etiam ostendere disceptationum forensium, etc.***

[Loehe:] See a strange passage concerning **secularization** of the office of bishop from Gregor and Geyser in Hutter l.c. p. 41. Concerning **independence from worldly power**, which is not even desired, see Luther WA 15:2380; Hüffell I, p. 37. [Editor's note: See also Ziegler, *Diaconate*, chapter 16.]

If it does not please him constantly to be scolded, least of all by his spiritual superiors; if he has the ardent wish to hear the fatherly tone of pious and wise fathers and bishops, despite the almost unavoidable office language that goes with his position, the *judicia ecclesiastica magistratuum territorialium*;[13] then let him not deserve his fate because of the tone he uses toward his subjects. He ought not to permit the rudder to be snatched out of his hand if it belongs to him. Let him not be a comrade to his cantor or deacon, nor use the familiar *Du* in addressing them, nor drink a toast of brotherhood with them.[14] But let him be fatherly, friendly, brotherly, civil and helpful. Let him not be above making a humble request in order to receive gladly what he could have gotten with stern words, but only grumblingly. In short: Let him be pastor and never lord. Let him leave the worldly imperative to the secular authorities, since God's command, the power of His Word are on his side.

F. In Social Life, Orient Yourself Right from the Start So That You Can Always Press Onward

57. As things are now, there is no doubt that the pastoral estate has the most opportunities for continued education. While the jurist, the physician, etc. walk in very limited spheres of life and are almost forced to one-sidedness through their occupation, the pastor, through his office, is guided toward contemplating the general interests of humanity. He has the chance to take part in every intellectual movement, more so than other professions. That is also the reason why, in every area of human knowledge, amateurs from the ranks of the clergy have excelled. That is also the reason why members of the clergy are gladly seen in society and one expects something lively and refreshing from them. Especially in small cities where there are families with a higher degree of education, it is almost required and expected that the pastor should be a member of the society. If he is, he receives respect and applause from the honored and educated class. Perhaps they even want to

---

[13] [Loehe:] For this one ought to look up all the places that are listed under "*Konsistorium*" in A. H. Francke's *Collegium pastorale*.

[14] In modern Germany some of these barriers have softened. Laborers and students still use familiar speech among themselves, as do family members. Yet some offices have implemented informal speech among professional colleagues and office workers. Nevertheless, there remain important social situations where formal language is required, even when the parties have known one another for decades. A toast of brotherhood (*Brüderschaft trinken*) is a formal ceremony in which two people intertwine arms holding glasses. They introduce themselves by forename to each other and then drink, arms still intertwined. They then use familiar speech with each other from that time onward. English speakers should know that terms like *Herr Pastor* (or whatever other profession) are not used to signify lordship, but to express formal, often mutual respect for the pastor, doctor, and so on. In the U.S., German Methodists were among the first to attack the use of the formal *Herr Pastor*, suggesting that it impaired personal religious liberty and experience.

please the good entertainer and come to his church once or several times during the year (New Year's Eve)! If he is it not, as a rule—at least in the beginning—he has to bear the ill will of the august members of society.

58. Now one cannot doubt that there are still societies in the world where honesty rules, where the name of the Most High is mentioned with reverence, and where a pastor can show up without having to leave at home both his devotional character and the office that can never be separated from him. There is also no doubt that in **such kind** of societies a pastor **is permitted** to make an appearance, if in doing so he does not neglect any duty of his office, any sick person, any instruction, any sermon preparation, etc. He can do this **if** love for the Lord and for his congregation directs him to no better activity, and **if** he might not, **to offer in particular a bad example from the present day,** neglect his family life and the education of his children.[15]

However, this kind of society is rare, **very rare.** Societies of the opposite kind are more frequent, **very frequent.** Since a pastor **is unable** get to know the public societies of his town right at the beginning, and usually does not hear the truth about them, the best advice is not to participate at all at the beginning, until one has come to know one's surroundings in other areas.

Of course one may offend if one does not respond to common courtesy in this area, refuses invitations, etc. However, it is hardly a sign of life in divine things if, through thoughts of concern about possibly generating a bad opinion, one is led away from this kind of wisdom and its consistency in order to see everything only as a means to further the office.

Do what is right for your office; live in such a way that you do not stop your course! Do not easily step into a society, unless you are convinced that you do not have to retreat from there again. Do not behave in an unfriendly way, but keep yourself free from all social pressure, so that any approach will be seen as a sign of free love! Would God only make it that one would have that much courage at the **beginning**! It is still possible to find likeminded people! One would not become lonely! At the beginning it is hardest to resist the enticement! In the beginning one sins the most! One sins in the good name of Christian freedom! One sins—yes, unfortunately, and out of love for the social circles one loses the trust of one's people, who have enough tact not to seek their shepherd in societies![16] If only we would be wise enough to

[15] [Loehe:] One finds the most natural recreation, the most pleasant of all, in being with wife and child. Whoever has no taste for this does not make his wife and child happy and he is not happy. He is also to blame for the stubborn misbehavior of his children.

[16] [Loehe:] The customary invitations for the pastor to attend a wedding, a baptismal banquet, etc., are something completely different. If the pastor is aware of an honest intent; if he has a manly soul that easily influences others; if he does not imagine disorder and all kinds of embarrassment; then he will do well not to refuse such invitations. He should not expect any great effect from his being there, but neither should he despise a small one, which his presence there may have—namely **prevention of evil**. It remains well indeed if he is permitted to involve all present in his conversation, and in a friendly way keep

understand that here is as much a matter of one's own soul as the salvation of the potentially weak people. If only we would stay away from the social joys if they cannot be enjoyed in the Lord and for the good of the congregation.

The virtues of a man are prudence, justice, courage, and self-control (Wisdom of Solomon 8:7). They are **great virtues for pastors**. If one lacks the last one of these, can he be a man and a good pastor? Will he not miss the first three also?

An overseer must be . . . self-controlled. 1 Timothy 3:2[17]

---

everything in a good atmosphere! If the pastor is not there, a wicked teacher or some other evil-minded person may well use the opportunity to sow bad seed, incite the congregation, etc. All this cannot happen if the pastor is in charge of the conversation (see S. J. Baumgarten, *Kasuist. Pastoraltheologie*, p. 863).

[17] Δεῖ οὖν τὸν ἐπίσκοπον . . . εἶναι, . . . σώφρονα.

Chapter Three

Conduct

Lest after preaching to others I myself should be disqualified. 1 Corinthians 9:27[1]

A. Introduction

59. All official work of a pastor, be it done ever so well, will not earn him the respect of his congregation if a truly spiritual conduct is lacking. Thank God that in the consciousness of our people, teaching and life are still so inseparably connected that they desire to see a living sermon in the example of the pastor. That should be a real incentive for a pastor to lead a worthy life. The requirement of the people is for him to be an echo of his own sermon and a proof that he did not preach it in vain. In this demand, the preacher, who rarely knows how to preach for himself, also has something of a sermon, for which he ought to thank God.

60. Conduct has two sides: It is either **hidden** or **public**. Hidden conduct is thus called because it is **hidden from people**. Either they **cannot** see it because it takes place on the inside and is visible only to the All-knowing; or they generally do not notice it because, even though it may be outwardly visible, it is not in a way that would provoke the eye of the neighbor. Public conduct is shallow and empty if hidden conduct before the eye of God is lacking. Just like a dead body is different from one that still has a soul, a purely outward respectability is different from the holy life of a man who is filled with the Spirit of sanctification, both inwardly and outwardly, in his secret and in his public conduct.

61. If the outward and inner forms of conduct agree, the word of the apostle is fulfilled: "If our hearts do not condemn us, we have **confidence** before God" 1 John 3:21. Confidence and a good conscience before the Lord are needed by the one who is to proclaim to Israel its faults and to the people

---

[1] μή πως ἄλλοις κηρύξας αὐτὸς ἀδόκιμος γένωμαι.

of God its transgressions. On the other hand, God will reveal and avenge a secret shame, if one teaches differently and becomes disqualified. A good conscience makes a quiet, clear, confident, courageous, and manly soul. And that is exactly what you need for the Holy Office.

62. Pure conduct before God and men, and the good conscience emanating from it, is so much more necessary for a pastor, since he has to walk in an evil world and is hated by the devil. Because of this he cannot avoid **slander**. The person who always comes up with "something always will stick" at every rumor has little experience.[2] The slanderer sometimes is happy to use a little truth and turn it into a great lie. But often he lies and makes things up, and his children talk, as they say in the country, "just what they want." Therefore, no one will remain blameless for long, until any old rascal has the idea to blame him.

That easily can happen to a pastor who administers his office without preference for any person. As soon as an invective is spoken in a devilish and shameless way, it just as soon gets in circulation. Then everybody also will believe "what he wants." In short, there is no one on earth and in heaven who can escape the attack of evil tongues. This often hurts a poor person so much, especially when he realizes how important a good example is for the office. Then it is well if "his heart does not condemn him!" After a while, one gets used to everything, and once one is used to living under the attack of evil tongues, a good conscience will find its right and might. The joy of a faithful pastor is then like that of a unicorn, and his rest like that of a rock.

B. HIDDEN CONDUCT

63. We do not want to mention everything pertaining to hidden conduct, nor are we able to do so. But some things should be mentioned here. The source of all spiritual life is the Word of the Lord. Therefore, the apostle exhorts his Timothy to "pay attention to reading." Exegetical studying sometimes leads to a beautiful hour of devotion. But as a rule, it is a part of a pastor's work. It is quite different with cursory reading, when one does not pay attention to individual difficulties, but looks at the total context and lets it make an impression. Older theologians have praised the cursory reading of Holy Scripture very much, and saw to it that they would read continually and finish Holy Scripture in a certain time period.

In recent times, when one no longer seems to have the steadfastness and strength of will as formerly, the suggestion to read the Bible in a cursory way, to finish a certain amount in a predetermined time, and eventually finish the

---

[2] The complete Latin phrase is: *Audacter calumniare, semper aliquid haeret.* "Slander boldly, for something always will stick." It is apropos to see this advice in light of today's ideologically biased broadcast media, the calumnious tendencies of social media, and the indefatigable spirit of flame warriors in the Internet.

entire Bible, was considered a limiting of Christian freedom. As if one could force another one to do this! As if it were not possible to read the entire Bible as a free Christian! As if there could be danger involved if one freely chooses daily to read the divine Word! As if it had been a danger for the fathers! One never tried or practiced it and yet one considers it dangerous! Ignorance, lack of experience, laziness, and realizing one's own inconstancy—that is what keeps one from the great blessing of regular reading of Holy Scripture. But let one find inner quietness and practice in simplicity what the ancients practiced for a while, and one soon will stop considering those objections to be wise, which clearly lack any wisdom.

64. A pastor should read Holy Scripture. But let him also use **human devotional writings** that can feed his soul. Unfortunately there are only a few. There are almost no devotional books for evangelical pastors.[3] Yet the work and the needs of a pastor would justify writings of this kind much more, than, for example, devotional writings for women or virgins. If only we had a evangelical book as excellent as the Roman breviary is in its own way, a great lack would disappear and a rich source of blessing would open up. But since something like this does not exist and can hardly be expected, let the evangelical pastor be so much more eager to use the manifold **ascetic literature** of the Lutheran Church. Let him not despise these sweet fruits of the Holy Spirit, which have not been recognized nearly enough.

True, the expression of many famous Lutheran devotional books are of a strange manner. Therefore one cannot recommend them to those who get so caught up in the strange form of speech that they either want to imitate it, or are repelled by it. But we do have authors who are excellent in form and content, who deserve a place in the history of German prose, just as surely as the hymns of the Lutheran Church have already found their place and their laurels in the history of German poetry. We do not want to talk about one who in this area is revered by all parties, namely Luther. But do remember Scriver, Philipp Nicolai, Meyfart, etc.[4] Truly, with these and many other

---

[3] Most Germans knew of Starck's prayer book (*Gebetbuch*) and devotional book (*Andachtsbuch*). Not only in the LCMS but also elsewhere, the works of Spener, Rambach, Caspari, and others were in circulation. The LCMS certainly did its share to reprint or create devotional books, albeit the time of floration was near or after Loehe's death. Loehe's desire in this paragraph has been met today in works like *Treasury of Daily Prayer* (St. Louis: Concordia, 2008).

[4] Christian Scriver (1629–93) was a pastor, hymn-writer, and transition theologian who helped prepare the way for pietism. He is best known for his devotional works, especially *The Soul's Treasure* (*Seelenschatz*). Pastor Philipp Nicolai (1556–1608) is best known for his chorales, *Wachet auf, ruft uns die Stimme* (*All Awake, the Voice Calls to Us*) and *Wie schön leuchtet der Morgenstern* (*How Lovely Shines the Morning Star*). Johann Matthäus Meyfart (Mayfart, 1590–1642) was a pastor, professor, and sometime rector of the university at Erfurt (1635–36). His specialty was eschatology and he became a strong opponent of witch trials. Such processes had emerged after the 1484 papal bull *Summis desiderantes* of Innocent VIII. The growth of mysticism, the Great Plague, and the rediscovery of

authors we possess rich, lovely gardens of paradise, full of tall trees and beautiful, fair-smelling flowers, full of precious fruit and fresh springs. The richly gifted pastor, as well as the one with fewer abilities, can find in them blessing, progress, riches, strength, comfort, and encouragement. There should not be a pastor who is not well acquainted in our rich gardens. Provisions should have been made long ago that those who want to enter here would find guidance and counsel. Long ago there should have been a history of the spiritual literature of our Church, and a collection of the most glorious and best. This indeed would be the best beginning, the best preparation for an evangelical breviary.

But even to bring about these advance preparations, we would need praying, devout, celebrating souls, who read for their own devotion, who know how to prove and to measure everything they read, and find the strength for this in a soul that is living and worshiping in God's Word. May many young pastors take the necessary admonition and encouragement from what has been said here. May they begin a holy sweet, devotional study in their young years, to which one should be able to dedicate the quiet hours of one's entire life, without finding any lack or boredom.[5]

65. **One particular** exercise and expression of our inner life has been lost altogether among us, namely, **meditation,** the reflection of divine words and truths before the face of God. What is required in contemplating the text for sermon preparation, which in any case aids **structuring,**[6] ought to be required of everybody reading the Bible, especially of the pastor. Meditation brings many riches to the soul, and a pastor would often save the trouble of finding new things, if he would not despise to live in meditation **for his own sake.** He would find out that godliness is good for all things, also for the Holy Office. The one who considers in meditation the height and breadth, the

---

pagan sources in the Renaissance fueled a witch craze whose carnage that lasted over two centuries among Protestants and Roman Catholics. The Lutheran Benedict Carpzov (1595–1666) was a strong proponent of witch trials in this period. Meyfart is also known for the hymn *Jerusalem, du hochgebauter Stadt* (*Jerusalem, O City Grandly Built*).

[5] [Loehe:] At this occasion one may also recommend the use of the writings of the ancient church fathers concerning devotion. Whoever wants to experience the blessing of this kind of Christian literature may use, e.g., the following book in a prayerful way for a while: *Precationes ex veteribus orthodoxies doctoribus, ex ecclesiae hymnis et canticis, ex psalmis denique Davidis collectae, et nunc recens recognitae et auctem per Andream Musculum D. Lipsiae, anno 1573* [*Prayers of the Ancient Orthodox Teachers, Collected from the Hymns and Songs of the Church, Also from the Psalms of David, and Now Newly Recollected and Augmented by Andreas Musculus, Doctor of Leipzig, 1573*]. Early editions were soon out of print, even among Lutherans to whom they were dedicated, namely in the first decades after the Reformation. Unfortunately we would hardly be able to offer anew a Latin prayer book to the present generation, no matter how excellent it may be.

[6] Loehe uses the term *Invention* here, a German term derived from Latin that refers to the plan and structure of a sermon as it pertains to the rules of rhetoric, dialectics, the purpose of the sermon, and the outline structure that fulfills that purpose.

length and depth of divine love—he will certainly not have any lack of thoughts for his sermon.

The sainted **Calvör**[7] edited three devotional writings in 1691, later in 1711, under the title ***Christian Cloverleaf*** [*Christliches Kleeblatt*]. The third of these is titled: ***A Way Prepared toward Rest in God*** [*Gebahnter Weg zu der Ruhe in Gott*]. In this he engages

1. The inner **prayer of the heart,**
2. The so-called **ladder of devotion,**
3. The devotion of sighs.

A "small school of prayer" follows as an appendix there. The author of these pages puts down the main thoughts taken from the three main parts of the *Prepared Way* in a tract that he titled "Sabbath and Fore-Sabbath." It was printed for the second time in 1851 as Number Six of Part II of the tracts edited by the Society for Domestic Mission According to the Understanding of the Lutheran Church [*Gesellschaft für Innere Mission nach dem Sinne der lutherischen Kirche*] by Beck in Nördlingen. May the author be permitted to insert here, from pp. 36–41 of the modest little book, the part that deals with the **ladder of prayer** or **devotion,** or, what is the same thing, of **meditation**. The matter has become so unknown that a simple, thorough instruction can best show what is meant and how it is meant.[8]

CONCERNING THE LADDER OF DEVOTION, OR OF HEAVEN:

1. What do you mean by the ladder of devotion or of heaven?

   The true, blessed use of the divine Word, leading to devotion and to heaven, as it is found in Holy Scripture or also in human books, such as the Catechism.

2. I must confess that I still do not know what you mean.

---

[7] [Loehe:] One ought to recall here an older book, formerly much in use. In one of its many editions it is titled *Praxis Pietatis*. That means *Practice of Godliness*. Originally it was written in English by Doctor Lewis Bayly, bishop of Bangor, and printed thirty times. Because of its dignity it has now been re-edited (Lüneburg, printed and edited by Johann and Heinrich Stern and heirs, 1670) Its second part "includes the excellent practice of godly and devotional meditation, namely how a pious Christian can practice the consideration of divine and heavenly matters at certain times, and thereby may gain hearty joy and continued delight in this fragile life, and in the following eternal one. That comes together with a useful introduction concerning the examination of the conscience, and some beautiful examples of such meditations. It is brought into our German language from the English and French." The whole book would be worth having a new edition. [Editor's note: Caspar Calvör (1650–1725) was a Lutheran theologian, church official, and school inspector. The Anglican Bayly (d. 1631) influenced John Bunyan (*The Pilgrim's Progress*).]

[8] The subsequent excerpt is found in *Löhes Werke*, vol. III/1:93, line 29, to III/1:96, last line, as well as in the original 1852 published work.

Look here, the blessed use of divine truth consists in three parts: 1. **in contemplation,** 2. **in testing,** 3. **in prayer.** One can read Scripture quickly, and that has its own advantage and is necessary. But one also should not neglect those three parts of the blessed use of Scripture. Much depends on it!

3. Alright! So how do you practice contemplation?

    a) I take up a well-known passage, the verse of a hymn, a piece of the Catechism, a prayer, etc. I do not let a single word pass by, but I think about and take to heart each one after the other.

    b) In order to penetrate ever deeper and more thoroughly into the meaning and understanding of the words that I took up, I repeat them and think about them slowly, with devotional attention, several times. I also divide the verse into certain questions. I ask about all the circumstances: who, what, where, why, etc.

    c) Then I remind myself of other passages from Scripture, the hymnbook, and the catechism that agree with the one having my current attention, and I move these also within my heart.

    d) I consider what teaching, admonition, and comfort I can take from my passage or verse.

4. How do you practice this testing?

    I ask if this passage is also for me. This I learn especially if I look at the persons[9] addressed by this saying. If I belong to them, the passage belongs to me also. Then I apply it completely to myself, as if it were spoken to me especially. All the questions that I asked during the contemplation I answer once more as applying to me. But if I am not one of those persons to whom the saying is addressed, I do not apply it to myself. If it is a word of comfort, I do not apply it to myself until I have become the kind of person that can accept this comfort. Therefore I immediately start improving myself, by sighing to God for grace and conversion. If the saying that does not pertain to me is a pronouncement of punishment, I do thank God that He has preserved me from the sin that is being punished, but I also ask Him that He would preserve me further and that He would graciously forgive my other sins and weaknesses.

---

[9] [Loehe:] In the same manner one can research the virtues and the burdens, etc., of which the topic is comprised, and test oneself if one has them for oneself, etc.

5. How do you practice prayer?

   Whatever I have found in my contemplation and testing I sum up in a prayer.

6. How do you go onward from this preparation to a devotion of the heart?

   The virtues of the inner life of which the passage reminds me—these I use immediately for my **heart's devotion,** for the peaceful, blessed work of my inner Sabbath. The sins and vices that are mentioned—these I look at closely, curse and reject them, and ask God that I may be able to do this more and more with my whole heart, and that my soul may be far from desire and love for them. Thus I have come via the first three steps of the heavenly ladder to the fourth, i.e., through preparation I have come to the true devotion of the heart. And once I have been strengthened by moving away spiritually from evil, by coming near to the good, through the blessed moving of my soul in heartfelt prayer I go about my daily work and practice the good outwardly also, and let go of the evil.

7. Really you do not tell me anything new with this so-called heavenly ladder. One should always use Holy Scripture this way and let it lead one through the festive hours of the inner life to a foretaste of the eternal life.

   Of course it is nothing new. But who uses Holy Scripture in this way? What is easier than this contemplating, testing, praying—and what makes one wiser, stronger, and more blessed in what is good? Oh, how one becomes aware of the powers of the future world lying hidden in the Word! Oh how the Word becomes sweeter than honey and the honeycomb!—This is not a new thing. But for many Christians the practice may be very new. Oh that God would have it that this heavenly ladder, this use of the divine Word would be more common, more practiced and more loved! One would feel it in all places and everywhere.

8. I wish you would give one or several examples of how to use this heavenly ladder.

   First I would like to exhort you to try it yourself. Perhaps later I could give you one or several contemplations, tests, and prayers. One learns more from other examples if one has found those points by trial and experience, which are especially difficult.—And by the way, the practice is very easy after the given instruction.

9. I am asking you for just a single example. How would you apply contemplation and testing to the verse in John 3:16, "God so loved the world," etc.?

Questions for contemplation are these:

> **Who** has loved the world?—**What** has he loved?—**How, how much** has he loved it?—**What does it mean:** "He gave his son?"—**What was his intention** when he gave his son?—What does it mean "to perish?"—What does it mean "to have eternal life?"—Who is not supposed to perish?—What does it mean "to believe in the Son"?—Who among believers in Jesus is excluded from the promise of eternal life?—What other verses agree with this verse?, and so on.

In examining this, one may say:

> Does this verse apply to you also, oh my soul? It does apply to you; first of all because **you belong to the world** that God has loved so. The wonderful "so" applies to you also. For you also, the Son—the only begotten—has been given. So you also should not perish, etc.—But you would perish, if you did not belong **to the believers**. The blessed promise of eternal life does not pertain to you, if you do not believe in Jesus Christ. Does the verse with its blessed promise really mean you? Do you believe? Is your faith genuine?

10. But is this not a pure catechesis?

    Yes, but it is the kind where teacher and pupil are the same person. That means the questions sound totally different, and the answers also. This comes mightily from the heart and goes to the heart.

11. But it can also be a pure matter of the head.

    It can be so, but then that is the fault of the person himself and then, of course, it is purely something pedantic. But just practice it seriously, in isolated quietness, as one who seeks God. You will find a great blessing. Nor do you have to question **everything**. And even less does everything have to happen in **questions**. I just pose questions for the sake of brevity. Just practice on your own and you will soon notice that a blessed freedom is ruling in the whole matter. Anything anxious and slavish will soon disappear.

12. I have not yet asked you to show me how, after contemplating and testing John 3:16, one can sum it all up in a prayer.

You have done well. For this does not need a pattern. When you are praying, there should be even less anxiety than during contemplation and testing.

13. So you refer me to practice and experience?

Completely! Any judgment other than the one that comes from experience does not count here.—*Go on, test and practice* what you have learned!

66. In the foregoing excerpt on meditation there is already the idea that one should use the Word under reflection also for **self-examination.** There is also a self-examination that is independent of the contemplation of the Word. One could call it examination of sins. In the heart of a Christian there should always be an equal degree of light and power of the Word, whether or not he has an open Bible before him, that when he looks into his heart and at his conduct, he will find where he moved away and distanced himself from the Word and will of God. Wherever he goes, a punishment of the divine Spirit should go with him. He should know and feel that he is in the discipline and under the punishment of the Spirit.

But he should not only carry within himself this unavoidable consequence of a life that is directed toward the Word, or suffer it. No, he should meet the humbling effect of the Word and the Spirit with diligence in searching for his sins. Whenever he feels the punishment of the Spirit within, he should pray Psalm 139:23f.: "Search me, O God, and know my heart; test me and know my thoughts. See if there is any wicked way in me, and lead me in the way everlasting." It is especially befitting a pastor to live in constant self-examination, sorrow, and repentance—for the sake of the **sins that come with the office.**

Whoever does not live all the time in serious testing can carry many sins with him without knowing it. On the other hand, there is great humility and a sincere turning to the One who justifies the godless and makes them holy, in a heart that never misses the duty of self-examination. This goes especially for the pastor. If he lives in self-examination, the whole complex of his duties will be in his soul, ever new and ever more. Many things he will not overlook habitually, and not as frequently: things that everyone sees in him and disapproves (except for him), but that could often get away from him because of human weakness and forgetfulness.[10]

67. The self-examination of a Christian, especially of a pastor, should not be limited to his sins, but also include his **gifts** and their **measure.** Nothing is more common than to overestimate one's own gifts and the disgusting arrogance that goes with it. This often happens with men of small gifts, and they

---

[10] [Loehe:] A salutary practice! Set up examining questions concerning works and virtues of the office. Search yourself often based on these or a list of questions. Every profession has its own special table of questions.

show it with overconfident behavior. **Every** pastor pictures himself (and of course, his own flesh and blood, his wife, pictures him) as a speaker who in no way lacks importance, an able teacher, and a wise counselor. If, therefore, he has little influence on his congregation and small success in his office, he puts the blame on all kinds of reasons, only not where it often would be correct.

One should think that it would give comfort if one could blame meager achievement on meager gifts. But then, how can one be comforted with what brings the most bitter disappointment and the most shameful "humiliation"? No, then one would have lived in vain! One has gone through school, through the university, and the years as a candidate and has suffered so much. If all this was meaningless, it would be better to have chosen another profession. One cannot accept that. No, no! It is not because of lacking talent that there is so little success. The congregation just does not see the gifts of its pastor—there is a lack of appreciation of what is there—the people are to blame. Thus thinks the proud heart of the pastor. His own and his personal friends agree, and in the whole congregation no one has "the heart" to tell the truth that everybody knows to the one who should hear it. Thus the poor pastor walks around his congregation with a complaint and under pretensions about which everybody laughs behind his back.

The arrogance of the self-righteous is shocking, but that of the conceited is laughable. Both, however, are equally unpardonable, yet the latter is harder to remove than the former. It is easier to find a sinner willing to repent, than a person who is pie-eyed over his little talent and importance, and yet is happy and content in the community where he is only a small light, and is known as such.

That is how people are! A person is prouder of the gift that he thinks he has than of his righteousness. He would rather be called a thief than be called stupid. He would rather forgive that sort of thing than such rumor. And yet, how much does a pastor stand in the limelight, especially one blinded by arrogance about gifts!

If only he would recognize where his gifts lie, and where not. Truth and humility would make the congregation inclined to appreciate the existing gift so much more. He would save himself work that is often in vain. He would no longer try laboriously to raise figs and grapes from thistles and thorns. He would work more happily by forming and nurturing the truly existing gift. Even a small gift would have a better chance to grow if it is correctly recognized and then receives the **kind of help** that can be beneficial. Of course one should also educate, form, and strengthen the small gift. But just as one does not educate a little child by treating him like a man, the small gift also will not amount to anything if one expects things and sets goals that are not appropriate.

Besides that, the humiliation that one feels when coming down from flights of fancy is painful only for a moment. It leads to the truth, and whoever **is willing** to be led to the truth finds a **fortune**. The true opinion that a person receives about himself makes him modest, quiet, happy and joyful in the existing measure, and just toward others. In short, it is blessed like any truth, if one has the courage to embrace it. Therefore have this courage and open your eyes for yourself and your gift! Examine yourself in the light of God! Read and study the apostolic passages that deal with gifts and their measure, and ask God to grant you, not to want to be more than what you are by the grace of God. But then, let it be with power. Fill out your place and be happy with it. One does not require more from a steward than that he be faithful.—Preach sometimes for others and for yourself about the good fortune of becoming small and being small. You know that this good fortune makes the greatest among those born of women a darling of all. Be happy with your small measure and people will love you more and learn more from you, then if you puff yourself up while being nothing.

68. There is not much to say about the **prayer of the heart,** because everybody is convinced of its necessity and importance, and it would really be a shame to instruct those who are to introduce Christ's sheep and lambs to it.[11] Yet we allow ourselves the following:

A) We remind you of the places that we recommend to pastors for the practice of silent prayer:

a) Every house should have a **prayer chamber,** especially a parsonage. Since this is not the case, the **study** has to become the prayer chamber of the pastor.

b) The **sacristy** of the church is often misused for all kinds of things. Often it is the place for gossip for pastors, deacons, and custodians. Often it also has to serve as a study, and the pastor memorizes in it until he goes up to the pulpit. How much better it would be if it were used for a quiet place to pray from the heart, for prayerful preparation, for intercession on behalf of the congregation, and for all the needs of the Church and of the world! To this end a sacristy should always be lonely, lockable, furnished with a prie-dieu (*Betstuhl*) or an altar. One can pray without all this. Nevertheless one should not despise the kneeling position that a prie-dieu provides. It invites prayer and makes it more comfortable with its armrest.

c) Especially easy opportunities for the prayer from the heart are offered during **official walks** [in order to do a pastoral act]. Nowhere is one more lonely than on the way. Nowhere is one less exposed to a listener, if one is used to pray out loud. And there is great loveliness connected with the *Ambulando* prayer. Just try it once!

---

[11] [Loehe:] Yet it might be good to get to know the instructions of our pious fathers concerning the prayer of the heart from the above-mentioned writing of Calvör (point 66), the tract "Sabbath and Fore-Sabbath." One can pray from the heart without these instructions, and it would be awful if this were not so. But why despise an instruction that is based on thorough experience?

B) In the second place, we remind you of the blessing of **intercessory prayer. Martin Boos,** from whom we can learn a lot—even if we cannot always put him up as example—claims that all his former success in the office is something he received through prayer. "Behind the main altar in Wiggensbach," he often wrote in his letters to close friends, "I received through prayer my living faith and all the graces and gifts that the Lord granted me." (See Gossner's *Martin Boos*, p. 34).[12] What else were his prayers for grace and gifts except intercessions for the congregation, toward whose salvation and blessing all the graces and gifts he asked for should serve? But besides the success of receiving a true answer, the prayer for blessing and salvation of the congregation is a necessary consequence of true love toward God, who wants such prayer, and of true love toward the congregation, which needs such prayer. Whoever is not praying for the sheep is not a true shepherd. Intercession is simultaneously a duty of the office, and a duty of love.[13]

Yes, praying is the unconquerable urge of the heart within a true shepherd, and one that cannot be refused. A true shepherd will pray, even if he does not feel that he is heard. Nor does he pray only for his own visible activity. When Boos was pastor near the Rhine, in 1820, a friend visited him. Boos took his friend on a walk through the area and said: "Look here, on these mountains, there is hardly a place where I have not laid on my face, wept and implored the Lord that He would give me the grace again joyfully to open my mouth, and to proclaim His Word with the blessing that hearts may be awoken, but I find no answer." He had to pray, he could not do otherwise. And he was heard, more than he knew. And certainly, what his biographer says, is true (p. 11): "Without any doubt here, in Sayn on the Rhine, the Lord has worked more through him than elsewhere—at least on him—but He did not want him to know. It was supposed to happen quietly." Let us take notice of this to our shame! But may the Lord improve His servants and teach them

[12] Martin Boos (1762–1825) was a Bavarian priest who also served in Austria. He had a story similar to some Lutheran pastors in the German Revival period (*Erweckung*). Like Martin Stephan Sr. he was an orphan who was given a mentor and a good education. Like Walther he went through a period of ascetic, rigorous life to find a more evangelical faith. He developed a pietism that led to friction with Roman Catholic authorities but won him popularity among the laity, including some powerful patrons. He spent 1812–17 amid church legal processes. He was offered a professorship in Düsseldorf by the Prussian government in 1817 and a pastorate at Sayn two years later. Johannes Gossner edited his autobiography in 1831, which was translated to English in 1836. Boos has been identified among those who consider themselves to be "evangelical catholic" among Anglicans, Lutherans, and Methodists. Despite any similarities, he played no formative role in the LCMS.

[13] [Loehe:] For the godly pastor the list of his members becomes an admonishing register for necessary intercession. He also will do well to make an excerpt from this register for his daily quiet half hours, and keep making new ones in which all persons and matters are listed which must not be forgotten in intercession. Our love-memory is unfaithful and deceiving and needs admonition and help.

to be repentant and seek cleansing from their sins! May His Holy Spirit teach them to pray!

C. QUIET LIFE AND PUBLIC LIFE

Strauss once stated correctly that the life of a pastor is and has to be both the most public and the loneliest.[14] In the right alternation between loneliness and being in the public, according to **Thomas à Kempis,** there is not only a wholesome measure for every Christian, but it is especially a secret of the often miraculous effect when a pastor appears.[15] The office does not permit one always to live quietly and withdrawn. It makes the pastor the center, the rallying point of the congregation. At every official act and in fulfilling his duties it puts him in the center of the congregation.

On the other hand the office does not require that he would constantly live among the congregation, but it forbids it. Consider the **pastor himself.** If he were to lead an ever-present life in the midst of his parishioners, he would risk the danger of losing **perspective concerning them**. Whoever sees a thing only from close up will only see that thing at the end. He loses the comparison with other things, no longer is aware of their connection with others, and no longer sees the thing's true form. Thus the pastor no longer recognizes the true form of the congregation if he totally lives among and with them.

This is the advantage that the pastor has over the schoolteacher. The latter is closer to and in the midst of the congregation. In details he may often have more insights into the conditions of the members and can thus often correct the judgment of the pastor. But the pastor can have a more correct and better total judgment over all, and over the individual parishioners. Therefore it is easier for him to find out the right way to treat the congregation. And that is important! As far as the **congregation** is concerned, it will be harder to keep the respect for the pastor if it sees him always close up. It will have the same experience with the pastor as the pastor will have with it. Just as he will forget the true form of the congregation, the congregation will lose the **true** form of the shepherd. All relationships cease if one is **too close**. As for the official acts of a pastor who lives too much in the midst of his con-

---

[14] Loehe refers to Gerhard Friedrich Abraham Strauss (Friedrich Strauß, 1786–1863). He was influenced by the mediating theology of August Neander and became court preacher in Berlin. He influenced Prussian King Friedrich Wilhelm IV.

[15] [Loehe:] No one appears safely in public unless he relishes obscurity. (*Nemo secure apparet, nisi qui libenter latet.*) Thomas à Kempis, *The Imitation of Christ.* Book 1, chapter XX.2. [Editor's note: Thomas à Kempis ("of Kempen," Thomas Hemerken; 1380–1471) was born in Kempen near Cologne. He attended the Latin school in Deventer 1392–99. In 1406 he joined his brother at the monastery of Mount St. Agnes, where he served as a copyist and writer. He was ordained a priest in 1413. As a Canon Regular of St. Augustine he helped further the influence of the Brethren of the Common life. Four of his booklets were collected together and published under the title, *The Imitation of Christ,* whose influence was widespread.]

gregation, they will lose their impression because of the above truths, but also because the right quietness and rest for the preparation is lacking.

70. Experience proves that a pastor will win the most correct opinion of his congregation only in a quiet life interrupted only by official activity. This quiet, separate, yet always wakeful, attentive, observing life gives the pastor the **high vantage of an overseer** (*Episcopus*) and watchman. And he ought not to be without this high vantage point. Out of necessity, he must live above the congregation in whose midst he lives. This is true if he wants to oversee it and its needs, notice approaching dangers and take care to prevent them.

The people would be impressed by a quiet life as being **something befitting**. It would make a thoroughly **favorable impression**. They do not **require** their pastor to be a comrade; they talk negatively about such a thing. Yes, one can well say that only the pastor who has found the right proportion of **space and distance** from his congregation can be popular in the best sense of the word.

In order to appreciate correct behavior in general, we want to point out a specific case that belongs here. One pastor goes out a lot, even if only to make house calls. Another one goes out only as the duty of his office requires it; otherwise he is seldom seen. Taken for granted that both are friendly and congenial, the latter one definitely is more respected by the congregation. The former will be less effective, the more he comes. The latter, because he comes less frequently, will find more attention, more willingness, and more emphasis. The less frequent trips of the latter will remind even those who only see him walking about the heavenly calling that the pastor represents because such trips are always in a certain relationship to the needs of the congregation and are requested by the people. One will pay little attention to the former, because his trips are based more on caprice, on mere human goodwill than on the duties of his office. He will be considered by his parishioners as one who is too busy to do anything but the business of this world. One can check with experience whether or not this is so.[16]

---

[16] [Loehe:] "One should not be seen at the wrong time in order to be seen at the right time." That was the principle of Martin Boos. If a friend invited him, he would say: "Let us not do this. We should never be seen outside of our profession in the presence of the people. If they see us too much and too often outside of our profession, they do not see us within our profession—which is how they should see us. We are messengers of the Lord. Therefore we should stay out of sight of the people if we do not happen to bring a message. We should never show ourselves or be seen, unless we have orders from the Lord and the opportunity to deliver them, so that, when people see us in the pulpit or at a sickbed, or otherwise in our profession, they believe that we fell directly from heaven, i.e., that we spend the remaining time with the Lord communicating with Him, that we come from Him, and what we tell and bring them, we have gotten and heard from Him, and thus we are true witnesses of the Lord." Gossner, *Martin Boos*, p. 33. One has to understand Boos and not entrust any foolish conclusions to him based merely on vainly jumping to conclusions. When that is the case, then he certainly is right.

71. Finally, concerning fitness for the office, it is strengthened tremendously if a pastor likes to lead a quiet life in order to learn constantly for the good of his congregation. Whoever has to give constantly needs always to have something to give. And since he cannot draw forth anything out of himself, he always has to be at the source in order to draw something forth. Many a truth, once you have it, grows on its own, even through life itself. But its development is rich in a double and threefold way, if life is quiet and public, inward and outward at the same time. The divine Word and the theological sciences can grant quiet studying that is far from false knowledge, which estranges one from the office and makes one unfit for it. [True knowledge] all the more prepares the pastor for the office, empowers, strengthens and gives a foundation. It will assist his experience, clarify it and enlighten it, opening up for him continually new vistas into the glory of the one truth that is being preached. It will preserve them from the misfortune of many lazy pastors. Once these [lazy ones] have mastered their profession in a mechanical way, they get sick of it. While the honey of eternal life should flow from their lips, they confess to the ears of good friends that Christianity does not solve their greatest questions.

Therefore a pastor who is just starting out should fulfill the duties of his office with the greatest diligence. The rest of his time he should faithfully spend in studying and preparation. It should be so much easier to follow this rule, since the relation of the pastor to his congregation will become more frequent, the more familiar the pastor becomes with it, and there will be less leisure time for pursuing the truth in quietness.[17]

D. Furnishing the Parsonage, the Table, and One's Clothes

72. We are not talking here about rules for diet, clothing, and so on, with respect to the pastor. Pastoral medicine, if there were such a discipline, could establish those. We are simply talking of what is appropriate. We speak of pastoral wisdom that, even in ordinary life, knows how to put everything, even outward matters, in relationship to the Holy Office.

Of course diet and clothing and all furnishings of outward life depend on the wealth of a man. Since most pastors come from the poor or middle

[17] [Loehe:] Whoever does not appear among the people will not be effective because he does not know them and they do not know him. Whoever can be found wherever there are people will lack trust. From the office to the study, from there to his office—that is the way of the pastor. This is as necessary as water for the one that wants to water. The condition for teaching is learning. To be able to comfort requires considering and overcoming one's own temptation. And the impulse and dedication of one's life is a praying heart. Solitude is the source of all streams and nothing glorious is born publicly (*publice*). Not always learning means not always teaching! Teaching and learning—that is how you penetrate and move forward.

classes—and in the office one hardly gets rich if he lives faithful to his calling and practices love and mercy—pastors will be limited by their circumstances. But the office and its circumstances themselves seem to point in the following direction: A pastor in his daily expenses should consider himself as belonging to the **middle class.**

Both a rich life and one that is too poor present difficulties and troubles. Whoever feasts sumptuously every day is hardly fit to be a pastor of [the beggar] Lazarus and his friends. Even if in his mind he would stand above his glory, it still would not be good if all his furnishings and his life would exhibit riches and plenty. A pastor may have great riches if through a benevolent life he is to satisfy the poor in a congregation. But a rich pastor will hardly escape the accusation of avarice. As long as he did not become poor through giving, he usually will be considered stingy, even if he himself would give beyond his means.

But poverty is almost worse than riches. It is hard to take care of the spiritual needs of a whole congregation if the worry about the daily bread constantly nips at your heels. If one is poor, one also becomes much more receptive to gifts and the moral (immoral) impression they convey. The order of the Lord remains: Those who preach the Gospel should **be fed** by the Gospel (Luke 10:7ff.; 1 Corinthians 9:14; Galatians 6:6ff.). This remains the right instruction for those congregations that want to bear the name Christian. The best prayer for pastors is to say with the rich king (Proverbs 30:7ff. [ESV]): "give me neither poverty nor riches; feed me with the food that is needful for me."

One should also accommodate **diet** and **clothing** according to this general view of the pastor's situation. Let everything appear as neither poor nor rich, but **modest**. One should not show off either abundance or lack, if the latter can be avoided. Not abundance, even if it were present, for it would only provoke the congregation and others to expectations and demands that cannot be satisfied. It gives an impression that is contrary to the office. Not lack, insofar as that is possible. Lack awakens sympathy from the congregation and a benevolence upon which one can become too easily dependent. If one is poor, it is easy to become a beggar.[18]

73. Perhaps it would be best to be able to describe all of the pastor's furnishings with the word **simplicity**. Diet, clothing and surroundings of a pastor should keep away from both seeking the present fashions of this world and from seeking the time of the fathers of old through a rejection of the pre-

---

[18] [Loehe:] A guarantee for keeping the right middle ground is brought about through a simple way of life. [That involves] a heart that has become free from the needs of the children of the world, content in the practice of a poor life. Whoever does not care for the worldly desires sees the true needs of life and seeks to satisfy them without being impure and selfish.

sent time. Neither the rich nor the poor should be scared away by finding the pastor's style of living to be too distant from their own.

[Have consideration for people of] one kind as well as another. It certainly should [feel] wholesome in the dwelling and in the family circle of the shepherd; [that shows itself] if one person is not spoiled and the other too depressed. Let an interesting intellectual life prevail and let one forget what is lacking in comfort and fullness of the temporal life. The fullness of eternal goods that is present should make up for everything. Everything in a parsonage should preach of independence from the temporal, of dedication to the eternal. A pastor's motto should be: "May integrity and uprightness preserve me, for I wait for you" (Psalm 25:21 [ESV]). This goes for personal conduct and everything else mentioned in this chapter heading.

74. Perhaps stating an admonition to be **orderly** in the parsonage would be just as fitting as it should be superfluous. It should be taken for granted that the servant of the One who is a God of order himself should love order. He, whose inner life is ordered in knowledge and desire, will also seek to be surrounded by outward order. Experience shows that a certain degree of inner disorder and confusion can be removed by putting outward things in order. A man who has much correspondence often may remove the unrest and lack of clarity of his soul by putting his letters in order. Here the mutual effect that exists between outward and inner things becomes clear. This also explains and justifies the mistrust toward disorderly men and women, and especially toward disorderly clergy families.

75. As for **clothing,** in particular it has become fashionable for clergy to wear dark colors, especially black. In countries where most people wear black, the clergyman certainly does not stand out. The question is whether or not in this case, or even otherwise, he should seek a form of dress that would make him stand out. One should not confuse this question with the other one: "Should the pastor **seek** something by wearing a different kind of clothing?" The latter question easily is denied. The former becomes acute every time the pastor needs new clothing. The question is unimportant, although in practical life perhaps not as unimportant as it may seem. In any case, once it has been asked, it must be answered correctly.

In recent times it was found to be unseemly for pastors to make "courtesy calls" in a surplice (*Chorrock*).[19] One debated if they should have another specific garment for solemn occasions when they were not supposed to show up in a surplice. [Such a garment] would not be appropriate for daily life. But one forgot this would mean a hefty expense for the pastors who, on balance, tend to be poor. This would be avoided if they were allowed to make official visits either in a surplice or to make it the **usual practice** to show up wearing

---

[19] Here "courtesy call" (*Aufwartung*) refers to a pastoral visit during which no official acts are performed.

elements of regular pastoral garments.[20] The latter may be better. The surplice designates an official function, but not the office. A "courtesy call" has nothing to do with official functions.

Yet it is proper for the whole temporal life of the pastor to be in harmony with his official life. This life should appear consistent, as if molded in one piece; this is the common desire of the congregation as well as the inner demand of the conscience and the command of the divine Word. One should give more than just a negative rule for the dress of the clergy, insofar as [the above statements are true]. [Such a rule might be], "to avoid anything indecent and fashionable." It takes but another step to give a positive rule, and one should give it simply, without making a big deal out of such an external matter.

Of course among us [in the Bavarian Territorial Church], all too often there exists such an obvious ineptitude for such things that in the end it might be best to permit the pastor to wear the wide-brimmed hat and the long black cassock for common occasions and also for official visits. This dress would be dignified and appropriate for the profession and it also would avoid an acutely obvious difference from other classes. If the clergyman wants to be recognized as such, a standing or double collar and a long double row of buttons would be enough to mark him.[21] For the dirty roads in the country, long boots would be better than long pants. They look better anyway. For official visits one can still go back to shoes. In any case, the frock coat, which is as uncomely as it is tasteless, deserves a death sentence.[22]

E. HOBBIES

76. Often one finds that pastors take up hobbies. Can one mention any area of human knowledge and achievement without someone, even if he knows just a few pastors, thinking of one who was occupied with it and therefore became notable? [Consider] philosophy, philology, law, photography, politics, natural sciences of all kinds, botany, mineralogy, geography, flowers, economy, hunting, fishing, and so on. In short, [with] everything you can mention, a pastor has tried and excelled in it.[23] The question now is:

---

[20] *Visitengewand* refers to official clothes in which one appears in public.

[21] The cassock (*Überrock*) was worn over the habit of the order in Roman Catholic orders. A standing collar is a white, round clergy collar. The similar double collar has a black outer band and a white inner band, recalling the tab collar. These developed from the ruff collars of civil servants. *Beffchen*, preaching bands, came from the wide *Mühlsteinkragen* and are related to the French *jabot*.

[22] C. F. W. Walther and other Saxon immigrants greatly favored the frock coat. Walther's formal pictures often feature him either in a suit or in a frock coat. See also *Law and Gospel: How to Read and Apply the Bible*.

[23] In the twentieth century, major advances and specialization have caused the language used by scientists and others to become highly technical, thereby creating a gulf between

Should one praise or criticize this; should one warn a future pastor against this, or encourage imitation?

77. Certainly no scholarly discipline occupies so much space, and has so many points of contact with the other sciences, as theology. None [of the other disciplines] gives so much opportunity to occupy even the richest spirit. Nor is any so inviting [for one] to enter foreign areas as theology itself. In none of the other sciences would one so take it for granted that he should stick with his own field. And yet it is theology that is the first to permit detours and excurses. A theological appreciation will find confirmation of theological truth everywhere. One can reap gains for theology from all the other sciences. But on the other hand, theology does not need another science in order to stand firm.

Since these things are the case, one cannot really criticize a pastor who enters any given area, especially a related one, in order to get a break from his proper professional studying and in order to win new inspiration. Any bow that has been strung, if it is to remain in good shape, needs to be unstrung again. One cannot do the same thing all the time, least of all in the highest regions of human knowledge. St. John needed a partridge, and even Adam in paradise cultivated the land during his life full of heavenly contemplation.[24]

Yet without doubt, it is and remains blameworthy if the side occupation becomes the main occupation, a favorite amusement and a passion. A pastor has to guard himself well, lest anything would turn him away from his love for the Holy Office and the theological studies. It is a great sin, and great ingratitude, if a man whose eye and heart stand under orders to pasture themselves by contemplating the highly praised beauty of the Triune, instead prefers something less instead of this calling. Let him take care of his own, and leave it to other Christian scholars to build up their sciences for the good of the Church, to confirm its eternal truth.

Even the laziest pastor in the ministry still is so occupied that he cannot turn to another science with his full strength. For as many examples that may exist of pastors who occupied themselves with a different discipline, etc., it is seldom that one can find one who achieved something great in a different area. Whoever occupies himself with trivialities is not completely filled with his profession. He does not accomplish what he should, and in the end [he does not accomplish] much in the trivialities either. Thus he wastes his life and exposes himself to the worst charges.

---

the sciences and the humanities. See also Ian Barbour, *Issues in Science and Religion* (Englewood Cliffs, NJ: Prentice-Hall, 1966).

[24] John Cassian (c. 360–435), known for introducing Egyptian monasticism to the Latin West, influencing the Benedictine tradition to the present, and being called by some a semi-Pelagian, gives the legend of St. John, the partridge, and the huntsman in *Collationes patrum in scetica eremo* (*Conferences of the Desert Fathers*) 14.21.

78. Unmarried pastors or those without children especially should guard against hobbies. Experience proves that those who do not walk in the ways of an orderly, truly human love for wife and children, blessed by God, are inclined to choose disorderly love. The low-minded person then falls prey to coarse sins while the higher-minded one falls for more subtle errors, for spiritual hobbies. But both sin before God without any difference. Therefore the single or childless pastor must dedicate his strength so much more to the service of the Church, 1 Corinthians 7:32. Yet they all have to realize that there is no office burdened with so much sloppiness and laziness as the spiritual one. Neither does any make such great demands of its servants. The higher the office, the easier it can be misused, and the more difficult it is to be used in the right way. The pastoral office needs the full, undivided love and strength of those who bear it, if it is to be practiced rightly to some extent.

Therefore nothing is more natural, more beautiful, than if a pastor lives for his office and the studies of the office, nothing else! That does not mean to criticize the partridge of St. John!

F. Gifts, Collections, Confessional Fees, and Accidentals

79. Almost everywhere a pastor will receive gifts that may be more or less voluntary. Some voluntary gifts have become customary, e.g., collections of flax, eggs, and the money paid for confession. A pastor ought to know about these things right at the beginning of his office, if he does not want to spoil his position in the congregation right from the start.[25]

80. As far as **gifts** are concerned, they are given either out of pure gratitude and love, or with the intention to get something for them. If the pastor is the inspector of the school, he might show a favor once. He may show special consideration when it comes to assigning pew seats, etc. The people then seek such things with gifts. It is good if the pastor knows the difference, so that in all cases where there is a hidden intention, he should not accept any gifts, neither if he can guess that the person wants to receive something, nor if it is gratitude for fulfilling some pastoral duty.

A reputation of innocence is so helpful for a pastor that he should pursue such a reputation with a definite fervor. St. Paul knows and honors the Lord's commandment that those who preach the Gospel should live by the Gospel.

[25] The issue of money and the church has a long and tumultuous past. Protestants proved to be just as mercantilist as their Roman Catholic adversaries. With the introduction of pews (French *puie*, from Latin *podium*) amid the Protestant Reformers' focus on the sermon, families began to pay regular fees for pews. Confessional fees arose from Roman Catholic customs as part of the *satisfactio*, the final restitution phase of their sacrament of penance that also has contrition of the heart and confession of sins. Early Lutherans broke with Rome over such practices, yet later Lutherans adopted the fees they formerly opposed as a sort of mandatory gratuity without the formerly-claimed sacramental benefits.

Nevertheless he declares it his glory, which he will not let anyone take from him, that he served the congregations freely, without reward, that he earned his own living. The circumstances that drove him to do this can often be found with others also, but not always the selfless attitude of the holy apostle, who is happy in poverty.

But the kind of innocent gifts, which from times immemorial have been given to the pastor at special occasions and at certain times, are something completely different. Just as one should not and may not refuse them, nor should one express the kind of pleasure that gives the hint that one would like more. Not only is the gift often a genuine indication of love, which one cannot refuse rudely; often a kind of pride manifests itself if one never accepts any gifts. The honor that a pastor receives with the gifts points to the beautiful, holy, patriarchal relationship that a pastor should have to his congregation. By refusing such honor, along with its signs and expressions, one can kill such honor—and not only for one's own time of office, but also for the successor. One does not have the right to destroy his proper relationship to the congregation, let alone cause him temporal loss of justly deserved income. There is a way to receive gifts and remain in the most beautiful thankfulness toward the congregation without becoming the least dependent. One ought to seek this way!

81. It is similar with the customary **collections** of flax, eggs, etc., mentioned in section 79 above. These still exist in many areas. One can practice them in an avaricious and demanding way, which often becomes a burden to the people. Then one really can admire the people in their great patience and longsuffering. One can also practice collections in a proud and arrogant way, accepting the gift unwillingly and without thanks, making it to be understood that one would not even bother with it if it was not for the sake of the successor. Many have also tried to change such collections into monetary gifts, which they raised from the congregational treasury, or let the mayor collect them.

All these different ways to make collections or get around them certainly cannot be approved. Not the first greedy one; everybody understands that. But not the other one either! A humble pastor will not despise to do his own collections, or let his wife do it, which would be very appropriate for her. He gladly appears as one asking and thanking, and is happy to teach how to ask and thank through his example, and to show love in receiving, just as he gladly shows love in giving. Yes, these very collections give an occasion for the most friendly and personal meetings with the parishioners. Here everybody sees the pastor or his wife in a lovely, purely human relationship, and talks with them. Because of a habit, sanctified by tradition, one gets to go into all the homes and finds open hearts. That is, except where people run away from the pastor in order not to have to give anything.

Often one can find out about a spiritual or physical need of members of the congregation in this way. The poor person who cannot give anything, but nevertheless is visited at this occasion, will feel the friendliness and turns to the pastor in love, and at times will open his heart. One can find out how the children are disciplined, and in general how the parents relate to their children, so that the pastor can offer both help and comfort. In short, the visits at the occasion of the collections have all the virtues that could be ascribed to house calls and other personal contacts between the pastor and his parishioners, while they lack many disadvantages that can be found with less justified and motivated visits.

One can also practice much compassion at these occasions by **not accepting** the gifts **but instead by bringing several gifts.**[26] By going from house to house as one expected to receive, one can be an angel of God who does good secretly where it is not suspected, nor expected. For this very reason one should not do away with such collections. In only the least possible case should one consider changing them into a sum of money. It would be less trouble, but it would forever change a blessed opportunity into nothing but a small benefit for the pastor. It appears as something heartless and loveless, just to save a little trouble, a little humiliation, to put oneself outside of the friendly social intercourse with the congregation.

Such a pastor cares for himself, seeks only his own, and if he introduces permanently the act of taking money instead of gifts, in an irresponsible way he also prevents his successors to do what was previously beautiful and better. The life of a modern pastor already has only few traces of the intimate, patriarchal essence that should be its due. Why then take away these last traces, which in the hand of true clergy families can be used beautifully and be rich in blessings?

82. Regarding **confessional fees,** there is a great difference between introducing them and doing away with them. Certainly it would not be wise to introduce this where it does not exist. But it is equally unwise to do away with this practice where it still is practiced. Usually one says in opposition to it that it would be too easy to consider it payment for the Absolution. But **this** error can easily be corrected by teaching the people. It would be tasteless to pretend that people did not see it this way. If it is recognized, or prevented by instruction, one cannot see what is bad with the confessional money. It is a gift for the father confessor, given to him for his trouble. And what is

---

[26] [Loehe:] **In general** it is a weakness to reject such gifts, or accidentals, or stole fees. It is never appreciated. It is considered to be ambition, or even calculating greed, and it hurts the successor. On the other hand, **in individual cases** one can **negotiate** based on one's right with even greater emphasis. This will be accepted with thanks, and one does not tie down one's own hands or those of others. See S. J. Baumgarten, chapter 1, p. 341.

One can find too much strictness in collecting gifts more frequently than too much largesse on the part of the pastor in remitting gifts and accidentals. Even if no one would deny the fact that, in certain cases, a pastor would be permitted to bring suit because of his outstanding dues, such cases should be kept to a minimum. It is only proper to act mildly in a self-denying way. See Deyling, *Prud. Past.* p. 242.

wrong with this? Are we—confessors and confessing—so ashamed and picky that a small gift already hurts, when it is only given **near** a great, inestimable gift? And how much can this be? In most places it is a dime, not much more! One rather should think that, as close as it is to the eternal good, all appearance of payment through an earthly trifle would have to disappear![27]

83. This also goes for the so-called **accidentals** or **stole-fees.**[28] When one instructs the people, anything objectionable should fall away. As little as there might be anything remarkable in the apostolic word, that the one teaching the Gospel should live by the Gospel, so there can be nothing remarkable in a gift that is given for the maintenance of the pastor, according to existing orders when official pastoral acts are performed. "If it is right to give a salary in kind for sacred work, why could something not be given for a special act?"[29]

As to the **strictness of the demand**, our fathers made an influential difference between the accidentals and the stole fees:

---

[27] Here one sees a marked difference between American Lutheranism and European Lutheranism. In the 1890s a protest in the LCMS arose over the yearly membership dues. At the 1899 general delegate-synod a submission (*Eingabe*, overture) asked to modify the mandatory collection. Augustus L. Graebner's committee responded that an overture that seeks to modify a point in the constitution and bylaws is invalid and that a constitutional amendment must be used (a technicality revisited as recently as 2004). The result was to funnel the energy of the protest into a movement that changed the constitution and bylaws, eliminating such dues. Whereas the "voluntaryism" of American Christianity bristles at fees, European Christians are more likely to accept them as part of the social order. See also Sydney E. Ahlstrom, *A Religious History of the American People* (New Haven: Yale UP, 1972).

[28] [Loehe:] See Deyling, part II, c. III, § XVII; Hartmann *Past. evang.* bk. IV, c. I; bk. III, c. XXIII, p. 641ff.; Seckendorf, Christenstaat v. III c. VI § 3; Spener, *Theologische Bedenken* I, 71; II, 438; IV, 6.6; Letzte Bedenken I 601.606. See Böhmer's *Ius Parochiale* section VII, c. II; *Ius Eccl.* T. I, part VII, 2.5.610; part II, 3.176.300; I, part VII, 2.11; Brunnemann, *Ius Eccl.* bk. II, c. V § 7; Balduin *Tract. cas. consc.* c. X case V d. 1120; Dunte *Decis. cas. consc.* p. 432–33, 513; Roques, [*Gestalt*] *eines evang. Lehrers* part 1, essay 1 § LV–LXIV. Compare Baumgarten, *kasuist. Pastoraltheologie*, p. 333ff. [Editor's note: Justus Henning Böhmer (1674–1749) was a jurist, both civil and ecclesiastical, as well as a professor at the University of Halle and government official. In 1701 he published *Ius Parochiale* on church property, tithes, and clergy; the *Ius Ecclesiasticum Protestantium* appeared in 1714. Johann Brunnemann (1608–72) was a jurist, part of the Brandenburg consistory, and professor in the university at Frankfurt an der Oder. He had continual friction with Benedict Carpzov. *De Iure Ecclesiastico* was published posthumously with Samuel Stryk in 1681. Ludwig Dunte (1597–1639) served in the area of Tallinn, Estonia. His works include the 1636 *Decisiones casum conscientiae* and the 1648 *Decisiones mille et sex casum conscientiae.* Pierre Roques (la Roque, 1685–1748) served the French congregation in Basel, Switzerland. He published *Le Pasteur Évangélique* in 1723. In 1741 it was translated into German by Friedrich Eberhard Rambach with a foreword by S. J. Baumgarten. Loehe has *Geist* instead of *Gestalt* in the German title.]

[29] *Quando igitur pro laboribus sacris salarium in genere recte datur, quidni etiam pro actu speciali aliquid dari posset?* (Deyling *Instit. Prud. Past.* ed. III, p. 240).

> At one time the name **accidental** had a broader meaning than **stole fee**. For it spoke in general of any donation that one would accept for extraordinary official functions, without referring to some special office, e.g., what is given by parishioners out of mere liberality to the ministers of the church on New Year's Day. This cannot be enforced by any law. In contrast, the law of stole fees legally can be enforced perfectly by any special official act rendered.[30]

That means: The concept of the accidentals somehow goes together with that of the stole fees and stands opposite of the essential salary (*salarium substantiale*), which contains certain payments and requirements (*certas pensiones et praestationes continet*). But as far as there is a difference between accidentals and stole fees, the concept of the former is wider, since it refers to voluntary gifts, which are given at a certain time without reference to a certain official act, while the stole fees are given for certain official acts. Therefore it is clear that one cannot **demand** the accidentals. But the stole fees one can legally request if they have been refused.

But even here there are differences. The more an official act is necessary and important for eternal life, the less a pastor can make it depend on payment or complain later because it has been refused. Baptism, Absolution, and the holy Eucharist cannot be postponed under any condition because the fee has been refused. Rather, the pastor may request other fees:

> Based on the rightfully introduced stole laws, the pastor has a right—either by law or by custom, to request some (things). This pertains to proclamation, church weddings, public prayers, conducting funerals, memorial service or funeral sermon. But other accidentals, such as offerings for Baptism and administration of the Lord's Supper, he may accept as long as it is confessional money spontaneously given, but he cannot extort it from those unwilling.[31]

Perhaps it would be good to extend the prohibition of extortion (*invitis extorquere non potest*) to all proper stole fees.

85. Anyway, in our days there is **one** stole fee that either should be done away with or substituted in some other way that does not oppress the poor.

---

[30] *Latius aliquando patet nomen* ***accidentalium*** *quam* ***iurium stolae****. Illa enim vox in genere de omni emolumento, quod ratione officii extraordinarie percipitur, accipi solet, sine respectu ad officium aliquod speciale praestandum, e.g., quod a parochianis ex mera liberalitate tempore novi anni ministris ecclesiae datur: qod nullo iure perfecto exigi potest. E contrario iura stolae iure perfecto exiguntur ob speciale aliquod officium praestitum.* See Deyling, p. 239f.

[31] *Ex iuribus stolae parochus quaedam suo iure exigit virtute vel legis vel consuetudinis rite introductae. Quo pertinent proclamatio, copulatio sacerdotalis, preces publicae, deductio funerum, parentatio, vel concio funebris. Alia autem accidentia, e.g., pro baptismi collatione ac S. Coenae administratione, quin ob nummum confessionalem sponte oblatum accipere quidem, sed invitis extorquere non potest.* See Deyling c. I p. 240f.

We mean the fee for **communing the sick and dying**. Because there is a fee involved, the sick person often has to go without enjoying the Sacrament until all hope of living is extinguished, and therefore also the hope of receiving Communion in church where the fee is smaller.

And then, how often is the sick person no longer able to receive the Sacrament! And how many leave this world without having received the Sacrament once more, just for the sake of the fee! This and others are unbearable cases. And it does not get much better if the poor are released from the fee. For who is poor, and who is not? There can be different answers for this question, and there can be different ways to handle it. Therefore, the fear of the fee remains for most people, as experience proves. But on the sickbed, or the bed of the dying, such fetters and bonds should no longer bind. The enjoyment of the Sacrament should be freely given and made as easy as possible. And therefore, the most insufferable of all fees, the one for communing the sick, should be dropped wherever possible.

86. **Perhaps in general**, one could support the pastor in some other way, not through accidentals and stole fees. True, they stem from the **oblations** of the ancients, which they deposited on the altar in order to have a consideration for guests and onlookers regarding individual cases of pastoral acts for the good of the poor, or the support of the pastor, etc.

And one should rather institute **oblations** than eliminate them and their last remembrance. We could be tempted, to recommend with Chrysostom (*Homil.* 86 in Matthew) to support the pastors with free love. "The Church and its ministers never had it as good as when they received their sustenance from gifts, which often were large and copious."[32] But unfortunately, as far as the majority of our members is concerned, love and fellowship (*κοινωνία*) is dead and totally gone. A pastor would likely suffer hardship these days, were he to live merely on gifts of love. Despite existing rules, pastors often have to fight with their congregations for their meager wages.[33] Therefore, as a rule, no blessing is lost if accidentals and stole fees are done away with, and some other way for the care of the pastors is found, if that is possible. Even though true pastors find nothing objectionable—on the contrary, they see it as something heartfelt and intimate when they receive love and gifts from members at such occasions—when the pastor has served members in a special way, there should be other opportunities to show him love and kindness.

---

[32] *Numquam ecclesia earumque ministris melius fuit prospectum, quam ubi sustentationem suam ex oblationibus habuerunt, quae admodum fuerunt largae et copiosae* (Deyling, p. 224).

[33] [Loehe:] However, one should not forget that at the present time there is no way to make the congregations support their pastors. If this would be the case, this would bring to life the reason for giving and for contributing to the support of the pastor. Our endowments and rights do not permit to let this reason come up. Examples show that it would be awakened if there is a real need.

This also would permit them to get closer to him in an intimate and heartfelt way. The high yearly festivals, anniversary of the church dedication, anniversary of the pastor's installation, etc., would also give an opportunity, even if that were not **as** heartfelt as the present opportunities for giving gifts. Sometimes one **might** wish that confessional money and accidentals could be avoided, if one considers chasing after penitents, whom one nevertheless neglects, and the shameful dealing with accidentals, which here and there are the order of the day. If only one could think of a human relationship where there is no misuse, no shameful and selfish behavior! But that is not even possible with a completely fixed salary. Even if one did away with all possibly wholesome uses of the present institution for the sake of negating detestable misuse, nevertheless, avarice and venality would always find new ways. Therefore it still is best to keep the old custom and to stigmatize its misuse.

G. Appendix to the Previous Section

87. Since the matter of accidentals and their removal is by no means unimportant, especially in our days, let us add here the appropriate question and answer text from S. J. Baumgarten's *Kurzgefaßte Pastoralteologie* (Halle: 1752, p. 332ff.):

> Can accidentals, or payment for certain official acts, be legal, and can they be demanded?
>
> This question should be answered in the affirmative. But with the decision there are three things that must be observed:
>
> 1. The limitations of the question to be decided;
> 2. Reasons for the decision.
> 3. Objections and how to answer them.
>
> The **limitations** are the following"
>
> The **first** contains an **explanation** of the thing itself. What are **accidentals**? We want to mention **two** characteristics that make these incomes of a teacher [of the Church] different from the other regular ones.
>
> The **first** characteristic is: These incomes are paid to the teachers [of the Church] by individual hearers, either at a certain ordered time, or for acts of divine service performed for individual persons.[34]

[34] A longstanding Lutheran practice refers to the Church as teachers [pastors] and hearers [laity]. See also Martin Chemnitz, *Examination of the Council of Trent, Part II* (St. Louis: Concordia, 1978), 682–88.

This kind of accidental income for teachers in the divine service emerged with the occasion of public **oblations** or congregational offerings in the early Church. All members were used to do this during regular worship or Holy Communion. From the beginning, these **oblations** served for the support of the teachers and the poor. But gradually it happened that these **oblations** were borne by individuals for [the performance] of special acts in order to spare other invited guests the cost. And since it was very little, it was given exclusively to the teachers to make them more willing to perform these acts. This should explain sufficiently that from the beginning this was not payment for the divine means of grace.

The **second** characteristic is this: Such incomes should be ordered by church law, or confirmed by it, in order to differentiate between [official ones] and those that have been introduced on their own.

The **second** limitation concerns a rule that has to be observed when these things are demanded: All transgression of common duties, also the appearance of avarice, must be avoided. One cannot multiply acts of divine worship and burden the listeners to one's personal advantage.

The **third** limitation is this: One cannot measure the willingness to serve the hearers through the [pastoral] office according to whether or not everything will be paid for. This would cause many to fear a visit by the preacher. **Nor should** the effort itself, and the reason for it, be measured according to the advantages one receives, or at least hopes to receive.

With these limitations it is legal to give and to receive such accidentals, for the following reasons:

It is part and parcel of the support of the teacher. The duty of the hearers to support their teachers includes this, especially if the regular salary is insufficient.

Such regulations are part of the legal authorization of a religions society or government. Therefore they can be observed by the teachers without sinning.[35]

God, in connection with the Israelite worship in the Old Testament, orders that in addition to the regular tithe, a portion of the sacrifices should be given to the priests. This makes it clear that, **on the one**

[35] This notion of church as a *societas* or *Gesellschaft* is based on longstanding statute law, part of the legal complex that defines the "established Church" as such in European Christian society. See also Franz Adolf Marbach, *Ein Wort über die Rechtscharakter der Actiengesellschaft* (Leipzig: Teubner, 1844), 13f.

hand, it could not be illegal, and, **on the other hand,** according to the wisdom of God, it was considered one of the easiest means to support the teachers.

Objections against this are not proper:

First, because this is not a **sale of divine things,** as some pretend, and therefore they use the occasion for all kinds of hateful remarks. It is an acknowledgment of the efforts of teachers in individual cases. This is not improper, since there is no way to acknowledge in a general way acts of divine service given to individuals. And then, the objection tries to prove even more, namely that it would not be right for the whole congregation to come up with support for the teacher. Nevertheless this is clearly ordered in Holy Scriptures.

Second, the words of Christ in Matthew 10:8 do not stand against this. First, because the context shows that the Savior refers only to miraculous gifts here. Second, in the subsequent text the Savior Himself answers this objection. He orders the disciples to accept sustenance from everyone wherever they may go, without making an exception for the good will of the people with whom they are.

Third, the words of Peter in Acts 8:20 do not prove that it would be sinful to accept anything for acts of divine service. The whole context of this story shows that only the sinfulness and illegality of the act and the purchase of the divine office is condemned.

Fourth, the passage in 1 Timothy 6:5 certainly can exist with this custom. First, the context shows that the discussion is not about teachers, but about everyday Christians who want to attract others by burdening them with new opinions and other exercises of divine service, and receive some gain for this. Second, there is a great difference between conducting a trade with godliness and the reward for special efforts in the divine service. The latter has been ordered in this same letter.

But in order to avoid all misuse, the following rules should apply:

First, it would be better, and also easier for teachers and hearers, if such incomes could be done away with altogether, either through a rich benevolence of the members of the congregation and a willing contribution toward the upkeep of the teachers, which would not be connected with the performing of acts of divine service; **or also**—and this would be even better—by a different regulation for a richer support. This, **on the one hand,** would give less offense to those who consider preachers a burden on society. On the other hand, one would not have to impose all kinds of individual forms of service to the people.

Second: A teacher does no wrong if he gives up this right, either because his conscience bothers him, or to avoid offending his listeners, or because he worries that they may not have the means while he himself has enough for his needs, or in order to further the good trust of his listeners, or for the sake of the prospering of his office. But it is better if he does this only in individual cases instead of giving up everything or making a public proclamation before the congregation, because:

1. That would avoid a disadvantage for the successor, or other teachers, who do not do the same, nor are able to.
2. This would confuse the listeners in regard to their duties in other cases as well. They can easily go farther and consider the entire support of teachers as something that is illegal.
3. It is easier for a preacher to fulfill his purpose to do good if he uses that right only in individual cases.
4. After one renounced this right solemnly and publicly, it is much more difficult and connected with a greater collision of duties, if he must reinstate this right in case of need and because the former happy circumstances have gotten much worse. It is much easier if it happened only in single cases with individual persons.
5. I have learned from the experience of others that even the best intention of a teacher who gives up all accidentals will be judged differently. It can be considered to be a secret ambition and therefore cause many obstructions to the blessed conducting of his divine office, which could easily have been avoided had he practiced the opposite.

Third: For the reasons above it also would not be right to leave these matters up to the congregation, even if (the money) would be designated for putting up public buildings. The congregation could suffer a great embarrassment at the next calling of a pastor if this would have to be considered as part of his job.

This will also help to decide the following cases:

1. Could a preacher in good conscience bring suit to the government for the collection of his income? This would be permissible and just in matters that are owed him legally, and the government would be obligated to order in court the continuing of such income.

2. In case a pastor is called by a congregation where the predecessor has publicly renounced such income, is he justified to request it again and to make the required presentation to the congregation? This is to be answered in the affirmative.
3. Due to the special behavior of a teacher, does such a congregation, have a permanent right to deny accidentals to all future teachers? The answer is **negative**.

H. GIVING

88. If the income of a pastor would be paid in cash at regular times, be it monthly or every quarter, etc., this would achieve a certain regularity for the household of the pastor, even if the total is just a small sum. If a man knows that he can spend half a guilder a day for his household, and if he really has it in his hand every day, he can stretch out under his blanket, as good as possible, and yet to a certain extent without worries.

It is much more difficult for the household, especially of the younger and inexperienced pastors who have less income, if their salary is not only cash, but mainly natural products that are not available before harvest time. That results in having plenty at certain times of the year, while during the rest of the year there is great need. As long as the scarcity lasts, a pastor has to bear it, suffer lack, and borrow. Once the time of plenty returns, he has to pay, later only to suffer want again. True, there are some characters that quickly understand this problem and find it easy during times of plenty to plan things in such a way that the total income is distributed evenly during the time of famine. Many a man whose attention has been called toward this (and this is the intention of these words!) considers this matter before starting in his congregation, as soon as he is aware that his income depends on the course of nature.

Some have enough talent in economical matters, so they get into trouble only once, if they are not hit by exceptional disasters that rob them of their money. But many will never get straightened out for the rest of their lives. They constantly have to worry about being solvent at some time, without being able to make the courageous decision, in the name of God and under these circumstances, to remain insolvent for a while. This situation causes many to be constantly unhappy with their congregation, even though this cannot be explained, since their total income may not be inconsequential.

Here wisdom, accounting, and a firm consistency when it comes to giving are necessary. Whenever possible, one should not go above the going rate of the time in question; neither in times of plenty, nor in times of lack. If, despite all the faithfulness of the steward, the regular income is not enough, then one can lift up the eyes in quiet hopefulness to the One who is rich beyond measure.

89. It should be most painful for a pastor if he were unable to give daily wages to his **day laborer,** and let him wait past Sunday when he needs the money exactly for the Sunday needs of his family. Not to be able to give the poor man what is owed him—not to be able to do it at the right time—is a bitter drop in the cup of a man who blesses the household of another with these words: "You shall eat the fruit of the labor of your hands; you shall be happy, and it shall go well with you." Such experiences truly can teach the meaning of this: "By the sweat of your brow you shall eat bread. In toil you shall eat of it until you return to the ground. For you are dust and to dust you shall return." Of course a pastor does not have sweat and tears running down his face, as does the farmer. But it hurts even more if sweat and tears are running down inside.

90. It is less hurtful, but full of the pain of bitter regret, if a pastor has to tell himself that his insolvency, his lack, stems from the fact that he did not restrict himself with **presentations** and **gifts**—not to mention **luxury articles** that are not appropriate for a man with middle or small income.

91. **Presentations** are often required of the pastor. From the start he should firmly abide by the principle that his estate could never demand what his fortune denies him. Let others do as they wish; this should not disturb a faithful steward! You may not, and should not do what you cannot do, that is it! And that is how it should remain, as difficult as it may be, and as seldom as people act accordingly, as seldom as one remains here guiltless, without punishment, without bitter regret.

The same goes for **gifts**. It is hard to refuse when one often is asked so imploringly. However, it is not a virtue, but weakness. It is even more than that. It is almost malice to give beyond one's means. Wife and child then have to suffer when a pastor—when a pastor here and there—gains the reputation of being merciful. Once you have taken care of your wife and child, you may do with the rest as you please. But see to it that you do not become unmerciful toward the members of your household by being merciful toward others.

Here a school of holy renouncing is opened for the pastor. If it is absolved cheerfully, it makes the man experienced and leads without doubt to a secret perfection of the poor, nevertheless recognized by God and his angels. People do not have an eye for this. The noble thoughts that may fill a pastor's heart here are not meant for the public. But that Day will make it clear!

A pastor who does not give anything because he cannot give always appears to his people as merely being stingy, as long as his poverty does not go so far that he lacks the most necessary things. A pastor knows that. If against all prejudice and suspicion of his people he is to exhort others mightily to show compassion, this requires a noble soul, especially if his soul would much rather that he would lead on with a mighty example of showing mercy. There are many similar tests of sanctification by fire for a pastor in his office.

92. Here one must also say a word about loaning and borrowing. Nothing is more common than someone desiring to borrow money from the pastor, or take merchandise (grain and other fruits) as a loan. A pastor is encouraged by sayings like "Loan, so that you not hope (for a return)!" On the other hand he can clearly see that he and his own will suffer lack with this kind of loaning. He also knows that those who want to borrow from the pastor, as a rule, are those to whom no one else will give a loan. They are the poor who cannot give any security for paying anything back. These poor people should not borrow, but honestly ask for gifts. But they hope to be able to return, where there is no hope. They borrow with the good will of wanting to pay back, but there is no probability that this will happen. What can you do?

A pastor who is well-off should loan, and according to the Lord's commandment without interest, when poor people stand before him. A poor pastor should openly confess his poverty according to the principle that he cannot spend more than is absolutely necessary for his own support. (He should mention) that his income is often irregular and meager; that he cannot loan what he does not have, but that he would gladly give if he had something to spare. For it might be that he could not risk to loan a greater amount, but that he could give a smaller one.

To be consistent in this manner has a great blessing. One will be appreciated, if not immediately, then at least in the long run. More and more the pastor will be spared the requests of his poor and his actions will be in harmony with his preaching. More and more he will be known as benevolent according to the measure of his circumstances. More and more he will do good according to his own judgment, quietly and without any fanfare, with what he can spare. From the pulpit or under the pulpit, a pastor can also discuss these rules that guide his actions and explain how this is according to the wisdom found in the Scriptures.[36] Thus he helps the congregation to understand and avoids a misunderstanding more quickly. The same is true as in other difficult situations: God gives success to the upright, and an honest explanation of the circumstances will bring a fairer understanding of the same.

93. Our time is a time of societies.[37] One society after another comes along, and no matter what kind it is, one counts on the pastor as one who

---

[36] Speaking under the pulpit refers to the typical raised pulpit (lacking modern audio systems) and the fact that pastors often delivered catechetical talks (*Christenlehre*) at a position under the pulpit as a godly instructor.

[37] [Loehe:] Section 93 should not be a demonstration against associations (*Vereine*). When some decades ago there was a great increase in Protestant associations, It was not immediately clear to the writer of this book if it would be proper for a Lutheran pastor and Christian to work along with associations. This was due to the danger of works righteousness, into which the associations easily fell. However, it soon became clear that it would be unwise to support works of the Church alone, only using some personal acquaintances, without any

should lead the way in good works. It can easily happen that one is asked to participate in some ten or twelve societies. Just add it all up. For many pastors this is hardly an exaggeration. If a pastor just gave 2 gulden per year to each of these societies, it would add up to an amount that would be very significant according to his income. It is not a trifle if a pastor gives 20 to 25 gulden to societies. It would be the twentieth or thirtieth part of his income.[38]

This is not doing something special for the societies, and yet he deprives himself of what he **owes his poor parishioners according to the duty of his office.** Therefore he should never obligate himself to a regular contribution, which would lessen his power to care for his own circle of influence. First of

---

[organizational] form. [At the same time,] Christians of all denominations were getting together in associations. Form is necessary for any kind of work where one's own personal strength is not sufficient. No good man loves to work without any control, i.e., without any form. Acting without form at one's own risk makes it hard to be aware of a good conscience. But even apart from promoting works of the Church, the associations also serve a pastoral use, and for its sake they deserve to be not just tolerated as outgrowths of church life, but they should be faithfully nurtured and diligently supported. Of course the Church is the association willed by God, in which all others should be absorbed. But even if the Church would be what it is supposed to be, it would only achieve its purpose if it would let its children, with their various gifts and strengths, come together and work together for individual works of love. But in this world things are not what they should be. Especially in our days [such problems] are in the majority in numbers and influence. The Church everywhere hovers in the greatest danger of having its sweet dough permeated completely by sour dough. Since all of this is the case, one must use every means that can bring the better ones at home together and strengthen them. That makes it clear that Christian associations can be used for this purpose. Christian meetings and devotional hours nurture the fellowship of faith, but Christian associations teach the children of the Church to practice love with combined strength, and thereby fill a hole that the Christian life would have without them. True, the normal life in congregation and family opens a wide field for all virtues and their practice. Even for works of mercy there is enough opportunity. But the activity of the associations permits more of a view of human misery, awakens eagerness to help, brings the like-minded together, unites not only their strengths, but also their hearts, and teaches the Christians to learn to say the little word "we" in the meaning of churchly love and unity. Far be it from the writer that longer experience would have taken him away from organizational activities. On the contrary, he became thoroughly convinced that a pastor owes it to challenge his parishioners to join associations, and to lead them. But it is self-understood that one cannot join all organizations. That would be counterproductive to the pastoral goals of the associations. But any Christian should seriously belong to one or several organizations.

[Editor's note: Association-related work in the U.S. arose on a strongly interdenominational footing. Therefore the LCMS preferred to promote mercy ministries within the Synodical Conference.]

[38] Before 1870 Germany was neither united nor did it have a single currency. Currency centers included Berlin (*Thaler*) and Vienna (*Gulden*). Bavaria used imperial gulden (fl.) valued at 24.5 to 1 Cologne mark weight of fine silver (7.51728 troy ounces U.S.). A gulden was 60 *Kreuzer* (xr.) and each *Kreuzer* was four pence. One gulden was equal to about 40 cents U.S. In 1886, an annual starting pastor's salary in the LCMS was $100 (250 fl.) to $400 (1,000 fl.). In 1852 Loehe suggested an annual income of 400–750 fl. for a starting pastor, in addition to which there were the mandatory gratuities.

all, he should watch over **his poor and sick parishioners**; then he can do with the rest according to his free will and good conscience. A good pastor will always keep in mind the support of needy fellow believers and the mission among the heathen. His greatest joy will be if he is able to do something, or do much, which will give testimony of his joy to those sacred works of love and can affirm his public admonition to do them. But here also, most of all, he will act according to his ability and will not be confused by a possible misjudgment. If he does this, the pastor will be spared a bad conscience and keep his soul free of worries, as far as this is possible. The good deed that he does under such guidelines is truly a good deed; otherwise it is just a pain.

With all this, of course we do not have in mind rich and stingy pastors. There is no excuse for their sin. We are only talking about how the great majority of poor pastors, **out of necessity**, should act right at the beginning of their office, so that they do not get into more and more embarrassing situations out of misunderstood charity. This would put them into poverty, obstructing their office, putting them into ever new embarrassments, and [pushing] them to the limits, perhaps beyond the limits, of honesty.

94. This may also be the place to point out briefly two things that happen rather frequently in the life of a pastor.

First of all, we consider **buying** and **selling,** which happens to all people and also to pastors. It is quite annoying and a disadvantage to the office if a pastor or his family will bargain and deal in Jewish fashion (*jüdisch feilschen und handeln*) for ordinary purchases.[39] As much as one might be provoked by the dishonesty of profiteering merchants, nevertheless it is better for the office to be a bit more accommodating instead of being rather too cautious. But it is even more disgusting and hurtful if a pastor uses the methods of this world when he sells his farm produce.

Most of the time—if not always—a pastor receives an ambiguous reputation if he sells his farm produce at higher prices than his parishioners. At times there may be some rather innocent reasons for this. However that may be, a pastor should not demand the most for his wares. Even dire need should not cause him to appear like a profiteer. He cannot do everything that others can. All things are lawful for him, but not all things are beneficial. And a pastor's life absolutely must be beneficial for others, even if it is to his own detriment. There is an old saying: "A pastor must come off badly!"[40] Therefore new pastors (who perhaps often need the opposite warning) should not become guilty of being too eager to run after income, not even in the case of need that a beginning household often brings. One should not be able to accuse the pastor of neglecting or wasting his property or being too strict

[39] Anti-Semitic remarks of this kind must be avoided by those in the pastoral office in the present day. Loehe, like Walther, was a man of his era, with all its biases. See also *Law and Gospel: How to Read and Apply the Bible*, 288, 435–36.

[40] *Ein Pfarrer muß Haare lassen!* [Literally: A pastor must leave (shed) hair.]

(with the books). A saintly, simple, honest mind—with the counsel of more experienced ones—easily can find out what is fitting for the sacred office. Experience shows that blessings often come specifically to an open and straight simplicity. Here also the rule is: "Godliness is valuable in every way, holding promise for both the present life and the life to come."

95. In the second place, we still have to mention the following: Our time follows a more faithless time, during which most pastors generally sought to eradicate what is good, what might have been left from former days, especially by distributing poisonous **devotional books**. As a result, the new pastor may have to get rid of evil books in his congregation and, out of necessity, replace them with better ones. If he has been blessed in any way from the beginning with the attention and benevolence of the congregation, his recommendation of good books will be gladly received, and it is easy for him to order them for his congregation. Everybody will gladly receive them from his hand. One will ask him to write into the book a verse, a dedication, the name, place and year, etc. If he does this the right way, he only does what is proper. He may well do the ordering of the books. This gives him the chance to offer a better price, or get free copies for the poor. This is not putting the bookbinder at a disadvantage, for the books must be bound anyway.[41] It is not a crime to sell them cheaper than the book stores and bookbinders, if one is able to obtain them legally at a discount. If the bookbinders themselves become interested in a cheaper distribution, so much the better!

But it is bad if a pastor permits **borrowing**, or otherwise does not keep **order** in the distribution of books. Both things will hurt him, often considerably. This is hard to bear and no one benefits from it. There are many thoughtless people who, without the intention of cheating, would rather borrow a good book that they would never buy. There are many wicked ones who intentionally want to cheat. The wicked one will laugh when he does so; the thoughtless one, who has not been questioned about his ability to pay or not to pay, will be estranged from the pastor by the very fact that he was loaned (a book). He is afraid of being admonished and ashamed if he is not admonished. Inwardly his conscience accuses him. Thus he avoids the pastor, goes out of his way, and misses even opportunities where he could meet [the pastor], like on the way to church, etc. Thus his ear and his heart become estranged and distanced from the Word. Yes, there are examples that such borrowers (and not only borrowers of books) start hating the pastor and his word, **simply** because they cannot pay the few gulden or *Kreuzer* that they owe. Just ask those with experience whether this is not so! We only mention this as proof that nothing is gained by loaning, but great damage is done to one's own treasury and to the souls of others. That is not to mention

[41] In Germany at this time, as even in the U.S., one firm might typeset and print a book, while another might bind and sell the book. Before 1874, the production and retail sale of books were done by different firms in the LCMS.

the damage that results from the wasting or measureless giving away of books. The books will be despised if they are given too freely, and a pastor, without noticing it, can cause a great loss to his household that would not have been necessary.

96. The best thing for the pastor is to **be clear about his task.** The evil books have to disappear, that is certain. Yet it is just as certain that they have to be replaced with good ones. First, this should not be with **many** instead of a few; second, this should not be with poor or **mediocre** ones. Mediocre books just contribute to ruining the minds and the aesthetics of the people. They do not elevate; they do not help. Only powerful books can lift the people out worldly desire, need and lassitude!

Many books will prevent the one or the other. To read many books hurts the people. It is a good thing that, as a rule, they neither do this nor are able to. A people's library is quickly assembled: the Bible, the Book of Concord, a sermon book, a hymnbook with psalms for singing, a book for confessions, a prayer book for good days and days of sickness, the Catechism with Bible verses, the calendar with festival days. That is sufficient for the daily feeding of souls.[42]

In order to maintain wholesome stimulation and to keep the congregation together as a whole, it would be good if the head of the household would buy a Christian book once a year, acquire the most important tracts of the time, and read one or several Christian journals. The pastor ought to guide his congregation in this process; that should be his goal. He may perhaps get that far. The better part of the people will gladly follow him in this matter.

It is good if [the pastor] does not recommend exactly the same thing to all, but advises some variety and choice. If it is only the same thing, knowledge in the congregation will be too uniform. Exchanging of books, a comparison of different voices, and some movement of thoughts ought to be possible. However, the circle of recommended books should not be too great. In sermons, catechesis, and in pastoral care, one should refer to this people's library and make it alive and effective. This would not happen if there are too many books in the congregation. Most people will not understand what the pastor is talking about when he refers to these books. Let him select a few that hit home. Let him recommend and advertise what he has chosen. Let him not betray any special concern in his recommendations, for then the people would suspect self-interest. Let him not be too hasty and ambitious, not act as if he owned a bookstore, or as if salvation would depend on the purchase of books. Let him not loan out new books meant for sale, nor borrow. Let him not easily make gifts and let him conduct all business of this

---

[42] In keeping with Loehe's recommendations, Concordia Publishing House offers a collection called "The Essential Lutheran Library," which closely follows this outline of a people's library.

kind simply and briefly. Let him keep the strictest order in income and expenses and not re-order before he is able to pay.

All this is easy to see and everybody knows it. But the one who does it is spared so much trouble! [Consider] how much more respect people will have for an orderly promoting of books. How much more of an impression this will make than the sloppy dealing with books by a thoughtless person.

I. HOSPITALITY

97. "Show hospitality to one another without grumbling" says the apostle to all people (1 Peter 4:9 [ESV]; cf. Hebrews 13:2).[43] Therefore, without any doubt, pastors have to apply this apostolic commandment mainly to themselves. However, every commandment has a special application for different circumstances. Hospitality in general is part of giving. But giving always depends on receiving. Just as, in general, one cannot give what one does not have, no one can extend hospitality farther than his circumstances and his **financial situation** allow.

The inexperienced one does not know what great expenses an extended hospitality requires. But experienced house-fathers know it. Precisely for these reasons, an act of considerable hospitality on the part of such as these is more valuable and honorable than on the part of a thoughtless and carefree beginner who extends such an offer. Blessed is the beginner who from the start acts in such a way that he does not later have to stop or limit himself! The early pleasure of having one's own household can easily lead to an excess in practicing hospitality. And some learn this only after the damage has been done. One who restricts himself from the start will not easily be misunderstood. On the other hand, a person who first opens his house and then has to start doing less becomes greatly exposed to the judgment of people.

And by the way, one can do too much, not just by receiving too many [people], but also by giving up simplicity when hosting someone. If, generally, the pastor only can be counted according to public standards as member of the middle class even if lives in good circumstances, then how much more does he have to consider his fortune if he is a beginner and his income and salary is meted to him very sparingly. Even if the English custom of demanding that guests fit exactly into the working of the house does not have

---

[43] [Loehe:] In addition to the passages mentioned above see also 1 Timothy 3:2, 5, 10; Titus 1:8. The φιλοξενία (love for strangers) to which the holy apostles exhort is different from what we usually understand with hospitality. [We think of] the Christian pilgrim who is looking for fellow believers in order to strengthen himself with them in love and the most sacred fellowship—or follows his calling abroad and is also seeking the love of the homeland with his brothers in the faith. [Such a person] usually is not the guest who comes frequently and makes the commandment of hospitality something important and difficult. Our guests and the intention of their visits are of the kind where it is questionable whether or not they fall into the category of φιλοξενία.

to be kept as strictly as in the English fashion, nevertheless it could be the **rule** for a pastor. Exceptions can easily be recognized. Simplicity in all things—simplicity in hospitality—is the proper thing for a pastor. He cannot strive for anything else because of his means! He should not strive for anything else because of the estate to which he belongs.

98. When it comes to hospitality, consideration of the means of the pastor is important, but it is not the only thing. Two other considerations have to be emphasized: One regards **the office.** The other regards **the children.**

In order to do good work in his office, a change between solitude and being in the public is good and necessary for the pastor. Solitude locks him up in his house. It requires not only quietness in being there, but according to the need of most pastors, [it requires] the absence of all, being alone, true solitude. The realization that one is in unusual surroundings is often very disturbing, even if everything is quiet. For many [pastors], even the realization that one is not completely alone, even having a beloved person nearby, is already disturbing. But if this is so, how can hospitality agree with this quietness and solitude? When the guest becomes the center of all in the house, then everything revolves around him, and even the pastor has to consider him. In an inn, the guest who enters is lord; the owner of the house becomes the servant. This must not be the case with the hospitality of a pastor. The sacred office that he administers requires the consideration of all visitors. One must treat with consideration the pastor's work, and therefore also the peace of his soul. The congregation will get to feel every inner disturbance, every dissension, and every episode of fatigue.

For this reason, whoever enters a parsonage has to give up the claim to have the pastor all to himself and constantly to be noticed, accompanied, and considered by him. But since many visitors are so demanding, the pastor has to watch out all the more that the practice of hospitality will not be to the detriment of his office. The more he gets upset by visits; is torn out of the peace of his soul; becomes restless, confused, worn out, and tired; then the less can he open his house to guests. His congregation and the office should always come first. Everything has to be subordinated to the office.

99. The other consideration that the pastor has to keep in mind while practicing hospitality regards his **children.** Even if he has enough strength of character and clarity of the spirit not to let himself be disturbed in his holy office, there is still the question whether or not he can be completely clear concerning his duty toward his children—his own or some that just happen to be in his house.

Precisely because the study is so necessary in a parsonage and solitude is so necessary for the pastor, and because his office so often leads him to the church, to the school, or to homes, the pastor's children—especially the younger ones—miss their father quite a lot instead of not enough. If, additionally, consideration for visitors takes even more of the father's heart, eye, strength, and time from the children, then, oh, how much are the poor children to be pitied! They feel unsupervised, not watched, and so they behave as they please. Their bad behavior either is noticed or not noticed by the father. In the first case the children have to be punished in the presence of the visitor, else they will be affirmed in their wickedness. Punishing and not punishing in front of visitors are both unpleasant.

And if the misdeed is not noticed, this is even worse. The visitor notices it so much quicker, but as a rule he will not discuss it in the father's hearing. If the children are beyond the age when one can punish them in front of strangers, then instead of youthful high spirits there will be untamable loutishness. Then the father easily will become more bitter toward the children than is good, especially since he is not without guilt in regard to this evil. But if none of this is the case, the children who see many strangers in the house learn to behave all too freely, and that bashfulness toward older people that is so becoming to a child is wiped out much too early.

In short: If the father too often is taken away from the children because of visitors, it is very likely that the children will suffer serious harm. Even if it should be possible to keep the children away from visitors due to supervision and the existing space—that would be in the best case—the disadvantage would still remain. It remains true that visitors can hinder children in their development, while grown sons and daughters can profit from visits.

100. **What then is a pastor to do**? Even if he could and would want to, he cannot live entirely without practicing hospitality. The more he is serious about always giving a good example, the harder it will be for him to withdraw from the general commandment of the apostle. So at first he has no other recourse than to find the right measure befitting of his office, his family, and his income; and to find the right simplicity and stick to it.

Every guest should be the householder's brother or son, and should be treated as such. The adult children may meet the guest like a father or brother. But the little ones ought to stay in their play room for as long as possible, as long as there is necessary supervision. If they have to come to the living room they should not be permitted to make themselves noticeable or to be drawn out from their undemanding existence by the guest. One should make it clear to the guests, who may not know this, what is customary in the house in this case. And the children should not be permitted to cling to the strangers all too trustingly and to converse with them. The children should imitate what appears from the part of father and mother as friendly respect toward the guest. [The children should do this] by showing deference and reverence. A father also should teach the children concerning the respect that one owes the stranger according to the Word of God. [He should do this] especially at a time when there are no guests present. Of course it is understood that relatives who come as guests will not behave like pure strangers to the children.

In this way the house of a Christian pastor should be a guest-welcoming glory (*ξενοδοχεῖον*) to the Lord, **as far as his circumstances permit.** It is well and good if not only the clergy or educated stranger of equal status can be received, but also the poor one who has been recommended, makes no demands, and is happy with what he can receive. Even toward strangers who have not been recommended, the pastor, using care and wisdom, may show an eye and a heart full of compassion and love. And the less demands a stranger will make, or is able to make, the more the sacred duty can be fulfilled in his person, and the less objection can there be based on income, office and children.

J. VAGABONDS AND SECTARIANS

101. Today there is a resurgence of "awakened" people everywhere, and where they are, one also finds also their opposites.[44] Those opposites are desperate people whose business it is to roam around the country and to look up all "Christian friends," especially all pastors who have the reputation of being Christians. They confuse the communion of saints with camaraderie and make every effort to know all determined Christians, i.e., to have seen them once or several times. The subjects that they usually discuss with all Christians are the so-called adiaphora, the future, the end of the world, the Revelation of St. John, perhaps also mission work, and especially the Basel or Leipzig [mission societies], etc.

They love to stir up emotions, also sharp denials, revival sermons in Methodist power, tears, sighing and grimacing—in short, one can find all the lusts of religious fools speaking and working in them. They also might choose the career of a door-to-door salesman in order to calm their conscience. Thus they are completely justified to take their spiritual gifts also from house to house. In their home town they often have considerable followers, often rule over the "awakened" people there, and their voice is also

---

[44] The German revival (*Erweckung*, "awakening") emerged during the last quarter of the eighteenth century as a reaction to crass rationalism. It developed two major foci. Northern Germany saw the rise of mission societies and social work under the influence of Hans Ernst von Kottwitz (1757–1843). Southern Germany experienced a neo-pietist, personal, spiritual resurgence influenced by revival preacher W. G. Ludwig Hofacker (1798–1828) and Reformed Erlangen professor Johann C. G. L. Krafft (1784–1845). August Tholuck (Friedrich August Gottreu, 1799–1877) and Schleiermacher helped revive a rationalist spirituality that Semler previously had helped to extinguish at Halle. With the 1817 publication of the anti-Prussian union theses of Claus Harms (1778–1855), three foci emerged: mercy work, individual spirituality, and a Lutheran neo-orthodoxy that strove to uphold Scripture and the *Book of Concord*, yet filter that through the lens of human experience and the Church. One could be "awakened" and yet be a cross-denominational mercy worker, a sort of enthusiast (*Schwärmer*) focused on personal spirituality agnostic of any particular theological confession, a Lutheran or Reformed seeking a mediating sort of spirituality, a conservative Lutheran in the territorial church trying to deal evangelically with rationalist influences, and even an expatriate Lutheran seeking to revive pre-rationalist orthodoxy in North America, South Africa, Australia, and elsewhere without what was perceived as a corrupt church-political structure.

heard in wider circles by the likes of them. They talk about pastors and their work, about their sermons, catechesis, and prayers in a masterly fashion. They beatify [their own saints], the bishop of Rome notwithstanding, and they are just as quick to condemn. They circulate the same kind of good and evil rumors that St. Paul and his successors always had to go through. With the confidence of welcome friends they enter parsonages any time of the day, and whoever asks them to sit down, or even listens to them while standing, should see to it how he can get rid of them again. They love to listen to themselves, especially if, besides their own, they can also find other willing ears. In the same tone, and with expressions of their favorite pastor, they present their judgments, praises, warnings, their apocalyptic deductions and apodictic commands concerning Christian freedom.

If they find approval, they become miraculously confidential, full of friendship and all kinds of personal offers of help. If they are treated benevolently, they can even take a little objection and admonition. The friendship and acquaintance of yet another famous pastor is not paid for too highly, even if one has to suffer a little. They keep coming back, and if they can, they seek to make themselves somehow pleasant, perhaps even indispensible. At times they bring up some rather unusual matters, e.g., the restitution of all things, the first resurrection, etc. If one treats them in this with consideration, in order not to anger them or in hopes to gradually disabuse them gently of their error, they cling to that error all the more, even if in sermons, etc., they hear the opposite teaching. The good pastor then is judged mildly, he just does not know any better, or he "will come around in time," and so on.

102. Against this easily recognizable vermin[45] in God's vineyard and all similar babblers within and outside of the congregation, nothing is better than to just refuse those visitors that are known, and for others, to set a definite time during which one is willing to speak with anyone, while promising oneself to take time for the practicing of pastoral care by day and by night. Confidently, one should ask those who come for their wish and desire, and one should refuse those who have not come regarding matters of the office or of pastoral care, openly confessing the lack of time.

---

[45] [Loehe:] Far be it [from anyone] to be soft on those pastors who do not abhor any visit or conversation as much as that of people of the lower class who experienced an awakening. The way some of them talk often lacks the education that some identify with a true revival and true religiosity. They are clumsy; they have customs and manners that cannot claim an inner divine life as their origin. Nevertheless this is no reason to doubt the honesty and uprightness of these people. Sometimes there is a jewel in a hard, clumsy, awkward shell. A pastor should have the sense, love and gift to find it and free it from its hindrances. Woe, if the pastor cannot tell the difference, and treats the simple visitor, the precious child of God, like a hobo, sectarian, and separatist! [Editor's note: Here again one sees a sharp difference between European class-consciousness and the sort of classless outlook held by many American religious groups.]

Even that often angers the vagabonds. But if they come during office hours, they know in advance that the pastor will close at the end of that time, so they cannot become too wordy. Sometimes they meet other people who also want to be heard during that time. In addition to that, the very order of such an hour demands that one be brief. The shortness of the office hour also affords the pastor, without giving offence, a good reason to firmly require shortness of presentation and also to inquire into the reason for the visit.

If one squarely refuses the people of the above mentioned sort, this does not make them any better. Their offended pride will drive them to greater obstinacy and to slander. If one receives them in the way just mentioned, one can serve them with the truth and practice the love that is wholesome for them without losing much time and without earning any ill repute through them. The basic tone of sincere love and the tone of honest care for the salvation of those gossips have at times sounded together in such a way that the better part in the soul was strengthened and purified.

But in any case, a short meeting should be sufficient. One should not invite such people to stay or feed them; [one should] not invite them to come back. One should refuse kindly any personal offers and keep one's distance. One should not give them any insight into conditions in the congregation or in the family. In short, one should be very plain, as is proper for a loving pastor toward an erring and mixed-up brother.

One would practice hospitality in the wrong place if one would receive those whose pride would be fed if they could communicate with pastors, as well as their arrogance that they practice toward the likes of them. It is not right for the pastor to encourage sin.

K. Neighborly Relations

103. Concerning neighborly relations, we do not mean a neighborhood in the narrow sense of the word, nor the fellowship with those parishioners who live close to the pastor. [We mean] neighborly relations in a wider sense, **fellowship with neighboring pastors and their families**. We speak here mainly of the neighborly relations of country pastors. Whoever is familiar with the life of country pastors knows how much this kind of neighborly relation is practiced by many pastors.

Who would doubt that precisely this common life of neighboring families of country pastors could be very wholesome and beneficial, not only pleasurable and enjoyable? Neighboring country parishes stand in constant and varying relationship to one another. The fields, the meadows, and the woods border on one another. The common laws, customs, habits and traditions bring many connections. The congregations are in close contact. The same goes for the pastors and their families. They also share many needs and often can help and counsel each other.

They can walk together beautifully in their physical and spiritual life. It also gives the best impression for neighboring congregations when the shepherds agree and are friends. Certainly, one of the noblest advantages of the life of a country pastor is this living together of the pastoral families. If anyone ever had an evil neighboring pastor knows to praise the fact that "faithful neighbors" are a noble gift of God.

104. **However**—and this "however" should be appreciated none the less: Neighborly relations should not be used as a tasteless and boring society event. The pastors and their families should come together out of love, not for killing time; this should be especially for the practice of the spiritual and intellectual life, not only for common temporal needs. Since there is often a lack of variety in the life of a country pastor, one should not have unlimited conversation about daily events. One should deal briefly with temporal things, and proceed together to the higher interests of the Church of God.

There are areas where the pastors who often live quite close to each other have a veritable gossip club. Each day there is a place where the neighboring clergy gather, often literally from good old Sunday to good old Friday, if not also to Saturday, the good old study day. What could you possibly talk about every day? What kind of joy and relaxation could that be? Without a quiet life there is no social uplifting; without work there is no refreshing rest; without studying there is no deeper conversation; without lonely meditation there is no real, interesting discussion.

In short, whoever has social contact every day deprives it of its attraction and value, and is lazy to boot, and in the company of good friends he will have a bad conscience. Therefore pastors' families who live all too neighborly and are often together become totally secularized. Their conversation is a true barometer of their life. Such pastors are superficial in their office as well as in society. Nothing noble, nothing great, no common effort for the good of the congregation, no loving intention inspires them. The things that bind such societies are beer, tobacco and cards—when not some rather different things as well. One ought to leave them with disgust and indignation.

105. A young pastor seldom should be with his neighbor in the office. But when he is [there with him], then [let him be there for him] with his whole heart. What should keep him in his place are his office, his daily work, his life's goal, his study, his fatherly care for his house, and also the observation of his duty of residence,[46] which forbids frequently leaving his place. If friends, who enjoy seeing each other and look forward to the conference day, get together, let it be as if they were visiting the suffering and the sick. At first let them briefly deal with the temporal, talk about it, and order it. Then they should move on to the work of the office through which the saints are being prepared.

---

[46] [Loehe:] This is a term from Roman Catholic pastoral doctrine.

Of course, the men should start the debate and be the main speakers. But one should not begrudge the women a time of question and answer. It will be good for them to listen to the talk of the men and thereby for once be removed from the household sphere, being lifted up and advanced. No protocol is needed, nothing formal, no pressure. In a free atmosphere, within the beloved limits of what is decent and pure, one acts unembarrassed and harmlessly. One does not get joy out of debating thousands of things. What is being discussed will be dealt with according to ability and possibility. The attraction does not lie in superficiality, but in having fellowship while talking. One deals with the subjects of the discussion in a manner that is lively and happy, gladly tolerating speaking and answering, waiting for the latter and requesting it.

Objection leads to consideration, but not to bitterness; joy, but not offense; the inner calm is not bothered by it, only spiced and made attractive. Everybody may say what comes to his mind, even immature and imperfect subjects may be brought to the light of day. From the beginning it is stated that there are no men here who are perfect speakers. Therefore no one has to be absolutely right, no one is afraid to take back the wrong or misspoken word. Clarity and love are augmented in assuring, in making oneself understood, in taking things back. Judgment and voice will become more circumspect and fuller, with more insight and weight, and life will become more intellectual and more important.

This is how things are here and there with neighboring pastors and pastor's families. Blessed are the parsonages where such neighborly fellowship is practiced—not too often and not too infrequently. The example of free and holy Christian love is displayed there. God and his angels will rejoice over such meetings.

106. No **envy** should rule during such get-togethers of neighboring pastors and pastors' families. Envy kills love. But love is the certain death of envy. Therefore one should bring oneself to love the wisest man in the meeting, instead of envying him. The goal of all right conferences should not be majority, but equality and unity, and not just outwardly, but also inwardly. But if equality should mean that all present, each one on his own accord, would find and say the same thing with the same clarity, the same completeness and the same limitations, and say the same thing as the other, this would be the most unnatural request possible.

Wherever two people get together, one of them is more qualified and capable. If several meet, of course it is no less so. In that case the virtue of the more capable one is to prove his ability in a humble way. And the virtue of the others is a free consideration and appreciation of the best voice, a testing of all that happens, and holding fast to what is good. If it is otherwise, it is only the arrogance of weakness—and this weak arrogance provokes the arrogance of the one who oversees the others.

It is a miserable time when one knows no better revenge against the distribution of different gifts by the Creator than to make the puffed-up claim that one has equal gifts as the other, that the voice of the one has the same power and substance as that of the other. Therefore, experience teaches that often nothing is achieved because, against better knowledge and conscience, one is unwilling to concede to what is obviously better. May God grant all His servants the right humility here!

L. RELATIONSHIP TO WOMEN

107. We are not talking here about courtship and marriage—we are going to save that for another chapter. [We are talking] only about **friendship** that sometimes exists between men and women. The manlier and the more excellent a man is, the more he will be appreciated by women—even if there is nothing sexual in the relationship. It is natural for a man to honor beauty and grace in a woman, even without any selfish intentions. It is natural for him to consider every female virtue to be so much higher, when it appears in this light. In the same way, it is natural also for a woman to seek the inner glory of a manly, perfected character in a man, and to honor it. Exactly in this [behavior] lies the assurance of female value. This is why the more excellent women often seek fellowship with a male character. And especially in the spiritual estate they prefer to find such characters. Therefore it frequently happens that even quite noble and high born women find special joy in a personal relationship, or in letters, with excellent pastors.

The question is now: How is a pastor to behave in such a case? If we ask the **popular voice,** it will always disapprove. In a milder case it will call it a mistake or put the stamp of the ridiculous on it. If we ask **our own voice**, it will also not find anything natural in it. It is and remains a strange feeling to want to have a friendly personal relationship with women, or correspond with them. [That specifically means] in such a way that more than the usual interest of social life is taken. If we ask **older people**, they also will render the judgment that one should not entertain such liaisons for pleasure or simply out of friendship. They will shudder in the face of the possibility that one might enter a wrong sexual relationship. They will want to preserve for the pastor the quiet rest for his soul, save him from evil gossip, and know that his Christian freedom is limited by Christian wisdom. And who wants to say that they are wrong? Especially if the talk is about unmarried women—either older or younger ones—wisdom will give its veto, and a wise man will accept this veto joyfully. This also is the surest way for women also to find rest for their souls.[47]

[47] Consider the problems when one does not follow this good advice as illustrated by the salacious career of Martin Stephan Sr., as detained in Walter O. Forster, *Zion on the Mississippi* (St. Louis: Concordia, 1953).

108. Of course, one should understand that this only concerns relationships **apart from the [pastoral] calling.** Where the job of the pastor requires one to be closer to women—whether in writing or in person—a pastor may consider the possible temptation and guard against it. But he will not step backwards for this reason, nor hesitate to go on with his professional work. The God who gives his servants the office that serves all creatures can also make it easy for them to practice it with all people. It is not the fault of the office, but their own, if this brings them to any kind of perversion.

109. As far as **correspondence** is concerned, it always takes too much time for a servant of the Gospel to do it without proper reason. Old friends who are both pastors seldom will correspond regularly without a proper reason. It would be far less possible for a friendly exchange of letters to happen between pastors and women. In addition, a person is usually different in letters than during his ordinary life—and not only during the momentary excitement and uplifting [that occurs in writing], but also in his whole being. True, it is possible that a person is more truthful in letters than in life; this really happens often. What is inside is often so sacred that it cannot be demonstrated publicly and in front of many [people]. Thus one often finds truly tender souls to be clumsy and hurtful in their appearance. Often love is clad in a repulsive form. Then it can happen that the hidden person of the heart shows himself **more truly** in a letter than in his public contact.

But perhaps the opposite is more frequent. Yes, in letters that are only written in order to communicate something, there is often a conscious hiding of the truth, an artificial simulation and hypocrisy. And for some, a letter written only to communicate becomes a veritable temptation for a self-embellishing lie. When it comes to the two sexes, both are especially inclined to embellish themselves to the other, to become hypocritical. With a correspondence like the one we are talking about, a double temptation therefore can start. Therefore every pastor should be on his guard and what is healthy and profitable on both sides, even if it should appear less pleasing. Here also the saying is true: "I am human. I do not believe that anything human is foreign to me."[48] Whoever is sure of himself and of the others is free to follow this advice.

M. How to Behave Toward the Poor

110. The poor either are completely impoverished people and beggars, or they are still able to earn a partial living amid all their poverty. According to civil statutes that regulate care for the poor, under no circumstances should beggars be tolerated. Even the pastor, who as a rule heads up the poor relief for the state, should practice this (certainly impossible) regulation of poor relief in individual cases. It is his right, even his duty, to have the beggar

[48] *Homo sum, nihil humani a me alienum puto.*

arrested. If he has done this once or several times, he will be in little danger of having to do it again.[49]

Even though one should not praise begging as much as one should work against it, nevertheless it does not go with the spiritual character of a pastor to execute the hard measures of the state against the beggars. It is fitting for a servant of the Word to give the beggar his gift in a manner that it will encourage him to do good or confirm him in it; or to give [the beggar] the gift in a spiritual way. But no position within the poor relief of the state should make him use a measure that not only would make [the pastor] exchange the character of a shepherd of souls with that of a police officer. This also would make him different from the arch-shepherd Jesus, who calls the poor blessed, and who knows no other means but love when it comes to eliminating the differences between riches and poverty.

Therefore it is best if [the pastor] uses his position in the poor relief of the state to push for [the result] that all measures of the state should become superfluous through Christian works of love, and this with all his personal involvement and effort. How he will do this has to be left to his wisdom, since conditions are different everywhere, and thus different measures may be required. One will never succeed in eliminating begging altogether. There are worse and greater evils that cause it. They cannot be eliminated through forceful oppression, even if that would be possible.

It would be much better if, e.g., the great number of people who try to alleviate their lack by stealing would find relief by begging and imploring. Begging is honest; stealing is an evil that excludes one from heaven. Of course, if all poor thieves and chiselers would become honest beggars, one would see even more clearly what a boundless, unfathomable ocean of misery and of divine punishments is covering our fatherland. But the evil would be there already; it would not be originated or become greater through this. But a return to a more moral life, such as a change from thievery to begging, would also bring more strength to lessen the misery. In any case, [such a change would bring] more strength to bear it.

There may be some exaggeration in these sentences, but no doubt [they hold] something true; we wish not to be misunderstood. Societies of beggars are something horrible and one should strive against them. But one should never forget that there is a difference between [some] beggars and [other] beggars. Not everyone who is called a beggar can help his circumstances in any other way [except by begging]. [That case] should be counted as [being] a professional beggar.[50] The fear of hurting an upright or even pious

---

[49] In Germany the poor have legal access to basic needs and need not beg as if that were not true. Note also the entanglements with the state as an established church.

[50] Here *zünftig* means *committed* in the sense of being committed to an unalterable course of action. It does not convey being a professional con artist, although the latter meaning is perhaps more apropos for the usual meaning of *zünftig*.

Lazarus—the desire for a blessed cup of cold water that Christ mentions in Matthew 10:42, with its great reward—that should make a pastor eager and sharpen his senses so that he can discern among beggars and serve the pious beggar.

Of course that does not happen if one just gives something to every beggar and then comforts oneself with the thought that this way one cannot skip any pious and upright beggar. That is cheap benevolence. At least a pastor deserves what he gets if he does not know how to use his position as head of the governmental relief agency, thereby falling into the hands of the local police who are watching for beggars and being denounced as one who transgressed government statutes. He did not know what better thing he could do for the beggars, or he was too lazy to do it.

On the other hand it is totally within the authority of the pastor, as head of the local relief agency, to provide some **serious** help for the poor and the beggars. The governmental laws are not against this. On the contrary, the institutions and means of the state help at this point and only have to be acknowledged.

We are not talking about pastoral care for the beggars here, or about begging as something under the auspices of the pastor. And no one will claim that a pastor, who gives according to the above principles and uses his position as head of the relief agency, would be going beyond his sphere of activity or transgressing into a strange office. The beggar falls into the care of healing love, even of pastoral care, wherever he happens to beg. This is like the day-laborer from outside the area that gets sick in a strange parish and is taken care of by the local pastor [in the place] where God let him get sick. He will receive pastoral care for the moment by the pastor in whose area he was collecting gifts. It will be loving care, and then he will be faithfully sent back to his hometown pastor.

111. Formerly the care of the poor was totally, or at least partially, a **matter of the Church.** At that time the poor would receive a gift from the deacon according to the pastor's instruction.[51] (There were special permission slips for this.) Of course this came out of the church treasury. This enabled the pastor to serve the poor in the best way. They were referred to him. What he did agreed with the meaning of the office and in the name of a Christian congregation. The pastor no longer has this beautiful and somehow easy position. Especially in some areas where there are many beggars, it will be a difficult task for him to do enough with the little at his disposal, since now he is supposed to give out of his own means.[52] Then again, the task should not

---

[51] Throughout this work references to *Kirchenpfleger* and *Mesner* arise. According to function, we use the terms *deacon*, *sacristan*, or *custodian* in the ancient sense of caretaker. Usage depends on the context.

[52] [Loehe:] However, if it pleases him, the pastor can start an association against begging and can make a contribution in its name. This would be some kind of substitute for the

be considered as being too arduous! Many a pious parishioner will fill his hands. On the other hand, many a beggar will not want to be referred to the pastor if he knows that he will be exposed to a detailed discussion concerning his inner and outward situation.

Despite this, as difficult as the task may be, it is difficult only for the one who forgets all the time that in these matters he is not supposed to do more than he is able. It is easier for the one who can put himself under God's guidance and His poverty, being humble and reverent even in giving. In magnanimity he will dare to appreciate his own contribution, which he gives in the name of Jesus, because Jesus honored it and honors it still. He will joyfully change his sighing over his small ability into praying for the poor.

112. So far we talked about the behavior of the pastor toward beggars, i.e., toward **unfamiliar** beggars [from elsewhere]. He has to take the poor and beggars of his own parish into more thorough treatment and continuous care, just like other poor ones in the parish. With them, even more than with strange beggars, he will have to look for the source of poverty. Begging is to be considered as the single consequence of the whole miserable condition and some kind of radical cure has to be started.

In his behavior a true pastor will be able to combine those sayings in the divine Word that claim there will be no beggar in Israel with the word of Jesus, who says: "The poor you will always have with you." [The pastor] will destroy begging and take care of the poor, especially in his own parish. When he researches the sources of poverty relating to both the local poor and those from other parts, he will be led from that point to digging into the religious and moral conditions of the poor, and thus learn the difference between godly poor people, and the others. How he then is to treat the pious and the godless remains another matter. Here we only talk about the general standpoint and the personal behavior of a pastor toward his poor. The pastor cannot waste his time with stubbornly godless poor people or with unrepentant sinners. **Whatever else** he still has to do depends on the circumstances.

However, he will deal in the most friendly and considerate way with the godly poor, i.e., those who bear their poverty in a Christian way and try to alleviate their bitter fate as much as possible through their own industry. He treats them exactly according to what he teaches in his office concerning poverty. But he presents pious poor people as the jewels of the congregations, as their true treasure. [He does this] according to [the example of St.]

---

loss of the former position. Such organizations are good and necessary wherever there is too much begging going on, even in rural parishes. A pastor kept a list of the journeymen to whom he gave gifts and found that it was always the same ones who came back at a certain time. It was the same with other travelers and beggars. The formal handling of this [matter] brought [with it] the advantage that he got to know his people and the value of simply giving. One could be on guard and give the beggars the better gift, one that they did not seek but needed: refusal and admonition.

Lawrence, as challenges of God for love and mercy, as people who have from God the precious calling that they should require love. And he gladly will apply the word of the Lord in John 12:8 [ESV]: "the poor you always have with you." [He does this] in order to present the generation of the poor as immortal for this world, a generation in which Christ himself will be honored until he visibly comes again, Matthew 25:40. To bear poverty appears as following the poor life of Jesus.

On the other hand, the generation of the well-to-do and the rich is exhorted to do works of mercy as a **blessed** action, according to the word of the Lord: "It is more blessed to give than to receive" [Acts 20:35, ESV]. Their whole place in life is pictured for them in the light of the heavenly calling toward continuous mercy. Just as the poor person gives the first sound of love, the one that demands, the rich person supplements it with the second sound, [the answer of] love that is helpful and giving. The Lord wanted to have rich and poor people. He ordered them to be points of origin and also the center of active brotherly love, without which life would lack the most intimate and most blessed mutual relationships. One should consider the other as necessary in the kingdom of God and appreciate him. Each one should honor and promote the other in **his own** way and in **his own** humility. Through such certainly true understanding of poverty and riches, the poor are given a very honorable position within the congregation. All the virtues of the poor, as well as those of people who have much, are being advanced. Mercy and thankfulness are recognized as duties of brotherly love and thus transfigured. In this way a pastor teaches and accts accordingly.

His living within the congregation gives him the opportunity to get to know the poor and their needs. He can counsel them, help them discreetly according to his ability, and be their advocate with others. If he knows how to divide up the burdens, he will find open ears as advocate for the poor. Nobody would believe from the outset how easy it is to solicit voluntary gifts even from people who at other times are not eager to do good. If a pastor knows how to use this lever, he will hardly need to enter many poor people into the public conscription lists for the poor. All the needs of poverty are covered much better and more gladly through voluntary love rather than through the orders of the state.

113. Of course one can also run into great **obstacles.** One thing we want to mention once more, as a supplement to section 110. If for example, the local situation of a congregation causes lack of wood, straw, and herbage, then as a rule the poor, and often also those who could easily help themselves in some other way, steal what they need. In such areas the well-to-do and the rich often give in to the traditional theft, but are not moved to **give,** not even as much as can be predicted to be stolen.

More than that: With this common stealing the poor person offends even many of the well-to-do, even if he does not steal, but claims merciful love. If he steals, he is a bother to some, but the claim for support offends all, even if this claim has not yet been pronounced, but only feared to be so. (And how great is the fear of the farmer in this regard!) It is quite possible that the poor person of greater godliness, who struggles against the common custom of stealing and suffers more than others, hears this not only from other poor but even from the wealthier ones: "Steal something, then you have something!" Then it is hard to help either the rich or the poor.

The one has a hard time not stealing, the other has a hard time giving. Greed and avarice are like old rust, which does not just sit on the iron, but eats it up. They are hard to eliminate. Thievery that has been practiced for generations loses its name and is hardly recognized. Whoever gives it up often winds up with a worse reputation than the one who still practices it. Whoever wants to better himself is stamped as a scoundrel—to better oneself becomes almost impossible. The victory and triumph of Christianity is hard to come by. It seldom happens, and when it does, one hardly rejoices the way one ought to because so much evil remains, so much evil and sin of the same, almost unconquerable kind.

Oh, here is a dark spot in the lives of pastors in congregations, the way they are put together among us. Thieving faces peer from all sides—and very little conscience, very little help! May God and His holy Gospel help here! But blessed is the pastor, who on the one hand does not become hardened against these horrible evils and keeps a sensitive soul toward them and a holy judgment. But on the other hand, he also keeps patience and goodwill toward the poor slaves of sin, and prays for them ardently.

114. A pastor especially should keep an eye out for the poor that are **sick**. For the sick in general, but especially for the **poor** who are ill, the pastor is a dear person. The people believe that a blessing emanates from him. A simple soup from the parsonage is received like a medicine full of blessing, and greatly appreciated. The drink that the doctor ordered and the food that he approved will be received as a doubly precious gift if the pastor sends it.

Here a cheap way of helping is opened for the pastor. May this be recommended to him. **However,** he should guard against wanting to act as a **physician,** even though he cannot help gathering more experience. His kitchen should not become a pharmacy. He should not interfere with a foreign occupation. **Let him be content with his own and honor that of the other.** In medical matters he should always be the willing servant of the doctor, as far as his conviction permits, and should always refer to him. To interfere with the medical profession often is punished by a shameful failure, and always by a restless conscience and worrying about the success. Even if no damage is done, perhaps the right kind of help is delayed, which could have happened, or would have been sought, if no one unauthorized would have entered. This is even true with homoeopathic means. Whether they do damage or not, damage does happen because the sick person delays the time before he goes to the doctor as a result of the quackery of unauthorized persons. If they do not damage, they do not profit either, which is what they ought to do. But regardless of benefit or hurt, no real man will occupy himself with what he does not understand and is not called for.

It is too bad that pastors, especially rural pastors, cannot combine the profession of a doctor with their own, nor are allowed to do. The pastor as doctor—how comfortable that would be for the sufferer, how much cheaper! How advantageous the combination of both callings in one person would be for the mental and pastoral care of the sick! But what good does it to think this, since it cannot be? Let each one practice his profession, and leave the other his responsibility.[53]

It is something totally different to ask whether or not a pastor should have as much knowledge of the human body and its diseases as is necessary to understand the mental effects of the diseases that often mask the pastoral condition of the patients. One would have to answer this question in the affirmative. If the preachers would care about **as much** medicinal knowledge,[54] they would be more qualified for the pastoral care of the sick—without being permitted or called to prescribe things, or even be qualified to do so. Even within the limits established for them at sick beds, they would still find ample opportunity for personal acts of love. For example, how much more compassion could be practiced if one gave himself to the **care** of the sick, not only spiritual but also physical? Here is an area that more than just the physician should be competent in, since there are many sick people who never consult a doctor.

Air, light, warmth, shelter, food, etc. of the sick—how many thinks one has to consider! How often must the pastor say something, overcome by the need of the sick? How much sin can happen in this area, and can also be avoided! How helpful a pastor can be here for his parishioners! How much responsibility will he have to bear, if he does not at least try to counsel and to help? Books like ***Notes on Nursing*** by **Florence Nightingale** can call a pastor's attention to many things that he himself may not see, but which he can use for his poor people, as soon as he is made aware of it.[55]

---

[53] Here one recalls the history of LCMS professor Alfred M. Rehwinkel and his wife, "Dr. Bessie." See Alfred M. Rehwinkel and Bessie Lee Rehwinkel, *Dr. Bessie: The Life Story and Romance of a Pioneer Lady Doctor on our Western and the Canadian Frontier* (St. Louis: Concordia, 1963).

[54] [Loehe:] Bering's *Psychische Heilkunde* [*Mental Health Medicine*] is to be recommended. Leipzig, Barth. 1817.

[55] Loehe refers to the authorized German translation of this work, *Die Pflege bei Kranken und Gesunden: Kurze Winke, den Frauen aller Stände gewidmet* (Leipzig: F. A. Brockhaus, 1861). Florence Nightingale (1820–1910) helped to shape modern nursing after being influenced by Lutheran pastor Theodor Fliedner (1800–64) and the deaconess community at Kaiserswerth-am-Rhein, the topic of her first published work. Her social reforms advanced the role and treatment of women, provided hunger relief, improved sanitation, and improved healthcare. Her achievements as a statistician include the development of the pie chart.

N. THE PASTOR AND HIS SCHOOL

115. "These are the ones who will take our place some day!" These words were spoken by an old pastor to his congregation, referring to the youth assembled for their finals. These words express the whole importance that youth has for old age. All change, all progress, all improvement, and all deterioration of the [present] time will be shaped by how the youth is turning out. Now if youth were like some kind of material that one can use to make anything one likes, those of mature age could prepare the future time according to its pleasure. One could rear the youth to produce the future.

But that is not how things are. These young people can be educated and exposed to the instruction, the example, and the influence of the generation that is on the way out. That [waning generation] therefore carries a high responsibility for them. However, not only do these young boys and girls all have their individual and innate character; they also have their own will. [This will] enables and empowers them to resist the entire influence of their fathers. In addition, each generation has its own motivation. According to those winds, [each generation] sails the seas of life without [fully] understanding [such motivation] and without being understood by older people. The generation on the way out may understand its own marvelous drive that it different from its predecessors; yet it does not understand the new drive of youth, nor the goal that the spirit of the times desires. Nor does youth itself understand their motivation, the pull that rules them, or the time that is formed by it. In this way old age does not understand youth, and youth does not understand old age. Youth does not simply surrender to old age or let itself be guided by it.

The secret of our immediate future meets here together with much sin. They turn the hint of the old pastor concerning youth, given above, into a pronouncement of great concern and great worry. For old age, youth seldom is the **hope** of the future. Nor can it be—least of all in our days. The spirit of the world is marching along so mightily; evil develops unstoppably; and the young people are so receptive to this progress that we cannot put our hope in youth.

The inexperienced young preacher quickly finds out about the difficulty of pastoral influence upon adults He thinks that he could at least form the young people in such manner that a congregation [shaped] according to his wishes would result from it. He hopes that things will look different over his grave than what they looked like over the grave of his predecessor.[56] However, this does not happen, or at least only in the most isolated cases, if all factors of the product are combined.[57] Usually the spiritual influence is

[56] Loehe refers to pastors being buried in the parish churchyard.

[57] The factors of a number are combined as a product of multiplication. Prime numbers have only themselves and one as factors; composite numbers have more.

wrested away very quickly. It can happen that the same pastor who wanted to build a paradise with youth gradually will choose the old again as fellow builders. If not a paradise, he will attempt to build with them, at least God's lodge in the cucumber field of the world.[58] In any case, one cannot **hope** for too much from the youth, as important as they are for the future.

116. Despite this, youth remains a focal point for the faithful diligence of a pastor. It is fortunate if he gets in the midst of the children right at the beginning. [He should do this] without any sanguine hopes, but [he should] listen all the more seriously to the words, "feed my sheep." The pastor must not have any part in the corruption of youth. If he cannot do anything with the young people as he wants to, if he is hindered by the willfulness or obstinacy of the youth, as well as by the spirit of the coming time, he nevertheless has the duty to rear the youth in the discipline and admonition of the Lord. He chooses the best seed, spreads it at the best time with the wisest hand, waters and nourishes his seed with holy care, and prays for it without ceasing. His heart is turned unshakably toward youth. The increase is in the hand of the Lord. We do not have to answer for it, but we are responsible for our work. Therefore it has to be done with greatest diligence, enduring to the end and with the kind of wisdom that we are able to apply according to our gift and experience. This has its promise and its gracious reward.

117. A pastor seeks the young children everywhere: in the family, in the school, in his own classroom, and in the church. Yes, he seeks the children before they are born. He cares for the **newborn** children by calling the parents' attention to their sacred duties toward them and by praying for the unborn. He teaches the young parents spiritual care for the newborn. He teaches them to pray with and for the children. He blesses the babies. He approaches the under-aged in order to become acquainted with them. He gets to know all little children and takes care that he, the pastor, will be known to them from early on. His eye is watching over them—over their playgrounds, their games, whichever way it can be. He accompanies them to school and visits them in school, and always in the same identity—the best he has—as **pastor**, as curate of their souls. If the school inspector is different than the pastor, the young people will have a hard time understanding who he is. But as pastor, his people understand him best, even the young ones. As pastor he is and always remains the most blessed, perhaps even well-tolerated by those who do not appreciate his influence on the school.[59]

---

[58] This is a reference to Isaiah 1:8 in Luther's Bible, literally, "as a night lodge in a pumpkin patch."

[59] The judicial trend in the U.S. since the 1948 *McCollum v. Board of Education* case has been to interpret the disestablishment clause of the First Amendment broadly through the Fourteenth Amendment in favor of atheists. The 1980 *Stone v. Graham* case that generated an extraordinary *per curiam* opinion of the U.S. Supreme Court resulted in the posture that any material considered to be "devotional" in an unqualified sense was barred from public schools. Lutheran Supreme Court Justice William H. Rehnquist saw this as

Indeed, it is just right that a pastor should pasture his congregation, including the lambs. A wise pastor will use his position. He goes into the school, exhorts toward all good, prays with and for the children, and blesses and teaches them. He will not permit another to give religious instruction without checking what and how it is being taught.[60] He will not permit anything destructive. With all the power of his office and his entire position he fights against any temptation and protects the lambs of Jesus against the wolves with every appropriate weapon. [That includes Bible] verses, the Catechism, hymns, Bible history and Bible reading, spiritual singing, and prayer. As long as they are being taught, these make every school an outer court of the church, a workshop of the church, a part of the church. They impress the seal of Jesus on the school. These [teaching principles] will be observed, practiced, guarded, and carried in the heart of a faithful pastor under all circumstances.

The entire spiritual instruction will be regarded and portrayed as a way to confirmation and to the Sacrament. Way and goal, school and altar, will be shown to the children again and again in their relationship. The pastor considers all [the days] of [one's] youth to be a preparation for the Sacrament. He also teaches the children to consider this in like manner. He endeavors to awaken in all children the understanding of the goal and center of all spiritual and church life on earth, the Sacramental fellowship, and to keep it awake. Thus confirmation class and sacramental instruction become the high point of all relationship between the pastor and young people.

Even if a pastor delegates much of his teaching, he still can remain basically in the posture toward the young people described above. But he will give the Sacramental instruction (in Franconia often called the "six week instruction"). [He will do this] with great seriousness, with fervor, with prayer, and [with] imploring, awakening his entire gift to teach, to punish, to guide, to strengthen, and to educate. His entire intention and his diligence serve the purpose of educating parishioners, penitents, and brothers and sisters to become saints of God. When their youth is past, they will stand before God, act

---

dangerously biased in comparison with *McCollum*, a path that could gag Christianity in the public sphere, which the authors of the First Amendment never intended. Whereas Loehe spoke of pastors interacting with public schools as civil servants, the role of pastors in the U.S. remains greatly limited to parish schools. See also Terry Eastland, ed. *Religious Liberty in the Supreme Court* (Grand Rapids: Eerdmans, 1993).

[60] Religious instruction (*Religionsunterricht*) was part of the German public school curriculum. Often the local priest and the local pastor each taught the students who were registered to their respective parishes. Even today, the German government registers people according to geographic location and collects the church usage fee (*Kirchensteuer*) for the geographical parishes in which people reside. For example, by moving across the Rhine from Mannheim to Ludwigshafen, a Protestant registered in the territorial churches automatically switches from being Lutheran to *Uniert*, the Lutheran-Reformed amalgam imposed by Prussia in 1817.

with Him, walk with God, and be able to work out their eternal salvation [together] in fellowship with the pastor and the congregation. Nothing is more certain than the fact that just a few weeks after confirmation spent in ordinary worldly surroundings are sufficient to destroy any fruit of an entire [course of] pastoral guidance. But as often as one has this experience, a good pastor will press on diligently, seeking the sheep of Jesus as if none of them would ever be lost; at least those who are presently in his care must be saved. Only here does he seek to do the right thing—anything else he leaves up to God.

118. Nevertheless, no matter how great and difficult it is, all this will turn out well if God gives to the pastor a teacher with whom he can work together toward the same goal. [Such a teacher needs to have] the sacred restraint over himself to work with his pastor as the second one following the first. This gift, especially in our days, is of such high and great significance to the office and the life of a pastor that it is worth the most incessant and fervent prayer. In fact, [this gift] seldom is given. The teacher does not feel the difference in being educated, but in having followed a different course of education. There is also the difference in position and the outward living conditions that do exist, and [the teacher] feels them often with envy and anger. To be subordinate to the pastor often is very hard, especially if he has gifts, perhaps in an area where the pastor has none, or if he lives in the present illusion that he and his profession are the more useful and blessed.

How many pastors could talk about this! But how many are up to the task of conquering their teachers with love, patience, and longsuffering? What a heavy task, and how seldom is there success! Nobody will have a good word for the current training of teachers if he is convinced that the school can only prosper as an organic part of the church. But even though it may cause many difficulties for the school itself, for the relationship between school and church, and for the church itself, the difficulties are not insurmountable. Therefore a newly-installed pastor should make every effort to overcome them, and to win the teacher for the church and as a friend. Can there be anything more beautiful, more blessed, more joyful and sweeter for pastor and teacher than for them to be in the right relationship with one another and to keep this relationship as faithful friends and brothers? Therefore, let every young pastor be wise and careful, not to spoil this good fortune for himself, or to make its acquisition too difficult through his first behavior!

Above all, the pastor should acknowledge the profession and the gift of the teacher in all honesty and joyfulness—in words as well as in deed. Then he should seek a decent, frank, and open relationship; he should make it clear how he, as pastor and school inspector, should behave toward the teacher. Both he and the teacher should make their entire dealings with one another open and clear. In honesty there lies the wisdom of serpents who always find their way forward and backward.

According to Jesus' rule [Matthew 20:26], the leader should serve the others (the Church prays, "whoever serves **you** also rules"). Let [such a servant-leader] acknowledge himself to be a willing helper and servant of the teacher in everything where the latter serves Christ and His Word. Wherever the teacher desires it, one should grant him help and one should not put him under pressure through unnecessary inspections and supervision. But wherever the wellbeing of the youth, of the congregation, or of the teacher himself require it, a pastor should not shy away from proceeding energetically against the teacher's ideas. The teacher must know that the willing service of the pastor is not weakness. In any case one should remain quiet, without passion, in control of his word before God, and not speaking anything wrong. But if it happens, he should take it back immediately, always sticking with the truth, placing the glory and honor of honesty and truth above everything else. And one should pray for the teacher without ceasing and not let the sun go down before casting anger aside, if at any time one had reason to be angry. One always should keep a faithful, good heart toward the teacher, a heart that does not give up hope easily. The Holy and Almighty one will bless such faithful and priestly behavior. Or, if it rebounds from the teacher, it nevertheless calms the soul and the Lord will have pleasure because of the faith that thus shows itself in good works.

O. HIRED HELP

119. As a rule, parents love to place their children in parsonages.[61] This should apply at least to rural folk. The honorable position of the pastor within the congregation partially rubs off on the servants. The service usually is not very burdensome, and at least it is more profitable than elsewhere. The main thing is that, regarding morals, the parents believe that their children are safer in pastors' families than elsewhere. Servants also like to be in parsonages, unless they are already too independent, stubborn, or hardened in their sins. Yes, there are examples where entering the service of a pastor becomes a turning point in the life of a hired laborer [that lasts] for the rest of his life. Pastors' families still have this kind of attractive and wholesome influence on the congregations, even in our days when so many old bonds are loosened.[62] As a rule, therefore, when it comes to hired help a pastor is luckier than others. At least it happens quite frequently that one finds pastors' families who are satisfied with their servants. From the opposite [stand-

[61] This section was written before current labor and education laws were enacted. Today it is unlikely that parishioners would seek for their children the position of a servant. Still, some points here could apply to cases where a pastor allows someone to work as a day laborer at the church instead of just handing out cash and food.

[62] One should remember that serfdom did not start to decline broadly until the eighteenth and nineteenth centuries. This institution, born amid the death-throes of a dying Roman empire, forged social ties and customs that endured about 1500 years.

point, one finds] servants who are satisfied with pastors' families. Therefore a pastor has to be very careful to retain the old positive reputation of parsonages in this regard.

120. A pastor has no need to act very engaging toward his servants. His office alone and his living conditions are engaging and friendly enough to create a joyful atmosphere, even for his servants. That is the reason why, even if the pastor is a very serious man, this does not prevent a person from finding his heart and mind. Yet one should not have to be stern to a point beyond a serious moral attitude. Much ordering, scolding, or forbidding is not needed. The sermon and the catechetical instructions still resound in the house, and even there, these will speak to the heart. A manly attitude of the pastor is sufficient to keep a parsonage in order and infuse respect, unless conditions at home are too mixed-up. In this latter case—one need only think of a single pastor's household, whether he might be unmarried or widowed—there will be a difficult task to solve. This will require not only a manly attitude, but also manly decisive action if the whole household is not to perish.

121. More than is necessary in other services, a pastor has to watch out especially for the **faithfulness** and **morals** of his servants. He should teach them that there is a certain degree of mistrust in every human heart, and he should ask them not to feel like they had to trust right from the start. On the contrary, they should be permitted to ask and to inquire. Once and for all, right from the start, the following are forbidden: roaming around in the village, visiting markets, visiting dance halls, and other opportunities easily seduce toward sinning.[63] The first servant who sins against this prohibition will be removed without any exception. If there is strictness right from the start, people will get used to it. In this way every new servant will know right from the start what he can expect. Whoever does not care for an orderly life will take heed and will not enter into a service position that he would not like. As time goes on, only with ever-decreasing frequency will one encounter a servant of the pastor who does not rejoice in the Word of God and a quiet family life. Then there is no longer a need for exceptional strictness. Love and peace will rule ever more quietly and, simultaneously, ever more permeating. If there is still the necessity of a change, one will always say: "like takes pleasure in like."[64]

---

[63] Before the mass production of phonographs in the 1890s, popular culture only existed insofar as books, newspapers, and magazines had any influence in a household. One had to visit saloons, theaters, dance halls, brothels, and the like. That is why Walther, Loehe, and other Lutherans preached the biblical doctrine of avoiding places where one could be tempted. By the 1940s some LCMS clergy were ridiculing their forefathers and arguing that general pop culture was relatively harmless. Fifty years after that, one can get all manner of sin transmitted directly to personal electronics. The urgency of avoiding temptation has new acuteness.

[64] *Similis simili gaudet* („*Gleich und gleich gesellt sich gern*"—*sagen wir Deutsche*).

122. It is usual for our congregations that they fear especially that those who come and go in the parsonage will bad-mouth, betray, and gossip. Most of the parishioners have burdened consciences and get nervous at the very thought of someone possibly talking to the pastor about them. Something that no one knows might come to the ears of the man whose word and eye are feared more than justice and judgment. If it were possible, one would love to have a fence and a wall around the parsonage and close it off against all but official visits. One would love to refuse entry to anyone who does not go to the pastor in his Sunday suit with hat and coat to announce a Baptism, a proclamation, a marriage, or a funeral. But that does not work. Therefore the mistrust increases all the more.

As often as the pastor says something that strikes home, whether publicly or personally; any time that he digresses from the text wherein nothing is written about a person still living; and as soon as he gets mixed up in things that do not directly concern him; then [people conclude that] obviously someone must have talked to him. [They claim that] he must accept gossip and libel; for even a perfectly true matter is called libel if it is told by a strange mouth and uncovers a sin. Whoever has some experience knows also that we have not become guilty of any exaggeration with the sentences above. How much one could lament and speak about this here, if one would want to! One considers it to be quite natural under these circumstances that the suspicion of gossip will fall on the servants in the parsonage. There is probably no way to keep oneself and one's servants completely free of any accusation regarding informing and gossiping, as long as God's Word hits home and the pastor is not a silent dog. It is also completely impossible to keep any news in the congregation far from the parsonage, and completely impermissible to condemn the servants to complete silence because they have to come and go and, out of necessity, they have to hear this and that.

The simple thing is to look for good servants, to familiarize them with the fact that people love to blame the pastor because of gossip, and to exhort them that, with their hearing and talking, they should not make trouble for the office. They should be slow to speak, slow to anger, silent with their tongue, and not speak useless things. In everything they say, they should first let truth rule, then mercy and mildness. They should consider it as sheer disaster if a servant of God, through their fault, is stamped as a rapscallion and rascal, and his fatherly word [is stamped] as gossip. Besides that, a pastor should punish any gossip of his servants harder than anything else. He should preach the eighth commandant to his own with emphasis and great care. He himself should strive with unrelenting eagerness to gain the reputation of a "perfect man," even though this may never be achieved completely. He should not fail in the Word, keep a bridle on his own tongue, and turn everything for the best, as far as this is possible. He himself and his virtue, his upright and noble behavior among the miserable reproaches of his parishioners who always feel betrayed,—those are by far the principal parts that matter. The longer he does it, the better a godly and wise shepherd will know and practice the art, whereby in word and deed he frees himself and remains free of the accusation that he listens to gossip (at least among wise and well meaning people).

P. ADMINISTERING THE GLEBE

123. It happens more often in rural congregations than in the city that tithes and some directly-owned property belong to the glebe,[65] and that the income of the pastor must be gained from them.[66] That means that one has to find the right way to gain an income from tithes and properties. Either the tithes and the farmland **are rented out,** or the pastor **does his own farming and collecting**. It has long been a subject of much debate regarding which of the two ways is not only the more advantageous, but above all, the one that is more fitting for the pastor and more beneficial for his office, and will always remain so.

124. To rent out the tithe and the land apparently is easier. Once the lease is signed, one is rid of all the trouble. At least it seems that way. Since one does not have to deal with farming in this way, the danger of doing something wrong seems to be gone. On the other hand, to do one's own collecting of the tithe apparently is more troublesome, as well as one's own administration of the glebe. There is so much worry and trouble—the danger is real and great that one will be pulled down from the height of the spiritual life into the mundane. In addition to this, if one does not have trustworthy people (as is usually the case), one will suffer not only worry and danger to one's soul, but also temporal loss, and one has to live amid much fighting and aggravation. All this is avoided if one rents out.

125. Not only does the convenience of renting seem to make it advisable to do so; but it also urges one to do more, to rent out the glebe for **as long a time as possible**, perhaps as long as the pastor serves there, and even to fix the tithe [at a given charge]. Thus, in addition to the other advantages, the

---

[65] The English term *glebe* refers to a plot of land or even a farm assigned to a benefice, the usufruct of which is intended for the support of the parish priest. The German equivalent is *Pfarrwittum*, derived from *widmen*, to dedicate. It is a medieval development where a tenth of the profit from the land (the *tithe*, from Anglo-Saxon *teogoþa*) went to support the parish. Since all people benefit from agriculture, this provided a stable income.

[66] [Loehe:] Oh, how old is the tithe, and how much worthy of a **defense**! There is nothing more beautiful than a **voluntary tithe**! Although the old tithe derived from [medieval grants and statutes] has been abolished among us, here and there, where new congregations are started, one gets the idea to combine the endowment of the parishes with a tithe and real estate. It is too late for a Bavarian pastor to write a defense of the tithe based on divine and human rights, history, and experience, because it would only be a farewell. But truly, even aside from the usefulness [of the tithe], it is a pity that, by doing away with the tithe, an ancient work of love—one of the most beautiful, based on divine commandment and faith—is being trampled in such a coarse and unknowing way.

tithe is fixed perpetually and the bothersome business of renting has been removed.[67]

126. But now it is certain that by fixing the tithe, one will limit those who also have a right to address these matters, yet of whom it is impossible to ask. [By that] we mean one's successors. Centuries later, [successors] complain bitterly if some predecessor introduced something that turned out to be detrimental. Whoever experiences and recognizes this will agree to fixed tithes only under duress, and not without protesting.[68]

In addition, if one keeps his right to receive the tithes *in natura*, one is dependent on the hand of God, giving us both fruitful and unfruitful years. But this divine uncertainty is better than a human surety and certainty. No matter how certainly one might fixate things, common disasters hit the pastors harder when they have to take their income out of the **purses** of other unfortunates instead of the ground and the soil. Of course, wars, crop failures, lightning strikes, and the like have influence on fixed tithes—as long as the people can pay them. But it can also happen that the bloody sweat of the poor people is clinging to the money. If nothing is fixated, the pastor shares the same fate with the people. He weeps with those who weep, rejoices with those who rejoice, shares everything God gives with the congregation, be it good or bad fortune. But if there is a fixed agreement, one can imagine enough circumstances when the baseness of people questions the right of the carefree pastor to his income, that it be reduced or done away with. For why should the rights of the pastors be less subject to the resistance and the injustice of people than the rights of thrones? One could say: "If ever things come to this point, even the right concerning ground and soil is no longer secure." But it is and remains more secure than the right to the purses of the congregations.

127. As to **renting** the tithe and the property, there may be no other help for the one who has no trustworthy people, no talent for farming, succumbs too easily to the cares and the burden of the business, and feels that at least his office would suffer if he himself would handle these things. It is simply a fact that not everybody can handle this matter easily and skillfully. Also, in

---

[67] The tithe was variable in England until the Tithe Commutation Act of 1836, when it was converted into fixed rent charges and later, annuities. The church tax (*Kirchensteuer*) in Germany goes back to the Final Recess of the *Reichsdeputation* (1803) that redistributed sovereignty within the Holy Roman Empire and secularized territories formerly governed by established churches. The churches originally levied direct fees on their members, but the national government took control over that process with the rise of the Third Reich. Article 137 of the Weimar Constitution and Article 140 of the current *Grundgesetz* [basic law] are the basis for this tax.

[68] [Loehe:] These sentences, written several years before 1848, are no longer important for Bavarian pastors. For we have been forced to accept fixed income. But [the author] did not want to change anything, because here and there, where this little book is being read, there is no coercion yet.

truth, it is seldom that pastors can find faithful and devoted people. There are not enough servants who could handle the tithe, even if they cling faithfully to their pastor. More people, other people are needed. And often the poor and the needy are happy to come, who do not mind a little cheating.

128. In any case, it is not a good thing if the pastor or his wife must go around collecting the tithe. As things are, people do not like to give the tithe. They all forget that when they took over their property, they also took on the pastor's property. They all act as if the **tithing pastor** had no right. All kinds of tricks are used in order to withhold even a little something. And if the pastor or his wife constantly must be on guard for thefts or cheating, a kind of hatred and ill will awakens in the hearts of the people, so that they do not like to see the man in the pulpit or at the altar. He knows too much of the individual weaknesses of his parishioners; he saw them and had to see them. Also, the question of "mine and thine" stirs up in the pastor himself an unworthy excitement that lures him to sin, often over little things. If the pastor then has to take matters into his own hands, this truly can be dangerous for him. But there are some characters that, in such temptations, can stand up most worthily.

129. If the pastor can find reliable people to work his tithe and his fields, it always seems best **not to rent** because:

a) **He can control many things if he does not rent, whereas if he does rent, he will have no control over them.** Thus he will fulfill the oath to do his best when taking over the glebe in the most honest way. The property can be administered and improved in the best way, and thus the richest possible income can be passed on to the successor. On the other hand, renting out the property is altogether detrimental to the general income. Not only does every [tenant] who rents a field take out of it as much as he can with the least effort; not only are the fields quite neglected toward the end of a long renting time; not only do they deteriorate more and more and pay less and less; but also at such an opportunity the borders are narrowed; often the property of the neighbor, who also likes to rent property, becomes unlawfully enlarged—and through all this a glebe of great value is brought down. Whole pieces of land sometimes have been stolen in this way. The same happens with the tithe land. The renter lets disorder sneak in, does not pay the tithe here and there, and thus establishes facts for the future from which later on it can be proven that the pastor has no right for this or that field, while on the contrary it belongs to him.—All such dangers fall away if faithful people do the work under the pastor's own supervision.

b) **In such a manner, the income corresponds to the harvest, and thus is the most honest, and in many cases also the richest.** In the renting process much cunning is perpetrated and much clever collusion of those who are eager to rent. Others—and often not poor but rich renters, will laugh at the advantage of the pastor, sin and let the pastor get stuck with the damage. It is different if you do the work yourself. If there is much growth, the pastor gets what is his. If there is only little growth, he will have little. But he will not be bothered with requests for remission or extension. In God's time he will receive out of His hand his modest part. Even if the rent contract states specifically that there will be no remission or extension, such wording only gives an excuse before human courts, if the pastor looks out for his own property in cases of disaster. But his conscience forces him to have mercy. And then he has to be merciful to such an extent that he cannot be accused of avarice—and that means hardship for the poor pastors, especially since the country folk are often very saucy and shameless toward the pastor. In addition to suffering scorn and contempt, he still gets cheated and suffers a loss, which for his circumstances is very painful. All this is avoided if one can take care of one's own income.

c) If the pastor can reap his own, he not only gets to know his parishioners in circumstances where their sin and their virtue are most often and most clearly recognized, but **he himself can practice the duty of justice and fairness in the most beautiful way.** In the worst case he can give the best example. The more he recognizes the sin of his parishioners and faces them blameless under the same circumstances, the more powerfully he can lead them to the recognition of their sin and call them to repentance. It is a dangerous position for a dishonest pastor, but a triumph for a good one.

d) If he reaps and manages by himself, he not only learns best the conditions of the farmer from his own experience, he also finds out **where the greatest problems are for the farmer**.

e) Doing his own work also enables the pastor to **take care of many poor,** namely through employing them, which at the end is always the best way.

f) Nothing shows the pastor in his **patriarchal dignity** more beautifully than when he does his own administrating. The richer and more frequent the relationships of the house father are to his family, his domestics, his day-laborers, and his workers, the more they give the pastor opportunity to stand in a manner that is spiritually beautiful among his people. His esteem grows, his judgment is honored. A truly spiritual man who walks without reproach in purely human conditions also will awaken greater trust in his office. If the pastor lives outside of rural connection, it is often said: "He would talk differently, if he knew our situation better." If he now knows it and yet remains faithful to the holy Word, his word goes deeper to the heart with a human weight.

As to the danger of **becoming more like a rustic,** we will not deny that many a pastor is not up to this temptation. But many noble men have proven themselves gloriously. Many developed excellent working habits in their office, continually educated themselves, taught their children, and administered the glebe. Who would cause him to lose out?[69] If only God would have it that there were more pastors of this kind!

But alas! Constantly seeking for a new call already prevents one from taking root in the congregation. Such activity [as considered above] brings about and demands [such roots]! Then there is the question about who has more of the mind of a hireling. Is it the one who never finds the right congregation, or the one who, though tempted, remains and lives in faithful love and seeks his income through better use of his property?

[69] Literally, deny him the victor's palm (*ihm die Palme verweigern*).

Chapter Four

MARRIAGE OF THE PASTOR

A. CELIBACY OR MARRIAGE?

130. Everybody knows that celibacy was never forbidden to the Protestant pastor. It needs not to be mentioned. How could one forbid celibacy, or as the ancients said, the "virginal life," to those who are called to lead the people in all praise and virtue? [This is] especially [true] since more than one passage of the divine Word can be found where this life is decorated with praise and honor. One cannot overhear Matthew 19:11–12 and 1 Corinthians 7:20ff. These passages could make us wonder whether the virginal life is not often considered to be unimportant within the Protestant Church. The exaggerations of the ancients and the indifferent silence of the Protestants are both extremes.

The judgment of Christ, and of St. Paul, lies within both of these well defined limits (see 1 Corinthians 7:4–9). Let us consider to be valuable what God the Lord considers to be of value. He praises and honors it, and has called and made it His gift alone. By the grace of God there is a pure celibacy. In times of persecution or in especially difficult tasks of life in the office, such celibacy can be very beneficial. The celibate is more mobile. He dares and overcomes dangers more easily, since he faces them only by himself and no one will suffer loss or harm through his temporal death and departure. The daring of the Roman Catholic mission among the heathen certainly can be credited to celibacy, and it can furnish many a proof to 1 Corinthians 7.[1] If only all the young, yet unmarried Protestant pastors who sigh during persecution or amid difficult tasks of their office would learn what there is to learn from 1 Corinthians 7 and the example of the Romans. [They should learn] to

[1] [Loehe:] Whoever looks at the Roman mission stations in North America will find that the Roman mission to the heathen is still ahead of colonization. It exceeds even the activity of the Methodists, whose principles always urge to move forward. Places that we never considered already show the cross of the Roman Catholic missionaries.

search for their gift, and if they find in themselves the gift to remain celibate, listen to what, e.g., Sarcerius says in his excellent *Hirtenbuch* (p. 137): "**Whoever has the high gift to remain chaste, let him use it; for the time is short (says the Apostle) and the present form of this world is passing away.**" (παράγει γὰρ τὸ σχῆμα τοῦ κόσμου τούτου. 1 Corinthians 7:31.)[2]

131. But just as **celibacy** is not forbidden for the pastors, neither is it **commanded.** The Roman concept of celibacy and the unclean opinion of marriage, which can be found quite early in the ancient world, have remained strange and distant for our Church. Based on the apostolic word and example, Matthew 8:14; Acts 21:8, 9; 1 Corinthians 9:5ff.;[3] 1 Timothy 3:2, witnessed by many Church orders of the sixteenth century, [our church] has recommended marriage for priests. Yet they did not do this as did the Greek Church, in misinterpretation and exaggeration of the apostolic passage, for it does not make the marriage of priests a commandment. (See Guericke's *Allgemeine Christliche Symbolik*, Leipzig 1839, p. 533f.)[4]

In order to prevent dangerous errors, oppose the exaggerated evaluation of celibacy—which during the history of many centuries unfortunately did not bring about much praise—and in order to witness by deeds against impure celibacy, our side praised and recommended the marriage of priests. Indeed, there was good and solid reason for this in 1 Timothy 3:2; Titus 1:6 (cf. also 1 Timothy 4:3). Neither the Old nor the New Testament contains anything from which one could prove that the marriage of priests would not please God! Even during the first centuries, there were witnesses of great fame who with the truth opposed false ascetic exegesis, or rather perversion, of those apostolic passages! The split between the Orient and the Occident was challenge enough to let the Holy Scriptures, in their simple wording, decide between the two! And the adversaries find themselves compelled to

---

[2] Erasmus Sarcerius (1501–59) was a Lutheran theologian who served as rector of the Latin school in Lübeck as well as a *Superintendent* for several territories. He suffered persecution as a result of the 1548 interims, clashed with the Philippists, aided the refutation of Andreas Osiander the Elder, Georg Major, and Huldrych Zwingli at the 1557 Colloquy of Worms. His publications include a catechism, Bible commentaries, explanations of the main points of Christian faith, pastoral helps, and orders for ordination and visitation. Loehe refers to Erasmus Sarcerius and Wilhelm Sarcerius, *Pastorale oder Hirtenbuch: Darinn das gantz Ampt aller trewer Pastorn / Lehrer / unnd Diener der Christlichen Kirchen / beidet ihr Lehr unnd Leben belagend / beschrieben wird* (Frankfurt am Main, 1565).

[3] [Loehe:] See Baumgarten's *Kasuist. Pastoraltheologie*, p. 224.

[4] Heinrich E. F. Guericke (1803–78) was a Lutheran theologian and professor at Halle (1829–34), deposed for his opposition to the Prussian Union. He served various Lutheran congregations, was forbidden to do so, and then was reinstated at Halle in 1840. He helped found the *Zeitschrift für die gesamte lutherische Theologie und Kirche*. He was known for *Neutestamentliche Isagogik* and *Handbuch der Kirchengeschichte* in addition to his symbolics text.

borrow the praise of celibacy in part from pagan and Mohammedan guarantors![5]

132. Since the Holy Scriptures permit both celibacy and marriage to all people, and therefore also to the servants of the Church, each pastor has to decide for himself whether one or the other is more advantageous for him and his work.[6] It is predictable that the majority, rightly knowing themselves, must needs will choose marriage. To live in celibacy without the temptation of the flesh is a special gift of God and rare indeed, even though it may be certain that many a man will ignore or deny the gift in a frivolous way. The gift is more frequent than it seems. Petulant curiosity often prevents one from seeing it. The punishment for having entered marriage in a frivolous way involves much marital disaster of those who should have remained celibate. If temptation exists and the precious gift is lacking, marriage certainly is the medicine for body and soul, ordered by God. It is much better to marry, and thus to be rid of the temptation of the flesh, than constantly to complain, as do Anthony, Hilarion, Pachomius, and others.[7] Therefore, apart from times of persecution and other heavy workloads, whoever finds in himself the direction and urge toward a holy marriage and does not follow it will find himself in spiritual danger. To succumb to them is the heavy liability of those who know the will of their Lord, yet do not do it.

133. The inner vexations and outward temptations that a pastor who is not gifted with celibacy has to overcome will prove to be much more troublesome and disadvantageous. This will cripple the man's strength and rob him of the undivided attention to his holy calling much more than all the disadvantages that one ascribes to the marriage of priests.

---

[5] [Loehe:] It would be good in this place to point at a very rich book, written in the Protestant understanding, even though long forgotten, namely: Georg Calixtus, *De Conjugio Clericorum Liber, etc.,* emended and edited by Heinrich Philipp Conrad Henke, Helmstedt 1783, Parts I and II. See especially p. I c. II, *Utrum coelibatus clericorum sit apostolica institudionis?* p. 9ff. [Editor's note: Georg Calixtus (Callisen, 1586–1656) was a German Lutheran of the progressive party in Helmstedt, often opposed to Wittenberg and Jena. He tried to approach divisive theological categories with a minimalism that used the Apostles Creed as a metric. Abraham Calov (1612–86) accused Calixtus of syncretism. The latter's ecumenism and his idea of a *consensus quinquesaecularis,* the supposed doctrinal harmony of the first five centuries, became popular with Anglican Latitudinarians and provided part of the basic approach for the modern ecumenical movement.]

[6] See Loehe's Works volume V/1 pp. 237–39.

[7] Anthony of Egypt (Antonius, c. 251–356) became the topic of a *Vita* (saint's life story) by Athanasius in 360. Anthony's anti-Arian position was bolstered by this greatly popular work that helped to spread and promote the idea of eremitic monasticism (solitary hermits). Hilarion (291–371) was an anchoritic (cell-dwelling) ascetic monk who imitated Anthony. Pachomius ("the great," c. 292–348), is considered to be the founder of coenobitic Christian monasticism that emphasized a common, communal life. Celibacy was stressed and popularized by these men.

On the other hand, in marriage and through it, one gets to know not only married life and its essence, but also one's own heart, one's own strength and weakness, in a way that will remain a mystery for the pastor who never gets married. Pastoral care of married people takes place mostly on a level that is best understood by the one who knows it from his own experience. The celibate one, or better, the one who has never been married, cannot be the same kind of counselor as the experienced one. The latter sometimes will be able to advise many troubled married people, especially the younger ones, with but few words and with simplicity. He does this without infringing on the sacred euphemism and the noble use of language that concerns the marital secret that is affirmed by all pious married people. Unmarried pastors will often be embarrassed when dealing with female parishioners and women making confession. They often will not become free of the sickly and sensitive desire that clings to many who never had their own wife. The married pastor, on the other hand, should feel more innocent, free, and confident when he deals with the women entrusted to his care. What do other women matter to the faithful husband?

134. And not only this! Marriage is not only recommended in regard to **pastoral care for women**; marriage also enables the pastor to give an all-around **example** of what is decent. Given the grace of abstinence, it is easy to walk through life alone. One is rather free from Adam's plague of worry and sweat of the brow. But it requires a different strength and nobility to live together with a wife and with a growing family. One must find for himself a second soul with all her idiosyncrasies and particularities, with all her virtues and weaknesses, and with tender love. One has to let oneself be improved and bear everything for the best of the beloved. In all the changes that occur in matrimony, one has to prove himself capable in the office, in days of fortune and misfortune, at the sick beds and death beds of one's own family, in poverty and in plenty. Oh, how many and varied situations there are, where one always has to be the same, the Lord's faithful servant! Looking at it this way, in this [part of the] task the unmarried pastor lags behind the married one, even if all other things are equal. Far be it that the married one would be richer in strength and virtue, but he is in a much stricter and thoroughgoing school of sanctification. And what a holy confessor is he, if he recognizes his task and solves it!

135. The question of whether the celibate life or the married one is more **comfortable** can be answered from the preceding paragraph and the casual remarks there. The pastor has a life that is marked by diversity of relationships and by a large number of the most diverse claims from the outside. Despite apparent restfulness, there is much unrest, a life full of many plagues. Therefore, he needs support, help, and care, more than many other men. Also, one should not begrudge the sick, tired, old, and dying pilgrim a faithful hand that wipes the sweat from his face and closes his eyes. This is better than to follow the counsel of Jerome in his letter to Nepotian: "In case you

are sick one of the holy brethren may attend you; also your sister or your mother or some woman whose faith is approved by all."[8] No one is more suitable, without reproach, to serve a servant of God, than the helpmeet whom God created to be with him, a pious wife!

But if one excludes these exceptions of suffering and shaky health, of sickness and dying, one has to confess that the unmarried man can lead the most quiet, most comfortable life. He can indulge his own opinions and his own tastes in life while the married man always has to give in and has to limit himself, no matter how independent he may be. Help and care during tired hours and sick days are outweighed by all the grief and trouble that he bears out of love and faithfulness to his wife and child.

136. The pastor is free to marry, even [to have] a **second marriage** after the death of his first wife. The passage in 1 Timothy 3:2, "husband of one wife" (*μιᾶς γυναικὸς ἄνδρα*) does not talk about successive polygamy, rather, [it rejects] contemporaneous polygamy, if indeed it is proper to call the successive one polygamy.[9] It also forbids a man to be made bishop or presbyter who has trampled underfoot the rule of Christ in Matthew 19:9 and the requirement of being above reproach (*σεμνότης*) that is necessary for a pastor. [Such a man] willfully dissolved his marriage (divorce) and lustfully entered into a second one, as was customary with the Jews and Greeks. Also, in the beginning one found no prohibition of a successive, second marriage in the apostolic word. Jerome writes in his letter to Oceanus:

> A Spanish bishop named Carterius, old in years and in the priesthood married two wives. [He married the first] one before he was baptized. After she died, [he married the second] after he had passed through the washing [at his consecration]. Now, you are of opinion that he has violated the precept of the apostle, who in his list of qualifications to be a bishop commands that a bishop shall be "the husband of one wife." I am surprised that you have dragged this into the light, while in the meantime, the whole world is filled with persons ordained in similar circumstances. I do not mean presbyters or clergy of lower grades, but I speak only of bishops. If I wanted to enumerate those [similar cases] I would be able to gather a sufficient

[8] *Aegrotanti tibi quilibet sanctus frater assistat, et germane vel mater, aut probatae quaelibet omnes fidei.*

[9] [Loehe:] Whoever once had a wife but does not have one now is no longer married to one wife but to none, thus, a widower. These things go together. Therefore if the wife is taken away, the related matter of being married is also taken away. (G. Calixtus c.I p. 41). [*Qui uxorem olim habuit, nunc autem non habet, is non est iam unius uxoris maritus sed nullius, atque adeo viduus.Relata enim se mutuo ponunt et tollunt. Sublata igitur uxore, tollitur correlatum, quod est maritum esse.*]

> number to surpass the crowd that attended the synod of Ariminum (which was quite well-attended).[10]

Such historical facts prove even more than the judgments of excellent fathers who do not consider the facts, that in the earliest times one was not upset about the marriage of pastors in general, nor about a second marriage. One can find such fathers, for example, in the book by Georg Calixtus mentioned above. It was not apostolic orders, but decisions according to church orders of later times that treated the clergy differently than other men. If the present Greek church orders the first marriage for the clergy, but forbids the second one even to the extent that it orders them to go into a monastery as holy monks (ἱερομόναχοι), such practice is based on a double, though ancient, misinterpretation of the apostolic passage in 1 Timothy 3:2. Against this, and for a simple exegesis of the famous passage, one again can quote a word of Jerome [from Calixtus]:

> When the apostle says "**husband of one wife,**" we should understand it in this way: We should not believe every monogamous man to be better than one that is married twice, but consider whether he can be exhorted to monogamy and continue and profess the example of the one teaching him. What if there were a certain young man who lost his wife after but a brief marriage and, overcome by carnal necessity, he took a second wife, whom he then got rid of immediately and afterwards lived in continence. Another one kept matrimony and the use of a wife to his old age, enjoying happiness, as most people think, and never being without the work of the flesh.
>
> Which of those two seems to be better, more chaste, more in control? Certainly it was the one who was unhappy in the second marriage and afterwards lived chaste and saintly, and not the one who, even in old age, was not without the embracing of his wife. Therefore, whoever is chosen to be monogamous should not applaud himself for being better than anyone married twice, since he has chosen more happiness over free will.
>
> Some think here this way: It was a **Jewish** custom to have two wives, or even more, as we also read in the Old Law about Abraham and Jacob. And now they want to have this as a precept, lest the one to be chosen as bishop would have two wives at the same time. Many who

---

[10] *Nosti problema tuum. Carterius Hispaniae episcopus, homo et aetate vetus et sacerdotio, unam antequam baptizaretur, alteram post lavacrum, priore mortua, duxit uxorem et arbitraris, eum contra apostoli fecisse sententiam, qui episcopum unius uxoris virum praeceperit ordinandum. Miror autem, te unum protraxisse in medium, quum omnis mundus his ordinationibus plenus sit: non dico de Presbyteris, non de inferiori gradu; ad episcopos venio, quos si sigillatim voluero nominare, tantus numerus congregabitur ut Arimiensis synodi (quae numerosissima fuit) multitudo superetur.*

> are more superstitious than truthful believe that those should not be elected for the priesthood who, when they were gentiles, had one wife whom they dismissed after the Christian Baptism, then married another one. If this is to be observed, then those should be even more prevented to become bishops, who after satisfying their roving lust with prostitutes were born anew and accepted a wife. Fornication with many is much more detestable than to be discovered as a bigamist. In the one case there is [only] marital unfaithfulness; in the other there is lasciviousness prone to sinning.[11]

In a similar manner, Theodoret [writes, according to Calixtus] (ch. 1, p. 42f.):

> It seems to me that this "husband of one wife" has been correctly explained. In former times both Greeks and Jews had sexual relations with and were married at the same time with two, three, or more wives. For even now, when the imperial laws prohibit having two wives at the same time, there is such a thing with concubines and prostitutes. Therefore they have said the apostle taught that whoever lives with only one wife should be worthy to be ordained as a bishop. Nor does he reject a second marriage, since this happens frequently.
>
> (A list of apostolic proof texts follows, and then:)
>
> If someone expels his first wife and is joined to another, he should be most severely reprehended. He is by law accountable to every accusation. But if the power of death has separated the first one, and the natural urge compelled him to be joined to a second one, then he

[11] *Quod ait apostolus "**unius uxoris vir,**" sic intellegere debemus, ut non omnem monogamum digamo putemus esse meliorem: sed quo is posit ad monogamiam et continentiam cohortari, qui sui exemplum praeferat in docendo. Esto quippe, aliquem adolescentulum coniugem perdidisse et carnis necessitate superatum accepisse uxorem secundam, quam et ipsam statim amiserit et deinceps vixerit continenter; alium vero usque at senectam habuisse matrimonium et uxoris usum et, ut plerique existimant, felicitatem, et nunquam a carnis opera cessasse, quis vobis a duobus videtur esse melior, pudicior, continentior? Utique ille, qui infelix etiam in secundo matrimonio fuit et postea pudice et sancte conversatus est; et non is, qui ab uxoris amplexu nec senili est aetate. Non sibi ergo applaudat, quicumque quasi monogamus eligitur, quod omni digamo sit melior, quum in eo magis sit electa felicitas quam voluntas. Quidam de hoc loco ita sentient: **Iudaicae,** inquiunt, consuetudinis fuit, vel binas habere uxores, vel plures, quod etiam in veteri lege de Abraham et Iacob legimus: et hoc nunc volunt esse praeceptum, ne is, qui episcopus eligendus est, uno tempore duas partier habeat uxores. Multi superstitiosius magis quam verius etiam eos, qui, quum gentiles fuerint, et unam uxorem habuerint, qua amissa post baptismum Christi alteram duxerint, putant in sacerdotio non legendos; quum utique, si hoc observandum sit, illi magis ab episcopate arceri debeant, qui vagam per meretrices ante exercentes libidinem, unam regenerati uxorem acceperint, et multo detestabilius sit fornicatum esse cum pluribus, quam digamum reperiri, quia in alio infelicitas matrimonii est, in alio ad peccandum prona lascivia.* See Calixtus, c.l part I, p. 43f.

> proceeded to a second matrimony not voluntarily, but because of circumstances. Considering this, I admit the interpretation of those who understand it thus.[12]

Everything depends here on the apostolic quotations and their correct interpretation.[13] The preceding shows how the simple exegesis of 1 Timothy 3:2, in harmony with the rest of God's Word, is just as old and even older than what stands against it. Scripture and the earliest time are in agreement. One cannot see why the consciences of the Protestant Church should be made unsure and disturbed through the Roman and Greek practice.

B. SELECTING A BRIDE

137. This is an interesting chapter for all pastors, whether they are single, married, or widowed. It is hard to really know a woman before marriage. It is only through marriage that what is in her is revealed. There is such a difference between the virgin and the wife that one might hardly recognize her anymore. The reason for this is that a woman was created for the man. She is perfected in a right harmonious way only when she is joined to the one who can make up for the lack and weakness of her sex, and really does so. This also applies to the man, even though what has been said cannot be applied so exclusively and in the same measure as is true for the wife. A man's life calling is not completed in and through marriage, as is the case with the woman.

But marriage influences his entire life's calling mightily. The influence of marriage is formed depending on the profession, but no profession escapes it altogether. A young man generally is driven toward married life. But there is more to this driving force than what many think, based on its disastrous misuse. There is a drive toward completion. If young people would know what marriage is all about, they would not be so hasty getting into it. It takes so much, with everything it gives, and it burdens with so much. But the Lord

---

[12] *Illud unius uxoris virum mihi videntur quidam recte exposuisse. Olim enim consueverant et Graeci et Iudaei cum duabus et tribus et pluribus etiam uxoribus simul jungi matrimonio. Quin etiam nunc, quum leges imperatoriae prohibent duas simul uxores ducere, rem habent cum concubinis et meretricibus. Dixerunt itaque, divinum docuisse Apostolum, cum qui cum una sola uxore habitat, dignum esse, qui ordinetur episcopus. Neque enim secundum reiicit matrimonium, qui illud saepe fieri.*

Si quis expulsa priore uxore alteri esset coniunctus, dignus foret, qui reprehenderetur, omni iure accusationi obnoxius. Si autem vis mortis priorem disiunxerit, et urgens natura, ut secundae coniungeretur, coegerit, non ex voluntate, sed ex casu processit secundum matrimonium. Haec considerans admitto eorum interpretationem, qui sic intellexerunt.

[13] [Loehe:] Namely for the one who does not consider them to be antiquated church orders, no longer applicable to the present time. However, the interpretation is difficult, resulting in different opinions during the first centuries. Gentle action is required where the word is not completely clear.

ordered it so, that no one can grasp the public mystery of marriage unless he has experienced it. Indeed, it is precisely these experiences under which manly souls will mature. Marriage itself does not complete a man, but **without it,** will all the strings of his being be tuned to a holy, God-pleasing harmony? With all due reverence for so many saintly and great souls who served the Lord and his children in a virginal life—with all humility toward them, this question should be allowed, and the answer should be unreserved.

138. "No one ever hated his own flesh, but nourishes and cherishes it, just as Christ does the church" Ephesians 5:29 [ESV]. It is the man's honor to nourish and take care of the woman. As long as he cannot do that, he should not reach out for a woman. But a man will be able to handle his temporal calling, which enables him to feed himself and his own, only much later than he usually finds in himself the desire and push toward a married life. Oh, how little assurance can a suitor often give the chosen wife—that she would be safe with him, that he would be able to nourish her and take care of her.

One should not misunderstand these words. I do not want to praise a marriage made of money. The question of food and clothing should not be made the first one of a suitor or a virgin, whom one desires as wife. Nor do we mean that a man already should be able to offer his chosen one a life of riches and plenty. Sweat of the brow and worrying about food are part of a marriage and cannot be avoided. They make a marriage healthy and happy, even though this sounds strange. But the man has to be able to offer the wife at least an expectation of temporal things. There has to be strength, a basis, and a hope for success, even if success means just getting by, having food and clothing. Whoever cannot offer that much to his chosen one whom he is courting does not love her by wooing her. He acts in a manner unworthy of a Christian gentleman and arouses the suspicion of being imprudent, if not worse.

Here lies a struggle for the young man and also for the young pastor. While on the one hand, nature pushes toward marriage, wisdom and spiritual as well as worldly caretakers and guardians pronounce an important veto against thoughtless and hasty steps. There occurs an involuntary celibacy, which as a rule is not purer than the maligned one of monks and nuns. This celibacy and the often long and fierce struggle required to maintain it, sanctify it, and purify it, is the serious task of the young man. To prove oneself here in holiness and honor, in innocence and a cheerful mood, is the greatest honor of the Christian young man, and blessed are those to whom the words of 1 John 2:13 [ESV] apply: "I am writing to you, young men, because you have overcome the evil one." Here is the patience of saints and of virginal souls!

139. That brings us to the question if an early **engagement** would not be a means to lighten the struggle—some kind of bridal estate during which time one resigns himself right away to wait and to endure. Not only in secular walks of life but also among the clergy, there are many examples from

ancient and modern times that seem to affirm this. Among these examples there are names of splendor and dignity. One should think of Heinrich Bullinger, a J. J. Moser and others.[14] In our present time, one does not have to search very far. It would be difficult to find out if there are many students and candidates who already have "brides," or none.

It seems that one can assume that an early engagement could pull the mind of a young man out of longing and seeking, fix the eye [on one person], and help him walk in a certain direction. Nor should it be denied that certain characters have succeeded when making an early choice. But if one is in a situation where one cannot say the best thing about engagements that have already happened, but instead has to give advice, one will have the confidence to encourage it only with great difficulty, or very seldom.

Indeed, the young man has been pulled away from looking around. He knows his future wife by name, communicates with her, gets to know her sufficiently before the wedding (sometimes to the point where he gets sick of her all too early), influences her, and is influenced by her, and so on. But this in-between condition also brings special, great temptations with it, especially for some natures. And since the knot has not yet been firmly tied, at least not so **firmly** that a dissolution might not be possible, even under mutual agreement, [this really means that] neither the fixation of thought is complete, nor has the direction even been decided on.

A long engagement is something uncertain, full of temptations, and often sinful. In general, one cannot advise it, but only criticize it. Besides, it is something irritating that does not bring any good. The citizen—the farmer—does not know a real difference between the love affair of a young pastor (also of a young pastor's daughter) and that of his own son or daughter. In most cases one must doubt whether there is a difference. In both cases he sees a very common **love affair**. If the one is allowed, the other is also. One can think good or evil of both. Why does the young clergyman preach against the love affairs of the rural folk and the bourgeois youth if he himself has a love affair? Or does he not preach against it because he would have to preach against himself? Are there some other things he does not preach against because his soul has lost sharpness and cutting edge due to his own frivolity and transgression? In the one case as well as in the other, it is a pity if a young pastor is engaged at an early time. It really would be better not to have a serious girlfriend or a fiancée or a bride as long as he is not able to marry.

140. On the other hand it is also true—and experience proves it with many examples—that **postponing the selection of a bride** until the time when one can promise her a certain temporal existence can also become an embarrassment. By that time a person usually is beyond the years when one

[14] Heinrich Bullinger (1504–75) was the successor of Huldrych Zwingli as head of the Zurich church. Johann Jacob Moser (1701–85) was an important German law professor and politician connected with the pietist tradition.

chooses boldly (because one is still unaware of what consequences this step will have). Choosing then becomes a vexation. The more dignified and lonesome one has been living, the less acquaintances one may have among the female sex. The group from which one can choose is small, and at the end one may pick exactly the wrong one. All this is aggravating enough. But this may happen, or something different and better may happen, and often does. May God rule!

All in all, it is better to avoid doing what one is unable to do. It is safer, more honest, and nobler first to become a complete man by having employment. [That] enables [both] the woman one wants to woo and her father to understand the step that they should take, so that they can answer reasonably with *yes* or *no*. What comes then, may it come in peace and for peace. Among marital ties that turn out well, there may be more that have been concluded at the right time, not at the wrong time, i.e., too early. But even if not, for most people it will be better to wait for the right time for all things.

141. But whether the choice happens sooner or later, no godly young man will act so secretly that he would hasten toward the goal of his honest desire **without the counsel and the blessing of his parents.** When considering the step that is the most important and full of consequences for one's own life, it would be the most shameful ingratitude that one could imagine, if one were to exclude the very people to whom one owes everything that one is and has and now wants to give away, but who also among all the counselors have the most faithful hearts and a loving attitude beyond all doubt.

In addition, later sufferings, which will not remain absent, will present themselves to the conscience as divine punishments for having chosen in an unsanctioned way. This will make them heavy and burdensome. A young man of better upbringing will consider that, in marrying, he is leaving father and mother anyway in order to cling to his wife. There is a separation, come what may. For this very reason he will be happy to be of one mind with the beloved parents in this step that leads to separation.

142. When choosing a bride, a young man will do well to set **high requirements** for personal excellence. Often enough, the heart runs away from reason in these matters and the flesh runs away from the spirit. Seldom will the one who is inclined to set **high** requirements be competent in his own case without having his judgment influenced. It is good if at least the internal drive to choose excellence will cause mistrust of one's own judgment and prevent one from acting too hasty. And without question, a man should choose the woman to be a helpmeet, who, because of her qualities, can help him the most. To strive for excellence in this case is a virtue, especially if the man is bright and reasonable enough not to make impossible demands, but to measure excellence according to his own qualities, his own reason and profession.

Therefore, one should understand excellence to be neither youth, nor beauty, nor station, nor riches as such. All these things certainly will retain their value. But even if all of them would be combined in one person and nothing else added, the poor seeker nevertheless would remain a defeated man for the rest of his life. Education would be greater than all of these. But even if this would be added to the other four just mentioned, there still would not be any help for the man. When it comes to his wife, a pastor primarily ought to require the fear and love of God; secondly, education and capability; third, understanding of his standing and calling. Last, but not least, she should be intimately attracted to his person. For what is marriage without that attraction!

143. Talking about **attraction**, let us repeat this requirement separately. Attraction is blind; it is foolishness if it is the beginning, middle, and end in the selection process. By itself it is not decisive, but is worth its proper, full effect among the persons with whom one has found the right qualities, with the counsel of the parents and faithful friends. We emphasize and repeat that a marriage without attraction is gruesome—one could almost say it is a vicious thing. But an attraction to someone unworthy is a deception, which soon enough will turn into misery or even hatred. And woe then to the disappointed man and the disappointed woman!

C. The Pastor's Wife

144. The frequently used term *Pfarrfrau* (parish wife) has to be criticized as improper, if one understands the word according to its meaning. It would be better to use the more modest names ***Pfarrerin*** or ***Pfarrersfrau*** (pastor's wife).[15] In contrast to the latter, the former expresses the whole error and the whole coquettish over-estimation that one so often finds these days regarding the *Pfarrerin*. One likes to assign to the *Pfarrerin* a more influential and important place in the congregation of her husband than this used to be. Some even want to claim that the place of the *Pfarrfrau* should not be missing in any handbook for the ministry. Therefore, it should not be missing in this little book either, even if only in order to get the *Pfarrerin* out of the handbook and into the most agreeable, least disputable part of her calling as house mother.

145. It is a willful claim, without foundation, that the pastor's wife should be a **deaconess** (in the biblical sense) in the congregation of her husband. One can argue about whether 1 Timothy 3:11 refers only to the wives of deacons, or also those of presbyters. In any case, the only thing written there is that not even the wives of deacons ought to be deaconesses, but that they should walk worthy of the office of their husbands. And yet, the wife of a deacon could more naturally be recommended as a deaconess than the wife of a presbyter.

---

[15] Since the introduction of female ordination, a practice completely unknown in Loehe's time, the term *Pfarrerin* now refers to female pastors.

Deaconesses are supposed to be childless widows who use their remaining lifespan and their accumulated life experience for the special service of the poor and the sick, see 1 Timothy 5. It is very natural that they ought to be widows, since the job of caring for the poor and sick cannot be combined with that of wife and house mother. A wife and house mother can have the most loving heart for the poor and the sick, but she cannot make the care of the poor and the sick to be her life calling since she already has another calling. As much as she may do and work for the benefit of suffering people, it all is done only as a sideline. It ranks below her calling as house mother and wife. Taking care of the poor and sick will burden the deaconesses and demand sacrifices that often eliminate the professional work of the house mother, or make it impossible.

146. The *Pfarrerin* is wife of the pastor, mother, and educator of his children, his help in achieving the apostolic demand to manage his own household well and have obedient children, 1 Timothy 3:4. The more perfectly she is that help, the more perfectly she will be what she is supposed to be. Look at the apostolic admonition in 1 Timothy 3:11 [ESV]: "Their wives likewise must be dignified, not slanderers, but sober-minded, faithful in all things."[16] To prove herself in this, to become more perfect in it—that is her calling and the goal for her life.

The greatest respect of her congregation and of others will follow her if she faithfully pursues this apparently small, modest goal, and has achieved it. It is a modest goal in comparison with what unreasonable well-wishers have assigned to the *Pfarrerin*. Nevertheless, it is a high goal and includes many good works, through which she can embellish her faith all the way into the next world. Her quiet walk of life, which transfigures her house and makes it into a pleasant cottage of peace, will in the long run be recognized by others also. Without being aware of it (it cannot be achieved if it is attempted intentionally) it will make a deep impression even on those who do not believe the words of their pastor. Her quiet way of life will make an even deeper impression, the more she herself is filled by the glory of the profession carried by her beloved. All of her actions and her refraining from action will carry a reflection of his holy office. One will always be able to tell that she is a pastor's wife. Her husband will have honor and joy because of this. Just as he is to be an example for the priestly people, she also will be a good example for the women. That is not because she affects it with a great effort, but because, regardless of the eyes, the appreciation, and the admiration of all people, she is [simply] the pastor's wife, and cannot be anything else. This is how she is, and it is the way she acts. She serves her Lord in the most beautiful lot among women. She has received a beautiful heritage. Her yoke is easy and her burden is light. Even if things are hard, her joy and her strength are to do good.

---

[16] σεμνάς, μὴ διαβόλους, νηφαλίους, πιστὰς ἐν πᾶσιν.

She has found her nest at the altars of Jesus and she blossoms in the court of his sanctuary.

147. As much as a pastor's wife may live quietly by herself, nevertheless, with time she will become more acquainted personally with her husband's parishioners. It cannot be avoided. Without looking for it, she will get to know the domestic conditions of the individual families. Her womanly sympathetic eye will quickly become aware of every need and misery. These qualities will make this godly disciple ever more the darling of the congregation: gracious words that well up from her heart because God's Word is bubbling in it; lovely gestures in harmony with the spirit of her heart reflecting it very naturally and immediately; unpretentious helping, which gives her the most innocent joy; a heart full of love and friendliness; a heart full of prayer when helping is not possible. Soon people will look for her, as soon as they know her. Soon every trouble that befalls a parishioner will point a finger at the good helper, and her name will be remembered in connection with all kinds of good works. A good Christian woman in the position of a pastor's wife does not have to cause attention. She will be noticed anyway.

148. The official business of a pastor is more popular than that of any other man. Everybody keeps an eye on it, everybody takes part. **How should the pastor's wife not take part in it?** She is also a parishioner and she stands at the head of all female parishioners, so to speak. Her marital relationship does not bring her that close to her shepherd that she would forget that he is her shepherd. Yet her participation in everything that concerns the congregation and the Holy Office is heightened by her intimate connection with the pastor. Here, in the relationship of the pastor's wife to the office of her husband, lies the most beautiful affirmation. The borderline between closeness to her husband and reverence for her shepherd and his office is the line of beauty and propriety for her. To combine this *near* and *far*, that is her art.

The extent to which she can go in this art is also the metric by which one measures the pastor's wife. Here lies her dignity and her commonness, her majesty and her baseness, her virtue and her vice. No domestic excellence, no education, no other superiority can be a substitute for a lack in the recognition of this borderline between wife and parishioner. [Nothing] can cover up a rude understanding of her relationship to her shepherd. If she as *Pfarrerin* takes the most intimate part in the work of her husband, without elevating herself to be a mediator between him and the congregation; if she is completely his, his wife and his friend, and yet also his respectful child, his daughter; nearer to him than anyone, but as parishioner not nearer than any other; if she is afraid of the possibility that she might influence her husband in matters concerning his office; if she always listens with comprehending joy to the Lord's holy "Woman, what have I to do with you?" and if it is her main concern to be **only** her husband's wife, his friend, and **only** to be a parishioner and penitent; if she is that and no more, if she **succeeds in being that and**

no more—then she is what she should be and she will not be unaware of her influence of innocence and simplicity upon her husband.

The more this is the case, the more he will refrain from forgetting that he is the shepherd, both in his marital relationship and all the more so in his official one. A beloved eye, full of love and reverence, is testing his works, and seeking confirmation of her love and reverence, and therefore [she seeks] womanly satisfaction and true marital fortune in his excellent behavior.

[There is, however, a different behavior. This occurs when,] on the other hand, the pastor's wife takes the side of her husband; if it is not the office that she honors in him, rather, perhaps she honors the office for his sake; if perhaps it is a very common love of self that makes her defend the work he does for his office. [It happens when she claims that] he is always right because he belongs to her; [that] his sermons, catechesis, and speeches are the best and the most beautiful because he has the good fortune, or misfortune, to be her husband. [It happens when] she is his representative against everybody, a mediator between him and everybody. [When this occurs,] if one can turn to her and win her over—will she then become his Eve that seduces Adam to do or not do things?[17]

[With this sort of behavior,] oh, what a base sort of wife she then becomes! Political wives are the most insufferable of all, and the pastors' wives who take the side of their husbands can only be the most insufferable among all who are insufferable. Who is going to respect them? Those who need her will seek and use her. Others will shy away. They are without respect.

This is not to say that the pastor's wife should never be assigned a task by her husband that would further his office. She is her husband's first student. On his side she grows in experience and knowledge, and the more she grows and finds and guards the above-mentioned border line of what is proper, the more irreproachable she will be if she fulfills a temporary task, or even a permanent one, especially in the pastoral care of women. There are some things a pastor cannot talk about in front of women. In that case the only one he can talk with should become an interpreter of his love as a shepherd. Then she is also truly a deaconess, even if not in the biblical understanding.[18] But with all the joy about such service, she should never forget the joy and love for the humility and modesty that goes with her natural position. A godly man will help her, and he also knows how to keep his godly wife in what is proper for her.

---

[17] Loehe refers here to Jerome's letter to Nepotian that he quoted in §135 above. Jerome spent much of his life benefitting from the patronage of rich women. Yet his attitude and conduct toward women polarized the Roman population in his time.

[18] Yet the pastoral care of women in such cases definitely was part of what the early Church considered to be the biblical sense of being a deaconess. See also Ziegler, *Diaconate*, chapter 19.

149. The Lord will require an accounting from those pastor's wives who pamper their husbands, their breadwinners, and know no worry, except how to keep the head of the family healthy and alive; who cripple the steps of men out of pure carnal love and anxiety for their own fate; who hinder their husbands in the sacrificial pursuit of the office; who take away his strength—like Delilah did to Samson—and count it a gain to tame the strong and make them effeminate and soft. They will not be able to give an accounting for all this. May there be a horrible woe sounding in their hearts, that they may desist from loving their own life and that of their husbands to such an extent that they lose it!

On the other hand, if a wife has the misfortune to have a lazy pastor, may she be his prophetess and shout a *forward* to him, and encourage him to work. How shameful is it to stand by the side of a lazy man, and a lazy pastor on top of that! Even from her deathbed the pastor should hear encouragement, the admonition to faithfulness, diligence and sacrifice for their Lord and his sheep.[19]

D. Child-Rearing

150. One should not have to mention much about disciplining children in the parsonage.[20] Perhaps only this, that a pastor and his wife have the common duty of parents to educate their children well. They should keep in mind especially the word in 1 Timothy 3:4 and fulfill it. Basically, no class has to strive for more than the others when it comes to education. Even the kind of education in the middle class, to which most pastors belong as far as their outward position is concerned, is pretty much the same, unless there are individual special conditions.

151. It is mainly because some mistakes, which easily happen in the rearing of pastors' children, that we do mention something under this heading. However, here as elsewhere in these pages we talk less about conditions and virtues of mistakes of city pastors; rather, we talk about rural pastors. Without any doubt, everybody watches the rural pastor in his congregation. Every virtue of his shines brighter, but every mistake falls all the more under a critical eye. Whenever a rural pastor makes a mistake, this is sharply noticed, very much taken amiss, often criticized out of proportion, but nevertheless very seldom reprimanded to his ears. This also applies to mistakes made in rearing the children.

---

[19] [Loehe:] See in the appendix the "Points to Remember" for pastors' wives. [Editor's note: See Appendix A.]

[20] The terms *Zucht* and *züchtigen* refer to discipline, yet also to *ziehen* and *treiben* in the sense of providing a climate for growth and maturation. They are related to Latin *castitas*, chastity, and the verb *castigare*, to chasten. *Kinderzucht* is not just the discipline of children, but also the general rearing of children toward a positive goal.

152. The children of the rural pastor must feel that they are better than the children of other parishioners. The father's position and the life in his house present a sharp contrast with that of the rural folk. From the start, the children of the congregation look up to the pastor's children and give them a preference and the right to be heard first, unless they have proved themselves especially unworthy.[21] If the pastor's children live together with other children in town, they usually rule over them, lead them, but also accept things from them. That is why the children of rural pastors do not often reflect the father's education, but often an ugly, disgusting mixture of farmer and city habits: bossy, rude and common, for which there is no name. It would take pastors' families of a very high intellectual level for these remarks not to apply.

The task of the rural pastor when educating his children is to guard his children from this mixture of commonness and nobility. On the one hand he gives them a good education, but on the other hand [he teaches them] simplicity, humility, modesty, and friendliness toward the farmer. This is a difficult task, especially since a complete separation of the pastor's children from the village youth is hardly possible, and should not be. Also, there are only few parents who know how to use the advantages of a rural education in such a way that will awaken and strengthen for their children the understanding of the low and the high, the small and the great, so that in an outwardly modest life, they can pursue the glory of a Christian education that leads to heaven.

153. For young children during their first years, even up to their confirmation, the conditions of a rural pastor could prove to be especially beneficial and blessed. Once the boys are older and their parents no longer are able to be everything for them, there is no other choice than to send them to school in the city in order to make up for the means of education that city children enjoy—only few fathers or mothers are able to do this. As many disadvantages as life at the [boarding] school may have, for many boys it is no less dangerous to live in a small town, be a leader among the local youth, and catch rural vices. One should guard his son and remove him, as soon as his personality requires it. Everyone who would become a pastor or occupy some civil office has to go through the schools anyway. They must acquire the kind of education that happens to be a stereotypical demand for the purpose mentioned. To weather the dangers of [boarding] school and to go through its temptations is the calling of the boy. One should make this clear to him and help him through it. If there is a good family life in the father's house, the feeling for his home will be strengthened in the separation, and in spending

[21] This again illustrates the class-consciousness of Europeans. In the U.S. the rural pastor's children may experience isolation and intimidation precisely because congregational polity gives certain laity the power of the purse. Their existence in church and community may be contingent on such power arrangements.

vacations at home it will be refreshed, even kindled anew. Also, being away from home, he will become more versatile in his life and in a more varied society he will learn to move more freely.

154. As for the **daughters**, it is easier to keep them away from the village youth than the boys. As long as father and mother are what they are supposed to be, living and growing up in rural circumstances can be very profitable for them. A woman's education grows out of family life as certainly as women should be trained for family life. And the family life of a rural pastor is just about the most beautiful there can be. Besides that, every family of a rural pastor has so many connections with city families that, using them wisely, the rural one-sidedness, which one must fear, can be avoided.

If the country girl grows up in the parsonage and if she is just the right kind [of girl], she will stretch herself toward managing a larger household. If she does that, she has the advantage of a more multifaceted female training. The city girl has no motivation to learn about rural households while the daughter of a rural pastor has enough reason to supplement and enlarge her greater ability by taking notice of city education. Even to acquire a so-called higher education, as far as one could wish that for women, is not as difficult for the daughter of a rural pastor as it seems, especially if the parents from the start have the courage to let go of what is forced on city girls as a vain and useless decoration. It may be true that among daughters of rural pastors there could be many who are lacking culture and a finer education. But who has compared their number with the number of city daughters who are also lacking in this regard? And on the other hand, how many daughters of rural pastors later on have adorned the most respected families as house mothers? And how many men with the noblest education do not gladly fetch a wife without reproach from the quietness of a rural parsonage? All in all, one rather could envy the situation of a rural pastor's daughter instead of pitying her, because in her youth, she has godly and educated parents as guides.

Chapter Five

Final Thoughts: Emeriti

155. It has been claimed that there is nothing more venerable than a godly pastor in his old age. If he stayed a long time in one place, his parishioners were baptized, instructed, confirmed and married by him. They all are his children, so to speak. Their being used to him has turned into honor and respect of the highest degree. And how much one can say about the dignity and influential blessed position of an old pastor, be it truth, half-truth of falsehood! For in the end it only fits a capable man, who lasted for a long time in the same congregation.

Yet frequently that is not the case, especially if one considers the word "capable" in its more precise meaning. Even in other professions where skill is the most important thing, old age is considered a great handicap. How much more that is with the calling of a pastor. There skill means the least, but a fresh, active, continually alert spirit has to be appreciated so much more. It is seldom that one [always] has enough strength to take care of the office. It should be the crowning glory of an old pastor, should he not insist to set aside the shepherd's staff only at his grave, as if he wanted to outlive himself. He should know when it is proper and honorable for him to become quiet, to keep himself [limited] to praying for the congregation and to the liturgy, to step away from everything that cannot be done without manly strength and freshness, and to make room for the strength that alone is worthy to occupy it.

Wanting to continue working in the pastoral office does not evoke pity from the people, nor [does it provide] excuses. The people will feel greatly burdened by the stubbornness of weakness, and rightfully so. On the other hand, they do not begrudge the old man his rest and they crown it with reverence and love.

156. Perhaps [the influences that] wrongly advise old pastors not to put their office into younger hands occur just as often namely, the joy of living and the fear of being reminded of death—which seems to be nearer when retiring—as well as poverty or avarice. Therefore old pastors, especially if

their weakness seems great, should be encouraged to take on a vicar or an adjunct. One should support them in this, as indeed it happens here and there. If the pastors would not know anything else, apart from the fact that they simply had to take on a vicar, then the passions that fight against it would go away from the start. The heart would get used to it and in due time obey. Many an old man gradually would find out the beautiful side of this. How beautiful it is, gradually to be able to say good bye to the office. After all, one did not take it on for eternity! How wholesome to die little by little, before one dies, in order to live when it comes to dying! Even a younger pastor should make the firm resolution to quit at the right time, not to put any burden and weakness of his old age upon the congregation, so they also must suffer.

157. But often there are other reasons besides the weakness of old age that could oblige a servant of the Gospel to consider himself to be an emeritus and to renounce the office. Often these include a chronic disease and infirmities, a diminishing memory, or the impossibility to make a living in the place, etc. In such cases there is nothing to criticize in a resignation. But sometimes it is also the flight from hard work, the boredom of disagreeable things, and the love of being wealthier.[1] In that case it is the soul of a hireling that moves away from both office and congregation. For no one called himself. Everybody should commend his woe and suffering to the Lord and bear his burden as long as it pleases God.

158. Emeritus in a different sense, worn without praise and merit, applies to the one who preaches false doctrine without letting himself be taught and converted; or remaining in a sinful life, obstinately wrong, without repentance and correction; or neglecting his office, causing a schism, etc. Such a pastor is an eyesore and a disaster for the Church. Not only is the soul of such a person in danger, but the souls of whole congregations. However, according to the apostolic instruction in 1 Timothy 5:19, it is only proper to accept a complaint against a presbyter from the mouths of two or three witnesses and to proceed slowly because lies and calumny, also wrongful accusations, often cling to the bearer of the pastoral office more than to others. But the Church should not become guilty of proof that is to lengthy, a process that is too slow, a late sentencing. Too much is at risk when a wolf claims the right of the office in a congregation. Against this, all pastors who carry a better conscience in their hearts should protest unanimously and seriously.

Yes, all better people in general should rise, with the combined power of witnessing, against the administration of the office by incorrigible false teachers and open unrepentant sinners. This should be an unbreakable principle: "Whoever is an incorrigible false teacher, an unrepentant, public sinner, is through with his office."

---

[1] *fuga laborum, taedium adversitatum, amor status pinguioris.*

It often happens that pastors who cast aside all good and do much evil are deeply rooted and cannot be removed, while those who draw disapproval only through an excess of good, making unintentional mistakes, are quickly removed so that their place does not know them anymore. Pastors to whom the government of the Church has been entrusted excuse themselves with the lack of any clear complaint and accusation against the first [case], yet in the second case [they find] justification in the urgent and truly existing complaints against the latter. It should be otherwise.

Those who hold the office of bishop should not have to wait for complaints. They should open their own eyes. Since they are overseers and masters, they should also watch and practice oversight and look for evils in the Church. Wherever a great many sins that cry to heaven present the challenge of ridding the poor flock of Christ from wolves and guarding against them, the "**eyes of the Church,**" i.e., its defenders, should find and judge the evil with sharp eyes.

But if this does not happen, ought not one find godly and brave men who have the courage to bring an accusation? Cannot one find men in great peace, in firm rest and confidence of their souls, who will capture the wolves that attack and devour the poor flock? Would it be noble and generous to spare the evildoer and his house, while the house of God, the congregation of Jesus, suffers harm? Is there no longer anyone who would call out "emeritus" when shepherds do not just let their flock perish, but ruin it themselves?

What good is anything pastoral if it is being mocked without any punishment, whether verbally or in the life of rapacious wolves? In such manner, thousands are being robbed of its fruit. The faithful work of pious servants of God is largely rendered ineffective when wolves remain unpunished in the office.

> We now know well how we are to act and to walk in the house of God, in the congregation of the living God. But Thou, O Lord, have mercy upon us and forgive all of us our sins and misdeeds, wherewith we have sinned against Thee and Thy holy Word and office. But give us, all Thy servants, great power, and strengthen in us Thy life, that all of us, ready and dressed for action to promote the Gospel of peace, may walk in patience, casting our seed, and work and wait for the precious fruit of the earth! Amen.

Appendix A: For Pastors' Wives

Points to Remember

[These points were] written by a young pastor's wife in 1837.

1. Every pastor's wife ought to understand her calling properly. She does not participate in the [pastoral] office with her husband; rather, she participates in the household with her husband, as does every other wife. Her area of help does not fall primarily in the office; rather, her area of care ought to be in the home and regarding the management of the household, so that everything should consistently conform to priestliness. That should not be in the sense of Word and preaching. Rather, she can support her husband in his office in the manner of godly conduct. In 1 Peter 3:1–2 it is written that those who do not believe the Word nevertheless might be won over by the wife's conduct apart from the Word (compare 1 Timothy 2:11–12).

2. However, the wife's conduct, when unlike others it must be according to the mind of God, is no small or easy work. A wife has primarily worldly cares in the household. Indeed, because of that it is difficult for her to behave in temporal matters so that she does not lose the eternal matters. On top of all that, she has her children to look after. To obtain salvation in that activity according to 1 Timothy 2:15 is an impossible task if the Lord is also not helping with it. In sum: A wife who fulfills her calling is just as honorable as her husband who fulfills his calling. She does not need to covet after her husband's calling.

3. A wife who butts in on the calling of her husband has lost the crown of her wifelihood; for a proper wife **cannot** be masculine and **does not like** that. Wifelihood and humility go hand-in-hand. It is the greatest disposition of a woman when she possesses humility, that is, "pride to serve." One who is patient in this seems to have received a gift from a Kingdom in which the preeminent one, the eternal King, became a servant of all even unto death. A woman readily should allow herself to be governed, and to stand and go about under the authority of her godly husband. She should consider that to be good fortune, even as the Church considers her salvation, to live under the governance and spirit of her eternal Bridegroom (1 Timothy 2:12).

4. A wife who sets herself over her husband and, instead of him, wants to practice his vocation (for that is what it means to set oneself above the husband) corrupts the soul, insofar as she is the cause. This soul is the one for whom she has been created as helpmeet unto eternal life, namely, **the soul of her husband.** [One of two things will occur.] On the one hand, it will be that the husband himself knows it is his humility to be the man in the name of the Lord, but he acts effeminately, thus causing great distress and many opportunities for sin against her. On the other hand, the man bows before his wife,

for which his wife also becomes guilty of his great sin that he has ceased to be in accord with the image of God. It is the same with the wife as with the congregation; one should call either of them Delilah, because she enfeebled the soul of her Simeon and stole from him his Nazirite vow!

5. A pastor's wife is a holy wife; she conducts herself in humility in a manner like her husband—in purity of heart and in the holy ordering of the internal life. Where there is no purity of heart there is **vulgarity**—and the man who has a vulgar wife is just like a bird with its wings clipped. Where there is no ordering in the internal life, where one does not conduct oneself diligently according to the salvific order of God, immediately there exists a wasteland and emptiness, a rapid aging of the soul, inconsolable sighing, and all that because one has found no fulfillment and indeed, believes oneself to have lost the very reason for living. If a pastor has such a wife, he has a miserable wife. It rather would seem to be the husband's greatest misery on earth to have such an unfortunate wife.

6. A pastor's wife must offer proof **in her own external appearance and in her household** that internal purity and order dominate. That puts the rule to the test. At any time or hour, one must be able to evaluate both her and her house, and in doing so, see that here dwells a servant of a pure world and the *Kodesh layhovah*[1] must lie upon the household; yet not merely with letters meant for show to the reader. Were the pastor's wife to consider how much respect that a priestly character gains for the pastor, she would pray right away for a holy heart full of heavenly order just on this basis alone.

7. A pastor's wife has (ought to have) a **calm heart and a confidential mouth.** A husband who has a gossipy and unruly wife is unfortunate (1 Timothy 5:13). This is doubly so when she possesses that corrosive vice yet does not recognize it herself! With such a wife, such a man has a millstone hung about the neck of his office, one that pulls it under through hindrances and dilemmas, from whence it becomes difficult to get it back afloat.

It is well known that the Word of God sometimes strikes hearts quite sharply and quite deeply. The listener who is hit does not know who delivers the blow; he knows nothing of the sword (Hebrews 4:12–13). He only sees the pastor when he considers the wounds that he has received, and he comes to this judgment: "Someone must have betrayed my confidence!" The more sincere and honorable the pastor's behavior is, so that one is not confident that he might question the gossipers, so shall the fault fall all the more upon the pastor's wife, as if he could have heard something that she got from the gossipers. When the pastor's wife does not have calm conduct and a confidential character, but rather struggles against that and provides opportunities

---

[1] In Hebrew, *qodesh l'Yahweh* means holy to the LORD. The Rabbinic spoken word *Adonai* was substituted for the written word Yahweh. Non-Hebrew speakers merged the vowel points for *Adonai* with the name Yahweh to create "Jehovah," which does not exist in Hebrew. Thus *qodesh l'Yahweh* became known as *kodesh layhovah*.

for such gossip and for making excuses for souls that have been affected, she is at fault when the pastor is seen as one sucking up to the women and God's double-bladed sword is seen as the sword, skewer, and nails of the slanderer. With that he loses much of his effectiveness. A pastor's wife therefore ought to be careful to remain at a distance from the congregation, to a certain extent. That is so anyone who might wish to do so may approach her, namely those in some sort of misery, yet so no one could even come to think that she might be mixed up in some sort of unworthy confidence with any women in the congregation, such as female schoolteachers, wet nurses, or anyone else.

8. In her judgments concerning the members of the congregation, a pastor's wife **in no manner should allow herself to be influenced by preferential treatment** and should not have any favorites. Whoever might speak to her face-to-face about her husband—meaning that he praises her husband to his face; compliments his sermons and pastoral administration; covers up his faults; speaks ill of his predecessor, the members of that person's household, and neighboring pastors, etc.; and places immeasurable hopes upon the work of her pastor—she should see as being disrespectful and be on the lookout that this person might be attempting to sneak in part of his agenda, something that he might have little hope of achieving, were he to proceed honorably. She ought to engage such a person with all seriousness and say to him—with the greatest of humility, indeed, in a cute and roundabout manner—that her husband is not in need of any praise from her, that she would be ashamed to receive any praise in his name or on his behalf, and that people who attempt this sort of thing make her afraid and she must therefore forbid that sort of loose talk.

9. One often has observed that pastors' wives have attended more to the comfort and bodily care of their husbands than to the faithful administration of their official duties. One can differentiate in this matter between a faithful maidservant of the Lord and a self-serving companion of her husband thus: **She can have and express continual pleasure in her husband's performance,** warn him against becoming used to idleness, encourage him to be diligent, and in every way, care more about his eternal crown of glory than a long [and prosperous] life (and thus one full of vanity). It should be more important to her that she behold him but once in the light of heaven, as the stars shine always and forever, than to have him perpetually at her side for a long time. And yet she should not neglect her husband's physical appearance for such reasons. Rather, she, like all wives, should have a husband who needs the easing of his burdens, because he must plow the field [so to speak] in the sweat of his brow. The Lord gives grace to the one with a childlike faith to see into this matter clearly and to help in the right proportion—the name "helpmeet" includes both: to encourage good works and to offer alleviation of burdens.

10. A pastor's wife is **diligent in her calling,** is domestic, and is not afraid of such work, not even the small things. Proverbs 31:10–31 is for her a

mirror in which she delights to look. To be praised by her husband according to God's command (vv. 28, 30) is something that is lovely and to be treasured in all humility. A lazy pastor's wife shames her husband's office and makes him blush and fall silent—both in and out of the pulpit—and that more than once. Her quiet diligence, however, gives him a cheerful face, wins praise, and also gives him motivation to praise his wife both at home and in public. Even in this matter, a pastor's wife ought to live out according to what her husband preaches, and when he praises feminine virtue, the eyes of the congregation reflexively ought to turn to the pastor's wife with pleasure, or at least be able to do so.

11. A pastor's wife likes to pitch in with work and is happy to do even the most lowly and least things, when that has to be, **yet her character is not ignoble.** When she works, she does so in humility and out of unconstrained love, not as an indentured maid. She does so rather that one might recognize the noble spirit of the housewife of a pastor. She works, yet she also lets others work, so that her own work might not be seen as being closefisted, but rather as a virtue, which it indeed ought to be.

12. A pastor's wife **offers hospitality** according to the command of the apostle (1 Peter 4:9; Hebrews 13:2). Indeed, she does this without complaint, but only to the extent that her spouse permits the circumstances. She does not try to be ostentatious; rather, she maintains the simplicity that reigns continuously in the parsonage also when guests show up. She is not hospitable in order to be something in society, rather, she enacts love for others. She is therefore dearest when it comes to the needy and through those to whom others express no love. She is thus so, and together with her husband she has sufficient freedom of the soul to take no notice of those who like to flit about visiting here and there in worldly social circles.

13. A pastor's wife is **frugal** in managing her household and only considers those things that are within means. Yet she does not do this merely to balance the checkbook; rather, she tries to have enough in reserve in order to give more than she receives, especially that she might have something to give the needy.

A pastor has considerable temptation to be and to become tight-fisted. Many pastors indeed become so, as experience proves. And yet he should be the last one to become so. There is no one, with respect to his person and his office, which can be harmed by this more than he. Unfortunately, experience also teaches that, as a general rule, women provide ample opportunities and indeed motivation for the miserliness of men. Yet with instruction from James 1:5, a godly wife easily can become wise. A wise wife can be very effective on behalf of her husband and his office, both in saving and in giving.

14. By divine providence, a godly pastor's wife is the assigned **helper** for the pastor in special cases of pastoral care for ladies and for girls, insofar as she is permitted by her main vocation, the administration of her household. Daily she prays with her husband for the congregation and in this she indeed

does no less than her husband—in such quiet, behind-the-scenes ways she helps him mightily in the pastoral office. Wherever he may go in his official duties, in the silence of her heart she also accompanies his way with prayers: that his office may succeed in its efforts. And when success is found, she prays that her dearest might have humility. When there is no success and the Lord withdraws His blessings, she then prays that her husband may be found to be only faithful and might have God as his comfort. For the office and the blessing are the Lord's. He may bless wherever He wills it—and He can test the servant who is not permitted to see any blessing, to the end that he might take hold all the more of eternal grace that is revealed in the Word.

The godly pastor's wife helps in additional ways with her husband's office. To the same extent that she avoids going around to the houses of congregational members without any reason, save perhaps for conversation, she eagerly and diligently visits the sick, the poor, the widows, the orphans, the needy, and the elderly. She pours oil and wine into their wounds [cf. Luke 10:29–37] and is a spring flowing with comfort to the miserable and an angel of God in their humble dwellings. In such occasions she also maintains confidentiality, and her words bring forth blessing.

FROM THE DISTANT PAST

Thus says Clement of Rome [Epistle to the Corinthians 21:6b–8] concerning pastors' wives and pastors' children, according to Clement of Alexandria:

> Let us direct our wives to that which is good. Let them exhibit the lovely habit of purity [in all their conduct]; let them show forth the sincere disposition of meekness; let them make manifest the command that they have of their tongue, by their manner of speaking; let them display their love, not by preferring one to another, but by showing equal affection to all that piously fear God. Let your children be partakers of true Christian training; let them learn of how great avail humility is with God—how much the spirit of pure affection can prevail with Him—how excellent and great His fear is, and how it saves all those who walk in it with a pure mind.[2]

[2] Here Loehe includes an untranslated Greek text of Clement, but it differs from the text in *Sources Chrétiennes* as well as from the text in Kirsopp Lake, *The Apostolic Fathers*, Loeb Classical Library v. 24 (London: Heinemann, 1913). Lake's text follows: τὰς γυναῖκας ἡμῶν ἐπὶ τὸ ἀγαθὸν διορθωσώμεθα. 7. τὸ ἀκιαγάπητον τῆς ἐπιεικὲς τῆς γλώσσης αὐτῶν διὰ τῆς σιγῆς φανερὸν ποιησάτωσαν, τὴν ἀγάπην αὐτῶν μὴ κατὰ προσκλίσεις, ἀλλὰ πᾶσιν τοῖς φοβουμένοις τὸν θεὸν ὁσίως ἴσην παρεχέτωσαν. 8. τὰ τέκνα ἡμῶν τῆς ἐν Χριστῷ παιδείας μεταλαμβανέτωσαν· μαθέτωσαν, τί ταπεινοφροσύνη παρὰ θεῷ ισχύει, τί ἀγάπη ἁγνὴ παρὰ θεῷ δύνατι, πῶς ὁ φόβος αὐτοῦ καλὸς καὶ μέγας καὶ σώζων πάντας τοὺς ἐν αὐτῷ ὁσίως ἀναστρεφομένους ἐν καθαρᾷ. The translation is from Alexander Roberts and James Donaldson, eds., *The Ante-Nicene Fathers* (New York: Christian Literature Company, 1895) 1:12.

Appendix B: Parish Registers

The following is an excerpt from a family register or register of souls. It contains selected locations and families:

House Number 24, Füntel

No.	Baptismal Name	Birthday and Baptism Day	Wedding Day	Occupation (*Stand*)	Death	Comments
1.	Michael	Born in Rettersdorf on 7 May 1784	Dahler, on 20 April 1807	small farmer[1]	27 April 1848, funeral text John 16:33	family originator, blessed by the Lord Jesus
2.	Anna Margareta, née Röderin, wife	Dahler, born on 19 Aug. 1778	the same	—	16 May 1848, funeral text Phil. 4:6	pious matron, of blessed memory
3.	Margareta Barbara, daughter	Dahler, 29 Feb. 1808	married around Easter 1846	wife of widowed farmer J. M. Stäublein in N., N. parish	—	respectable
4.	Johann Michael, son	Dahler, 17 July 1811	Dahler, 17 Mar. 1846, see No. 7	small farmer; church board director (*Kirchenvorsteher*) since 1850	—	respectable, Christian, churchly, very strict
5.	Magdalena, daughter	Dahler, 6 Nov. 1816	—	—	1 Feb. 1847 in the night from dilated cardiomyopathy that no one had noticed	a pious virgin
6.	Marla Magdalena	Dahler, 9 April 1819	married in March 1851	wife of widowed brickmaker J. L. Holz in N., N. parish	—	respectable, faithful to Jesus
7.	Wife of 4: Ursula Barbara née Hollmännin	Lippersdorf on 13 May 1821	See No. 4 17 Mar. 1846	praiseworthy farmer's daughter		

[1] A small farmer (*Halbbauer*) worked about a half-parcel of land, while a farmer (*Bauer*) usually worked a parcel or larger. Some of the vocation names referred to here tended to be specific to Bavaria and southern Germany.

No.	Baptismal Name	Birthday and Baptism Day	Wedding Day	Occupation (*Stand*)	Death	Comments
8.	First child of 4 and 7: Maria Magdalena, daughter	Dahler 1 April 1847 baptized same day				
9.	ditto, second, Maria Barbara, daughter	Dahler 26 April 1848 9:45 PM baptized same day	—	—	11 May 1848	
10.	ditto, third, Johann Konrad, son	Dahler 13 Mar. 1849 at 5 AM, baptized same day	—	—	25 Mar. 1849	
11.	ditto, fourth, Maria Barbara, daughter	Dahler 13 Feb. 1850 at 5:30 PM, baptized 14 days later				
12.	ditto, fifth, Johann Leonhard, son	Dahler 1 July 1851 11:45 PM baptized 2 days later				

HOUSE NUMBER 73, FÜLL

No.	Baptismal Name	Birthday and Baptism Day	Wedding Day	Occupation (*Stand*)	Death	Comments
1.	Johann Michael	Helpersdorf near Dieten-burg, 4 Oct. 1806	Dahler, 24 Oct. 1841	subsistence farmer[2]	11 Jan. 1848, 3:45 PM from typhus	A laudable Christian soul. He made a pact with Christ that He should be master of the house and Füll His servant, that he should fulfill all his agricultur-al duties according to the mind of Christ.
2.	Anna Apollonia, née Stegerin, wife	Dahler, 28 June 1820	the same	single small farmer's daughter		

[2] A Bavarian farmer on less than a half-parcel was called a *Gütler* because he subsisted on the usufruct (*Gütl*) of the land.

No.	Baptismal Name	Birthday and Baptism Day	Wedding Day	Occupation (*Stand*)	Death	Comments
3.	first child Maria Barbara, daughter	Dahler, 14 Jul. 1842, bapt. next day				
4.	ditto second, Johann Bartholomäus, son	Dahler, 10 Jun. 1845, bapt. next day	—		12 Jun. 1845	

After Füll's death, the widow sold all her goods and departed peacefully. The house and goods came to:

SCHNÖRR

No.	Baptismal Name	Birthday and Baptism Day	Wedding Day	Occupation (*Stand*)	Death	Comments
1.	Johann Georg	Bettelswurf 9 July 1823	Dahler, 3 Dec. 1848	small farmer		The birth certificates of both parents are with the certificate of manumission[3]
2.	Margareta Barbara, née Schreierin, wife	Margraviate Schallersdorf, born on 24 April 1822	the same	farmer's daughter		
3.	born before the marriage: Christine Margareta Barbara, illegitimate daughter	Margraviate Schallersdorf, born on 19 Sept. 1847	—	—	—	according to the vaccination certificate[4]
4.	Johann Jakob, son	Dahler, 4 Dec. 1848 3:30 PM				
5.	Christine Barbara, daughter	Dahler, 24 Oct. 1850 10:30 PM				

[3] *Ledigungsschein.*

[4] *Impfschein.*

The family sold in 1851 and moved away, without subsequently being missed by anyone. The current owner is:

No.	Baptismal Name	Birthday and Baptism Day	Wedding Day	Occupation (*Stand*)	Death	Comments
1.	Johann Georg Lall	Weißenzell, 1 Dec. 1782	17 Dec. 1820	retired farmer[5]		widowed 30 March 1839

[The following is an] excerpt from a confessional register [for receiving the Lord's Supper]:

HOUSE NUMBER 24, FÜNTEL

Confessional years and days:

No.	Names	1850	1851	1852	1853	1854
1.	Füntel, Johann Michael, b. 17/7/11	Invocavit Holy Thursday Ascension Pentecost 23 Trinity Christmas	Septuagesima Holy Thursday Pentecost 6 Trinity 23 Trinity	Oculi Holy Thursday Ascension Pentecost		
2.	Ursula Barbara née Hollmännin, b. 13/5/21	Invocavit Holy Thursday Ascension — 23 Trinity Christmas	Septuagesima Holy Thursday Pentecost 6 Trinity 23 Trinity	Oculi Holy Thursday Ascension Pentecost		
3.	Maria Magdalena Füntelin, sister	Laetere Pentecost 22 Trinity Christmas	Invocavit Per N. parish N. transferred			
			Easter M. B. Meierin, maid Leonhard Scholl, servant N.B. Confessional certificates[6] shown beforehand			

[5] *Altsitzer.*

[6] A confessional certificate (*Beichtschein, Beichtzettel*) is a document from a pastor attesting that a person has made private confession before him and therefore is ready to receive the Lord's Supper. In this case, the servants likely made confession to a different pastor, received these certificates, and presented them before the service.

Booklet Two

Viewpoints on the Various Areas of Work of the Pastoral Office

[FOREWORD TO THE FIRST EDITION]

Dedicated to the graduates of the two closely connected planting schools, the Evangelical Lutheran Preachers Seminary in Wartburg at St. Sebald at the Well, Iowa, and the Evangelical Lutheran Mission School at Neuendettelsau in Middle Franconia.

The first part of my so-called *Evangelical Pastor* originated from notes that I dictated a few years ago to the students of the Mission Institute here. This was part of their education. Later I reworked these notes so they could be published. A second and a third part was supposed to be developed in the same way. The dictated notes, whose contents were to make up the second part, have been ready for years. However, the time necessary for a more detailed reworking before publication simply never materialized. Either I had to give up the idea to form these notes into the second part of the work mentioned above, or I had to have the courage to present them to you, my dear younger brothers, and to those who are still able to show an interest in something so incomplete.

Basically, they are the unchanged notes dictated in 1853. I dared the latter. I have known for a long time that I am not able to write a book of a really scholarly form. Even if I would have rewritten the dictations, they would still have the aphoristic form that you already know, although perhaps to a lesser degree. And then today it is no longer true that one could only dare to do it with the conviction of presenting something perfect when it comes to publishing written works. Printing today is not much more than writing or speaking. Whoever is resigned from the start not to bring anything special into the world, but only to stimulate and cause others to do better, may just as well deal with printer's ink as he would with the writer's ink. Thus the second part of this *Evangelical Pastor* goes out in the poor form it has, and I am happy if I have rendered a service to you, my dear ones, and to those like you, be it ever so small and humble.

The nucleus of this little volume is the second part. But as you can see, this second part in its entirety has a similar shape as the first. The first part hides behind the famous poem of Valentin Andreä about the good life of an upright servant of God, as if it was a shield.[1] The second does the same, hiding behind the circular letter of the good Eberlin von Günzburg. You will have the same experience with this circular letter as with many writings of that time. One feels touched and elevated, not only by the guileless language,

---

[1] See the Editor's Notes regarding any omissions and changes in content.

but also by the pure gold of the content, without having to subscribe to everything.

But I think that you, whose profession often makes you break up the fallow ground and sow anew, will find yourself related to Eberlin in a special way. Basically, he only instructs us how to sow and how to work in such cases. Nor is it only my idea to republish this old letter. It has been brought to light a number of times, the last time, as far as I know, by August Hermann Francke in his *Collegium pastorale.* Just look, dear brothers, whether Eberlin is not truly a man of the right measure. And what about us, who strive in all things to seek the right measure, regardless of the opinion of the modern "human day"? Should we not do rightly if we receive the old Eberlin into our brotherhood at least in likeness? If he did not always hit the mark, it does not matter. No man of the right measure will always hit it squarely. And I confess that people who are always right make me more suspicious than the Pharisees who met with Christ's disapproval. There has to be something in a person that can still be improved, as long as he still walks this earth. All of us, as holy as we may be, walk only through faults toward perfection.

As an appendix to the first part of my little book there appeared a word about the pastor's wife. The appendix to this second part is something I dictated for deaconesses. The deaconess, at least the ones in the ancient world, may very well appear close to the pastor, and now as always should be the right hand of a steward of the divine mysteries among women. But concerning this appendix itself, it has no other intention than to lift up the great significance and importance of the mental conditions for pastoral care at the sickbed, and the necessity for all who practice pastoral care to become acquainted with them. But if this little book may cause one at times to pay attention to this point, and realize how difficult pastoral care at a sickbed is, and how one is neither mature nor capable when one comes into the office right from the university, my purpose has been achieved.

Of course one can ask me whether I consider a young woman, serving as a deaconess, more capable than a young man fresh out of school and in the office. I simply answer: "No. I, an old pastor, am not such a fool that I would claim pastoral care only for myself and the likes of me. I am angry with my church council and parishioners if they do not help me take care of souls, and therefore I can also permit the deaconess in my congregation, if she practices noble pastoral care. But precisely because I can permit it and want it, and see that she knows no more than the young man new to the office, I instruct the servants of Jesus. I believe that in the dictation, which I mentioned first of all, I put something useful into their hand."

And by the way, I did not learn it all on my own. In the text I mentioned Vering, my chief authority.[2] While he seldom served me with the mental means to be used, he often served me with the description of the mutual influence between body and soul. I think that for you and whoever else is willing to learn, it is much better that I had a medical authority than if I had taken everything from my own experience.

Thus, dear brothers, take this little book and use it as best you can. Step on our shoulders and raise yourselves to higher wisdom. Remain faithful to your teachers and ancestors, but not to the point where you no longer want to continue on our way. Keep what you have. But if the Holy Spirit adds a new blessing to the old one, or refreshes what we have forgotten, do not imagine that in eternity we would be angry about that. We often told you that God, over against creation, is an immeasurable ocean of knowledge, and there is an eternal progress, both in the knowledge of God and in the recognition of the sinful life that ends here on earth. But whoever talks about an eternal progress cannot be angry when those who come later also make progress.

We also, in our time, acted like that toward our fathers. Twenty or thirty years ago, one no longer wanted to know anything about what we had gained from the sixteenth century. One would only despise it. Then we did what we could, in order to call the army of Christ back to the old symbols. We were not alone, but we were among others. We still do that now, and especially in these days we not only call back to the old symbols, but also for the Church to act accordingly. You know how little success we have in this regard. It just becomes apparent that just to change one's opinion is not the same as true repentance and change of life. The call to the word of the old confession has had more success. But since many remain content with just the change of their opinion, finish their day's work, and will not permit new progress on the old road, even if God's Word and guidance require it, we insist with the same seriousness and emphasis on the ***forward*** as well as on the ***return.***

To the so-called Lutheran, that is the true catholic Christian, belongs the entire past, before and after Luther. The future must belong to him as well. All things true and scriptural are his, when and where they are spoken. The *norma normata* of the sixteenth century is for him not congruent with the *norma normans* in the sense that the former exhausts the latter, and that God

---

[2] More on this topic is found in chapter 4, section C. Albert Mathias Vering (1773–1829) was a physician who set up a private clinic for the mentally ill in Liesborn after 1796. The field of pastoral medicine helped to explore issues of hygiene, the mental state of the ill, and the role of such conditions in healing. Today the questions asked in this field largely belong to theological ethics.

Himself would not be permitted to give something to his Church that either did not exist in the year of 1580, or was not observed.[3]

It is self-understood that in moving forward one has to be careful, and has to keep the guiding thread from the past in one's hand. And of course one can be wrong and in error. One therefore has to listen to warnings, even reproach and shouting from the left and from the right. One has to keep on reading, researching and praying. Yet the Lord will grant success to the upright and bless the direction in which we belong. May God grant that in such direction a better future will be found and comprehended—just like on the day when Mary was visited, when the Old and the New Testament came together on the mountains of Judah.

The birthday of the Lord stands at the door. Rejoice in the Lord always, and again I say: Rejoice! Let your gentleness be known to everyone. The Lord is near. Do not worry about anything, but in everything by prayer and supplication with thanksgiving let your requests be made known to God. And the peace of God, which surpasses all understanding, will guard your hearts and your minds in Christ Jesus. Amen.

Neuendettelsau, 17 December, on the eve of St. Wunibald, 1857
W. L.

[3] This point was a true bone of contention between the LCMS and Loehe. The LCMS took the position that the *Book of Concord* accomplished a full and final exegesis of those *sedes doctrinae* that it covers, and that the analogy of faith consistently maps this to the rest of Scripture. What the LCMS saw to be static and complete, Loehe saw to be dynamic and incomplete, using the Erlangen School criteria of Scripture, Confessions, and the Church's experience. Of the various rationalist schools among Lutherans, Loehe interacted with the most conservative. Franz Delitzsch (1813–90) and others used principles based on the *Critique of Pure Reason* by Immanuel Kant (1724–1804) to speak of an incomplete life of the Church over against God's complete revelation in the Church. The liturgy and sacraments helped conform the incomplete to the complete using the Gospel as "material principle." The more liberal approaches of Johann C. K. von Hofmann (1810–77) and especially Franz H. R. von Frank (1827–94) led to Gospel reductionism in the twentieth century, which used the Bible as a Hegelian "living document" to create actualized revelation events determined largely by the community as Church. In-depth exploration of these differences goes beyond the scope of this text.

Foreword to the Second Edition

When I read through this second part of my *Evangelical Pastor* in order to get it ready for a second edition, it appeared to me to be so insignificant, that I almost did not have it reprinted. After much hesitation I resigned myself to prepare it for a new edition. It happened with some sort of resignation. If there were people who knew how to use the first edition, which was worse than this one, I could also launch this one, which in my opinion is better.

The introductory writing by Eberlin of Günzburg remains. I do not think I have to fear any criticism for this. What I said in the foreword to the first edition is still my opinion. However, the appendix of the first edition concerning mental effects on physical deceases has been omitted for reasons that are explained in section 47 (chapter 4, section C). However, a part of it (section 63; chapter 5, section D) has been retained in this edition. Instead of the mental effects, this edition contains something else: *Dr. Hochstetter's Short Commentary on How to Preach Aright and How to Expound and Apply the Sacred Text.*[1] See the appendix. Perhaps the appendix to the first edition in all its imperfection has brought some fruit—and perhaps the appendix of the second edition will also bring good fruit. It seems to me that, in all its brevity, it nevertheless deserves friends and recognition.

The center of the whole, the proper second part of my *Evangelical Pastor*, is found in sections 1–63.[2] Even though it became richer and is worked more carefully, it still shows its old aphoristic nature. I cannot do more than that. A rascal will give more and better than what he has. I just do not imagine my readers to be young candidates with highly scholarly education. What would they do with my poor little book? I am thinking of people who go from the school to the office with a feeling of poverty, and are happy to hear this and that from an old pastor, which can save them from errors as they begin their practice. May I not have labored in vain, and may the Lord accompany this writing with his blessing! May it be on its way and accomplish what it is able to accomplish with God.

I do not know what more to say.

May there be peace with the reader! Amen.

Neuendettelsau, 24 April 1866.
W. L.

---

[1] *Dr. Hochstetteri de recta concionandi textumque sacrum exponendi tum applicandi ratione Commentariolus.*

[2] These are now alphabetically enumerated sections within chapters.

INTRODUCTION

An Open Letter
From Johann Eberlin, first preached at Ulm
To Johann Jakob, Pastor at Leipheim near Ulm
Reprinted from the Edition of D. Georg Coelestin:

HOW A SERVANT OF GOD'S WORD SHOULD BEHAVE IN EVERYTHING HE DOES, AND ESPECIALLY TOWARD THOSE WHO NEVER HEARD THE GOSPEL PREACHED, SO THEY ARE NOT OFFENDED.

Issued for the first time in the year 1525, with the advice
of D. Luther, but now beautifully reprinted
Anno MDLXXIII.

To the well-born, noble and honorable of both estates,
The lords and knights of the Arch-Duchy of Austria,
Deputies in religious matters, its gracious and benevolent lords,
Georg. Coelestinus, D.[1] and provost at Thum, wishes God's grace, peace, blessing and wellbeing toward eternal blessedness, offering first of all his reverence and his faithful services.

Wellborn, noble, gracious and benevolent lords: You so eagerly and diligently take care of faithful servants of the divine Word and spare no trouble or expense, so that they can continue to preach the dear Word according to the writings of the prophets and apostles, also the Augsburg Confession, pure and undefiled, and, as Peter exhorts, with fear and gentleness, without bitterness and blasphemy. This Your Graces are doing to please God and to build up the poor, saddened churches, also for your own blessedness. I also thank God for this faithfulness and benevolence, and I pray with all good Christians that He may graciously strengthen and keep Your Graces in such Christian work and purpose. Amen.

---

[1] Georg Coelestin (Himmlisch, Himmel, Uranius; 1525–79) was a Lutheran theologian and pastor. He wrote several books on doctrine, served as a church leader, helped with the process of putting together the *Book of Concord* by seeking an authentic copy of the Augsburg Confession (which the papists had destroyed), and helped to obtain signatures subscribing to the *Book of Concord.*

Your Graces were gracious enough to call me, unworthy servant of the Word, as a deputy in religious matters to Vienna. You also want to be comforted with my counsel and Christian assistance, and have asked permission of my gracious lord, the Prince-Elector of Brandenburg. But due to my present office and other reasons I was not able to come so quickly to Your Graces. Nevertheless, to get started and use the right of a teacher, I wanted to have this little book reprinted and to dedicate it to Your Graces. It tells how a preacher should act toward those who never heard the Word of God preached. This would give Your Graces a reason and a token how, and in what form, I meant to plant that Word, continue, and advance it. In the meantime, it would also give Your Graces' preachers, who did not know any better, an instruction to inform themselves in matters of God, gently and quietly. If it pleases Your Graces, as I hope that it will please all those who are blessed and peace loving, I will rejoice in the Lord. The restless and sure petty intellects and masters may babble about it and make of it as they please. For us, God's honor and the continuation of His Word is enough. On Judgment Day He will bring to light what, and upon what, everybody has built. To the faithful, eternal God I commend Your Graces for His protection, armor and blessing. May He keep you all together for eternal salvation. Written in the court camp of the Brandenburg Prince Elector, Cölln on the Spree.

Year 1573, the eighth day of September. On this day 1,500 years ago, the city of Jerusalem was mounted and conquered by the Roman soldiers of Titus Vespasian.[2] It was burned, devastated and torn down. Thus, according to the prophecy of the Lord Christ, not a stone remained upon another. And Josephus writes that not one Jewish hair remained there, a lesson and a warning for us, that we may pay attention to the time of grace during which God's Word is proclaimed and preached, so that we should not also be punished and destroyed as the Lord threatens in Luke 13: Unless you repent, you will all perish, just as they did.

2 Timothy 2

> The Lord's servant must not be quarrelsome but kindly to everyone, an apt teacher, who can bear the evil with gentleness, and punish all the fractious. May God perhaps grant that they will repent and come to know the truth.[3]

---

[2] Vespasian (Titus Flavius Caesar Vespasianus Augustus; 9–79) was Roman Emperor from AD 69 to AD 79. He rose to power in the so-called Year of Four Emperors and founded the Flavian dynasty that consisted of him and his two sons, Titus and Domitian. He is featured in the *Jewish War* of Titus Flavius Josephus (Joseph ben Matityahu, 37–c. 100), an important extra-biblical witness of Jewish history, former Jewish resistance fighter in the First Roman-Jewish War (66–73), and client of the Flavian family.

[3] Scripture passages in this circular letter are translated as they are from the source text. The intent is to let the letter speak as a complete document.

To the honorable Johann Jakob,

Pastor of the Christian congregation at Leipheim at the Danube, my favorite gentleman and dear cousin.

You know very well, dear gentleman and brother in Christ, how beautifully and masterfully the holy apostle St. Paul depicts a bishop and pastor in the two letters to Timothy and in the one to Titus, so there is no need to add anything.

But since such general instructions and exhortations are more useful and wholesome if they are applied according to occasion and circumstances, time and place, and special persons and happenings, I considered writing to you, not only out of Christian love, but also because we are related. Thus, with one of my two letters, I wanted to send you this little book that has been published. It is full of friendly Christian exhortations about how we can perform our holy preaching office in a God-pleasing way, fruitful and without giving offense, as far as God the Almighty will grant us grace. May God grant that with you and others, whom I would also gladly serve, it may bring much fruit. Amen.

But before I write any more, I want to remind and exhort you sincerely that you consider it to be something to which I do not want to add anything, unless it is firmly grounded in Holy Scripture, or can be demonstrated with tried, reasonable causes and proofs, as you will hear.

First, and above all things, you should never forget the great gifts of the grace of God. Through them you have been powerfully torn out of the gullet and throat of the hellish lion. He has sunk you so deep into the lust, honor and favor of this world that you easily could have advanced to many other vices without really trying, even to persecuting and despising the Gospel. But God our Father be praised. He has mightily broken all bonds of the devil, has overturned his seductive treachery, and has given you the knowledge of His truth, according to the saying: Thus it is given to you, not only to believe in Christ, but also to suffer for Him.

You have been put under the ban, yet God has ordered the ban in such a way that it would turn into salvation and blessedness for you and for your sheep. Every hour your life is in great danger. And yet, God gives you grace, so that you can preach His Word constantly and without fear, to the joy and desire of the listeners. Even the surrounding peoples are moved to emulate the Word of God, so that I imagine that the saying of the prophet Zechariah is now being fulfilled, who says: At the times of the Gospel the heathen will grab hold of the hem of a Christian garment and will say: We want to go with you, for we have heard that God is with you.

Yes, certainly God is with the people of Leipheim, where His Word is being preached. Rejoice, good Christians there, and may the 60th chapter of Isaiah be applied to you. Read it, and pray to God that He may fulfill His promises. This grace and gift of God [is something that] you should consider daily and esteem very highly, give thanks for it constantly, and pray that grace may be strengthened and increased. But beware, lest you be found ungrateful, that God may not complain against you as it is written in Isaiah 7; Amos 2; Matthew 12; and other places.

Second. Nothing should be as important and beneficial with you, than a constant, serious, hearty and confident prayer for yourselves and your listeners, for the highest and the lowest, for all friends and enemies. You know that in the Old and New Testament God exhorts us often, and in a friendly way, to pray in faith. For without prayer you will not achieve anything against the devil. Therefore St. Paul also counted prayer as part of the Christian armor. You should also exhort your listeners to pray, as St. Paul also prescribes for a bishop or pastor in 1 Timothy 2, where he says: I urge you that supplications, prayers, intercessions, and thanksgivings be made for everyone, for kings and all who are in high positions, so that we may lead a quiet and peaceable life in all godliness and dignity. This is right and acceptable in the sight of God our Savior, who desires everyone to be saved and to come to the knowledge of the truth.

When the people are gathered, you should tell them how we are in such great danger of body, soul, goods and honor, and how the devil, the world and the flesh lead an insurmountable struggle and fight against us, which no human wisdom or strength can resist. In Job,[4] God himself says of the devil that there is no one like him on earth. Even Christ calls him[5] a prince, and St. Paul[6] a god of this world. And St. John[7] says about the world that only faith in Jesus Christ can overcome the world. And St. Paul[8] complains about the flesh and says that nothing helps against it but the grace of God. You should read to your people from the sayings of Holy Scripture about the great dangers of these three enemies, and from daily experience you should exhort the people to pray to God for help and assistance against such vehement enemies.

You should also tell them that we are caught in such great injury, which we do not know, nor are able to discern, unless Scripture shows us. That is how blind and insane we are. Therefore you should exhort the people to pray for rescue from such danger and harm. Also, God daily puts so much misfortune on our necks that we have enough reason to pray for redemption. Also, one should exhort the people to pray for others as well, especially for those who persecute the Word of God, that they may desist in blaspheming the Word of God, so that they may attain salvation and life. Also, one should

4 [Loehe:] Job 41.

5 [Loehe:] John 14.

6 [Loehe:] 2 Corinthians 4.

7 [Loehe:] 1 John 5.

8 [Loehe:] Romans 7.

demonstrate to the people in that place the benevolence and goodness that God proves to us in our soul, body, honor, goods, friends and the like, as everybody has often experienced. And that we also thank God for His divine promises, which He has done and promised out of pure grace and mercy.

These elements should be presented to the people so that they take [this to heart]: in order that our heart may be moved to know our own misfortune, ask God for help, trust Him completely, thank and praise Him in all creatures, as Psalm 104, Psalm 148, and other psalms do. "For if the Holy Scriptures are read, preached or heard, but do not pull toward prayer and thanksgiving, all trouble and toil is in vain."

Third. Every day you should read a few hours, if it pleases you, in the Bible, i.e., the Holy Scriptures. But see to it that you do justice to the reading. First of all, you should consider the smallest word written in the Scriptures [to be] higher than all the goods of the world. For God's Word is a divine power[9] that saves our soul,[10] indeed it is God himself,[11] the Word made flesh and equal to Him in voice.[12] Therefore you should not just think of the letter, or the voice that comes from the word, but of the divine power that is hidden in it. Therefore have great diligence that you do not read Holy Scripture with any less reverence than when you receive the Sacrament of the body and blood of Christ. If you do any differently, God will disappear before your eyes. You will receive poison instead of medicine when reading the Bible, as God threatens in the prophet Isaiah, chapters 6 and 28, in Ezekiel 14, in Matthew 13, also in Romans 9 and 10.

[First sub-point].[13] Beware of belittling the Word of God, be it in thoughts or in words. Truly, truly, God will not let this pass without blinding you. He punishes with great severity such criminal, joyful mistreatment of his Word. For no fruit will come of it; there is no spirit in the person that would not be afraid because of God's Word, as Isaiah says in the sixty-sixth chapter. Whom shall I look at, says the Lord, if not at the poor and a humble broken spirit that is frightened by my words? Therefore you should not follow the joyful, rough, false Christians "who unfortunately make out of the Word of God a wives' tale (*Tischmärchen*), a useless babbling, a hair-splitting disputation, which only leads to pride and strife." Therefore God punishes

---

[9] [Loehe:] Romans 1.

[10] [Loehe:] John 1.

[11] [Loehe:] That means that it is God Himself who shows his power in the Word and through the Word.

[12] [Loehe:] That is how God reveals Himself in the Word become flesh; He reveals Himself also in the preached and written Word that witnesses to Christ.

[13] This subseries engages how one reads Scripture. It contains five sub-points. The main series will restart enumeration at point four.

them, so that they are full of all manner of vice, more than any papist,[14] whose fruits will soon break forth.

Second [sub-point]. Whatever you read in Holy Scripture, accept it for yourselves. What is written in Scripture concerns you the most; it touches your mind, your behavior, your being. Rule your body and soul according to the Word of God. Seek in Holy Scripture your counsel, comfort and help. Once you have instructed yourselves well, you already have dug out a fountain of strength in your heart and thoughts, even your members, which will never dry out or be exhausted, as Christ says in John 4 and 7. From this you may teach and give drink to the entire world, without a cumbersome and busy seeking and reading at a time when must preach or give counsel. For if one teaches only out of books, not out of experience or from the heart, none, or very little use will come of it.

Third [sub-point]. Make for yourself a short, small register in which you may write down the chief points and articles from your reading, so that the previous work will make the following easy, and you will always have at hand what serves your present need.

Fourth [sub-point]. Before you start reading, ask God that He may lead and guide you in Scripture, reveal what serves you, and hold back what does not serve you. Keep on reading.[15] Keep attention in your heart for the hand of God. Wherever He leads you, follow. Do not hasten. If He drives you away, then go away. If He stands still, you also stand still, as is written in Numbers, chapter 9.

Fifth [sub-point]. If you get tired of reading, stop; lest this boredom finally cause you to abhor and be disgusted with the heavenly bread, to the harm of your soul, as is written in Deuteronomy, chapter 11 and in Romans 12.[16] And do not desire to know too much, so that the manna will not turn out to be harmful for you, as is written in Exodus 16. If you do not get wise when reading, hearing or speaking the Word of God, you will suffer unspeakable harm. The Corinthians also wanted to play around with the Word of God too much. Therefore Paul warns them, lest they suffer harm.

Christ exhorts us to read the sacred Scriptures in John,[17] where He says to the Jews: Search the Scriptures, for in them you have eternal life, and it is they that testify on my behalf. Paul says the same in 1 Timothy 4 and 2 Timothy 5. Also, when he talks about the qualities of a bishop, he mentions, among other things, that he should be an apt teacher. And to Titus he says in the first chapter that he should cling to the certain word of doctrine, so that he may be able to exhort with sound doctrine and to refute those who contradict it.

---

[14] [Loehe:] Romans 1.

[15] [Loehe:] That means: keep doing it without ceasing.

[16] [Loehe:] It most likely should be 1 Corinthians 10.

[17] [Loehe:] John 5.

When you read in the Bible, look up the passages mentioned in the margins. Check in a concordance and look up what is written before and what follows in the chapter, and how it harmonizes.

Do the same with other books, and with teachers. Check the title of the book and see how the following speeches agree with the title, well or not so well. Check all the citations and allegations from the Bible in the original, as they say. If you do this for half year, you will have great benefit from it.

But this should be the order in which you are to read the Bible. Start with the Gospel of Matthew and read it all the way through, without any commentary, once or three times (*ein Mal oder drei*), so that you get to know it well.[18] After that the Gospel of St. Mark, which is a shorter version of St. Matthew's Gospel, and do not forget to look things up in a concordance. After this, read the epistle of St. Paul to Titus with great diligence, once or three times, then the two epistles to Timothy which explain the former. Then read the epistle to the Colossians with great attention, then the one to the Ephesians, which is a further exegesis of the one to the Colossians. Then read the one to the Galatians, also the one to the Romans, which is a gloss of the one to the Galatians. Finally, read the Gospel of John, which is like a blessing after the meal of Holy Scripture, also his epistles, which are nothing but fatherly admonitions concerning the things that are written in his Gospel. Thus you also find in St. Peter's first epistle a summary of all the things you read in the previous books, mixed and adorned with teachings concerning faith, discipline and love, so that it should be a form and a beginning when you preach to your people. The Acts of the apostles themselves will inspire the reader to diligent reading and knowing how the evangelical teaching continued and prospered. We should act accordingly in our times.

In the Old Testament, start with the fifth book of Moses, also called Deuteronomy. All of Moses is contained in it. Read diligently and check the concordant passages in the margin. No one without experience can believe what great benefit there is, if one checks the concordant and parallel passages here and there in the Bible. For in this way will become acquainted with Holy Scripture without trouble and labor. Once in a while one also finds something that will serve one in another place, something that one would have never thought of. The first four books of Moses are so much more fun to read because they have so many pleasant stories that make the reader happy. The same is true about the other historical books: Joshua, Judges, Ruth, Samuel, Kings, Chronicles, Ezra, Nehemiah, Esther and the like. But in all the histories, pay attention to how God always carries the believers in His hand and heavily punishes the unbelievers. In the book of Job there is a nice discussion about this question: Does God bring disaster not only upon the sinners and godless, but also upon the pious and God-fearing? The friends of Job talk and dispute about this vehemently. But Job is right in his under-

[18] The historic Lutheran lectionary places emphasis on Matthew and John.

standing, that God at times sends disaster to the pious also, as indeed it happened. In this dispute and action one can find many a good thing about God's power and wisdom, as it appears and is recognized in the creatures.

The Psalter should be your hymnbook, from which you can sing love songs to the dear God.[19] Therefore write down the sum and content of the psalms so you always have at hand what you need. St. Paul,[20] in the epistle to the Colossians, exhorts us to sing such songs when he says: Teach and exhort one another with psalms, hymns and spiritual songs in grace, and sing to the Lord in your hearts. And whatever you do, in word or in deed, do everything in the name of the Lord Jesus, giving thanks to God the Father through Him. Also in the epistle to the Ephesians St. Paul[21] says: Do not be foolish, but understand what the will of the Lord is. Do not get drunk with wine, for that is debauchery; but be filled with the Spirit, as you sing psalms and hymns and spiritual songs among yourselves, singing and making melody to the Lord in your hearts, giving thanks to God the Father at all times and for everything in the name of your Lord Jesus Christ. Be subject to one another out of reverence for Christ. If you do this for Him, the Spirit of Christ will give you such devotion that you will have the greatest joy in this. Believe me, no poet, no love song will please you as well as these very psalms, if the right devotion overcomes you. Let the Proverbs of Solomon be for you a primer in Christianity. Let Ecclesiastes be for you a mirror of the cosmos, and how there is no joy without divine knowledge, and how only the godly person can be well on earth. The Spirit of Christ should make you understand the Song of Solomon at the proper time.

Among the prophets I know of no rule or goal how to read them. For some start with the lesser prophets, with Hosea, and after that tackle all the lesser prophets. Some use the prophet Amos as goal and register, and the same with Isaiah for the great prophets. But I think that is someone has read Isaiah once or three times diligently and gathered some experience from it, he should also know how to deal with the other prophets.

There are also good instructions for some of the books, like: Doctor Martin Luther's explanation of St. Paul's epistle to the Galatians, of some psalms, of the epistles of St. Peter, the fifth book of Moses, and other books of the same kind. Also there are Philip Melanchthon's introduction to Holy Scripture, to Matthew, to John, to St. Paul's epistles to the Romans and Corinthians.[22] There are also Johannes Bugenhagen's commentaries of the psalms, his explanation of the short epistles of St. Paul, of Deuteronomy,

---

[19] [Loehe:] That means: Sing it in heartfelt love to God (Isaiah 62:4 and 5).

[20] [Loehe:] Colossians 3.

[21] [Loehe:] Ephesians 5.

[22] For the sake of brevity we will not cover in the footnotes the careers of Martin Luther (1483–1546) and Philip Melanchthon (Philipp Schwartzerdt, 1497–1560).

Samuel and others.[23] Once you have read the above explanations, you will well be able to continue on your own in the Bible, and it will no longer be necessary to read many commentaries. But with all your reading, use great diligence in studying *Loci communes theologici*, i.e., Melanchthon's common introduction to Holy Scripture, and look up all the verses in the Bible that he cites and quotes, so that you may comprehend a foundation of doctrine, which will be of great benefit for you.[24]

Here I also have to say something about the negative side of reading too much. The reason why some read a lot and have little or no benefit from it is this: They do not read and study because they themselves want to know and be taught in the things they read, rather, solely for other people so that they may find honor, glory and goods; or they do it out of idle curiosity. If that were not their reason, they certainly would give up reading. That should be understood in this way: The right understanding and knowledge of Scripture consists in this, namely, that one finds in his heart what one reads, and that the reader also might be of the same mind as what the lesson shows. Holy Scripture will not be understood by a great reasonable contemplation, but by an urgent longing and feeling of the heart, so that our heart and our conduct become of the same shape, and similar to what we are reading.

That means that all other knowledge in the Bible, even if one knew all verses as well as the Lord's Prayer, and could babble at length about it; even if he had memorized all the explanations of the fathers and doctors, it means no more than reading words without understanding them when compared with the feeling and finding the things one reads. Where the proper attitude (*Befinden*) is not there with the knowledge, everything else is nothing but useless babbling and disputation, useless questions and frivolous minds, against which Paul writes much in the epistles to Timothy and Titus.

But since there are only few that really look for what they read in Holy Scripture, it follows that there are also few that really understand the Bible. They turn into loose babblers, an offense for the simple-minded. For as St. Paul says to the Corinthians: The kingdom of God is not in word, but in power. Many who study just the human arts, not seeking the deeper knowledge, but chase after goods and honor and pay for their morbid curiosity, will forever remained unlearned, even though they may become masters and doctors. My first purpose was, and I started with it, to exhort you to start out on the right foot in the ministry. Perhaps I went too far in the above articles and points, however not without necessity and benefit, as I hope. But now let us look at the other points.

---

[23] Johannes Bugenhagen (Pomeranus, 1485–1558) was pastor at St. Mary's Church in Wittenberg. He introduced the Reformation to the Duchy of Pomerania and Denmark-Norway, becoming the most important Protestant reformer in the north.

[24] See also Melanchthon, *The Chief Theological Topics*, translated by J. A. O. Preus (St. Louis: Concordia, 2011).

Fourth.[25] If you thus will be reformed and informed every day, break down and build up your mind and morals, as St. Paul also teaches so beautifully in the epistles to Timothy,[26] especially when he says: Shun youthful passions[27]—if you discipline yourself completely, as a child taken on as an apprentice;[28] to teach, to move into and out of [the text] according to the rules of Scripture, you will get to know yourselves and will experience things within yourselves that all the world could not talk about. Therefore follow the Spirit who will well motivate you at His own time.

But in other exercises of your mind, through studying the human arts, histories, laws, natural things and the like, or in physical labor, you should keep order and rules. For without reasonable order you will accomplish nothing. Have also an orderly, appropriate time for sleeping and do not change it unless there is a real need so that you do not without sleep. Do the same with eating and drinking. If you do not have the proper regulation to take care of your body in sleeping, eating, and drinking, you will never have rest or joy, and you will not accomplish anything. St. Paul teaches about this in his first epistle to Timothy.[29]

The governance of your house and the servants should also be ordered well. Thus says Paul to Timothy:[30] A bishop, among other things, should manage his own household well, keeping his children submissive and respectful in every way, and he says: If someone does not know how to manage his own household, how can he take care of God's church? Your studying also should have an order, measure and goal, as you are being taught in other books.

Also be diligent in learning any other kind of work, to exercise the body and to spend the time wisely when you are not inclined to other exercises. Work is something honest. You can even find some princes who have learned the trade of a lathe-turner, or other joyful work, just to pass the time. For without physical work you will not be without damage to your mind, or take care of your business. At the end you will have to run out and walk back and forth for a long time, which cannot happen without noticeable hurt. Besides, it will be useful in your house. By doing it, you will drive away many melancholic fantasies. It is also better for your neighbor and for your listeners. It creates bad blood if the farmers, while working, think of the lazy life of the pastors, especially in our days. We read how diligently the great preacher

---

[25] Here we come back to the main series of points.

[26] [Loehe:] 1 Timothy 4; 5; 6.

[27] [Loehe:] 2 Timothy.

[28] Literally: under the spurs (*unter die Sporen*). In the Middle Ages, successful completion of knight's training earned one a set of golden spurs. Today a similar phrase (*sich die Sporen verdienen*) means having the first big professional success.

[29] [Loehe:] 1 Timothy 5.

[30] [Loehe:] 1 Timothy 3.

Paul worked with his hands in the Acts of the Apostles[31] and in the epistles to the Thessalonians.[32]

Fifth. There are two things that should take preference over any labor of studying: Devotion, and the need of your brother. If a good devotional thought comes to you about God, or about the salvation of your soul, or a good understanding of any verse in the Scriptures: wait upon it with all diligence and know that God pays you a fatherly visit, and now it is God's time to engage you. At such a time you should let go of all work as an obedient servant, if it is in the way. But if it is the kind of work that does not hinder you listening to God, then go ahead and finish your work little by little.[33] But beware, lest you let such a visit of God pass in vain. This certainly could not happen without great harm. For just to turn toward devotional reading or to prayer by itself does not help. But God Himself comes through the Word that is read or heard and He knocks. We should wait diligently for him; waiting is the best preparation for devotion.

This is how the holy patriarchs and prophets often heard God speak to their heart, but we no longer know anything about that, and therefore we are so godless. For this you need Holy Scripture, that you can tell whether such talk is according to Scripture or not, that you may know to tell the difference between wholesome and deceiving voices, according to the rule of faith taught in Scripture, how St. Paul says to the Romans:[34] If someone has prophecy, let it be in proportion to faith. He writes the same in the epistle to the Corinthians;[35] also St. John in his first epistle, chapter 4.[36] Therefore, read many good things in the book *Collationes Patrum*.[37] There is a good deal of Christianity in it, so that one can tell the difference between right and false devotion, between truth and deceit of the voices.

The other matter, which should take preference over all planned exercises, is the need of your neighbor, your wife, your children, your servants, your friends and enemies, local or strangers. You should serve your wife and your children above all, comfort them, help and counsel them. Show them works of love in health and in sickness. No other imagined exercise should

---

[31] [Loehe:] Acts 20.

[32] [Loehe:] 1 Thessalonians 2; 2 Thessalonians 3.

[33] [Loehe:] He does not mean an immediate inspiration, rather, that a person should pay attention when the Holy Spirit knocks at the heart through the Word, and wakes it for devotion.

[34] [Loehe:] Romans 12.

[35] [Loehe:] 1 Corinthians 2.

[36] [Loehe:] 1 John 4.

[37] This is John Cassian's *Conferences of the Fathers*. A period print edition was *Collationes Patrum Opus Ioannis Eremitae qui et Cassianus dicitur, de Institutis coenobiorum* (Lyons: Jacques Giunta, 1545). This helps show that Lutherans did not cut themselves off from the long patristic tradition, but saw themselves reviving it.

prevent you; nor should any shame pull you away. For what you do for your wife and your children, you have done to God Himself. Our parents did the same thing. After that you should help and comfort your servants, your neighbors, and others in need. Do their pleasure according to your ability. For [this reason] man has been created for the benefit of the other. Therefore, whoever does not help or counsel his neighbors as best he can is neither a Christian nor a human being. There should be no person in your parish who could not receive service, counsel, help and comfort from you.

Sixth. You should practice special diligence in order to comfort those who mourn. This takes great wisdom and sympathy. Dear gentleman and cousin, I ask you in a friendly way that you may accept kindly what I am writing, and that I thus teach and instruct you. Truly, I do it for your good, and that of many. I experienced it myself, and with others, how much danger there is in this matter.

Therefore you need, first of all, the virtue to be able to keep as a secret everything you hear from people who present their need to you. To keep a secret is a great art that only few people know how to do. Do not consider your wife, your children, and your friends so dear that you can talk to them about such things. Do not trust anyone, for the devil is always very eager to do mischief and spread rumors to the preachers of the Gospel. For if it would be known that you revealed a person's secret to someone else, he or other people would call you a rascal and a gossip. That would bring great shame to the Gospel. Nor should you laugh at a person because he told you his problems. Everybody is convinced that his own concern is the greatest. If ever you reveal someone else's secret or consider his complaint and trouble to be laughable, you frighten him and many others, so that they no longer dare to ask your counsel nor open their conscience to you. This would turn out to be a great and noticeable detriment to the saddened consciences. A pastor or preacher should be the last refuge of the saddened and frightened on earth, especially when it concerns their consciences, in such a way that, even if he finds no counsel of help with you, he should still be able to expect a friendly greeting, heartfelt sympathy, and a silent mouth.

Seventh. Until now it was seldom that one would bother a common lay preacher, as they were called, with difficult matters. It has been especially so, that wise and noble people have not done that. One would go to a great doctor, to a famous confessor, or to a preacher in a monastery, so that your kind would not have had much experience, nor would there have been any reason to go after great, heavy and difficult dealings in order to think, read or ask about them, in order to be able to give sincere, honest, faithful, good counsel. I know what I am talking about.

But as soon as you, and the likes of us, start preaching the Gospel, and many people are drawn to it, believing your teaching and no longer approving of the former counselors, they will start seeking your counsel in weighty matters. Therefore it is necessary that you receive the people in a friendly way, listen seriously and diligently, understand the matter, be disciplined in body language and words, do not pass on what you hear, do not criticize, blaspheme or despise anyone, and talk with everybody in a decent way. You will not know everybody. Many deceivers and false brothers will come to you under a good guise, women and men, and if they would find you undisciplined,[38] they would proclaim that to everybody, to the derision of the holy Gospel.

Not without reason did St. Paul teach so diligently in many places how a Christian should be well behaved and disciplined. Especially to Timothy[39] he says: Stay away from young widows, for when their sensual desires alienate them from Christ, they want to marry. And soon thereafter: Keep yourself pure. Above all things you should be found faithful, honest, and silent, and then counsel accordingly. For the Holy Spirit will make you careful and give you counsel in human matters, as is written in the prophet Isaiah.[40] If you do not know how to give a good counsel, it is better to remain silent so that you do not lead anyone astray, and that your carelessness will not be criticized. If you pray for God's Spirit, wisdom, reason, and intelligence, God will not forsake you, as Christ says in Luke.[41]

Toward this end the historical books in Holy Scripture, the teaching of Solomon, of St. Paul and other similar books will serve you well. Nor will it hurt you if at times you read pagan histories, the books of Seneca, Cicero, and others, also imperial, Roman, civil, and territorial law, which you all need in order to counsel in temporal, external, human affairs.[42] But those things that concern the conscience one should treat with the Word of God. Also one's own experience in much suffering and anxieties, in sadness and adversity can be very helpful. Therefore you should also read the book of the lives of the ancient fathers, *Collationes Patrum,* the epistles of Jerome, Augustine and others, some little books of Gerson, Kaysersberg, Tauler and others.[43] One finds in them great experience and faithful warning to comfort the anxious hearts and consciences that are constantly attacked by the devil.

---

[38] [Loehe:] That is immodest and thoughtless.

[39] [Loehe:] 1 Timothy 5.

[40] [Loehe:] Isaiah 11.

[41] [Loehe:] James 1; Luke 11.

[42] Lucius Annaeus Seneca (c. 4 BC–AD 65) was a Roman Stoic philosopher, statesman, dramatist, humorist, and tutor and counselor to Nero. His elder brother was the Gallio before whom Paul was tried (Acts 18:12–17). Marcus Tullius Cicero 106–43 BC) was a Roman philosopher, politician, lawyer, orator, political theorist, consul, and constitutionalist. Imperial law refers here to the laws of the Holy Roman Empire of the German nation. Territorial law refers to state laws.

[43] Augustine of Hippo (Aurelius Augustinus, 354–430) was a bishop, theologian, and philosopher who shaped medieval thought in the West. He is known especially for his *City of God* and *Confessions.* He helped to shape the discussion of many teachings, including original sin, human will, grace, predestination, and just war. Jean Charlier de Gerson

There also will occur manifold suffering, fear, trouble, sadness, adversity, affliction, sadness and temptation. For this you need divine wisdom, no matter how diligent you are.

Uncouth and loose people do not know what to say of this. They just talk, badmouth pastors and monks, reject all old orders, and babble about the Gospel without any experience, without any feeling for spiritual things. They know as much about the common human life as a cow knows about noon. They are without discipline, without honor and useless. They only know how to cause shame, vice, restlessness and misfortune, even "revile or hinder God's Word in other matters through their uncouth and loose life." But you, my dear cousin and gentleman, do not bring shame on Christ and on yourself by wanting to follow such rascals. And then, I almost forgot, to give you this advice: If you are not smart enough in a certain affair, do ask other faithful and wise people for advice, or refer your people to them with all good will.

Eighth. Learn from Paul in his epistles,[44] also in the stories of the apostles,[45] how sincerely and like a mother he has taught everybody with praying, weeping, and compassion; [how he has] admonished and comforted by day and by night. If you read those chapters, you will find in them very beautiful sayings. St. Paul also says in the second epistle to Timothy:[46] A servant of the Lord must not be quarrelsome, but fatherly to everyone, an apt teacher, who can bear up under evil people, correcting opponents with gentleness. And in the first epistle[47] he says, among other things, that a bishop should be diligent, sober, chaste, ethical, hospitable, capable of teaching, not addicted to wine, not snappish, not desirous of ill-gotten gain, but rather mild, not quarrelsome, and not greedy.

And in the Epistle to Titus[48] he says almost the same words: A bishop ought to be without reproach, as a steward of God, not thinking highly of himself, not angry, not a drunkard, not violent, not a lover of money, but hospitable modest, just, holy, chaste, and keeping to the certain word of doctrine, so that he would be capable to exhort through the wholesome doctrine, and to punish the antagonists. Dear gentleman and cousin, pray also to God

---

(1363–1429) was a French scholar, educator, reformer, and poet. He served as chancellor of the University of Paris, helped to guide the conciliar movement, and played a prominent role at the Council of Constance. Johann Geiler von Kaysersberg (Kaisersberg, 1445–1510) was one of the most popular reformist preachers in the 15th century, connected with the Strassburg humanists. Johannes Tauler (c. 1300–61) was a German mystic, Catholic preacher and theologian. He was a Dominican monk, a disciple of Meister Eckhart, although he deemphasized Eckhart's Neo-Platonism and was an influence on Luther.

[44] [Loehe:] 1 Thessalonians 2.

[45] [Loehe:] 2 Corinthians 1; 12; Romans 15; Galatians 6; Acts 20.

[46] [Loehe:] 2 Timothy 2.

[47] [Loehe:] 1 Timothy 3.

[48] [Loehe:] Titus 1.

often and diligently for people under temptation; for the pain and anxiety of the afflicted is great.

Ninth. Take great care that, with your counseling, you do not make people small or seduce anyone, so that you do not have to regret it continually for the rest of your life. Especially in the hour of your death you would have to fear, wondering whether God would have forgotten. Therefore, do everything with a good conscience, after mature reflection, as diligently as possible. Look at the hands of God. He will help you. What formerly was an anxious, troubled confession shall now be turned among Christians into a confident, faithful asking for and giving of counsel, out of brotherly love for Christ. For he says thus in Matthew: Where two of you agree on earth on what they should pray for, it shall be given to them by my Father in heaven. For where two or three are gathered in my name, I am there among them. O what a dear person this is, with whom everybody finds counsel, comfort, sympathy, faithfulness, a silent mouth and a Christian, loving heart, in his troubles and temptations! Of such a man Solomon says in his Proverbs:[49] The mouth of the righteous is a fountain of life. Also: The mouth of the righteous brings wisdom. One can find many such sayings in Holy Scripture. If you well consider the words of St. Paul in the epistles to Timothy and Titus, you will find the foundation and cause of all things.

Tenth, concerning the office of preaching. First, and above all things, ask God that he may put His Word upon your tongue, and rule [your tongue] according to His will for salvation and blessedness of the listeners. For your planning and undertaking is worthless here. God rules the tongue, as Solomon says in Proverbs:[50] Man will plan in his heart, but from the Lord comes the answering of the tongues. Pray God that He will not let you err, to the detriment of you and the listeners, as Ezekiel[51] says in the fourteenth chapter, and ask Him that He may grant you to keep in your heart what you teach with your mouth. For if the heart and the mouth do not go together, one will sin without ceasing, even if one talks of nothing but God and Christ. Whatever does not proceed from faith is sin, as St. Paul says to the Romans.[52]

Eleventh. Do not tempt God. Do everything that God has called you to do and for which He gave you strength. Read diligently, write it down, and compare it with Scripture. Consider beforehand whether it will serve the listeners or not, whether damage or profit will come of it. Then, after looking over a sermon twice or three times, you will often find how much you do not like in it and how necessary it is to pay diligent attention to the material and the words. One quickly can say something that will cause great harm, and one can never take it back. God will not permit scolding with His Word. The

---

[49] [Loehe:] Proverbs 10.

[50] [Loehe:] Proverbs 16.

[51] [Loehe:] Ezekiel 14.

[52] [Loehe:] Romans 14.

little word and the common phrase, "I did not think this would happen," is a mockery even for people. How much more is it for God, especially if it concerns God's cause and the salvation of souls. Know this for sure: Not one little word will escape the judgment of God. Stone and wood will testify about your sermon, for they have been created and kept through the divine Word that you preach.

Twelfth. Now I have said that without diligent, devotional, and continuing prayer you should not go up to the pulpit. For truly, the devil is not idle, he is going to prevent you from using good words, or he will drive you to say something harmful without your thanks, wherever he can. Great suffering will come from this, just as now there are many useless babblers who without modesty prattle from the pulpit. This will make them fall into great pain and suffering, unless they say: Yes, I suffer for the sake of the truth.

Not so; you are suffering for the sake of your foolishness and immodesty. When you are lying in the peril of death, your own conscience will deny you when you recognize yourself and say: It is not yet the time or the place, it was not necessary that I said this or that, so I earned God's wrath, and I suffer this not for the sake of God, but for the sake of my stupidity and foolishness, and before the [proper] time I stirred up the enemies to act against the Word of God and to attack it. In my arrogance I acted as if I was persecuted and have deprived the listeners of the Word of God. They could have learned in peace if my foolishness would not have prevented them.

How then are you going to stand, if your own conscience in truth does deny you? You certainly will cry out: O mountains, O hills, fall upon me and cover me before the wrath of God, which I have deserved with my preaching! Therefore, my dear gentleman and cousin, arm yourself from now on with prayer and other Christian armor, which Paul writes about in the epistle to the Ephesians.[53] For if you step up to preach, you are standing in the forefront to fight and to struggle, not against flesh and blood, but against the princes and powerful, against the rulers of darkness in this world, against the spirits of wickedness under heaven. If you lose against them, they certainly will not lose against you.

Thirteenth. You must preach God's Word with a serious, honest heart and bearing. Beware of a defiant, proud mind and bearing, or else you will fall into the devil's cords. One should teach God's Word, not in proud defiance, but with humility and gentleness. That will wear out the devil and tire him. The humble and gentle Christ wants to be preached humbly and gently. If you do otherwise, you sin against God and become a laughing-stock for the devil and before the world. If you preach the humble, mild, friendly Christ, you should also use humble, mild words and bearing, which is also the common judgment of men. Your inner eye should look more above yourself to God while you are preaching, as if you heard all the words from Him and

---

[53] [Loehe:] Ephesians 6.

speak for Him, instead of paying attention to something else. Keep and practice this little point, you will soon comprehend its use and benefit.

Fourteenth. The rhetoricians and professional speakers have written several things that may be useful for you, to show you the proper, formal presentation of your teaching, whose rules and ways are shown by rhetoric, as well as how to understand the writing of other teachers. You should not despise this. For the Holy Spirit does not use a miraculous funnel to pour things into you, as long as you can have a thing in a natural way. Therefore do not neglect to read what Cicero, Quintilian, Erasmus, Philip Melanchthon and others write about this, or have written.[54]

Fifteenth. Do not overwhelm your listeners with too many sermons as well as long sermons, or at the wrong time, as do those who daily want to make a long sermon, as if one had nothing else to do except listening to their sermons. They do not know that their audience does not listen with the ears of the preacher, but with their own ears. The holidays should be spent in resting the body, and in Christian activity, both in teaching and in the Sacrament. On other days one should have a short sermon on selected small subjects that a simple Christian can easily remember well. On that day can move them around in his mind and feed his soul with them.

I know an evangelist or preacher who was asked whether it would be beneficial, even in a small town, daily to have two or three sermons, even in the morning. He answered: It would be good, and quoted a verse of St. Paul in the epistle to the Colossians,[55] where he says: Let the Word of God dwell in you richly. This, I think, is like pulling Scripture by the hair, just to make it fit what we think is right and what pleases us. This preacher is still a young miller. He did not tie up many sacks. Therefore he is still young and happy, and is pleased when one listens to him. Before that, he was not used to have people come running, or to have fame. May God give him grace, so that he will not have the experience of Narcissus of whom the poets tell fables.[56] It would be good for him to read Gerson's *Gospel of Mark*. There he would find faithful admonition, which would be useful and necessary to know for a young preacher.

I have to say what I think. When Raimund Cardinal Peraudi once came to Heilbronn, the people were not used to such splendor, yet it pleased them

---

[54] Quintilian (Marcus Fabius Quintilianus, c. 35–100) was a Roman rhetorician from Hispania who started his career in Rome during Nero's reign. His mentor was Domitius Afer (d. 59) who led a stoic lifestyle modeled after Cicero. Desiderius Erasmus (1466–1536) was a humanist, theologian, and priest known for his Greek edition of the New Testament that Luther used for his 1522 German "September Testament." A priest critical of Roman Catholic abuses, he nevertheless clashed with Luther concerning free will. Erasmus is his baptismal name; he later added Desiderius, "one longed for."

[55] [Loehe:] Colossians 3.

[56] Narcissus is a character from Greek mythology. His beauty and pride caused Nemesis to lead him to a pool where he fell in love with his reflection and drowned.

well.[57] When the cardinal's people noticed this, every stable boy came out and wanted to shine like the cardinal himself. I and the likes of me do the same thing. God the Almighty has lifted up Doctor Martin Luther, Philip Melanchthon and others, in such great skill and knowledge (*Kunst*),[58] in wholesome teaching and an honorable life, even for the world, that all of Christianity is looking at them, So now I, and many a fisherman, come along and assume that we are Lutherans, or evangelical, as they say, and want to be held for no less than they, without any skill and knowledge, without any discipline, without any spiritual experience, and without Christian modesty. We want to scold priesthood and monasticism and trample on old customs (that may not do any harm to Christianity), and besides that we say so little, and in a cold way, of the kingdom of Christ, that one can easily notice how inwardly we are monkeys and donkeys, outwardly clothed with human or lion's skins, and that we are nothing less than Lutheran or evangelical.[59]

Yes, dear friend, one does listen to you, and should one consider you to be Luther? But the listeners think: *Vox quidem est vox Jacob, manus autem manus sunt Esau,* i.e., the voice is Jacob's voice, but the hands are Esau's hands.[60] Also: *Dat sine mente sonum,* i.e., it is a sound without reason. Also: *Sermo est, non virtus,* i.e., these are words without power.[61] If at first God leads you into hell with teachers such as these, and then led out again toward heaven, so that the world and even the devil will see God's power in you, then you can act like Luther and others. We praise the above not only because they drove the pope out of our hearts, but because they taught us the kingdom of Christ and portrayed it for us with words and good examples, and because in other ways they are wise and good people.

But we, who neither know how to cackle nor to lay eggs, and know more about drinking wine than about spiritual temptation, and do not know how to keep secret our neighbor's concerns that he complains to us, nor know how to counsel him, often deride him on top of it, and yet want gloriously be like such learned and excellent people and be honored like them: One can see that we are donkeys and not lions. But my dear gentleman and cousin, God the Almighty has given you modesty by nature, and God's spirit will still

---

[57] Raimund Peraudi (1435–1505) was a cardinal, commissioner of indulgences, papal legate, and political negotiator. He raised money and awareness to repel Islam. Heilbronn was an imperial free city; it lies on the Neckar River in Württemberg.

[58] As in the tree of the knowledge (*Kunst*) of good and evil, this use is related to the need of *cunning* (skill and knowledge) to make great art (*Kunst*) and artifice.

[59] This is a reference to the "Ass in the Lion Skin" fable that occurs in Aesop's fables as well as in some versions from India. See also the character Puzzle in C. S. Lewis, *The Last Battle.*

[60] [Loehe:] Genesis 27.

[61] Similar references appear in Walther's writings. See *Law and Gospel: How to Read and Apply the Bible*, 27.

augment it. Therefore beware of such obnoxious bragging, remain in the measure that God has measured out for you, as St. Paul shows to the Romans[62] and Corinthians.[63] Humbly preach the humble Christ, and you will have honor and praise from God and from the people.

Sixteenth. You already made a start, so it may not be necessary to teach you how modest the beginning of evangelical instruction should be. But to please other good friends who may benefit from this little book, by the grace of God, I will say a little about it. A preacher has to realize that there are two kingdoms: one of the devil, the other of Christ. The devil takes hold of a heart through godless demeanor,[64] with blindness, self-love, hardening, and other vices. All the senses and thoughts of man are turned toward evil, from his youth on. Therefore he is under the wrath of God; his conscience always trembles before God; he will not trust God, nor have love for his neighbor. He always seeks his own praise, honor, gain, and his all that is his own. He may try all kinds of strange things, manifold ways to serve God, but he has no heartfelt trust in the mercy of God. Many people are so blind and desperate that they never dare to deal with God. But if such a person starts to deal with God, he does not follow the Word of God. He only follows his own pleasure; he wants to buy the grace and the gifts of God with his own works, i.e., he trusts himself more than God.

Thus, such a person sins in everything he does or omits, no matter how good, how smart his cause appears to reason. And that person will not be dismissed as if he were in the wrong. To sum it up: Flesh and blood will not be despised in his judgment and undertaking. And that is truly the devil's kingdom: Not to know God, neither to fear Him nor love Him in truth. From this follows that such a person cannot know any creature rightly, nor use it well.

Against this kingdom of the devil there stands the kingdom of Christ, which consists in true knowledge of God, fear and love of God, knowing God's will and His commandments, knowing one's own sin and the mercy of God. Such a heart finds out how difficult it is to bear the deserved wrath of God, what unspeakable pain for the sinner is before his eyes, and how no person can counsel or help him. All power, counsel and help must come from God's mercy, without our free will and reason, without our useless good works. In short: Such a heart knows deep down how evil it is and how good God is toward it;[65] how God, out of grace, without our merit, has taught us His will through Christ, and has sacrificed Christ for us, also promised us all His goodness in Christ, so that all who have such trust in God through Christ should be from now on beloved children. God also gives us through

---

[62] [Loehe:] Romans 12.

[63] [Loehe:] 1 Corinthians 12.

[64] [Loehe:] Genesis 6:8.

[65] [Loehe:] That means: toward such a heart or such a person.

Christ His Holy Spirit, who presses such love and knowledge of God into our heart.

Such a heart begins to trust God in life and in death, wagers all his salvation on God's grace, despises itself, does good to everybody in view of the great, undeserved love of God toward it. If God now looks at such a person in grace, all the works of that person will also please him. God rules that person, and if he sins, God will lift him up again. Such a person knows that no work pleases God well, except to trust Him in such wise through Christ. In all things he will also look up to God's word as to a lamp in the night of this world, as the psalm says: Your Word is a lamp for my foot and a light on my path. St. Peter[66] says the same thing in his second epistle, the first chapter.

These two kingdoms—a preacher should take up and think how he could also teach his listeners to know them. Let him start to preach about the kingdom of Christ, that it consists in fear and love of God, and let him fit the talk according to the ability of the listeners. If the listeners are bold and daring, he should talk about God's wrath concerning our sin. Let him bring blessed fear to haughty consciences, so that graciously they will find joy in the mercy of God. But if the consciences are quite frightened by the wrath of God, let him preach about the grace of God, and let him thus pull the sinner with the word of grace into the kingdom of Christ, where nothing rules but grace. But if the consciences of the listeners are frightened, the preacher should begin to talk of God's mercy in Christ, so that all must happen through Christ. For this means to be frightened in a blessed way: To see the great wrath of God in Christ's suffering. No one can atone for this wrath. Christ had to do it with His blood and pay for the sin of the whole world. One will also find a gracious comfort in the suffering of Christ, that God gives His Son into death out of pure grace. And this means to preach God's kingdom rightly: To proclaim God's wrath before all things, and to know our sins.

Seventeenth. Here one needs to be careful not to pull a splinter out of the eyes of the listeners and prevent oneself and others from getting out a big plank. Thus there are some who yell at the people and provoke them against preachers and monks. They say that their whole being is evil and godless, their teaching false, their presence dangerous, that regular fasting, confessing, going to mass, receiving the Sacraments, praying, church attendance, and holidays are useless toward salvation. The works do not do it, faith alone saves. Then the listeners fall for it, accept it—not faith in Christ—but the error and the pleasure from this talk, so that they put aside the usual and see what kind of game they can play. They go ahead without any fear of God, without any conscience, and without any modesty, turn everything around wherever they can, become evil-doers and daring to do all things, and are happy that they have found a cover for their mischievousness, so that with-

---

[66] [Loehe:] 2 Peter 1.

out harm they can break down the fence of all discipline and decency, which formerly enclosed them to their displeasure.

Besides that, there stands an enthusiast in the pulpit and encourages the common rabble in their purpose, as if they rendered God a service. Formerly they did not like preachers and monks and everybody disliked discipline and honesty, and now they continue in that vein.[67] Wise people just look on, and while they weigh things, mischievousness takes over, so you no longer can get rid of it. The devil laughs at that and has won his game. For while formerly he was served by diligent keeping of the ceremonies, because of the godless condition of the heart, now he is being served by the insane tearing down of the ceremonies, since it happens without fear of God, without conscience, and most of such preachers and listeners know God less than any pope. They are fornicators, drunks, blasphemers, badmouthing, avaricious, and full of similar vices.

But if one finds honest, disciplined, conscientious people who are frightened by such crimes and do not want to get involved in them, the frivolous people will mock them and call them hypocrites and braggarts. Every sermon is directed against them, and there will be such misery in the world before one begins to preach the kingdom of Christ that one is almost forced to forbid doctrine as something hurtful, rebellious, and the like. Then we really got to deserve it. If one would start to prove to the heart its own godless being with the Word of God; holding it up in the fear of God and in love, we have achieved it in our devilish way that one cannot preach Christ nor the devil,[68] and that is the cause of the great ill will against the Gospel in the world. One assumes that the Gospel is an enthusiastic thing, as those people pretend. No, no, dear friends, that [sort of preaching] does not mean to preach in an evangelical way, but to land in deep trouble.[69]

Eighteenth. An evangelical preacher points the people away from their suspicious, self-loving heart toward a good trust in God through Christ, toward a benevolent attitude toward the neighbor. The Gospel scares the proud, wicked heart away from self-love, reason, strength, wisdom, wittiness, conspiracies and the like, and drives it to God's power, fear, wisdom, to consider these heartily and truly, and to come through fear to love.[70] Once one has brought home this main point and article for a long time, establishing it in the hearts and minds of the listeners, one gradually and decently should

---

[67] [Loehe:] That means: Therefore one continues that way with all mischievousness.

[68] [Loehe:] That means: Neither about the kingdom of Christ, nor of the kingdom of the devil, as has been shown in the preceding.

[69] Literally, "fry an egg for the devil." This is related to "*in die Küche des Teufels kommen*," to wind up in hell's kitchen, to be in real unpleasant circumstances.

[70] Here we see "Gospel" in the loose sense of the revealed Word, Law and Gospel. Its opposite is when God punishes via the Law by refusing to reveal His scriptural message and leaves a sinner's heart hardened and benighted.

show by what deeds or omissions, we act against God's fear and love. The listeners may notice it by themselves. Then one will be able to give counsel for outward abuses. They will daily fall, so much more as God's fear and love shine in the hearts, until our hearts and those of our neighbors become stronger in the faith. There are some things that one can let go of, as long as the inner heart has become new through the divine light.

And yet, those do not please God, even if they did away with all images, temples, cloisters, days of fasting, confessing, masses, and other outward things, for they do not remember the fear of God. None of them has ever been hit with the fear and judgment of God, or examined his heart before the judgment seat of Christ because of his breaking things, [asking] whether at the end he may stand before God or not. They run along as insane, raving people.

Nineteenth. I really would not like to counsel and offer help regarding the vulgar, idolatrous worship among the people without the Word of God forcing me, not any more than I would help murder someone. I am afraid that whoever helps here would not do it out of faith. Therefore the devil would be served here as well as there. And just as some rely on setting up the ceremonies mentioned above and think to render a service to God without any godliness and please themselves very well, others lead [people] astray by breaking down, relying on the fact that they helped destroy idolatry, and that now they are Christians, and never attain to true divine blessedness, as was said above. Yes, and whoever talks against them would have to suffer more misery from them than from the papists.

I would rather preach in a papist city, where there never was such an enthusiast, than in a city where the people fell away, became criminals and mischievous. But no doubt, we will have to give an account of our crime. I thank my God, who has led me to the good Mr. Philip Melanchthon, who punished such crime in me, and faithfully has taught me this modesty with which I now have written. And those who read Dr. Martin Luther's books diligently and listen to his teaching will not find anything else either. But if someone understands it differently and wants to defend his false understanding, one must fear that God's curse has already come over him, so that God's Word only serves to blind him, as the prophet Isaiah says,[71] and as Christ repeats it in the Gospel.[72]

Twentieth. Therefore, dear sirs, who have such enthusiasts as preachers in your lands and cities, see to it in time, before your people become mischievous and loose. The Gospel of Christ teaches patience, obedience, discipline, honesty, as one can find in the epistle of St. Paul to the Romans, chapters 12 to 14, and also in other places. A Christian will bear everything that does not hinder heartfelt trust in God through Christ. Dear sirs, if you want

---

[71] [Loehe:] Isaiah 6.

[72] [Loehe:] Luke 8.

to change or eliminate an order in your congregation based on common counsel, well and good. Your faith is your judge. If you do not want to do this, it is also good. But your listeners should not riot and want to change this or that. Everybody should reform himself according to God's Word and gift in reverent prayer, and should also exhort his neighbor to do the same. If it helps, well and good. If not, one should commend the thing to God in reverent prayer. He will make all things well. If one does this, God will be with us, and He will destroy the antichristian kingdom. Therefore, take for yourselves preachers who teach you Christian faith and discipline based on Holy Scripture, and get rid of the enthusiasts.

Twenty-first. I do not say this in order that one should refrain from offering serious resistance to those who want to tear the truth of God out of hearts. But read rightly the epistle of St. Paul to Timothy, where he says: The Lord's servant must not be quarrelsome, but fatherly to everyone, an apt teacher, patient, correcting opponents with gentleness. God may perhaps grant that they will repent and come to know the truth, and that they may escape from the snare of the devil, having been held captive by Him to do His will.

Notice: A servant of the Lord should not be quarrelsome, not put everything to the question, not pounce upon everybody, not plan to assail any resistance and fight everything with the sword. No, no, he should be fatherly to everyone, an apt teacher, knowing how to bear the evil ones and correcting the opponents with gentleness. One should be stern in gentleness. About seriousness St. Paul talks in the epistles to Titus[73] and Timothy,[74] but about gentleness in the second letter to the Corinthians[75] and in the above quoted words to Timothy.[76] Therefore act in this way: In strictness be gentle, and in gentleness be strict, as St. Paul says. Act with all patience and teaching, so that one does not get a scolding from you, but instruction. Street urchins and old women also know how to scold, but they do not know how to teach.

But you say: Who can mix strictness and gentleness in such a way and keep them together? Answer: If you cannot do this then give up preaching, plough the field, dig, and work. Christ may look on for a while, but at the end He will punish the mistreatment of His Word most severely. Yes, you may then say: The prophets, Christ Himself, the apostles, and even Luther are sharp and scold their opponents harshly. Answer: You want to pour out all their scolding, which you find in all their books, in one day. They may have done it over a period of many years. Also, they did it as the time required it, when they practiced the stern gentleness of the Spirit the most. Also, when Christ punished the Jews harshly in the garden, His heart nevertheless was

---

[73] [Loehe:] Titus 1.

[74] [Loehe:] 2 Timothy 4.

[75] [Loehe:] 2 Corinthians 2.

[76] [Loehe:] 2 Timothy 2.

gentle and mild, so that he restored the ear to Malchus[77] and even died for them. If we also would be so skillful, our scolding would fit us well and would bring more fruit among the listeners. But we are enthusiasts: We scold, despise, badmouth and more. By nature we have been this way since birth. This we practice now under the guise of the Gospel against the papists, and yet there is no Spirit in us, only flesh.

Dear cousin, I am writing so much about this to you and others, for I am also "too much inclined toward abrupt, sharp action, and have led many ships astray. I learned from my own loss. Once one has looked over the game, one will no longer protect bad advice with indulgence or harshness. No one wants to be wrong, but God is not mocked." No one should deceive himself; that is my faithful counsel.

Twenty-second. We should learn from the prophets and apostles how nicely and slowly one should proceed with preaching. Is not the article concerning Christ's divinity necessary for salvation? Yet Peter, at the beginning, says nothing about it in Jerusalem, as we find in the Acts of the Apostles.[78] Nor does he say anything to Cornelius at the beginning. Also: St. Paul is quiet at Antioch in Pisidia concerning the godhead of Christ. He only touches it superficially in a short little verse. He did the same in Lystra and Athens, as is written everywhere in the Acts of the Apostles. Christ also forbade His disciples to tell anyone before His death that He was the Christ.[79] The entire New Testament did not proclaim the article of the virginity of Mary, except Matthew and Luke. John and Peter are silent in their writings about the Sacrament of the Altar, and Paul talks about it in only one epistle, and yet all of them described the Gospel. In the same way the prophets also presented many articles very darkly.

Why is all that? It is because one has to go slowly. In the beginning one should hear about God's omnipotence, how He alone creates and does everything that is good, and also how all our possessions, our doing and omitting, come from God's power and order, and keep going. It takes much time and diligence to drive this into the listeners. For through this the heart is driven away from its own arrogance and learns to turn the inner eye toward God, and sees how much good He does for us daily.

After that one ought to explain the commandments of God and show the right reason for them. This also takes much time and work. Once the heart learns about its own sin from them, one should begin to teach Christ, how He was sent from God for our sakes, to die for our sins, and how He was appointed as Judge over the whole world, but will spare those who believe in Him. One should also say that, just as he rose powerfully from death and hell, our bodies also will rise again, and that our soul is free from death, hell and

[77] [Loehe:] Luke 22.

[78] [Loehe:] Acts 2; 10; 13; 14; 17.

[79] [Loehe:] Matthew 16.

the devil. One has to preach a long time about this part and often bring it home, until the listener wins a love and trust for Christ. Then it will be good to talk about other articles.

All the books of the New Testament have been written to those who already believed in Christ. Therefore it is hard to learn from them the right form and method to start preaching to those who do not know Christ in the right way. But in the Acts of the Apostles alone one finds such form to preach the faith. One can also learn how to start preaching from the way the apostles preached about the death of Christ. For we have to deal so gently with those who have not yet rightly known Christ, even though they were under the pope. We have to deal with them as with unbelievers, as the apostles had to do in the beginning with the heathen.

And once one has presented it in the right form and method, as the above examples of the apostles teach, and people now start knowing Christ, one should not hurry with the ceremonies, whether to have fewer of them, or do away with them. Peter and James did not do so either in Jerusalem. Read the Acts of the Apostles about this,[80] also St. Paul's epistles to the Romans[81] and Corinthians.[82] But this one ought to do: Preach daily how our salvation and blessedness does not lie in these ceremonies or outward orders, but in believing in Christ. Thus these ceremonies eventually will fall away, little by little, but more with some people than with others, according to each person's faith, without force or pushing, with peace and love out of faith, with a good conscience and the fear of God. Then the devil's kingdom will be destroyed with the Word of God, not with our misdeed.

Twenty-third. Let no one say: I will chase out the ceremonies just as Paul did. Dear fellow, you misunderstand Paul. The gentiles formerly did not have the law of the Jews, and then learned Christ with a will. After that, Paul prevented that one would put the strange law of the Jews upon the gentiles. For faith in Christ would be enough for their salvation, as St. Paul writes and explains in the epistles to the Romans[83] and Galatians.[84] The heathen also had enough local law for their worldly government, so they did not need the Law of Moses.

Paul also kept many of the heathen uses and customs when he was with pagans, so that he would bring the pagans to faith in Christ, as is written in the first epistle to the Corinthians, where St. Paul says: For though I am free with respect to all, I have made myself a slave to all, so that I might win more of them. To the Jews I became as a Jew in order to win Jews. To those under the Law I became as one under the Law so that I might win those under the

---

[80] [Loehe:] Acts 15.

[81] [Loehe:] Romans 14.

[82] [Loehe:] 1 Corinthians 8 and 10.

[83] [Loehe:] Romans 3.

[84] [Loehe:] Galatians 2.

Law. To those outside the Law I became as one outside the Law (though I am not free from God's Law but am under Christ's Law) so that I might win those outside the Law. To the weak I became weak, so that I might win the weak. I have become all things to all people, so that I might by all means save some. He also permits other Christians to go to a pagan inn and not to worry whether they might unknowingly eat of something that had been sacrificed to idols, as he indicates in the epistle mentioned above,[85] where he says: If an unbeliever invites you to a meal and you are disposed to go, eat whatever is set before you without raising any question on the ground of conscience.

But Paul deals differently with the Jews. Outwardly he kept the law with them, as in the Acts of the Apostles,[86] and as we now have heard in the first epistle to the Corinthians,[87] so that he would bring others to the faith. And since they already believed in Christ and did not want to let go of the law that soon, he ordered that one should not mock them on that account, nor reject or judge them, but bear and tolerate them, until they daily would be freed from the prison of the law through knowing about Christian liberty, as is written in the epistle to the Romans.[88] And for many years, the apostles had pity with the Jews in Jerusalem, as Paul did with the Jews in Rome.

But thus far, beginning with our parents, we have been stuck with the laws of the Pope. It is just as hard for us to let go of them as it was for the Jews with their law. It is no wonder that we do not want to get away from them so quickly. Therefore one should have pity with us, until we grow in the faith so firmly that we drive away the law from our heart, out of faith in Christ and not out of mischief. To keep the Pope's law or to break it, without true godliness, is the same. But if we accept godliness, or have not yet firmly grown into it, so that we would despise the laws out of faith, it is better still to walk with the law, but pray unceasingly to God that He would strengthen us in our weakness. Besides that, a preacher should "promote the Word of God modestly, in a friendly manner, and thereby show how our salvation depends on our faith in Christ, not on any law." [He should ensure] that no one should judge, despise, or provoke the other, whether he keeps the law or not. But one should bear the other until God helps, so that the mischievous and petulant rabble that keeps the laws simply out of enthusiasm, but does not respect honor or discipline, should "not mock or afflict other people who are honest, conscientious, but weak in the faith, yet good, who want to wait until they learn to despise the laws and human orders, not frivolously, but out of faith.

If the law of the Pope would not lie so hard on our conscience, we would not let it break in, just as Paul did not want the Law of Moses to fall upon the

---

[85] [Loehe:] 1 Corinthians 10.

[86] [Loehe:] Acts 16:21.

[87] [Loehe:] 1 Corinthians 9.

[88] [Loehe:] Romans 14.

heathen. But since unfortunately we were born and raised under the papacy, let us gladly and with diligence learn Christ until we can leave the laws out of faith. Therefore, dear preachers, go slow with us and nicely, have patience with our slow-wittedness. We are not as strong as you are, we do not want to let go of our ceremonies as freely and courageously as you. Praise your God that He has redeemed you, and teach us in a friendly way and wait patiently until our consciences also are strengthened by God. Unless our consciences grow stronger, we do not want to let go [of the ceremonies]. It would be frivolous, and that would bring great harm and burden our hearts. Pray with us that God may strengthen our faith.

"Just do not throw Luther against us. We do not consider each one of you to be a Luther. Some of you do not even know how to read Luther correctly, much less understand him." Not even the smallest number of you is as wise, as smart, learned, experienced, godly, and proven as Luther is. We also know how things are.[89] Besides, for three of four years Luther powerfully has disputed, preached, counseled, and ordered in Wittenberg, with the help and assistance of the modest and learned man Philip Melanchthon and others like him. Yet Luther did not want "to let anything be changed in public customs; he was afraid this would happen more out of foolishness than out of faith" and the devil would laugh about it. Only after a year did he begin gradually to discontinue one or the other thing, according to his ability. "And some unlearned, inexperienced newcomers fall upon us suddenly in cities and villages with new teachings. In a few months they want to do away with all ceremonies on our side; want to make us more frivolous than godly, and sick the rabble on you, who neither know God nor have any reason." And if we are not stupid enough to do this, we become their laughingstock and a target in the temple and the market place, at which they shoot their arrows.

I have to say one more thing. Dear friends, one should also say to some of our own people: We also must have patience with you, and you with us. We have not yet learned to eat meat on Friday, to give up [the papist] confession and mass, to stop saying our little prayers to the saints, and such. But we want to use all diligence to learn such things. Therefore, do not be impatient with us.

You, on the other hand, have not yet learned to do away with whoring, overeating, blaspheming, needlessly swearing, scolding, gossiping and other sinful things. Nor have you learned what serves toward a peaceful, disciplined life of a citizen. You do not practice it, and thus have only little experience in human and worldly matters. You do not know how to comfort us a little, and to teach about the kingdom of Christ. You are also much too weak to keep our secrets confidential, of which we make complaint to you from our hearts. There is little evidence of your love and compassion for us; you do not want to be instructed or admonished, as if you knew all things and

---

[89] Literally, what beets and pears are (*was Rüben oder Birn sein*).

could always hit things right [on target]. In all these things, which sometimes are very offensive, we bear you in patience. Therefore it would only be fair to have patience also with our imbecility. Truly, one can find some honest people who in truth would speak with me and the likes of me; inexperienced preachers might thus speak, and perhaps even harder.

All of this, dear gentleman, I wrote to you so much longer, and gladly. May you accept it from me in the best way, for I know how much you dislike such enthusiasm. But I have to add one more thing. If someone would remain wickedly in unbelief, and even prevent others from hearing sound doctrine, we should resist in modesty as far as God gives us grace. If this does not help them, we want to separate ourselves from them, and diligently practice good will, as St. Paul did with the Ephesians, as we read in the Acts of the Apostles,[90] and as Christ did with the Pharisees in the fifteenth chapter of Matthew.

Twenty-fourth. If you notice that a person has taken hold of God's Word, you should not worry about the outward change in his being and acting, as some do. With great diligence they counsel and push that the preachers should give up their parishes, the monks and nuns should leave their cloisters, and do other such outward things, as if there were no salvation, unless one threw away all this not only inwardly, but also outwardly. But outward things do not matter much, if only God's Word is kept in the heart. As long as it is there, it does not rest, and with time these things will fall away by themselves. Also, the biggest fight in the world, the one against the papacy, has been won, and every day one hears more and more about what the kingdom of Christ consists of and, thank God, one despises the kingdom of the Antichrist. Also, one is not upset much about the old, sick, helpless cloister people and preachers, who have no other income, whether they remain in their monasticism or stay with their parishes, recognizing their stupidity and anxious for the power of God and His redemption.

But the fact that I left the cloister two years ago had a different reason. For even if Luther had not stood up, I was in the sort of position that, according to all proper rights and by reason alone, I would have been discharged from the order. The Pope also would have given me a dispensation, if I would have had the money. I also was free in my heart through evangelical teaching, which was shown me through Lutheran writing. Since in my conscience I was free, and had enough cause before the world to leave the order, and it was now customary that many members of the order left without a scandal, I also went away without any papal dispensation and permission. Rome was too far for me, and I did not have any money. I did not doubt that the Pope would have given me dispensation and permission to leave the order if I would have given some money. Since it was right for me before men to acquire a dispensation with money, it also suited me before the world to leave

[90] [Loehe:] Acts 19.

without money. In my heart I did not need the Pope's permission. God had redeemed me a long time ago.

But if someone would want to remain in the cloister and knows Christ, but his affairs are not such that he could leave, I would not deny him God's grace. St. Paul says:[91] Neither circumcision nor uncircumcision is anything; but a new creation. To chase away all ceremonies is also a ceremony, and to live without a law is also a law, and even if they flee the laws, they make a law.

One also has to worry that a man could come into greater danger if he left his parish than before, if that same man is inexperienced, without knowledge and weak, and not used to a life of poverty. He would fall into begging, into unused work, trouble, and care. One could see how the devil would become active then. Not without reason does King Solomon[92] ask God the Lord that He should give him neither riches nor poverty, so that he would not become proud, or audacious and desperate. For thus he says in Proverbs: "Two things I ask of you; do not deny them to me before I die: Remove from me falsehood and lying; give me neither poverty nor riches; feed me with the food that I need, or I shall be full, and deny you, and say, Who is the Lord? Or I shall be poor, and steal, and profane the name of my God."

Someone might say: Yes, one must trust in God. Answer: Then jump with both feet into hell. If it is God's will, hell will throw you out again. If one should not guard against the devil in your meaning, I will not dispute with you. If God wants you to leave the cloister or the priesthood, He will arrange such means that you get away, not knowing how. If you are a Christian, you know that your food comes from your heavenly Father. But if you cannot get it through comfortable means, confess your trouble before men and lament before God,[93] ask Him for help and advice, trust Him, He will make it well, and wait for Him. Then neither cloister nor parish will hurt you.

I want to write to you the advice of a learned, Christian, enlightened man, which I believe will be very useful to preachers, namely that in the beginning one should not overthrow too much at once, such as mass, vigils, anniversaries and the like. Rather, one should start gently. One should say that one should read the mass for the sake of any gain, nor for honor, nor from habit, but one should only pray for oneself and for others for God's sake. Once someone has taught about this for a long time, friendly and seriously, he should continue and say that no other ceremonies should be used for pomp and circumstances either, be they daily offices or vigils. Nor should one seek any profit or honor with them, but only consider the prayer by itself. After some days one should teach the people why they should use confession and the Sacrament.

---

[91] [Loehe:] Galatians 6.

[92] [Loehe:] Proverbs 30.

[93] [Loehe:] Psalm 27.

In confession the sinner should come, not driven by any person, but by his own trouble, in order faithfully to tell his sins to the priest before God, to the best of his ability, without worrying about their number. He should receive the comfort of the Absolution from the priest and listen to his counsel how the poor, sad person should act from now on. For Christ has said in Matthew:[94] "Truly I tell you, whatever you bind on earth will be bound in heaven, and whatever you loose on earth will be loosed in heaven." And Christ says further on: "If two of you agree on earth about anything you ask, it will be done for you by my Father in heaven. For where two or three are gathered in my name, I am there among them."

Upon this promise of Christ let the sinful person, lacking comfort, come to the priest as to a Christian to hear God's Word, comfort, and counsel through him. Once you have taught this opinion often and well, and God's Spirit also works in the hearts of the listeners, they will soon understand how one should trust God's Word, spoken by the priest, and be comforted by it, more than by one's own confession. Therefore talk about it for a while, how a priest has this power, not because he has been consecrated by the bishop, but because he has been "anointed by the Holy Spirit in Baptism with the grace of God, like all Christians. And thus one should notice that all Christians together have the power to forgive sins,[95] to teach and to comfort, all in the same way. But though this power is given by God to all Christians,[96] nevertheless no one should publicly assume to exercise this power unless the congregation has chosen him for this. And those who have thus been chosen, one has called priests."

Such an election is indicated by the consecration of the bishop, if it is best, and not more. Thus one will daily come to the conclusion that one can skip the bishop's consecration, or keep it, as it pleases the congregation, and that one should not take any vow from the chosen priests, except that they will faithfully preach God's Word, with the help of God, that they will confess and do good and serve everybody according to their ability. Timothy gave such a vow and confession, as I understand the text where St. Paul,[97] among other words, says this: "But as for you, man of God, shun all this; pursue righteousness, godliness, faith, love, endurance, gentleness. Fight the good fight of faith; take hold of eternal life, to which you were called and for which you made the good confession in the presence of many witnesses." See, one has to preach a long time on these matters, with authority and modesty, that

---

[94] [Loehe:] Matthew 18.

[95] Loehe inserts a parenthetical doubt here: (?) we relegate that to the footnotes and allow Eberlin to speak unhindered, perhaps to the delight of Walther. Loehe's bias on these matters caused friction over the doctrines of the Church, the pastoral office, and Absolution during the first forty years of the LCMS.

[96] Again Loehe questions this with (?). Compare Walther's *Church and Office*.

[97] [Loehe:] 1 Timothy 6.

without any hurtful offense one can understand what confession is, and after that, when and how it is necessary or not. But if one would reject confession from the beginning, before one has taught and preached enough and well, you would soon scare away all good hearts from your teaching. And no honorable, reasonable man deals this way with doctrine, only shameless people who like to be seen, so that they can come up with something strange.

Do the same with the Sacrament of the body and blood of Christ. First of all, one should say that the Sacrament is a seal of the Word of God, so that a comfortless person may hear God's comfort, even if he is still weak in the faith. Let him receive the Sacrament of the Altar to strengthen his heart, trusting in God against all suffering and temptation. Also a person should show himself, as a comfort to all, as one who also confesses Christ by receiving this. That way others will be drawn and enticed to faith in Christ, and they will be willing to do all possible service and good deeds as an example of discipline and honesty for the whole world.

Do not pounce right away on the fact that one should receive the Sacrament in both kinds, and whatever else there is. Continue more and more to teach about the Sacrament, teach faith in the words of Christ with which the Sacrament was instituted. One should always use more diligence to point to faith in Christ than to outward signs. When the time comes, let one say a little about both kinds in the Sacrament, but one should not receive either one without faith. Say also that a person is not forced, either by God or man, for this Sacrament, but it should happen with a free heart and devotion toward the end and benefit that has been mentioned. Be sure to exhort the people that they should not omit to receive confession and the Sacrament lightly or with contempt. For the devil uses just as great a diligence to draw people away from confession and the Sacrament through thoughtlessness and carelessness, as formerly he was eager to drive them there by force in droves, without faith. In this way one will come to the point that the misuse of the Sacrament will be abandoned.

This will happen especially if one drives home what a sacrament is, namely this, that God adds a visible sign to His promise, through which man is assured of God's favor and grace.

Thus one can show and prove later that marriage, ordination, unction, and confirmation should not be called sacraments of Christ since they have not been instituted as signs by Christ. Only Baptism and the Sacrament of the Altar are signs and sacraments of Christ. Thus you will lead the people away from their error concerning the Sacraments, and toward the receiving under both kinds, without any rebellion or offence. Oh, if "one would have preachers who sought more the salvation of souls than their own gain and honor, one would hear God's Word preached well in our lands, without rumbling and unrest." For Doctor Martin Luther and some of his faithful helpers have cut away the biggest and heaviest stuff on the ground, and have opened the holy sepulcher of divine Scripture, so that in almost all places the horror of the papacy has been recognized and everybody is pleased with the Bible. Therefore we have no need of blowing the trumpet anew and chasing away fools uselessly and without need.[98] We would like to build upon the foundation that Luther laid with gold, silver, precious stones—good, comforting teaching of the consciences, honest and chaste morals and such. But I know from my own experience that the devil promotes "such rumblings, that he may have an easy time to drive away our teaching, or to prevent us from doing better things."

If you have done all these things, you may show from the words of Christ, preached so often, that the mass is no sacrifice for us, and that the priest, when taking the Sacrament (also in faith) does not do any more than a faithful lay person. Therefore one should not believe that the priest offers the Sacrament for the living and for the dead. All such understanding of the mass should be done away with as unchristian. Christ is our Priest; He sacrifices for us, not a human being. The priest is only a servant of the congregation and should take the Sacrament for himself and give it to others. The people should be able to comprehend this teaching, if you have taught beforehand what has been said above. Thus the votive and sacrificial masses will all fall away by themselves.

You should often and repeatedly say that "a Christian is unsure and uncertain if he accepts and believes something for which no Scripture has been presented to him." If this decision is well founded among the people, you may do away with many abuses in their hearts. Since Scripture does not mention any purgatory, or [any] ways and means to help souls, and no one is certain that one should preach about purgatory or believe in it, all anniversaries, vigils and masses for the souls will fall away without any trouble or work.

And because there is no teaching or example in Scripture to call upon the dead saints for help and intercession, one also should stay away from so many pilgrimages, little prayers, vows, and other foolishness that one has done with the saints, especially since such trust in the saints is often harmful for the faith in Christ, from whom we should expect all things.

Also, since God nowhere commands to keep monastic vows or to make them, and it is not certain whether to make such vows or keep them; for they are against God, because they bind and enslave the conscience, while our conscience ought to be free from all laws, ruled only by God's Word: It follows that if a priest or monk no longer wants to be celibate, let him get married and avoid much danger, as St. Paul tells in the seventh chapter of the first epistle to the Corinthians.[99]

After all this you may show nicely that, since Christ alone is the Head of the Church, as St. Paul says to the Ephesians[100] and Colossians,[101] neither St.

---

[98] [Loehe:] 1 Corinthians 1.

[99] [Loehe:] 1 Corinthians 7.

[100] [Loehe:] Ephesians 1.

Peter nor the Pope should be considered the head of the Christian congregation. And since Christ Himself is with us until the end of the world, as He promises after His resurrection in Matthew,[102] there is no need for a vicar. Therefore neither St. Peter nor the Pope should call themselves Vicar of Christ. Also, Peter and Paul do not call themselves anything but servants of the congregation and want to be considered as such, as they themselves write in their epistles and letters, especially St. Paul to the Corinthians,[103] where he says: Think of us in this way, as stewards of God's mysteries. Therefore our popes and bishops, if they are really pious, should also not be or appear as anything but servants of the congregation, not lords, but helpers for our faith.[104]

And since the councils are nothing but an assembly of Christians, and all Christians are born through God's Word and become Christians, it follows that God's Word is above all Christians, be they within or outside of the councils. Therefore no council should order or bind anything or comfort the consciences unless it is founded in Holy Scripture. But if something is ordered without this, it should not be valid. Now one already knows what to do with all councils, doctors, and schools, how to pull away and tear oneself away with God's Word. See now, how peacefully, better, and comforting one could teach God's Word if one starts this matter correctly. Not without reason, Paul writes to the Colossians[105] that one ought to entreat God that he may preach God's Word and speak as he ought to speak. Experience teaches how much wisdom it takes to speak God's Word as one ought to speak it. Paul also teaches Timothy[106] correctly to divide the Word of God.

Twenty-fifth. Before all else we Christians should ensure that we do not ourselves put a hindrance and persecution upon our neck while we are able to live peacefully in worship and Word, in all honesty, as St. Paul says to Timothy:[107] First of all, then, I urge that supplications, prayers, intercessions, and thanksgivings be made for everyone, for kings and all who are in high positions, so that we may lead a quiet and peaceable life in all godliness and dignity. But we do put a hindrance and persecution upon our neck if, without Scripture and reason, we start to mumble against common customs and traditions that only burden our bag, our money, our body, and our honor without damaging the soul, if only it believes in Christ: "Giving the tithe, paying taxes, bringing sacrifices, doing compulsory service. This does not hurt anyone's conscience, and no one should grumble less against it" than

---

101 [Loehe:] Colossians 1.

102 [Loehe:] Matthew 28.

103 [Loehe:] 1 Corinthians 4; 2 Corinthians 4; Colossians 1; 1 Peter 5.

104 [Loehe:] 2 Corinthians 9; 1 Peter 5.

105 [Loehe:] Colossians 4

106 [Loehe:] 2 Timothy 2.

107 [Loehe:] 1 Timothy 2.

Christians. For a Christian here has much higher comfort from God and expects more than anything earthly could be. A Christian should protect the Word of God, which is being hindered by unbelievers, priests, prelates, princes, and lords when they hear that we preach directly against their gain. This way they start to chase us away with the Word. Otherwise they would let us remain as long as we pay taxes and furnish compulsory service. And in many places that is the reason why we are being persecuted. A Christian should rather die than cause such disturbance. Is it not the devil's work that no one is found more unwilling and disobedient than some and many who call themselves evangelical and Lutheran. And yet, neither Christ nor Luther taught such. But if they understand this teaching in their own way, truly their own wickedness has blinded them, not this teaching.

Not without reason does Paul so diligently exhort the Romans[108] and others that one should honor the government, be obedient, and render dutiful service. The servants, subjects, or one's own people should show faithfulness and be obedient to their masters, and the women to their men, the children to their parents, so that the teaching of Christ is not blasphemed, as if it were the cause of such disobedience. Paul also orders his disciple Timothy[109] that he should exhort, as said above, that one should offer petitions to God faithfully for all in high position, that they may be well, that under their rule we may lead a quiet and peaceable life in all godliness and dignity. St. Peter[110] also exhorts us earnestly to do the same. And to wrap it up (*summa summarum*), as Christ says in St. Matthew:[111] Everything you want people to do for you, do it also for them. He says the same thing elsewhere:[112] Give unto Caesar the things that are Caesar's. He also said to St. Peter:[113] In order not to give offense to them, let us give the tax.

If God would give us gracious, godly princes, we spoil it "with our wanton ways, so that princes and lords, noblemen and cities often have to be ashamed of our sacrilege." Such wanton people are worse than the papists. And then the Gospel has to take all the blame, and those same poor people say: I suffer much persecution for the sake of the Gospel. Also, in this or that place one will not allow the Gospel to be preached. Now you really did it. "You do not suffer for the sake of truth and the Gospel, but because of your sacrilege and your arrogance, which you demonstrate arrogantly, and present without wisdom to the unknowing people."

---

[108] [Loehe:] Romans 13; Colossians 3; 1 Timothy 6; Ephesians 5–6.

[109] [Loehe:] 1 Timothy 2.

[110] [Loehe:] 1 Peter 2.

[111] [Loehe:] Matthew 7.

[112] [Loehe:] Matthew 22.

[113] [Loehe:] Matthew 17.

If the people would notice that in many places we wanted to be what we should be, according to the epistles of St. Paul,[114] one would gladly let us preach. But we have been defamed so much because of our enthusiasm, that we hardly are trusted anymore." And that is our fault. May almighty God not withdraw his Word, nor hinder good preachers because the enthusiasm of a few.

Twenty-sixth. Above all remember how Paul so diligently, so often, so earnestly exhorts Timothy[115] and Titus[116] that they should abstain from foolish, arrogant and quarrelsome questions, skimmed from the Scriptures, which only serve to make the spirits frivolous. A preacher should withdraw from such quarrelsome people. The devil now drives many people to do nothing but question, question, and yet they do not want to be instructed, but want to be seen more than others. That is devil's dung; it stinks especially badly. And if the evangelical preachers also want to start to occupy themselves with such questions, they become worse than any sophist. May God preserve us from this! Such questions also hinder good hearts, make them quarrelsome, uncertain, and unsure. Therefore one should drop such questions and commend them to God, and be more diligent to become more pious than learned through the Scriptures.

Twenty-seventh. Some among us are so eager, so obnoxious, so full of impolite gestures when we talk about Christianity that they think that one must be that wild. Yet St Paul[117] teaches and exhorts everywhere that a Christian should be mild, friendly and lovely in speech, especially a preacher. He indicates this when he talks about the qualities of a bishop in the first epistle to Timothy.[118] Also, if we are asked for the foundation of our faith and our hope, we should answer with gentleness and fear. I have been present when an evangelical preacher in a fairly large city was talking so provokingly, cheerfully, and in a quarrelsome way, even before many at table, that I felt ashamed. Afterwards someone said: I think that the evangelical teaching must require one to talk in such a way; for all those I hear talk about it act that way. I answered him: "No, but Paul teaches us to talk friendly and modestly about God's Word." But such forward ways are the fault of our own foolishness. Dear cousin, use your innate friendliness for the Word of God. It will please the ears "if one talks about the mild, humble Christ mildly and friendly."

Twenty-eighth. Do not despise this warning, dear cousin, but learn well its basis in Holy Scripture, and imagine nothing but this, that you should be for all people a mirror of an honest, godly, decent life, as Paul exhorts his

---

[114] [Loehe:] 2 Corinthians 6; Philippians 4; Romans 12.

[115] [Loehe:] 1 Timothy 1 and 6; 2 Timothy 2.

[116] [Loehe:] Titus 3.

[117] [Loehe:] Colossians 4.

[118] [Loehe:] 1 Timothy 3.

[disciple] Titus[119] when he says: Show yourself in all respects to be a model of good works, and in your teaching show integrity, gravity, and sound speech that cannot be censured; then any opponent will be put to shame, having nothing evil to say of us. For this also read the little book called *Pastorale Sankt Gregorii*, and Bernard, *De consideratione ad Eugenium.*[120] In a life that is disciplined and godly through faith you will understand much of Scripture and also get much wisdom to counsel others.

Twenty-ninth. You should have a wife, and if you are not allowed to have one publicly, you will find advice in the little book of Doctor Martin Luther, written to the Order of the Teutonic Knights.[121] Your wife, child and domestics should be ruled according to the rule that Paul prescribes in the first epistle to Timothy,[122] and this should be done for the improvement of the whole congregation.

Thirtieth. And not to forget my dear relatives, your parents: You should instruct your wife, children and domestics to honor your old and godly parents, so that these good people in their old age will find joy and support. Therefore God will give you His blessing, both now and in eternity, according to the promise that He has added to this commandment, as is written in the second book of Moses.[123] And thus all your children should learn from you how to honor father and mother.

Thirty-first. I will not neglect to remind you that all who want to live a godly life in Christ Jesus will have to suffer persecution, as St. Paul writes.[124] Therefore, as soon as you start preaching in a Christian way, great misfortune, anxiety, trouble, temptations, adversity, and persecution will follow you—threats here, insults there, secret snares, and more. "Therefore be warned, read some beautiful verses from the words of Christ and His holy

---

[119] [Loehe:] Titus 2.

[120] The *Pastorale Sankt Gregorii* refers to the *Liber regulae pastoralis* by Pope Gregory I. Bernard of Clairvaux (1090–1153) was a French abbot who helped found the Cistercian order. He was a papal advisor, preached the Second Crusade on papal request (for which he was later blamed), and a Doctor of the Church.

[121] Loehe rightfully doubts Luther with (?). The Teutonic Knights of St. Mary's Hospital at Jerusalem grew from a field hospital at the siege of Acre in the winter of 1190–91. Modeled after the Knights of St. John the Baptist (Hospitallers), they were asked to Christianize the Prussians in the thirteenth century. They became a governing force based in the Baltic, but could not marry. In 1523 Luther met with Albert of Brandenburg-Ansbach (of House Hohenzollern; 1490–1568), then grand master of the order. Luther wrote to the order at the end of 1523, where he suggests a biblically-approved monogamous living together in the specific case when human church authority forbids one to marry. In 1525 the order's territory became the Lutheran Duchy of Prussia under Poland, the future Kingdom of Prussia.

[122] [Loehe:] 1 Timothy 3.

[123] [Loehe:] Exodus 20.

[124] [Loehe:] 2 Timothy 3.

apostles, also from the prophets, to strengthen your heart in such trouble, and do not be afraid, do not soon give up." it is enough for you that God gives witness to your heart, that such action pleases him. And do not set your hope in any person; beware not to trust any master, any community, and any city; or God will put you to shame. Trust only in God; He will always help you with peace and joy.

Thirty-second. Finally, this is my faithful advice: Call the young children once or three times a week together, and tell them clearly and in a childlike way about discipline, honesty and the commandments of God, else they may not understand your sermon in the temple; they are too simpleminded. Be certain to believe that the greatest improvement of Christianity consists in diligently guarding and instructing the children. Read about this in the beautiful little book of Gerson, how one should guide the youth to Christ, and do not let go of the catechetical schools in your little town. To this the little book of Doctor Martin Luther, how to establish schools, should inspire you.

Conclusion

Thus, my dear gentleman and cousin, you have a long disorderly writing from me, an unlearned and disorderly person, in which is written my simple counsel about some articles that will serve you, me, and many others. I hope this little book will bring greater understanding and further meditating for many, and that they will pray to God for me also, for grace and help to better my life. For I sigh every day, how I may piously live in the Christian faith, but unfortunately I am making little progress so far. My steady prayer is that you and others may accept this writing in the best way, for I meant well from the heart. And if this makes you a better person, give credit to God Almighty, from whom all things come, and return thence. Pray to God for me and greet your parents, my relatives, and all other brothers in Christ Jesus, our Lord.

Given at Wittenberg on Maundy Thursday, 1524.
The grace of God be with us all! Amen.

Your dear cousin
Johann Eberlin

Chapter One

HOMILETICS

A. SHEPHERDS AND TEACHERS

Among the gifts that the Lord Jesus received from his Father at his Ascension and gave to his Church, two are mentioned specifically: The shepherds and teachers, ποιμένες καὶ διδάσκαλοι (Ephesians 4:11). With two words one and the same office is indicated: The shepherds are also the teachers. (Thus Augustine also understood it Ep. 59 *ad Paulinum*; Jerome. *ad Oceanum* Ep. 33; Balduin, p. 113). Therefore it is quite correct if one finds the **character** and the **highest of all the virtues of a shepherd** in the ability to teach, as Theophylact comments to the first chapter of the letter to Titus: "Doctrine is the virtue and the character of a bishop."[1] Hilary writes in book 8 *de Trinitate*: "The sum of all virtues of a bishop is knowledge and doctrine."[2]

From the fact that one and the same office is described with "shepherds and teachers," one learns not only the purpose of the office—to lead congregations to eternal life, as shepherds lead their flocks to green pasture—but also the main means that God gives the shepherds for this purpose, namely the divine Word. It comes out of the mouth of faithful shepherds as sacred teaching and must save the hearts of their congregations. In fact, the pastor has no other means to fulfill his office than the **divine Word**; everything else one might think of as a means for the Holy Office to become fruitful and helpful only in connection with the Word. Even in the **sacraments** it is not only the element, but much more the Word that everything depends on: "Water by itself is only water," eating and drinking accomplish nothing, but it is the "Word that is **added to** the elements" that makes the elements into bearers of heavenly goods. It combines both element and heavenly good, prepares the souls to receive, and makes them open and prepared for the enjoyment of the sacred effects and blessings of the Sacrament. The Word is

---

[1] *Est doctrina virtus et character episcope.*

[2] *Summa omnium virtutum episcopalium est scientia et doctrina.*

everything: It is the Word of the Lord through which the world was created and through which it is also renewed and sanctified. And therefore the servants of the Lord accomplish everything, yes, everything in their holy office through the Word.

After this, one could raise the question whether or not **experience in the office, dexterity, wisdom, eagerness, and use of outward conditions** in which a pastor lives also could not be **means to achieve** things. Could they not also be called means for the office? However, the answer is not difficult if one can rightly see the difference. Who would want to deny the fact that a pastor could use external conditions to further his work? As president of the relief work, the school, and charitable trusts, in a human way he can create attention and find a hearing for the word of his sermon. **Experience, dexterity, and wisdom** can remove many an obstacle that otherwise would oppose the Word. These qualities can prepare hearts psychologically and pedagogically in a human way for the reception of the divine blessing. And a holy **zeal** is able to find opportunities for the Word and quickly to use the occasion. To deny this would make any instruction for the office superfluous and useless. One would trample into dust the entire [body of] pastoral theology, which is yet worthy of all praise. Yes, one would forget that the Lord, the Holy Spirit, who gave to everyone a modest part of His gifts, calls some of the above-mentioned things his gift and power. (1 Corinthians 12:4–11): "Now there are varieties of gifts, but the same Spirit; and there are varieties of service, but the same Lord. . . . All these are empowered by one and the same Spirit, who apportions to each one individually as he wills."[3] One should not despise the gifts of the Spirit, but zealously pursue them. "But earnestly desire the higher gifts" (1 Corinthians 12:31 [ESV]).[4] As highly as one may consider the official behavior and the gifts of a pastor, and as greatly effective as they may be, it remains true that everything is salvific only when it is permeated by the divine Word and because that is so. The behavior of the pastor neither gives power to the Word, nor adds to it. It always is and remains the Word that brings forth such blessed effect. One could compare the excellent official behavior of a pastor and the gifts with a silver bowl in which the golden fruits of the divine Word lie. The bowl is worthy of the fruit and **commends it to people in a human way,** but in the end only the fruits of the Tree of Life, the good powers of the Word, can bestow refreshment and strength, as well as give and multiply life. Therefore it is also true that skill, zeal and a wise behavior, apart from the divine Word, may not be without effect, but can work in a destructive way. Yes, one can say that even the slightest moving away from the divine Word in the official behavior of a pastor has its harmful con-

[3] Διαιρέσεις δὲ χαρισμάτων εἰσίν, τὸ δὲ αὐτὸ πνεῦμα· καὶ διαιρέσεις διακονιῶν εἰσιν, καὶ ὁ αὐτὸς κύριος. . . . πάντα δὲ ταῦτα ἐνεργεῖ τὸ ἓν καὶ τὸ αὐτὸ πνεῦμα, διαιροῦν ἰδίᾳ ἑκάστῳ καθὼς βούλεται.

[4] ζηλοῦτε δὲ τὰ χαρίσματα τὰ μείζονα.

sequences. Take e.g., the case that a pastor in his official behavior defends or presents a good case, but lacks the right **moderation** that is needed, by being too eager and too fiery; this already is harmful. Just like someone driving a wagon will drive the animals with one hand, but with the other holds the reins to hold them back, the human will of a pastor also has to be held back by the divine Word, and then again be driven, if the work of the Holy Office should be done and not the opposite happen.

One certainly does well to differentiate among means of the office, gifts, and behavior for the office. It is easy to overestimate the official behavior in comparison with the means of the office. There is an important difference between a pastoral theology of the Church and those of a Gottfried Arnold and Baxter, etc.[5] The former looks more at the means, the other at the behavior. The [pietistic or liberal] ones also render an unhealthy, almost Pelagian judgment in regard to the extent that a pastor can apply his diligence and zeal, while the churchly theologians keep the extent of the sacred means within human extremes. How necessary it is to differentiate between means and ways on the one hand and behavior on the other! Especially those pastors should take this to heart, who through temper or guidance have come to a **Methodist** way of conducting their office.

Without knowing or wanting it, Methodist teachers often, put too much hope in one's own, human addition to the Word, in the official behavior. They lose the higher trust in the Word of truth and therefore fall into a hasty, restless activity and fishing for people. And yet rest and the quiet magnitude of such trust finally attracts the hearts of men more than measureless activity. The rest that was just mentioned does not have to end in laziness and the conviction that in the end, everything depends on the Word.

By no means does the grace of God have to kill the realization that, through wise acting, one can bring the light to the lamp stand, the gift to a thankful reception; but through a wrong start one can put the light under a bushel basket and cause the gift to be despised. Put together, this knowledge and conviction give to the true pastor his just measure. And **how much** goes with this! To stick with the parable above, a pastor who puts all his hope in **his own** work and forgets the heavenly co-worker would be like a coachman who only drives his horses and therefore comes to harm, but never to the

[5] Gottfried Arnold (1666–1714) was a Lutheran theologian and historian whose groundbreaking impartial history of heresies influenced the direction and writing of scholarly history. After he married and took a pastorate, he wrote a number of books on practical theology. At first a radical Pietist, he later moderated some of his views. Richard Baxter (1615–91) was an English nonconformist pastor and chaplain who wrote *The Reformed Pastor* (1656). Like other nonconformists after the 1662 Act of Uniformity, he faced several acts of Parliament (the Test and Corporation Acts and the 1689 Act of Toleration) that clearly favored the Church of England and the Tories. As a result, nonconformists (Presbyterians, Congregationalists, Baptists, and other groups) sided with the Liberal party.

goal. But a pastor who has the right measure is like a coachman who uses the whip to drive his horses, but also the reins to guide them, and thus comes quickly and safely to the goal.

The same goes for the **good example** of a pastor. Woe to him who neglects this and preaches the divine Word to the flock of Christ without recommending it through his example, or even hinders it through an evil example. An evil example truly is not just a human, but also a satanic hindrance for the Word. The multitude cries with a thousand tongues: "the life of the clergy is the Gospel of the people" (Acts 5:13).[6] [The multitude] has an evil eye; it will hardly leave a pure and holy example without criticism or giving it a name. It chases after every spot of a preacher, even if only to take offense, to quiet one's own evil conscience, to excuse one's own sin. Therefore, one cannot impress a servant of the Gospel enough to tell him what a responsibility it is not to contradict the word that he preaches with his own example.

But with all high esteem for the example, with all praise of the holy life of a pastor, the life and example only remain a human means that cannot be made equal to the divine means of grace of the Word. As it comes from a human source, it also works in a human way, perhaps here and there powerfully and overwhelming, but yet only in a human manner, merely human. Many an example simply drips from the divine Word, from which [such examples] have their origin. They can be compared to the body from which the water of life flows, according to the Lord's word. [Such an example] is being venerated, marveled at, and imitated. But will it lead to repentance, to faith, to sanctification? Will it truly work in a spiritual way, if it is not being explained through the Word, if the Word and its power is not somehow **separated** from it and is brought home to ears and hearts in the form of instruction, judgment, improvement, and discipline? Can a Christian life even be understood without the Word, no matter how well it pleases the contemporaries? Can the source of true discipleship be discovered without the Word?

Certainly not! The ancient ones had **this kind** of insight into the relationship between Word and example that St. Jerome, *ad Oceanum* Ep. 33 can write: "One's conversation should be innocent and without a sermon. As much good as one does by example, one does harm through silence."[7] This word sounds almost exaggerated, but in any case it comes from the correct conviction and experience that Word and doctrine are to be estimated much higher than the mere example. The former can work without the latter, but the latter cannot work without the power of the former, at least not for anything that is good. An evil example will powerfully promote evil, because it finds a soft and strong soil in the corruption of the human heart. Insight and

[6] *Vita clerici Evangelium populi.*

[7] *Innocens et absque sermone conversatio, quantum exemplo prodest, tantum silentio nocet.*

experience of Christian teachers should agree with all this, and thus the principle is established that even an example in the proper sense cannot be called a **means for the office** of the pastor. May many holy examples flourish in the Christian Church, but without arrogance, modestly, without the hope and claim that they have the same kind of effect that can only come from Word and Sacrament.[8]

"**Your Word is the right doctrine,**" the holy singer prays (Psalm 93:5 Luther). And what pastor should not rejoice, having this right teaching, and finding in it a powerful means for his office? Being happy because of this possession, we still want to go a little farther, looking at what the holy singer says here. "God's Word is the right doctrine." This verse from the psalm, on the one hand puts God's Word on the same level with other teachings; but it also lifts it above all others by saying: "It is the **right** teaching." Other teachings are not equal to it, not according to content (nobody denies this!), yet neither according to **power**, with which it turns the hearts of men. True, the Word of the Lord also appeals to the natural powers of man, to his natural ability of knowing. It also takes for granted the powers of the natural will, which tries to accomplish what reason has recognized as being right. That means it enters a person in the same way as any other human thought. And through the power of its arguments it works a human conviction in the human heart, just like any human thought. Nevertheless it is no mere human thought and it works in more than a human way. Nor is it a mere human conviction, but it brings with it a power that can put down the resistance of natural reason, or un-reason, and it can bestow on the Word an emphasis that enables it to grant a conviction capable of overcoming any resistance or doubt. It is called **faith.**

Just think of the power of Absolution. This is what the Church means when it says that the Spirit is given through the Word and the Gospel, that the Word is the organ and carrier of the Holy Spirit. Holy Scripture means the same thing when it speaks of an enlightening of the Holy Spirit through

---

[8] [Loehe:] Just as the pastor has no other means besides the Word to influence the soul spiritually and walking in the truth, thus **there is nothing in the whole world besides the Word.** To be torn away from the Word and not to be a carrier does not bring any creature to salvation. Many hope for great blessings for changing minds, **such as a change of time or place, of life circumstances, or the use of natural things, the contemplation of nature, of other acquaintances, etc.** None of this is able to bring a true change of heart. In Isaiah 28:9 (Luther) we read: "**Only temptation teaches us to pay attention to the Word.**" But it only teaches one to pay attention to the Word that is already there, and points to the Word, because by itself it is too poor to bring the desired change in human hearts. Other means can change the old man into different forms. But only God's Word and His creative power is able to make a new man out of the old man. Therefore to experience the Word is the most desirable and highest experience, the most blessed for time and eternity, while all worldly and human experiences have no truly improving power, quite apart from the fact that they are unreliable. [Editor's note: Walther and Loehe agree here. See also William Dallmann, *My Life* (St. Louis: Concordia, 1945).]

the Word, of tasting the Word of God and its powers, Hebrews 6:4ff.; [also] when it says about the Word that it is sharper than any two-edged sword, piercing until it divides soul from spirit, joints from marrow, and that it is able to judge the thoughts and intentions of the heart, and before it no creature is hidden, but all are naked and laid bare before its eyes, Hebrews 4:12f. From this we learn that the Word of God and its effects are more than natural. They are **supernatural** and **incomprehensible**. We see that the Word is both human and divine: Human, because it speaks in human language to human understanding; divine, for it works with divine power a heavenly knowledge for eternal life.

What a means for the office is given to the pastor once he is entrusted with the Word of God! True, it has been said that the word that a pastor speaks during his pastoral acts is not God's word in the **proper sense.** The content may correspond to the divine Word, but the presentation, the formulation of this Word is human work; only the apostles spoke of God's mysteries in words that the Holy Spirit taught them. This may be true in a certain sense. But does God's Word stop being God's Word through a correct human understanding? It may put on human form, but does that mean that God's power is no longer with it? Just one time, attentively read the pastoral letters of Paul and convince yourself about what divine power and what divine blessings have been added to the humanly understood words.

We remind you of a compelling example from the fathers.[9] The sunlight falls into a mirror, and it throws it back. Is true sunlight only **what** shines into the mirror, or is it also what is reflected from the mirror? Apparently, it is also what is reflected from the mirror. If this is true, it is also correct that the word that comes from the mouth of the preacher, as long as it is faithful to the word of Scripture from which he drew it, is basically nothing but one and the same Word of God, of which Scripture says that it shines brightly into our hearts, so that through us others may be enlightened as well. It is the will of God that his holy Word, in the hearts of his servants, would take on the form and shape of his servants, so that it would be preached out of faith, and in divine-human power create a faith that is also divine and human. It goes from faith into faith: The Word is preached in a living way and also creates life. Therefore the holy apostle reminds not only the apostles when he exhorts: "Remember your teachers who have spoken the Word of God to you" (Hebrews 13:7). Not only apostles, but also other preachers faithful to

[9] [Loehe:] See volume 2 of Löscher's *Vollständiger Timotheus Verinus* [2 parts, Wittenberg, 1718–22], I, p. 276. [Editor's note: Valentin Ernst Löscher (1673–1749) studied at Wittenberg while his father Caspar was professor. He studied church history in Jena, lectured at Wittenberg, and then later became pastor of the *Kreuzkirche* in Dresden. He opposed the Prussian plan to use pietism to unite Lutherans and Reformed. He argued that pietism ultimately opposes salvation by grace alone in his *Complete Timotheus Verinus*. A translation exists by Northwestern Publishing House.]

the Word can be comforted in having that great means for the office that we just talked about.[10]

[10] [Loehe:] There can be no question; rather, it is a clear and obvious truth that, even a simple father, a simple mother, and a young child can speak and preach God's Word with rich blessing. Who would want to make the power of the divine Word dependent on the office, against the witness of the centuries and of daily experience? The divine power that unites itself with the eternal truth dwells in it and works from it, no matter who preaches it. Nevertheless it is true that the Lord has given His servants certain promises to conduct the Holy Office. A co-working grace (ἡ χάρις [τοῦ] θεοῦ ἡ σὺν ἐμοί; 1 Corinthians 15:10; 3:10; Galatians 2:9; Ephesians 3:2, 7–8) is ascribed not only to the apostles; a gift (χάρισμα; 1 Timothy 4:14; 2 Timothy 1:6) is ascribed not only to the evangelists. To a simple teacher, Apollos, Paul ascribes the διακονία πνεύματος no less than to himself; that should also mean the πνεῦμα, the Spirit, without which the office cannot be a blessing. He also calls out in 1 Corinthians 3:5ff.: "What then is Apollos? What is Paul? Servants through whom you came to believe, as the Lord assigned to each, etc." And in v. 9 he says of Apollos as well as of himself: "θεοῦ γάρ ἐσμεν συνεργοί, we are **God's co-workers.**" But if Apollos is a servant and co-worker of God, then God, his Lord, working through him, is also his co-worker. Apollos and all like him, all the teachers of the Gospel, therefore are not alone when they execute the office, but the grace and the Spirit of the Lord, who promised all His servants special assistance, is with them when he said: "Lo, I am with you all the days to the end of the world!" Thus it is right to ascribe to all of them the office of the Spirit, and therefore one can say about all of them with Wilhelm Lyser [fl. Wittenberg, 1643]: "The call constitutes the ministry, so that a power that is above humanity is given to humans through it, and in this agreeable arrangement being made, humans become God's co-workers—so that they are lifted by their calling to the lot of doing what is beyond human ability. The minister does not do this publicly only as a sign of the divine; rather, God in fact executes these works productively through His own divine organs, etc., so that the energy of the organs, because they have descended as the principal cause joined and working together therewith, they elevate [these works] to produces a common fulfillment, which is truly worked by God, etc., so that from it a productive divine effect is produced." [*Vocatio ministerium constituit, ita ut hominibus per illam potestas super humana concedatur, et homines in grata dispensanda cooperarii Dei reddantur—ita ut ultra humanam sortem operatione Dei per ipsam vocationem eleventur.—Minister non tantum significative divinum quod indicat, sed Deus revera effective per illa ipsa organa divina opera perficit, etc., ita ut ἐνέργεια organi propter accedentem causae principalis confunctissimam cooperationem et elevationem concurrat ad commune ἀποτέλεσμα producendum, quod vero divines effectus est, etc., ut ab ipsis effective divinus effectus producatur.*] See vol. 2 of Löscher's *Vollständiger Timotheus Verinus* I, p. 290. If one does not deny that the Lutheran pastor possesses the divine Word as the noblest means for the performance of his office, one must admit that he has to enjoy special divine promises with the precious use of this Word. These promises, quite apart from the status of grace of the teacher, have to be ascribed to his performing his office as long as he does not distance himself from the Word of God. In the opposite case God's office would depend on human behavior, the divine from the human. Even though at times the trouble of a preacher may not be greater than that of a printer, who can print the entire Bible faultlessly, without making a blessed use of it for himself, nevertheless the trouble and diligence in this matter is not the salient point (*punctum saliens*; *der springende Punkt*) but the conducting of the office while being faithful to the Word. Besides this, experience offers enough examples [demonstrating] that apparently beyond question, the Lord did grant a blessed effect to the pure teaching even of immoral teachers. Let us not attack what is beyond question. Let us rather rejoice that it

B. THE GIFT OF TEACHING

Whoever wants to possess such a beautiful office and such powerful means for the office as God's Word and the Sacraments should also have the **capability** and the **gift** to use the office and its means. No one should receive the office without these. Therefore in 1 Timothy 3:1, St. Paul also demands of all bishops that they should be διδακτικοί, or able to teach. Word or teaching is a means for the office; **ability to teach** thus is a necessary gift for the office. Accordingly the holy apostle reminds Timothy in 2 Timothy 2:2 that he should pass on the teaching office only to those who are **capable** of teaching others. Yes, according to Titus 1:9–11 the elders of bishops should have the power **to exhort** through sound doctrine, **to refute** those who contradict it, and **to silence** the rebellious people, idle talkers, and deceivers.

However, one should not count the ability to teach among the special spiritual gifts that depend on the imparting of the Holy Spirit. It is a natural gift, without which no one should be considered for the pastoral office, just as no one should be admitted to any other secular profession without the necessary gifts and qualities. But to count the gift of teaching among the other natural gifts does not dishonor it. The gifts of the Creator are gifts of God, just like those of the Redeemer and the Holy Spirit. Yes, the natural gifts and capabilities often are not only purified, uplifted, and strengthened through the Holy Spirit, but also become bearers and organs of the proper spiritual gifts. Thus in 1 Corinthians 12:8ff., the gift to speak about wisdom is listed among the proper spiritual gifts, also the other gift, to speak about knowledge. As wisdom and knowledge that are mentioned here cannot be called natural gifts—and certainly [they] do belong into the area of the third article—the gift to talk about this wisdom and knowledge is not a natural gift either. But it is just as certain that it is a special effect and a gift of the Spirit of Jesus to be able to talk about the wisdom and knowledge of the New Testament. Who would not be able to see that proper spiritual gifts are attached here to natural spiritual gifts? They somehow are related as the crown of the king to the king himself. What is the crown without the king? One could also say: What is the spiritual gift without the corresponding natural mental gift, which is taken for granted by the former? All this is said only in order to lift up and praise the natural gift of the ability to teach, without which the great means for the office of the divine Word cannot be used or become effective and a blessing.

However, this ability to teach is not the same as **eloquence**, the ability to speak. One often gets these mixed up among us Protestants. As desirable as the gift of eloquence and the related gift of teaching may be, we think never-

---

is so. The means of the office have to appear even higher and more glorious and awaken even greater trust, the less they depend on humans, and the more, on the other hand, the human depends on the Word.

theless that one could possess the gift of teaching to a high degree while there may be a lack of a rhetorical gift. A servant of Jesus could have the greatest influence in a congregation because of his ability to teach, without ever making his fortune as a speaker. By holding on to this difference and the certainty (1 Corinthians 12:31) that even among God's mental and spiritual gifts there are differences, that some are greater, some less, some more excellent, and some less important, then one might well elevate the gift of teaching over eloquence, care for it, and cultivate it, just as any gift can be elevated and strengthened through care, but becomes smaller and less significant through neglect.

Of course there is also a **limit** to spiritual and mental gifts that cannot be passed, even through care and education. No one can pass beyond the limits that are given by the Lord. This realization brings us to the following conclusions, based on experience: Why do we have such manifold instructions concerning spiritual gifts in the sacred Scriptures, if not for the reason that we apply this instruction to ourselves? As surely as the Lord, the Holy Spirit lives, He surely lives in his Church; and as surely as the Church exists, it surely still has the gifts of the Holy Spirit, truly spiritual gifts. Of course we have no eyes to see them, and we do not search for them. However, even though they are less than formerly, according to the measure of our guilt, they would cause our eyes to shine with joyful brightness, if only we would open our eyes and **search** for the gifts. But who among us knows anything about his spiritual gift, or at least something certain and sure about it?

Surely it is the same with the easier recognizable natural mental gift. How many know what gifts they have in a very general way? Every choice of a profession depends on a gift. But because one does not recognize the gift, the choice of a profession often turns out bad. If a profession has been chosen, the discovery that the necessary gift does not exist is so depressing, as one might imagine, that one avoids it as much as possible and puts the blame for failing in the profession rather on other causes than on the true one, the lack of talent. A pastor who has no gift of teaching will be **the last one** to admit this. Friends and relatives, especially his wife, talk him out of it. Experience shows that a congregation is convinced that its pastor has no gift for teaching, while he himself and his own do not know it, nor want to know it. To recognize one's sins is easier than to recognize one's gifts, the humility of a poor sinner is a much smaller, much easier virtue than the humility that surrenders itself to the fact that one does not have the necessary gift, or only a small measure of it. How hard it is for a person to recognize the lack of his gift or talent! And yet the right knowledge of self could often be the beginning, [causing one to] bud and drive toward an improvement. But this also is often neglected, the last hope for improvement and greater success in the conducting of the office is taken away by the fact that one shies away from knowledge of self, does not like the ways of humility that lead to what one could become, to what is **possible.** [One does not] avoid harm that comes from the vain exaggeration and affectation of gifts and their measure that simply are not there. It is hard to imagine a more unfortunate person than one who is supposed to teach, but is unable to do so. There is no greater and more painful poverty than this, and indeed it does not get better if one imagines, as many pastors do, that one is not that poor, but rich. It will be hard to cling to this imagination once one is old and the congregation will more and more get tired of the poor speaker. At that time, a dying has to happen, which one could have been spared if one had chosen a more appropriate profession.

C. Different Forms of Teaching

If one takes the word teaching literally, it means nothing but the communication of knowledge, in the sense that is discussed here, the introduction to the knowledge of salvation. Any kind and form of communication for this purpose becomes teaching. Whether this purpose is achieved through a continuing and connected lecture, or in the form of a discussion, basically does not matter. Therefore one really cannot say that a continuing lecture belongs to the area of a homily,[11] while the form of a dialogue belongs to the area of catechizing. The catechesis of St. Cyril of Jerusalem, which from of old were held in high honor by the Church, are continuing lectures, while the homilies of Spangenberg, still much beloved by our people, preach in the form of question and answer. This widespread usage is similar to that of the *Book of Instruction by Goffiné* in the Roman Catholic Church, which nevertheless does not belong to the area of catechesis in any way.[12]

Not the form, but the content and intention divide the human lectures between the areas of catechizing and homiletics. If only knowledge is communicated, and there is no other intention than this, the lecture on **doctrine** serves this end in a specific sense. But there are also other intentions of divine and human speech, e.g., that of instruction, which is expressed clearly in 2 Timothy 3:16[–17, ESV], where we read: "All Scripture is breathed out by

---

[11] Loehe intentionally uses *Homilie*, from Greek ὁμιλία, Latin *homilia* or *tractatus*, a commentary on a Scripture passage, instead of *sermo*, German *Predigt*.

[12] Cyril of Jerusalem (c. 313–86) was a prominent theologian, bishop, and Doctor of the Church. At the First Council of Constantinople (381) he voted for the term *homoousious* (of one nature) regarding the divinity of Christ. He stressed a loving, forgiving God and was famous for his catechetical lectures. Cyriacus Spangenberg (1528–1604) was a prominent theologian and historian, a student of Luther who later sided with the error of Matthias Flacius, holding that some faculties of the human nature itself were corrupted by sin. Leonhard Goffiné (1648–1719) was a Premonstrant monk in Steinfeld/Eifel who in 1687 wrote his *Unterrichtungsbuch*, a compact postil collection that went through many printings and editions, e.g., *Goffine's Devout Instructions on the Epistles and Gospels for the Sundays and Holydays: with the Lives of Many Saints of God, Explanations of Christian Faith and Duty and of Church Ceremonies, a Method of Hearing Mass, Morning and Evening Prayers, and a Description of the Holy Land* (New York: Benziger, 1896).

God and profitable for teaching, for **reproof**, for **correction**, and for **training in righteousness**, that the man of God may be complete, equipped for every good work." Like divinely-inspired Scripture, human speech or writing of the servants of God serves not simply one purpose, that of instruction, but many, as is presented so perfectly in 2 Timothy 3:16. This has been acknowledged by the Church and divided in four parts. As soon as a lecture does not exclusively want to teach, but attempts to apply the benevolent powers of the divine Word in their multiplicity to the hearts of the hearers, as has always been the case with the lectures of the ancients and the modern teachers of the Church, it no longer is catechetical, i.e., instructive in a narrow sense. It serves the entire purpose of a Christian congregation and becomes homiletic. But with all this, one cannot deny that the dialogue, or conversational talk, is especially fitting for catechizing and the introduction into the teaching and knowledge of salvation. One must not think only of mere questioning and memorizing of answers, but of the living exchange between teacher and students, both sides questioning and answering, as Christ did among the teachers in the temple.

This is the most perfect way of reaching the goal of knowledge. No academic lecture can take care of all the hindrances or needs of the students. What that kind of lecture does not achieve can be accomplished by the honest question of the inquisitive student and the answer of the teacher through a detailed catechetical discussion. In the end, this may be the most desired form of instruction of doctrine, both for teacher and students, and serving as a pattern.

Like the dialogue form [is best] in the area of catechizing, therefore the continuing lecture in the midst of an instructed and believing congregation is the most natural, and recommending itself. The various needs of the congregation are expressed in the words reproof, correction, and discipline. Certainly they are best covered in a public gathering by the continuous speech of the bishop or pastor. Therefore one might well say: The servant of Christ who is able to teach will accomplish his purpose as well through a continuing lecture as in the form of a dialogue. If he wants to teach the congregation, or any larger group, the continuing lecture will be preferred. But in the case of teaching individuals or hard learners, the conversational form will rule. And since we seldom are in other circumstances, it is understandable why in catechetic instruction we usually take a conversational form, have a catechesis based on conversation, or speak of question and answer, a term that might not be better, but certainly represents what really goes on. True, questions and answers do not make a discussion, but they are what remains when the majority of our catecheses do not reach the level of a refreshing conversation.

At the time of the Reformers the level of knowledge had sunk so low among our people that, first of all, one had to promote **pure doctrine.** Ability to teach became not just the first, but the only requirement, almost a virtue of a teacher. All singing and speaking—truly singing also had to be used in the service of teaching, of pure doctrine. It could not be otherwise. The **liturgy** also had to become not simply something that contains doctrine; to a certain extent every mental (*geistig*) product of the Church has to accomplish this. But the spreading of pure doctrine also was assigned to [the liturgy] as its proper purpose. Of course the liturgies of the ancient and the modern Church have to be counted as sources of knowledge for those who are eager to learn the differences of church doctrines with the various Church parties. One also cannot deny that in general, young people gain rich treasures of knowledge from the liturgy that they grow up with. But is this a reason to say that liturgy is nothing but a teaching tool of the Church, or a means of an introduction into Church doctrine, or a special form of saving doctrine? Certainly not!

The congregation does not worship God just so that the ignorant would get to know God from their worship. When the congregation lifts its hearts to God, worship is not merely one of its intentions; it is quite simply **its intention.** Whoever calls on God in order to teach the ignorant how to call on God, should take care not to fall into the company of the hypocrites, who call on God in order to be seen and heard. The ignorant and the children who take part in the churchly life of the congregation certainly will learn much, but in an unintentional manner, just like one learns from everything in life. But it is a different thing if one asks whether liturgy can also teach, among other things, or if one asks whether the intention of the Church is to teach with the liturgy, if liturgy is a form of instruction. One does not live with the purpose of giving an example, even though one cannot deny that all life must become an example by necessity. In the same way, liturgy is never conducted in order to teach, no matter how much illumination and instruction may come forth from the liturgy.

The intention of the liturgy either is to act with the congregation in the name of God, or it is to act with God in the name of the congregation. Insofar as doctrine is an action between God or His representatives on the one hand and humans on the other, of course it can have a place in the liturgical life, and does have it. But doctrine is neither the only, nor even the noblest action of God and His representatives among humans—quite apart from the fact that the entire sacrificial part of the liturgy, according to its nature, can have nothing to do with teaching. Therefore, as certainly as we are going to deal in the following with the introduction of teaching and the gift of teaching into the activity of the office, it is also certain that this has nothing to do with liturgy, but with homiletics and catechesis.

D. Formal Preparation for the Office of Teacher

We have touched on doctrine, the gift of teaching, and the form of teaching. But we must not forget that there are also **preparatory studies** for the office of teaching and of the Word. Of course there are many great bearers of the office who have no recollection of these studies and have never gone through them. The great gift and the power of life have led him into the midst of the practice, without spending much money and without any harm. But for us ordinary people and our ordinary children, these **preparatory studies** that we now refer to are not to be despised, nor to be neglected.

When I was young, I had the good fortune to study in the Nuremberg Greek *Lyceum*, which followed the time in the *Gymnasium*. I learned logic, dialectics, and rhetoric; the letter in the sense and form of ancient times. I felt that **only this** gave value, clarity, and closing to the formal education I had received. Later the *Lycea* were discontinued; other graduates from the *Gymnasium* had to go to the university without this finishing school, where those formal studies were considered sort of useless for a formal education, according to the ways of the new time.

It seemed to me that the written products and the sermons of many candidates lacked nothing more than a formal education, no matter how many classical examples they had heard and read. As an adult and teacher (see below) I was so much happier to become acquainted almost by accident with Melanchthon's instruction books. My time at the *Lyceum* was revived. When later on I was no longer teaching, a man more able and more thorough for such things took my place, and he also liked those books no less than I. By that I mean the inspector of the mission school here, Mr. Friedrich Bauer.[13] Perhaps it will be given to him to make these noble writings accessible anew and enjoyable for our young students. In the meantime, may the following chapters of the first edition of this book serve to revive some desire and longing.

In these studies a young man of sincere diligence may find a faithful hand that may guide his gift into practice, so that it may become for him completeness, dexterity, art, and virtue. May this guidance soon become possible for the needs of our days, through the publishing of the writings of Melanchthon, and may it then be richly received and used!

E. DIALECTICS

All human thinking moves between concept and judgment. To define, divide, and conclude—compare and differentiate—wrong from right, that is what all who think and talk do all the time. They have to do it, even if they themselves were not even aware of it. This has been given by God the Lord as

[13] Markus Friedrich Wolfgang Bauer (1812–74) was a German theologian, teacher, missionary, and scholar in Germanic studies. He wrote *Grundzüge der neuhochdeutschen Grammatik für höhere Bildungsanstalten* [*Main Points of Modern High German Grammar for Secondary Schools*], which was continued by the notable scholar Konrad Duden (1829–1911), father of the Duden language resources. The mission school in Neuentettelsau (today: Mission EineWelt) trained men to send them to North America, benefitting the Missouri and Iowa Synods.

a dowry to all people of sound mind. But what [begins as] a gift in itself becomes skill, art, and virtue through education. This education gives to the willing student **dialectics** for the inner working of his reason. "Dialectics is an art, or the way to teach correctly, in order and clearly; to define correctly what happens, to divide, connect true arguments, and to untangle and refute what is badly connected or false" (Melanchthon).[14]

It is not everybody's thing to study the present-day philosophical textbooks, nor does it occur to this writer immediately to recommend the study of the same, especially since he hardly ever was able to occupy himself with them. In the end, most young pastors will be able to ascribe to themselves only very mediocre or small gifts for the philosophical sciences. Claudius thinks that to study the same, leads many astray, away from the desired goal, or at least deprives them of much time and strength without enabling them more for a profession or even for the Holy Office.[15] They remain stuck in hardship, without any reward for their trouble. On the other hand, some simple textbooks of formal sciences still exist from former days, [which are] less subject to philosophical systems. Even a mediocre brain with small gifts can easily understand them, and use them to great advantage for the training of the existing natural gift. The textbooks of Melanchthon [that were] mentioned above belong here. Indeed, they make it possible to understand how he came by that high honorary title of Teacher of Germany, *Praeceptor Germaniae.* Of special [value] from him we have a Latin writing, titled *Dialectic Questions Containing the Complete Art, Written So That They Can Be Stated Usefully to the Young.*[16] Besides a noble simplicity, one finds in this book a wonderful combination of classical and theological scholarship. Christ rules in this dialectics, even though he does not sit on the professional chair and Master Philip does not directly mention him. Also, the choice of examples is especially beautiful and fitting and the language of the good teacher makes learning easy, even for the one who has little skill reading Latin books. The author of these pages got to know the above-mentioned writing in a close manner only when teaching missionary students who had not received a *Gymnasium* education. Missionary students of this kind do need a formal education, even though the purpose for which they learn, their average age, and the schooling that they had do not make it possible or advisable to let them repeat *Gymnasium* studies. Therefore I found Melanchthon's

---

[14] *Est enim dialectica ars sive via recte, ordine et perspicue docendi, quod fit recte definiendo, dividend, argument vera connectendo et male cohaerentia sive falsa retexendo et refutando.* Robert Preus mentions this in *The Theology of Post-Reformation Lutheranism Volume I* (St. Louis: Concordia, 1970), 77–82.

[15] The reference is vague, but Loehe may refer to Friedrich Matthias Jacobus Claudius (1789–1862), a German jurist.

[16] *Erotemata dialectica continentia integram artem, ita scripta, ut juventuti utiliter proponi possint*; [Loehe:] e.g., [printed] at Wittenberg in 1581.

Erotemata very apt to fill the urgent need. At times it seemed to me that a diligent and thorough study of it would somehow provide **more** of a formal education than the study of the classics in the schools **without** the accompanying study of dialectics. Therefore one should dare to recommend the study of the above book to young pastors who become aware of their lack of education, and feel deeply that they lack the skill to teach in a proper, orderly, and clearly manner: *recte, ordine et perspicue docendi.* Whoever follows this advice, and **afterwards** blames the advisor, let him be in the right. But to this hour the advisor fears so little that he dares even more, namely to advise those already in the office to study the *Erotemata*, or something of a similar nature. He promises them that after studying this, they will feel the sinews of their gift steeled and the skill to use the gift increased and strengthened.

F. RHETORIC

If dialectics teaches how to speak **correctly**, it is the job of rhetoric to speak and to teach **purposefully**. This alone gives us an idea of how necessary and useful it is to study rhetoric for the one who wants to further his gift of teaching. If dialectics is a preparation for any kind of teaching, rhetoric prepares especially for the kind of teaching and speaking that is the subject of homiletics. In all His revelations, the Holy Spirit uses a language that, just as the language of human reason, corresponds to the natural laws of thinking, meaning the rules of didactics. The pronouncements of the holy prophets and apostles are no less formed in such a way that they do not contradict the common rules of rhetoric. Though the form of the holy speakers of God is very **different** from that of mere human speakers, yet this specific difference becomes most clear to the one who can compare the products of the heavenly gift of speech with the rules of the mere human art of speaking finding what is common to both.

The Holy Spirit sanctifies and transfigures the natural gifts, but He does not eliminate them. His work in the New Testament is a new birth, not a new creation. Thus He also takes human speech as it is; He does not eliminate its laws that He **Himself** created, but teaches to use them unblemished and worthy of the heavenly light. Therefore no one should feel ashamed to study the rhetoric of the ancients, especially if it is presented in such sacred meaning and with such gift of teaching, as the *Praeceptor Germaniae* Philip Melanchthon does it.[17] See his writing: *Two books of elementary rhetoric, recently rec-*

[17] [Loehe:] It is obvious that not everything found in Melanchthon can just be accepted. His books also are human. For example, who simply would copy his definitions? (See *On Definition of Many Terms in Use in the Church, Given by Philip Melanchthon*, Torgau and Wittenberg 1552 and 1553 [*Definitionem multarum appelationum quarum in ecclesia usus est, traditae a Philippo Melanth. Torgae et Witebergae. Anno 1552 et 1553*].) The same happens here as with the casuistry of the post-reformation teachers. How much one can recommend

ognized as being authored by Philip Melanchthon. With them the opposite Epistles of Picus and Hermolai Barbarus are rejected, together with a disposition of Philip Melanchthon. There is added a very rich index of things and words. With royal authorization. Wittenberg. Printed by Clemens Schleich 1582.[18]

G. THE SPEECHES OF THE ANCIENTS

The ancients, namely the Greeks and the Romans, did not give speeches for the purpose of religious instruction. Better: Their rhetoric does not give us any insight into the religious instruction in use among them. But they did speak before the assembly of the people and before judges. Their speeches were speeches of the state, speeches in court, probably also speeches to praise heroes, statesmen, etc. Therefore with them rhetoric has three categories of motives: demonstrative, deliberative, and judicial.[19] Melanchthon adds a teaching category, *genus didascalicum*, more because it suited **his** purpose than because he found it represented among the ancients.[20] Though many

---

this casuistry! But should one really rely on all the old casuistic decisions? Only the ignorant would say *yes* to that.

[18] *Elementorum Rhetorices libri duo, recens recogniti ab auctore Philippo Melanthone. His abjectae sunt Epistolae contrariae Pici et Hermolai Barbari, una cum disposition Philip. Melanth. Accessit demum Index et rerum et verborum locupletissimus. Cum gratia et privilegio. Witebergae. Clemens Schleich excudebat. 1582.*

[19] *tria genera causarum: demonstrativum, deliberativum, judiciale.*

[20] [Loehe:] "In general they count three kinds of motives: The demonstrative, which includes praise and reprimand; the deliberative, which moves between persuading and dissuading; and the judicial, which treats controversial forensic matters. I believe there should be added a διδασκαλικόν (a teaching matter). Even though it belongs to dialecticσ, where business matters are treated, it should not be overlooked, especially since at this time it has the greatest use in the churches, where one can have not only persuasive sermons, but much more often people have to be taught in a dialectic way about religious dogmas, so that they are able to know them perfectly" (p. 15f.). "The demonstrative contains praise and reprimand, but there is a big difference whether [it applies] to persons, facts, or things. If we praise a person, we tell the history; and in speaking we follow the sequence of things. Thus personal subjects are: The fatherland, sex, birthdays, genius, education, discipline, doctrine, accomplishments, rewards for accomplishments, and end of life. [Then there is the] opinion [about the deceased] after death" (p. 61). "Whether we are praising a fact or a certain thing: We change to topics from the deliberative category: honest, useful, easy, etc. . . ." (p. 63. 17. p. 57). "The deliberative moves between persuasion and dissuasion, admonition and negation, asking and pleading, consoling and similar tasks, where the end is not knowledge, but some action beyond knowledge" (p. 56). For the judicial, p. 28f., see footnote to section H below.

["*Vulgo tria numerant genera causarum: Demonstrativum, quo continetur laus et vituperatio. Deliberativum, quod versatur in suadendo et dissuadendo. Judiciale, quod tractat controversias forensesis Ego addendum censeo διδασκαλικόν genus, quod, etsi ad Dialecticam pertinent, tamen, ubi negotiorum genera censentur, non est praetermittendum, praesertim cum hoc tempore vel maximum usum in ecclesiis habeat, ubi non tantum suasoriae*

things will remain strange for us, especially when we read the rhetorical instructions of the ancients for our purpose, nevertheless there is still much we can gather for us. Not only the categories of motives will **remain,** changed for Christian usage, but also the **partitioning of the speech.** Let us think of a Christian speech—for the time being we do not talk of the sermon or homily, but of a proper speech: What parts does one have to assign to it? We will have to stick with the introduction, refutation, and summary (*exordium, confutatio, peroratio*); there are no other parts for a speech—and everything one can learn in Melanchthon chapter 1, from page 32 on, about the individual parts of a speech will **also be fruitful of the spiritual speech.**[21] As we soon will see, the sermon of the later Christian era until today did follow the speech of the ancients and their tradition closely; indeed had to follow. This again is another proof that it is good and necessary to study rhetoric before advancing to homiletics and not the reverse. Whoever knows Melanchthon's dialectics and rhetoric and is acquainted with their content will come well prepared to homiletics. And whoever compares examples of ancient speeches with what he has learned, which speeches Melanchthon in part brings extensively as an appendix to his *Rhetoric*, in part cited, will come to the specialized study of Christian speech with a rich measure of fruitful preparation.

---

conciniones habendae sunt, sed multo saepius homines dialecticorum more de dogmatibus religionis docendi sunt, ut ea perfecto cognoscere possint." P. 15f.—"Demonstrativum genus continet laudationem et vituperationem, sed multum interest, utrum personae, an facta, aut res. Cum laudamus personam, ordine narramus historiam et rerum seriem in dicendo sequimur. Sunt igitur loci personarum: Patria, Sexus, Natales, Ingenium, Educatio, Disciplina Doctrina, Res gestae, Praemia rerum gestarum, vitae Exitus. Opinio post mortem." P. 61.—"Cum factum aut remcertam laudamus, Locos mutuamus ex genere deliberative: honestum, utile, facile, etc. . . ." p. 63. 17. P. 57.—"*Deliberativum versatur in suadendo et dissuadendo, adhortando et dehortando, petendo et precando, consolando et similibus negociis, ubi finis est non cognition, sed praeter cognitionem action aliqua.*" P. 56.—*Judiciale, p. 28f. Siehe Anmerkung zu §8, S. 194.*]

[21] [Loehe:] Three things should be achieved in the beginning: We must make the listeners benevolent, attentive, and responsive to teaching (p. 32). Narration is an exposition of the fact, which is submitted right at the beginning. A proposition that sums up the matter must follow. The proposition must never be omitted (p. 351). Confirmation is the most difficult part of the work of the orator, for he must persuade this to be judged so that it agrees with the proposition (p. 38). Peroration is the conclusion of the speech, in which the principal proposition is repeated. For in part it establishes through repetition the proposition and the strongest of the arguments, in part through affectation (p. 40). [*Tria in exordio efficienda sunt, ut reddamus auditors benevolos, attentos et dociles. P. 32. Narratio est facti expositio, quae statim exordio subiicitur. Hanc sequi debet propositio, quae contineat summam rei. Propositio nunquam omitti potest. P. 351—Confirmatio difficillima pars est oratorii operis, haec enim persuadere iudici debet, ut propositioni assentiatur. P. 35.—Confutatio est dissolutio argumentorum, quae obliciuntur. P. 38.—Peroratio est conclusio orationis in qua repetitur proposition principalis. Partim enim repetition constat propositionis et potissimorum argumentorum, partim affectibus. P. 40.*]

H. THE FIRST WAY OF PREACHING

Under the proof and the power of the Spirit, the holy apostles **preached**, i.e., proclaimed to the world the **great fact of redemption** through our Lord Jesus Christ. For this they were sent by the Lord. Therefore even the first sermon that they would preach anywhere had to begin with the life or the **history** of Jesus Christ or the kingdom of God. Therefore Gospel and history had the closest relationship and were almost identical, as can be seen already in the presentation of the four evangelists. Whoever wants to classify under a *genus causarum* the apostolic sermon—or one of the four Gospels—would without doubt count them under a *genus demonstrativum.* And if one would now check pp. 61–65 in Melanchthon's *Rhetoric* and consider it, one would soon recognize how simply such apostolic preaching and the Gospel are ordered according to the rules mentioned there. It is not that the holy writers and speakers had rules before their eyes, but that, if one presents a **biography**, a **history** and great **facts,** one cannot proceed differently from what these rules prescribe. For these rules are not arbitrary, but taken from nature and experience. Even the untrained speaker will follow them without being conscious of it.

But as much as the Gospels and the first sermons have to be in the *genus demonstrativum,* it is also obvious that even the apostles could be forced to turn to another *genus*, be it the *deliberativum* or the *judiciale.* One should, e.g., examine the first Pentecost sermon of Peter, the speech of St. Stephen, the one of Paul in Athens, etc. As soon as this happens, one will also find the same principles that one can read in Melanchthon, p. 26ff.[22] about the *judiciale*, or p. 56ff. about the *deliberativum,* of course without any artificial method or manner, as was proper for the apostles and the living conditions from the soil of which the apostolic speeches had been sprouted.

Whoever is willing may study **the holy rhetoric and dialectics of the great apostles and their speeches, and compare them with what he learned from Melanchthon.** He will find the ancient speech transfigured. But what the Spirit infused in it appears so much more indestructible and worthy of honor, if it walks along in the brightness of the noblest usefulness for the Church of God.

---

[22] [Loehe:] Ecclesiastical disputations often have a certain similarity with forensic battles. For they interpret laws, dissolve what is against the law (or lawlessness), namely sentences that seem to struggle against outward appearances; they explain ambiguities; sometimes they dispute about the law, sometimes about facts; they seek advice for facts. Therefore this kind has great use in our customs (p. 26). [*Disputationes ecclesiasticae magis ex parte similitudinem quandam habent forensium certaminum. Interpretantur enim leges, dissolvunt αντινομιας, videlicet sententias, quae in speciem pugnare videntur; explicant ambigua; interdum de iure, interdum de facto disputant; quaerunt factorum consilia. Ideo hoc genus in his nostris moribus etiam magnum habet usum. P. 26.*]

I. SERMON AND TEXT

The sermon or proclamation of the Gospel by nature is **without a text**. What does the heathen care about the text of a book that he does not know or value? Otherwise he would not be a heathen. To him the sermon comes without any previous revelations. It hits him with its innate power, which cannot deny itself, even where the Word comes simply, without proof, in the form of a divine message and revelation, or as a prophetic, apostolic witness.

The missionary sermon to the **heathen** is **without a text**. The sermon to unbelieving **Jews** also does not need a text. Even though the great facts that are proclaimed to them are fulfillments of Old Testament prophecies, the holy apostles as a rule do not take a text from the Old Testament,[23] but use the Old Testament texts only as proofs for their Gospel, since to the Jews also it came in the form and power of a divine revelation. Therefore the missionary sermon to Jews is also mostly without a text. Individual texts in general become the basis of a sermon only when the sermon itself is no longer a **calling**, no longer **basic**, but when it is a matter to lead the already existing congregation deeper into the healing and sanctifying water of divine speech, accepted in faith. Yes, the Christian speech itself can be imagined without text because, being directed toward an already existing congregation, it no longer is a proper sermon, but has taken on more the nature of exegesis, or the form of the ancient speech. So there can be sermons with or without a text, and the latter not only with missionaries, but also within a congregation; e.g., the fifty homilies of Macarius, which contain admonitions to the ascetics.[24]

J. THE HOMILY

The **homily** differs from the sermons of the apostles and missionaries. It closely follows the pericope. From the beginning, the Church read selected texts from the Word of God in its assemblies, which were followed by a free speech of the bishop or presbyter. But the connection could be very different, and the need of the congregation quite naturally became a **key for the structuring** of the most manifold addresses. But as time went on and the free speech was juxtaposed more and more to the text, an emanation of the divine Word and a human parallel to divine thoughts emerged.[25] The purpose

---

[23] [Loehe:] But compare the speech of Jesus at Nazareth Luke 4:16ff.

[24] Macarius of Egypt (c. 300–91) was a celebrated Egyptian ascetic monk. The fifty *Spiritual Homilies* were ascribed to him relatively soon after his death, but modern scholars have put his authorship into doubt. These sermons influenced the Augustinian Spirituals, John Wesley, and the charismatic movement because they assert miraculous post-apostolic spiritual gifts.

[25] [Loehe:] See examples of this kind in *Doctor Haymon, Bishop of Halberstadt (d. 853), Homilies on the Lord's Gospels for the Whole Year and the Main Festivals, Recently Improved, with Many Errors Corrected. Antwerp, in the house of John Steelsus, 1559. Printed*

became the knowledge of the text, textual application, and according to this purpose it happened that the form of the ancient speech, whether the speaker knew it or not, became secondary to the development of the beginning. There was no longer an *exordium*, no *narratio, propositio*, etc. The text ruled, and the simple immersion into the Word of God was completely sufficient for the congregation living in the Word. That resulted in **homilies**, simple conversations about the Word, simple feeding with it.

Since we still read the divine Word in the congregation, just as in the beginning, and the explanation of the Word is the main business of every shepherd, now as then, we can also have homilies of the simplest kind, just as in the early days. In those the special needs of the congregation become completely **subordinated** to the text, and only once in a while they are satisfied and knowledge of the text becomes the main intention.

K. DEVELOPMENT OF THE HOMILY

Dr. Andreas Adam Hochstetter, formerly professor in Tübingen, issued a small homiletic in 1701 under the title *De recta concionandi textumque sacrum tum exponendi tum applicandi ratione commentariolus* [*Little Commentary on the Method for Rightly Preaching the Sacred Text, Its Explanation, and Application*]. This small, excellent writing[26] was forgotten, but pulled out again by others, and in 1767 it was issued for the third time by the Tübingen professor Christoph Friedrich Sartorius.[27] This little book is written in Latin, serving as an introduction to homiletics and emphasizing mainly the knowledge of the text. In section 4 it says: "The text of the sacred is recognized by its very nature through these five parts: One must first investigate

---

with Royal Permission. [*D. Haymonis, episcopi Halberstatensis (d. 853), Homiliae in evangelia dominicalia totius anni et de sanctis praecipuis, nunc recens excusae et a multis erroribus restitutae. Antverpiae, in aedibus Joannis Steelsii. Anno 1559. Cum privilegio.*] See, for example, the homily for Quinquagesima: "Haymo, Anglo-Saxon, blood-friend of Beda, best friend of Rhabanus Maurus from childhood, cell-mate in Fulda, abbot at Corvei and Hirsfeld, bishop of Halberstadt for 13 years." [Editor's note: Haymo also studied under Alcuin of York at the Monastery of St. Martin at Tours and wrote a number of biblical commentaries. He was also chancellor of the Benedictine monastery in Fulda. Rabanus Maurus Magnentius (Rhabanus, c. 780–856) was archbishop of Mainz. He wrote numerous biblical commentaries and scholarly works, as well as the hymn *Veni Creator Spiritus*, often used at Pentecost. Alcuin of York (Ealhwine, c. 735–804) was the dominant scholar of the Carolingian Renaissance who taught many of the greatest minds of the time. Bede (the Venerable, Beda; 672/73–735) was a Northumbrian monk best known for his *Ecclesiastical History of the English People*. It is unclear what Haymo being the blood-friend of Beda means here, but it is probably someone else or a figurative expression.]

[26] [Loehe:] Given as an appendix to these pages for the benefit of those who would like to adopt the right kind of preaching.

[27] Christoph Friedrich Sartorius (1701–85) was professor in Tübingen from 1754 to his death. He served as both rector and chancellor of the university.

the **object,** then proceed to **genus and species,** inquire in the **arguments,** and finally make a judgment from these about the proper **theme.**"[28] Those indicated individual parts are treated in the following sections 5–18. Reading this, one may often think that the author talks not about the text, but about the sermon. **Each text** is treated completely as a whole, as a sermon having a head and members. Even though this understanding may not apply to all the texts, it is based on something completely correct. The Holy Spirit also has spoken according to the rules of grammar, dialectics, and rhetoric, which He created. The Church only selected pieces as lessons, which together form a round whole. Therefore one will comprehend these lessons most correctly by seeking the division, the connection, and the composition; by searching, like in a human speech, for theme, partition, confirmation, confutation, perhaps even for an exordium or a peroration, and then presenting it to the congregation as a **well-recognized outline** presented in an understandable manner. This will increase clarity and precision, synopsis and insight. Once the homilist has finished his work, the soul that hungers for the Word will be satisfied and happy. The total impression of the whole will be strengthened through the knowledge of the beautiful division, just like one loves and appreciates a picture so much more, once the artist has pointed out and explained the individual parts.

That also is a homily. The clearer and more precisely the homilist has understood his text, the simpler he will be able to present it, and this art therefore will serve beautifully the heavenly meaning of the whole. The more perfectly such a saintly exegete is in his service, the less he will fall into a self-denial that he did not look for. At the end it will seem as if he did not do anything, even though he accomplished much, and one has to thank him that the text in its brilliance, bright as the sun, is powerfully penetrating the soul.

Here an **application** can follow as a second part. In it, while keeping one's own disposition of the text, one can let the light of the divine Word shine on [local] conditions, so that it accomplishes teaching, improvement, punishment and discipline. Whoever understands this way has a great and holy gift, which can hardly be equaled by any other gift of a preacher.[29]

---

[28] *Textus sacri natura ipsa ex his quinque dignoscitur: Investigandum primum* ***objectum,*** *progrediendumque deinceps ad* ***genus et speciem,*** *inquirendum in* ***argumenta,*** *ipsumque denique* ***thema*** *ex istis judicandum,* p. 6.

[29] [Loehe:] In contrast to this instruction for preaching by Hochstetter, which permits art as well as simplicity, the whole mess of Protestant ways of preaching stands as a warning. Balduin counts seven methods; Rebhahn 25; Carpzov 100; Löscher reduces the number to 25; etc. There is a Jena method, a Helmstedt one, an artificial and bombastic Leipzig one with three introductions, one from the Netherlands, an English method, a French method, a *methodus Loescheriana Balduina,* even a *methodus dassica* (from starting the introduction with the word *dass*), etc. One could think that all the seriousness of the sermon had disappeared in the face of such small things, and yet it is not so. This much one can demand from the patient Spirit and His holy Word and office!

L. THE CHRISTIAN SPEECH

The homily in both its forms is the opposite of the **Christian speech,** the presentation without text that concerns sacred matters within the congregation. With the homily, the speaker has no thought of his own, no other intention than to serve his text, to put it as a light upon the bushel. Thus the word of [John] the Baptist fits the homilist: "Christ must increase; I must decrease."

It is completely different with the speech. The speaker is independent of the text. He may have accidentally started with a text, or was inspired by it. He chose a Christian topic on which he now wants to speak, whatever the occasion or the need may be. His topic is either a *quaestio simplex* or *quaestio conjuncta.* In the first case, he goes **from the topic into the parts by defining and dividing.** The old saying, "Who, what, where, by what means, why, how, and when,"[30] will rule the partition, and what Melanchthon says about the *genus didascalicum causarum,* pp. 20–25 will be completely applicable.[31] In the second case the ***conclusio* of any syllogism is going to become the main point**. Major and minor [premises] will rule in the *confutatio* as in the *confirmatio.* In the end, everything will return to the topic, and the topic will rule the entire Christian speech.

A Christian speaker will only deal with **Christian** topics. All his definitions, divisions, syllogisms, enthymemes,[32] etc. will agree with Holy Scripture. Word and Spirit of Scripture will penetrate the entire content of his speech, but the form will be the **pure form of the ancient speech.** Here it will appear in transfigured beauty as a holy handmaiden of her Lord Jesus Christ.

This holy handmaiden is not in the service of a text, but in the service of Word and truth itself. In the end she may well be a sister of equal rank to the homily. She is like the converted person of the Occident, the Greek or Roman who, while keeping his lifestyle, serves the one Christ of all believers. The homily is like the person of the Orient. He seems not to keep anything of his own; is not diligent to keep his individuality; is totally absorbed in contemplating the divine; and precisely in this, without knowing it, he appears in the most beautiful brightness of his individuality. There the human is transfigured into the divine: Here the divine the divine has descended to the human and has totally overcome it.

---

[30] *Quis, quid, ubi, quibus auxiliis, cur, quomodo, quando?*

[31] [Loehe:] It is a very easy method, if one sticks to a mediocre exercise. *Methodus perfacilis est, si quis mediocrem exercitationem adhibuerit, p. 20.*

[32] An enthymeme is an argument in which one premise is not explicitly stated.

M. Combination of Homily and Speech

As different as their forms may be, Homily and speech still have found a **way to be combined.** For if one considers the special form and organization of the sermon used most commonly by our Lutheran fathers, one finds that they completely agree with the form and organization of the ancient speech. Only in place of the ancient narrative account (***narratio***) there is the exposition or commentary (***enarratio***), that is the homily, that is the explanation and presentation of the text.

The organization remains one and the same, regardless if one changes the measure of the individual parts of the speech, lengthens the *enarratio* in comparison to the ancient *narratio,* shortens it, or sums it up. There is a preamble (*exordium*), which leads to exegesis (*enarratio*). From this there is a transition to the summary statement of the issue (*propositio*), which is executed in the form of argument for one's position (*confirmatio*) and refutation of contrary arguments (*confutatio*). There is a closing (*peroratio*), which often has a powerful affect. In fact, one cannot see what really would be missing from a speech in the old style. Also, the nature of the speech is not essentially changed through its close connection to a text and the *enarratio*.

As peculiar as this form of the more modern Christian sermon seems to be, nevertheless it is more thorough, based more on Scripture and truth than that other, newer form, in which a sermon really is nothing but a speech. One starts with a text that serves as a motto. From there one proceeds unperturbed, unless during the process here and there one remembers the text, or other passages that have not been mentioned before. It does not have to become clumsy through the homiletic-oratorical arrangement mentioned above, especially if the *enarratio* is the first principal part, and everything following, summed up briefly like a connecting part, appears like an application.

The homiletic way of preaching is also called the **analytical** way. The other, oratorical one is called the **synthetic** one. If the clearly recognized and presented disposition of the text rules in the sermon, so that it is arranged to a beautiful whole, a combined echo of the text, it is the **analytical-synthetic** way of preaching. But if the content of the text is presented under a special viewpoint, under a special topic and included in a self-made partition, it is called a **synthetic-analytical** way of preaching. Each one can occur according to time and circumstances. Once this one, then the other may merit a preference. Where there is a **continuous reading and explaining of Holy Scripture,** as in the so-called Bible studies, where the reading has been recognized as the main task and the service of the homilist is necessary only to assist the weakness of the listeners, the simplest kind of homiletic scriptural explanation, the explanation of Scripture for its own sake, will be the appropriate thing to do. With the lessons of the main service,[33] the **homily of the second kind,** the analytical-synthetic, or also the synthetic-analytical will be the most appropriate. The synthetic way becomes compulsory for sermons at special occasions, such as baptisms, weddings, funerals and others.[34] But the speech without any text will always retain glory and honor at such occasions.

N. CHOICE IN THE MANNER OF PREACHING

As already mentioned, the choice of how to preach depends on the circumstances, but in part also on **talent**. But if someone is gifted in every way, wants to be trained for everything, or wants to make some trials to explore his gifts, one might perhaps give him the following advice for his sermons on Sundays and holidays.

For the first year of your preaching, stick to the homiletic style. Put down a foundation of your speaking in the office for yourself and your listeners by sticking to the text and explaining all its details. Strive for **distinctness**. During the first year you do not the congregation yet, nor do they know you. Therefore it is natural and good if you look less at the congregation and more at the text, as if the congregation would hear it for the first time, as if its content was something new.

During the second year, use diligence to make the text not only distinct, but also **clear**. Treat it as a well-composed whole. Point out its parts, yet in their connection, its main thought, and how it lives in all its parts. Doing this, you make the congregation own the text, under the impression given by the form, the summation as a whole, and the subordination of all details under the main thought. Thus your sermon, even if it did not have a special application, by itself it becomes practical and acceptable.

During the third year, put your texts under special **viewpoints**. Show the whole and its parts from the dogmatic and the ethical side, or use teaching, proving, correcting, and educating,[35] depending on the kind of text and its content. You can always pay attention to the whole and its parts, and there will also be the opportunity to use your knowledge of the congregation that you have gained by now, and to put it into effect.

After this course of the third year you will be able to take individual thoughts and topics from the text in as many courses as you desire according

---

[33] *Hauptgottesdienst*. In its most proper form it is a Divine Service with a celebration of the Eucharist. It is differentiated from matins, vespers, and the like.

[34] [Loehe:] In general, the synthetic way of preaching demands the least from the listening public. The Lutheran church orders that recommend it especially are correct, given the spiritual level of most of our congregations, including the present ones. A clearly-stated theme and the parts mentioned [above] support and make easy one's attention. The preacher also is forced by this kind of preaching to make things simple, clear and distinct. That still does not mean that the sermon always has to have three parts.

[35] διδασκαλία, ἔλεγχος, ἐπανόρθωσις, παιδεία.

to the needs of the congregation. You will never run out of ideas. The pastoral, truly practical preaching will come into its own. The preceding years will have been a good preparation for it. Finally, you will **return** to the beginning and be able to treat whole texts in a very practical way. You will also learn to preach analytical-synthetic sermons on a more exalted level. For this is certain, that no art is higher and more glorious than to be able to show in entire texts one's own condition like in a mirror, and in the light of a rich text point out the present in its true form and value.

O. STUDY OF SCRIPTURE

It is said that a sermon should be an *emanatio scripturae sacrae.* This indicates the relationship of the sermon to the text. But basically one also indicates with these words the right relationship of any speech to the divine Word, even the one without a text. "Whoever speaks, as one who speaks oracles of God," says Peter in his first epistle, chapter 4, verse 11.[36] How could it be otherwise? A preacher should speak in the name of God. Can he speak something in the name of God that is not God's Word? Does he not need the confidence that he can make the total claim to be viewed as a messenger of God, both for **what** he says and for the **divine mandate** to speak? If someone says what neither he nor the congregation can recognize as God's Word, he deserves no other name than that of a sacrilegious babbler for what is said without God's Word. Deyling is right when he applies to him the saying of St. Jerome: "chattering has no faith."[37]

But if this is the case, one cannot wish more for a preacher than that he may be a good *textualis*, to use an expression of the ancients.[38] But in order to become a good textualis, one has to do more than study one's sermon texts. That also, but the studying of a specific text has to be based on a daily, continuing study of the entire divine Word. Overview creates insight, and the individual passage can only be fully understood in its connection with the whole. Whoever wants to study individual texts without constantly striving

---

[36] *Loquntur eloquia Dei.*

[37] *Garrulitas non habet fidem.*

[38] [Loehe:] Doctrine should be sought from the very center of the biblical text. If this happens, the text is dealt with in order and is correctly explained. For the doctrines that flow out of the text are the best. Therefore the blessed Luther used to praise the textual theologians the most. For we can be certain that the Holy Spirit intended such doctrines that the text presents. Thus they affect us more sweetly, take hold of and corroborate the mind of the teacher, that he has not presented human figments, but the Word of God. Balduin's *Brevis institutio ministrorum verbi*, p. 148 s. 1622. [*Doctrina ex ipsis visceribus textus biblici petenda est, quod ut fiat, textus ordine disponatur et recte explicetur. Nam doctrinae, quae ex textu fluunt, sunt optimae, ideo beatus Lutherus* ***Theologos textuales*** *maxime laudare solebat. Nam de huiusmodi doctrinis, quas textus suppeditat, certi esse possumus, quod eas intenderit Spiritus Sanctus, ideo et suavius afficiunt, et facilius arripiunt animumque docentis corroborant, quod non figment hominum, sed Dei verbum protulerit.*]

for knowledge of the entire Holy Scripture will find it impossible to gain knowledge of individual texts and parts [of Scripture] out of the whole.

If this makes it certain that one must study Scripture and its content as a whole, first one must not recommend the **careful and slow** reading, but rather the **cursory** reading of Holy Scripture. For insight into the content and the connection of the entire Holy Scripture comes from the cursory reading of the divine Word. Of course, the cursory reading of Holy Scripture can also be started in the wrong way. Therefore one should avoid this mistake. Cursory reading has to begin with the study of **biblical history** and go together with what is called the **science of isagogics**. History of the kingdom of God, history of the people of God, history of the non-theocratic nations in the Old Testament, history of Jesus and His apostles, chronology, sacred geography, antiquity, history of the Bible and the biblical text, etc. create a capacity to understand the content of Holy Scripture. The introductions to individual books of Holy Scripture give more of a basis for the right progress in the knowledge of the individual parts of Holy Scripture than even the grammar.[39]

But then one should not reject the careful and slow reading of Holy Scripture. **Oversight helps very much toward insight. Yet insight also helps much toward oversight.** And did the Lord really want only the knowledge of the whole? Then why does His Holy Spirit put so many single verses and many a piece of Holy Scripture before our soul, which carries in itself the rounded nature of a whole in the whole (macrocosm—microcosm)?

The more one has recognized the great whole, the more his soul will rejoice when he accurately recognizes the individual part and becomes aware how completely the two fit together, how gloriously one fits in the other, how the great is mirrored in the small and the whole in its parts, and how therefore the whole is so very excellent and divine. Therefore the cursory reading and the studying that goes with it should be the soil from which grows a rich seed and harvest of a **careful and slow** reading.

Even those who have a better knowledge of the original languages will gain the fruit of cursory reading quicker from a translation, whether they use only Luther's translation or another one that might be of lesser linguistic and churchly value, but perhaps is more faithful to the text.[40] Even the careful and slow reading can be accomplished, to a certain extent with a faithful translation, so that even someone not familiar with the original languages can attain a deeper and more accurate awareness and knowledge of the divine Word from a faithful translation. If this were not so, it would not only be impossi-

---

[39] [Loehe:] Circumstances illumine what is said (*circumstantiae illuminant dicta*), Hilary of Poitiers. See Melanchthon's *Rhetoric*, p. 52f.

[40] [Loehe:] For example, the German Elberfeld translation: *Neue Uebersetzung des zweiten Teils der Heiligen Schrift, genannt Neues Testament. Aus dem Urtext uebersetzt von einigen Christen.* Elberfeld 1855. Zweite revidierte Auflage. Elberfeld und Barmen. In Kommission bei Langewiesche. [1864],—or the Authorized Version, if you understand English.

ble to be a pastor without knowledge of the original languages, as is often the case in North America, but the whole Protestant principle of reading Scripture in a translation would be in vain.[41]

Nevertheless, the study of Scripture in the original languages remains in **highest** honor. Truly, there is a tremendous difference between **any** translation and the original. Quite a lot gets lost in any translation. Therefore, whoever is able should learn and practice Greek and Hebrew to his grave,[42] and not just in a bungling way, but to the point where he can use it freely and independent of the commentaries. The measure of knowledge of the original possessed by most of our pastors hardly enables them to penetrate deeper into the divine Word than they could with a mere translation. There is some truth to what Balduin says in praise of the Lutheran translation: it is like a commentary (*commentarii instar*). With this he expresses the virtue of the Lutheran translation, but also its weakness, because **every** commentary only gives a human, often false or lopsided perception of the original. One is being advised, but is it always right? So what good is a **little** knowledge of the original languages? A little knowledge may make you doubt a translation, e.g., that of Luther. But a more accurate knowledge could at times bring the translation back to honor again. Luther wanted to let the Holy Spirit speak German, as he says. And the German at times seems to lie far from the text, while nevertheless hitting the nail on the head. The right linguistic knowledge sometimes reconciles one with the translation. But where this does not happen, one must yet praise it, because it renders the text without commentary, and therefore more correct and blessed.

As to the knowledge and the study of individual texts, what one has learned from Hochstetter about *analysis exegetica, dialectica* and *rhetorica* remains valuable. But it presupposes not only a continuing study of dialectics and rhetoric, but also of the languages. Without the latter, just using a translation, even dialectics and rhetoric will remain dependent on the translation. This will often cause an embarrassment, but can also lead to error.

Of great value for the study of the text, whether based on the original or on a mere translation, is the study of **parallel passages.** Scripture explains Scripture (*scriptura scripturam illustrat*). Light falls from the bright passages onto the dark ones. Therefore nothing is more useful for the sermon preparation of a pastor than a good concordance. The best kind has the main advantage of **completeness** and ease of finding things, and it also shows the

---

[41] [Loehe:] However, someone not knowing the original languages should practice modesty, especially in regard to the interpretation and application of individual verses, since so much wrong interpretation and use is simply based on a faulty translation. For example, one need only think of the usual misuse of the phrase: "Whatever does not come from faith, is sin."

[42] [Loehe:] The reader should not forget that this entire little book was originally dictated for mission students at Neuendettelsau.

bright summary of equal matters. Such a concordance (e.g., the *Handkonkordanz. Biblische Real- und Verbal- Konkordanz* by Gottfried Büchner) also has the advantage of the *loci communes,* much praised by our fathers (see section P below). If a concordance does not combine both attributes [of completeness and summation], one needs to buy one concordance of the first kind and one of the second kind. Besides Büchner, there is the excellent one by Lanckisch,[43] which indicates exactly which Greek or Hebrew word is used for the German in each place. There are so many expressions that are rendered with one word in German, with the result that the fine nuance of the original is lost.

It is not necessary to emphasize how much is contributed to a lively understanding of Holy Scripture not only by study (*meditatio*), but also by prayer (*oratio*) and trial (*tentatio*). Everybody agrees on this. Compare here Balduin's wonderful words on pp. 123–35 [of his work]. A blessed conducting of the office by the preacher requires living in the Word of God, and to be led into it in prayer and trial. Whoever would live and study only for the sake of the office, without feeling the personal need to do so, would **emit a hollow sound** in his sermons. This statement is always true: If you want to be the trumpet of grace, you first must open yourself to grace.

A preacher must read Scripture daily because his soul needs it. One can read the Word faithfully and daily, due to the office, without advancing and becoming pious. Therefore there is nothing one could wish more for a preacher than the spirit of meditating on Scripture and praying over it. The first application of Scripture must be to one's own soul, then only after that to the souls of the congregation. That way there will be a preaching from the depth of the soul, a heartfelt speaking that goes to the hearts [of people], while a mere official studying of Scripture produces cold sermons that do not grab the hearer, do not open up human trust, and give no ear for the Word of God that is being preached. There is no flowing forth of Scripture, no *emanatio scripturae*, without studying for one's own heart. And if Scripture "does not shine brightly into one's own heart," neither can anything bright **come out.** Second Corinthians 4:6 and Psalm 1 show the right preacher. In general it would be very desirable for preachers to understand the *meditatio* not just as a study but as a spiritual exercise, and that we would have a [theologian like] Löscher[44] who would change books as e.g., *Garcias exercita-*

[43] [Loehe:] *Concordantiae Bibliorum germanico/ebraico/graecae.* German, Hebrew and Greek Concordance Bible, etc. by M. Friedrich Lanckisch, newly revised, etc. by M. Christian Reineccio, Leipzig and Frankfurt 1718. 2 folio volumes. This work deserves its own little standing table in the study of German pastors.

[44] [Loehe:] Doctor Valentin Ernst Löscher's *Noble Fruits of Devotion, or 68 Selected Passages of Holy Scripture That Deal With* ***Devotion****, for the Encouragement of the Spirit, Completed in Many Sermons, According to XXV Different Methods, Wherein the Theologia Mystica Orthodoxa Is Presented in Six Parts, Together With an Introduction to the Theologia Mystica and Two Appendices: I. About the Use of the Theologiae Mysticae Against the*

torium into something Protestant. It would be useful for the pastors and a benefit for their souls, and become available for the congregations and dear to them.[45]

P. CONCERNING STRUCTURE

A spiritual speaker either talks with or without a text. In the first case the text is either given to him, as with sermons *de tempore,* or he must choose it, as e.g., for all sermons on specific occasions.

With the given text one must preach either analytically or synthetically. In the first case the preacher can have no doubt about what to preach. He presents the text, and the structure (*inventio*) falls into place with the analysis, which we already spoke about. But if he is to preach synthetically, he has to **find out** which main thought he should take. In the case of sermons on specific occasions, there is a *casus*, a reason that can give direction and measure to the thoughts. But first one must seek and find a certain **thought,** and then a **text.** If it is a speech without a text, at least the main thought has to be formulated. This entire activity belongs in the realm of **structure,** as well as finding the right **partitions** and **divisions** of the main thoughts one has found.

Of course one would think that a preacher would never lack material.[46] Scripture is an inexhaustible ocean of thoughts. The occasion, reason for preaching, the knowledge of the congregational circumstances and persons, etc., should make it easy to find what is right and needful in Scripture. One would think that the material for every speech or sermon would come as by itself, even be forced upon one. However, as much as life and experience relate to Scripture, and as much as this is a seething ocean of thoughts, one

---

Papists; II. About the Limits of Devotion and Enthusiasm [*Edle Andachtsfrüchte oder 68 auserlesene Örter der Heiligen Schrift, so von der* ***Andacht*** *handeln, zur Ermunterung des Geistes in so vielen Predigten nach XXV unterschiedenen Methodis ausgeführt, darinnen die Theologia mystica orthodoxa in 6 Teilen vorgetragen wird, nebst einen Vorbericht von der Theologia mystica und 2 Anhängen: I. vom Nutzen der Theologiae mysticae wider die Pabstier; II von den Grenzen der Andacht und des Enthusiasmus*]. Third edition, Leipzig 1741. See note 29 above [on the 25 methods].

[45] [Loehe:] *A Spiritual Exercise Book with a List of the Canonical Hours. Author: R. P. Garcia Cisnerio. With a Formula for Prayer and Meditation by R. P. Ludwig Barba.* New Edition, Regensburg. Completed by G. J. Manz. 1836. [*Exercitatorium spirituale cum directorio horarum canonicarum. Auctore R. P. Garcia Cisnerio, et Formula orationis et meditationis, Auctore R. P. Ludovico Barba.*]

[46] [Loehe:] Sirach 24, especially v. 28f. "No one has ever existed who has learned [Wisdom]—the Book of the Covenant—completely and no one will ever exist who could fathom it completely. For its thoughts are more abundant than any sea, and its counsel deeper than any abyss." [Editor's note: Loehe uses the Luther translation, but substitutes "the Book of the Covenant" for "Wisdom." This is analogous with the teaching of Jesus as the Word in John 1.]

cannot deny that man is lazy and that even a "man of God" (1 Timothy 6:11 [ESV]), a preacher, can easily become deaf and dull to find such thoughts through the habit of relationships.

In general it is certain that no profession demands such a measure of productivity as that of the preacher. And yet, the strength to produce is a rare gift. Even if it is there, it cannot easily be trained to become a skill and a virtue. Therefore one should not despise the part of dialectics and rhetoric that deals with **structure,** as well as the ancient doctrine of the *loci communes* and the **ancient topics.**[47] It should be **esteemed, learned, preserved,** and prac-

---

[47] [Loehe:] E.g., *Theological Topics from the Most Illustrious and Most Important Theologian D. Andreas Hyperius, Most Celebrated Professor of Sacred Literature in the Renowned School of Marburg. Wittenberg, printed by Petrus Seitz. 1565.* [*Topica theologica a clarissimo viro gravissimioque theologo D. Andr. Hyperio, sacrarum litterarum in inclyta schola Marpurgensi professore celeberrimo, Witebergae. Excedebat Petrus Seitz. 1565.*] Melanchthon says in the beginning of the fourth part of his *Dialectics*: The ancient division of dialectics is this: One part of dialectics is judging, the other inventing. The one called judging is the one that discerns the voices—it judges what is rightly connected, and what is not correctly tied together; it discerns propositions and judges when the members hang together correctly in syllogisms and other forms of arguments. The other part is called inventive. It exhorts how things should be investigated. Or, when things are put to the top, it teaches to choose those which illustrate the present material. This art is called τοπική, i.e., the teaching of places that are like lists of things to be investigated, or chosen, like a doctor through an outward sign, or the speed or irregularity of the arterial pulse, following the place from its effect, knows which is the cause of this sign that is the fountain of the pulse, namely the heart, and then searches where the heart is inflamed.—But often we use places, not so much for investigation, as for choosing the things whose greatest importance has been proposed, so that in the church of the teacher things do not get invented. For we do not give birth to doctrine. But when some part of heavenly gathering is proposed, a wise interpreter chooses the principal parts, and the commonplaces show in what order they should be explained, what definition is to be sought, what parts to be established, the reason for the flow, the effect of judging.—Later: The dialectical topic is the seat of an argument, or the index that shows us from what source the evidence should be taken, to the end that one might prove the proposition that lies in doubt. [*Dialectices vetus divisio haec est: Alia pars dialectices est iudicatrix, alia inventrix. Dicitur autem iudicatrix illa pars, quae discernit voces,—iudicat, quae recte connectantur, quae non recte iungantur;—discernit et iudicat, quando recte cohaereant membra in syllogismis et ceteris formis argumentorum. Altera pars nominator inventrix, quae monet, quomodo res investigandae sint, aut propotio rerum cumulo, docet eligere ea, quae praesentem materiam ilustrant. Haec ars vocatur τοπική i.e., doctrina locorum, qui sunt velut indices rerum vel investigandarum, vel eligendarum, ut medicus proposito signo externo, ut velocitate vel inaequalitate pulsus arteriae, sequitur locum ab effectu, scit signi huius quaerendam esse causam, hoc est fontem pulsus, scilicet cor, quaerint deinde, unde cor incensum sit.—Saepe autem locis utimur non tam ad investigationem, quam ad electionem rerum, quarum cumulus propositus est, ut in ecclesia docent non sunt res inveniaendae, non enim gignimus doctrinam; sed cum pars aliqua coelestium concionum proposita est, eligit res praecipuas prudens interpres, et loci monstrant, quo ordine sint explicandae, quaerenda definitio, faciendae partitiones, cruendae causae, iudicandi effectus.*—Later: *Locus dialecticus est sedes argumenti, seu index, monstrans, ex quo fonte sumendum sit argumentum, quo confirmanda est propositio, de qua dubitas.*] cf. the above mention *Topics* of Hyperius, p. 3—

ticed. One seriously should refer to the fourth part of Melanchthon's ***Dialectics***, also to the **first book of his *Rhetoric.***

Balduin also guides us wonderfully in structuring by showing from St. Paul in 2 Timothy 3:16 how one can and should find out from Holy Scripture and its texts what can serve in part as teaching (διδασκαλία), in part as proving (ἔλεγχος), in part as correcting (ἐπανόρθωσις), and in part as education (παιδεία). One cannot deny that this passage of St. Paul, from which the frequently used division of the entire content of Holy Scripture and its teaching is taken, is of the greatest importance. The study of what the fathers wrote about the *elenchus* and its different kinds is to be recommended. It will enable a person for structuring.[48]

Q. LENGTH OR BREVITY OF SERMONS

Length or shortness of sermons is **relative**. True, usually one considers half an hour to be right for a sermon, according to the judgment of Luther and others. It has often been said that it takes a powerful preacher for people to stand him any longer. But this very pronouncement points to an important fact, namely, the gifts of the preacher, without wishing to deny that there could be other circumstances as well. Experience teaches, e.g., that off and on there can be such a hunger for a sermon that even a mediocre or poor preacher not only can be tolerated, but also even can be heard with pleasure. Also a subject can be of such an importance that it can be dealt with for a much longer time than another, without tiring people out. There are also political speeches—one only has to think of the English Parliament—that go on for hours and are listened to with greatest attention. Even if there is a great aversion in the human heart against what is holy and good (see Luther's Large Catechism concerning *acedia*), why should there not be certain circumstances under which a churchly and holy subject fills hearts with greater interest and holds them for a longer time?

The question and answer about length or brevity of a sermon will sound differently, depending on whether they come from the **teacher** [pastor] or the **hearer**. The listener will make his judgment concerning the length of a sermon dependent on the material, gift, time, and circumstances. The pastor, on the other hand, would do well to measure the length of his sermons in such a way as if his talent were less, and therefore a **hindrance** to long sermons. Of course one could say very simply: "What I have to say, I speak, and when I am done, I stop." This rule, if followed conscientiously, would at least

---

Compare for further instruction, if you like and have the opportunity: *Themata concionum sive Sylva locorum in singula evangelia, etc.* by Andreas Pancratius von Hof. Frankfurt a. M. 1597.

[48] [Loehe:] Cf. Balduin p. 164 f. VI. Deyling p. 328f. *The True Teaching Guide, Considered According to the Scriptures* by Bernhard Walther Marperger. Dresden 1727.

prevent any babbling. However, this is not the only rule that exists, not even the most important one. In his presentation, a preacher necessarily must take into consideration the aversion of the human ear. He has to strive so seriously for the attention of his listeners that he would rather talk twice about a matter in an incomplete way than once in a complete way, if he has to fear tiring his listeners. He has to be master of the subject. The right measure of the subject then also will give the right measure of the time. If under this rule one has to speak too long or too brief, then too brief is to be preferred. It is better for the hearer if, at the end of the presentation he would have liked to hear more, than to have him wait for a long time for the Amen, which just would not come.

In 1525 **Eberlin von Günzburg** sent an open letter to Pastor Johann Jakob at Leipheim, titled "How a Servant the Word Should Act in All He Does."[49] In it he says: "The preachers who preach too long do not know that the listeners do not hear with his ears, but with their own." He also correctly compares such preachers with young millers[50] who have not yet tied up many sacks, and therefore tie them too large. In general Eberlin is a man who knows what right measure is. His chapters X to XVIII are especially to be recommended.

Finally we must not forget that a sermon that is too long **upsets the harmony and the purpose of the entire Divine Service**. One does not come to church only to hear. One also wants to **pray, sing, and come to the Sacrament**. Thus, one must not use the entire time just for hearing.

R. Influence of Personal Authority on the Tone and Language of the Preacher

As you know, the authority of the preacher is a divine one, namely, of the office that admonishes, speaks, and petitions in Christ's stead. Therefore one could claim that all preachers had the same authority and dignity. However, one cannot deny that the lack of personal dignity, which is based on natural gift, character, experience, virtue, etc. can be a great hindrance for the authority of the office. The opposite is also true: Personal authority will quickly make people acknowledge the one related to the office. Of course it is certain that personal authority, where it exists, will only be raised by official authority and hardly differentiated from it, rather, they blend together. Therefore even in a speech, some things that are flesh will be considered to

---

[49] [Loehe:] This excellent writing has been communicated in full as the introduction to this little volume.

[50] [Loehe:] But you find the same thing with many of the ancients also: They do not listen to anyone more gladly than themselves. Just like the monkey in his purple, so they please themselves in their gift of teaching [*Neminem libentius audiunt, quam se ipsos, et ut simian in purpura sua, ita ipsi in suo docendi dono sibi solis placent.*] Balduin p. 130.

be spirit. However, this cannot be changed in this world. One finally has to wish that no man who does not possess a natural authority would seek the office and its authority.

Even though personal respect by itself is not always spiritual, one should not underestimate the effect of mere human authority, especially if the one who has it is faithful to the divine Word. Everything that is humanly pedagogical has the blessing of the Fourth Commandment and leads to God. Even if one would consider the blessing of human authority to be unimportant, still, **the tone and the language** of the speaker especially depend on it. A preacher with small or mediocre gifts cannot and may not speak like one that is highly gifted, nor can a younger preacher speak like an old one, nor a novice like one who has proven himself, nor one with spots on his conscience like one with a pure heart, etc. Concerning age and its influence Balduin says (p. 120): "A man of great and authoritative character who is skilled in speaking bears much, so that he can speak to the heart of those listening, which otherwise would be received with derision if a younger man spoke thus."[51]

Therefore our fathers, not just Balduin, held the **modesty** of the preacher in high honor. For the preacher, modesty is a high and indispensable virtue. Whoever considers himself and his reputation to be always a good deal less than the old Adam tells him—he will do well to avoid burdening his conscience with vanity and will incite his listeners to say to him: Friend, move up higher. Everybody is inclined to trust a modest person, while the talk of the immodest one raises mistrust and drives away God's blessing. Whoever exalts himself will be humbled. Therefore, whoever would like to gain a great amount of trust should know above all that he does not deserve any trust, both by nature and through his life. Therefore let him adopt his standpoint **accordingly**, and not only for his youthful years, but for his entire life. He will benefit from this the most, especially if confidence and respect grow. Often to outsiders, life seems to present a proof and confidence is raised in the progress, while one's own eye, looking inward, will find more and more just cause for deepest humility. The Lord preserves his own little ones, but by doing so keeps them in **the truth** and **in endeavoring**, and in this way He makes them more faithful and more trustworthy. The saying will be true in their life: When you humble me, you exalt me.

Young pastors especially should learn this. They quickly come to a great admiration of their own gifts and achievements. There is hardly a more vain generation than that of young pastors. All successes are **their** fruits. Every good they see they connect with **their** activity. Others can see what little effect they have; only they themselves live in self-praise. In their young years they know everything, and not only from school, but—how ridiculous!—according to their experience.

---

[51] *Multa profert magna cum auctoritate vir gravis et dicendi peritus, ita ut ad cor auditorium loquatur, quae risu exciperentur, si dicerentur a iuniore.*

S. EXTEMPORIZING AND THE NECESSARY PREPARATION OF SERMONS

Different, mutually exclusive opinions have arisen concerning extemporizing and preparation of sermons. There was always the worthless, yet tolerable exaggeration that did not want to permit any speaking *ex tempore*, while the opposite one, according to which an extemporaneous speech is supposed to be the sign of a true speaker, could find no value in it.

Above all, it is an indispensable requirement that one who wants to speak must know **what** he wants to present and **how** he has to present it. Given that this is so, one may certainly talk about a **gift** where a man is asked [to speak] at the proper occasion. He may very well speak excellently and with the best effect, even without having written down or memorized his speech, even without any written notes. The speeches at the *Landtag* and in Parliament would furnish sufficient proofs for this.

But one can skip this altogether. The official activity of overburdened country pastors, who sometimes have to speak in public eight days in a row, once or twice daily, gives proof in superabundance. One only could wish that there would be such men, as is unfortunately the case, who have the gift of extemporaneous speech and who could speak in a relaxed manner with wisdom and knowledge, even without writing their sermons. However, not only does experience show that there are only few of this kind, but also the question arises whether someone who really has this gift should use it in an unlimited and regular manner. Of course a gift will be awoken, lifted up, and strengthened simply by using it. Thus the gift of extemporaneous speech also will reach a certain degree of improvement simply by using it. A man may succeed only if he really **lives in what he is going to preach** and if he works continually to improve his inner education and to enlarge his knowledge and his horizon. But would not a frequent, exact preparation for each sermon, which becomes a habit, strengthen the existing gift even more? That is especially since no one is tied to his preparation, but after a thorough preparation, one is able to speak freely and worry free. Will not the quiet meditation, which goes so beautifully with studying, planning, and writing, have a great influence on the soul of the preacher and grant him unction? Will it not augment the quiet disposition and that "original good feeling" from which speech flows like a mild and powerful stream and "forces the hearts of all listeners?" And besides that, who can always trust his gift? Who has never become bitter and lost a great deal of confidence and respect and could be sure that in the moment of his speaking he would be able to find the right goal, the right way, and stick to it? Many a highly gifted person has been bitterly humbled and punished for his vain self confidence.[52]

---

[52] [Loehe:] Cf. Balduin p. 145f. The timid preachers are the best (*concionatores timidi sunt optima*).—"Seek the glory of God in all simplicity; not glory and approval of people, and

One could say: "Preaching is not human work; a sermon is totally different from a secular speech. With the latter the human spirit alone rules, while the preacher has the assistance of a higher Spirit that helps him in his work." And surely, this is so; preaching is not human work. How often has a well-prepared man stood before the congregation in order to preach; either everything that he wanted to say had disappeared or proved to be insufficient, so that he became confused and stood before the congregation as a beggar and had to plead for mercy, rather than claiming that he was their teacher and preacher. And the opposite: How often does a preacher enter the pulpit, poor as a beggar. And behold: When the singing and the organ are silent, he has plenty of riches, feeds the congregation with bread from heaven, gives them wine and milk to drink, and he is lacking no gift. Many preachers have this wonderful experience again and again, and those who had it live more and more from the mouth of the Lord and His gracious mercy. But should these two kinds of experiences be allowed to strengthen the person in his laziness and his frivolity? Are not both quite according to the Lord's will, mighty exhortations to be diligent and to pray that the diligence may be blessed? Will the one who does not prepare himself easily be humbled when he fails? Whoever has to confess a sin of laziness at the start, will he easily accuse himself of poverty and pray that Christ would make him rich? If we have done **everything**, we are useless servants whom **the Lord makes useful**. It then happens to us according to the saying: "A diligent hand makes rich," namely, through the Lord's grace. The frivolous, lazy offenders against what is holy perhaps will be humbled neither by success nor failure, but the Lord will punish them more and more through failure and incompetence.

Thus far we kept a consistent view to men who **have** the gift of extemporaneous speech. Nevertheless we did not find it advisable that they should let this gift rule without having prepared themselves as much as possible beforehand. Who would hinder a gifted man who let his gift rule after thorough preparation, so that he would say something better, which is shown to him in the moment of need, or improve something he found. But what should hap-

---

pray that God may grant you wisdom and voice, and the listeners a good and pure hearing, and let God do the work. For this you should believe me that preaching is not human work. For though I am an old and practiced preacher, I am still afraid when I have to preach, and you certainly will experience these three things. 1. Though you have composed the sermon in the best way and have understood what it should be based on, it will still flow away and turn into water. 2. When you despair about your understanding and concept, God gives grace so that you may preach your best, please the people, but not yourself. 3. If you did not get it, so that it will please neither you nor the listeners, therefore pray to God and leave it up to Him. Luther. Conrad Porta's *Pastorale Lutheri*, ed. Cramer, 1729, p. 113. Note, ibid. "In a certain village a student of theology once preached and when the pastor wished him God's grace, he said he did not need it, for he already had preached a number of times and never missed. But it happened after this that he got stuck and had to come down from the pulpit again."

pen to those who have no gift to speak freely, and yet attempt to speak *ex tempore*? What a poor judgment of one's own gift! What blindness! As often and as usual as it happens, nevertheless it seems to have sprung from frivolity and arrogance. And what disdain of the Word, of the congregation, of the office, of the Lord, and of giving an account! The catechetical instructions of Cyril may have been given *ex tempore*. Chrysostom gave most of his speeches praising the martyrs extemporaneously. But of what use are such examples for the poorly gifted one? How much better is it to take Origen as an example in this regard? He also extemporized, but not before he turned sixty. Balduin rightly says, p. 136ff.:

> Least praiseworthy are the extemporaneous preachers, who draw praise for themselves because they are able to stand up and produce a sermon by blabbing something to the rude rabble out of their sleeve, so to speak. Such rashness is tempting God, fleeing from labor, and achieves not what is good for the listeners, but only its own little glory.[53]

Simply, no—one does not extemporize, or to say it better, one does not extemporize if one can avoid it. For indeed, it is not possible that a pastor who has to preach a sermon almost every day would have to write it, work it out, and memorize it every day.[54] One should not extemporize, but keep preparing faithfully, and never bring anything but a good conscience to the pulpit. One should not be pedantic, not hanging on a word, not clinging so closely to one's notes, so that if a single word or sentence is missing, one loses

---

[53] *Minime laudandi sunt extemporanei concionatores, qui sibi laudi ducunt, quod quasi stantes pede in uno ad rude vulgus aliquid deblaterare et quasi e manicis, quod dicitur, concionem excutere possunt. Quae temeritas tentat deum, fugit laborem et non auditorum utilitatem, sed privatam quondam gloriolam captat.*

[54] [Loehe:] "Dr. Aegidius d. Hunnius in *Methodus concionandi*, p. 19, 6ff. gives the advice that one should not rely on memorizing, but one should prepare a good structure and commit that well to memory." With strenuous and anxious memorizing it could happen that if someone misses one word, he might hallucinate in the whole context of the sermon (*si quis uno verbo impingat, ut in toto contextu concionis hallucinetur*). After a good preparation, whoever preaches on the basis of a good plan is much calmer and freer in his movements. Besides, the sermon and the action of the one who spends all his strength on memorized words rather than the things seems colder. It is much more impressive when the preacher first understands in his mind the things themselves and then leaves himself to the enjoyment of the words while he is speaking. [*Praeterea frigidior et sermo et action videtur eius, qui omnem vim memoriae verbis potius quam rebus addicit; multo enim gravior, quando concionator comprehensis animo rebus ipsis liberrimum sibi inter dicendum relinquit verborum delectum.*] Porta's *Pastorale Lutheri*, p. 112f. Very true, but in the above text we based a good conscience not on a completely finished concept and sure memorizing, but on faithful preparation. We did not make extemporizing the opposite of memorizing, but of faithful preparation. That is the basis for criticizing extemporizing. The worry about thoughtless chatter recommends strictness of preparation—for **young** preachers also a literal concept and memorizing.

all deportment and stands there helpless, like a child that failed in his memorized recital. But one should be faithful in studying, planning, writing, elaborating and, as far as talent requires and advises it, also in memorizing. On the road of the most faithful preparation one should advance to a free and decent movement while in the pulpit.

T. ABOUT THE *ELOCUTIO*

It has to be the intention and the wish of every preacher to be understood by his listeners. One cannot even think of any effect of his presentation without a clear understanding. This understanding, which is not the same as the dubious praise of popularity, is already being prepared if the speech is bright and clear in its parts, the thoughts are simple and follow one another, and therefore invite attention, further it, and make it easier as one goes forward. But much depends also on how **the sentences are built** and what **expressions are chosen.**

As to **sentence construction**: One can use either short sentences or a periodic way of speaking.[55] To write well in periods requires much talent and education. Among hundreds who have the courage to do it, hardly one succeeds. But to write in a bad periodic style means to scare readers and listeners away and to hide one's thoughts in tombs from which one does not even want to pull them out again. Who reads the books of Spener and Francke? They are inaccessible because of the bad periodic style of their time. Besides, the periodic way of writing and speaking not only serves to bury one's thoughts, but it also favors chatter. On the other hand, the simple, short sentence resists babble but is very well suited for presenting mature thoughts. Why is Heinrich Müller still being read today?[56] Why is he so refreshing and exciting? It is the way he writes in short sentences.[57] Without this he would not be what he is and what he accomplishes. Since one can be so easily understood with short sentences, and since it is easier to achieve perfection in this simple way of presentation than in the periodic style, it is advisable to practice how to express simple thoughts in short sentences, especially for those who have not received a formal education. Of course one should not

---

[55] In the nineteenth century, a florid style of delivery was not uncommon among politicians and public speakers. Like English, German can have both simple sentences and complex sentences. Mark Twain (S. L. Clemens, 1835–1910) gave derisive examples of the latter in his 1880 essay, "The Awful German Language."

[56] Heinrich Müller (1631–75) was a German devotional author, hymn writer, and Lutheran theologian.

[57] [Loehe:] *Stilus nervosus,* short-sentence style.—Johann Laesenius. Nervous, strong, lively. [Editor's note: The reference to "Laesenius" is unclear. It may refer to Pomeranian Lutheran pastor and devotional author Johannes Lassenius (Johann, 1636–92), son of pastor Johannes Lassenius (Johann Laczincsky, d. 1654).]

forget that the simple sentence can degenerate to laconic incomprehensibility and clumsiness, just like the periodic one can turn to babble.

By the way, one can also plan his sermon very simply and write in short sentences, and yet give the impression of something affected and unnatural. One can put people off if one **chooses words** of splendor and pomp instead of those that really bring home what one wants to say. Demosthenes is praised because he achieved his great successes with a way of expression that fit exactly his topic, while Cicero is criticized for his Asiatic pomp of expression.[58] With Demosthenes one forgets the speaker, while with Cicero one cannot get rid of the man, even if one is captivated by his topic. Here is a hint for a spiritual speaker—one could say a doubly strong hint. His subjects are not of this world, in any case, and they cannot be engaged in a conversational tone. They are exalted and make even a simple speaker seem to talk in grand style, the *genus dicendi grande.* Let him express himself as properly as possible and avoid allegories, images and figures of speech if they do not serve to advance the matter and the understanding, or to make them more pleasant. "Usefulness is the greatest rule of all."[59] This is a sentence that applies even regarding ornament and decoration of the speech, and one should not be enticed away from it even great examples. "Truth is put forward in the simplest manner," says Baldwin.[60] He and others speak against any kind of singularity of expression, and even the pure taste of Melanchthon fights against idle talk (κενοφωνία) and novelty (καινοφωνία). On the other hand there is the ancient advice that one especially should keep the standard phraseology of the Church and always express oneself in a way so that the hearers can determine that all preachers agree. Certain concepts and sentences have to be kept unchanged; like milestones of the truth they must never be moved.

Quite often, particularly poorly gifted preachers who do not have many thoughts of their own decide to use biblical expressions constantly. Their sermons are like a **mosaic of Bible verses.**[61] This is intolerable if a small man constantly wants to walk in the heavy armor of Holy Scripture, especially if

---

[58] Demosthenes (384–322 BC) was an outstanding orator and statesman of ancient Athens who rallied his city-state against the expansion of Philip II of Macedon and his son Alexander the Great, but to no avail. He committed suicide as a result.

[59] *Summa utilitas omnis regula.*

[60] *Veritas proponatur quam simplicissime.*

[61] [Loehe:] Antiochus in the cloister Saba, monk 629, is named the first forerunner of sermons based on biblical verses. *Pandectae divinae scripturae.* 130 short homilies, very simple. [Editor's note: Antiochus of Palestine (of Saint Saba, fl. early 7th c.) witnessed the Sassanid Persian invasion of Palestine in 614 and the massacre of 44 fellow monks at the Monastery of St. Saba. After the Persians conquered Ancyra in 619, he wrote *Pandects of Holy Scripture*, translated into Latin as *Pandecta Scripturae sacrae*. In the West it was mistaken to be a series of 130 sermons instead of its original intent as an abridgement of Scripture used by displaced monks who lost their books. The *Pandects* contain many extracts of works that have been lost.]

he does it to make it easy for himself. Even if he is a great *textualis*, whoever wants to put together a sermon from Bible verses often will set aside the meaning of a verse and say something with God's words other than what God says with them. There is nothing more difficult and having greater accountability than to state one's own opinion with the Lord's own words (*ipsissimis verbis domini*). Scripture is text, not sermon; the sermon is an explanation, not a collection of texts. At times one may use a verse different than the text as a proof and explanation, but an overflowing and unnecessary use of the divine Word is not appropriate. There is hardly a preacher so talented that he would be able to join together Bible verses like precious stones, so that the splendor of the individual ones is heightened by the reflection of the others without being altered. Therefore one should abstain from this and do the right thing, namely, give a simple, faithful, human explanation of God's Word with one's own words.[62]

Just as it is not proper constantly to talk with Bible verses, neither should one imitate the **expressions of former times and former teachers.** Some of our brothers in North America, for example, called it a Church style to make their way of speaking similar to that of Luther. They put on Luther's clothes and the armor of Saul without having the body that would fit with these. This can no more impress the unbiased than if someone at the present time would walk around in an outfit from the Thirty Years War, or with a big wig from the eighteenth century. About the times it is also said: To each his own (*suum cuique*). It is part of manly modesty to keep one's own peculiarity and to speak that way; to leave to the heroes their heroic sword and to use one's own. One could furnish proofs from American sermons showing how many crude habits instead of pearls were picked up with this Luther mania and Luther phonetics.[63]

[62] [Loehe:] The testimonies of sacred Scripture are not to be gathered up or numbered, but the words that apply to the matter especially should be selected. They should be emphasized and read aloud. Too many parallel sayings gathered from concordances and repetition from books and chapters are superfluous and fastidious. For what good is it to heap up verses of Scripture and of testimonies and to extend them like a thick cloud over the immediate argument that has no need of an elaborate proof. [*Scripturae sacrae testimonia non tam cumulanda et numeranda, quam apposite seligenda et illa imprimis verba, quae ad rem pertinent, urgenda et recitanda sunt. Nimia et immodica dictorum, quae parallela sunt, accumulatio et ex concordantiis repetitio ac librorum capitumque allegatio tam supervacua est quam fastidiosa. Quid enim prodest, sententias scripturae coacervare et testimoniorum veluti densum nimbum extendere in eiusmodi praesertim argumento, quod operosa non indigent probatione.*] Deyling. Also important.

[63] Loehe aims his criticism directly at the LCMS here. There is some truth to the fact that the early LCMS rejected most authors after 1750 and adopted a repristinationist stance in their educational system, worship, and theology. They felt the backlash from that when they adopted English and suddenly found themselves in a different world of thought. For their part, the LCMS criticized Loehe as a failure in not helping to establish a free church in Bavaria and as a sell-out to Harless. They criticized his limitations on the rights of the

Here among **us** in Germany some have attempted to imitate the way of **Scriver** or of **Valerius Herberger**.[64] From this comes their intolerable affected style that does not refresh anyone besides themselves and whoever rides the same hobby horse with them. The great word that also applies here is called **simplicity**.

U. Use of Sermon Books

If one hears how Charlemagne offered to the preachers a book for their preparation in his wonderful ***Homilarium***, one can pity the poor time when one had to train the preachers with a book of postils. It was indeed a wonderful book, and to this day the Church does not have another work that could be compared with it. But truly, we are living in a puffed up and hypocritical time! As if it did not happen today also that many, many pastors sit all day in their studies and brew their ragout out of someone else's stew! Even there are many, many who could neither live nor preach without books on sermons. I do not even want to call them postils, for we really do not have any that would deserve that name. Instead of acting noble and hypocritical, looking to former times, the gifted preachers should rather see to it that they put together for ordinary use (*in usum communem*) a collection of sermons or *Postille*[65] that would deserve **just** to lie next to the old Haymo of Halberstadt,

---

congregation of believers. They ridiculed his turning deaconesses from being Theodor Fliedner's nurses to being a spiritual order with a kind of nun's piety (*eine Art Nonnenfrömmigkeit*). They labeled him a chiliast and crypto-Romanist. Both parties referred to each other as "brothers" or ones "among whom the Spirit works;" yet they could not get over their mutual animosity. See also K. Georg Stöckhardt, *Die Kirchliche Zustände Deutschlands* (Zwickau/Dresden: Naumann, 1892), 69–79.

[64] Valerius Herberger (1562–1627) was a pastor in Fraustadt (now Wschowa, Poland). He is known for the hymn *Valet will ich dir geben* (*O World, So Vain, I Leave Thee*) and *Magnalia Dei de Jesu scripturae nucleo et medulla*, meditations covering Genesis to Ruth that emphasize Christ in the Old Testament.

[65] [Loehe:] A *postil* has its name from the transition between the biblical text and its explanation [homily]: "*Post illa verba evangelii*" (After these words of the Gospel). Charlemagne wanted to have the postil book translated either into German ([*lingua*] *theodiscam*) or into Late Latin (*rusticam latinam linguam*). Title of the *Homiliarium: Homeliae seu mavis sermones sive conciones ad populum praestantissimorum ecclesiae doctorum: Hieronymi, Augustini, Ambrosii, Gregorii, Origenis, Joh. Chrysostomi, Bedae, Henrici aliorumque. In hunc ordinem digestae per* ***Alchuinum levitam,*** *idque iniungente et Carolo Magno Rom. Imper., cui a secretis fuit. Nun ex vetustissimis exemplaribus ab innumeris mendis vindicatae, quod facile deprehendet is, qui hanc editionem cum prioribus contulerit. Adiectis etiam nonnullis homeliis, numquam antea impressis. Apud sanctum Ubiorum Coloniam Agrippinam in aedibus Heronis Alopesii. Ann. MDXXV.*—Newer collections for other purposes can show precisely how difficult it would be to produce a popular book of sermons of the same uniformity and glory as the Carolingian book of homilies, even if taken just from sermons of the Lutheran Church. [For example,] Wilhelm Beste's *Most Important Pulpit Speakers of the Older Lutheran Church*, 2 vols. Leipzig 1856 and 1858; or

and the less gifted should simply and openly use this collection. Here again one can say: "Usefulness is the greatest rule of all."[66] Why would the congregation care to hear the pastor's own work, if he is not able to write down and brew up such sermons that can benefit it and are worth to be presented? I have great respect for the eloquence of many a simple Christian, and would rather listen to his sounds without rule, than to the ruled, empty tone of a preacher who has studied but is anemic. I have great respect for the simple occasional speech of a less gifted pastor, but little or no respect for the so-called studied presentation that he had to labor for, wrestling them out of his poverty. He will put his farmers to sleep, and instead of lifting them up to the divine, he pushes them down to the common. Oh, if one would only have the courage to be wise and create something useful for the congregation!

A young pastor brought great blessing in his sermons and his congregation and people from the surroundings were inspired as long as he **studied** the sermons of one more gifted. He **reproduced** them inwardly and then **presented** them from his pulpit. But when someone discovered his source, and in a very arrogant way told him of this discovery, the good preacher felt humiliated, even betrayed. Instead of simply saying: *Summa utilitas omnis regula,* happily confessing what he did, and continue onward, to the blessing of his people, from then on he would suck a presentation out of his own quill and his own fingers, and that was the end of the blessing. Dare to know (*sapere aude*) and throw away the miserable prejudices, especially of those in the congregation who want to be the better educated ones and therefore can tolerate only an eloquent and gifted preacher. Both preacher as well as congregation should be taught and convinced once and for all that truly everything depends on the blessing [meant] for the hearers. The congregation deserves the best possible sermon, no matter where it is taken from, but not a lesser one, just so the pastor can present his own work.

Balduin speaks against the use of postils. But these days one has to fight against the opposite evil. He says very beautifully: "Novices use postils like bark, which eventually one has to throw away as one learns."[67] He adds: "For one has a slavish character to say that he would rather be led than to go himself."[68] But what good does it do to excite the pastor's arrogance when most of them in fact have a slavish character (*servile ingenium*) that only can become ennobled if it would rather be led for the good of the congregation than walk on its own two feet to the congregation's harm. Truly, here especially in

---

Nesselmann's *Book of Sermons and Speeches of Various Times, Countries and Confessions, Put in Order for One Year,* Elbing 1862.

[66] *Summa utilitas omnis regula.*

[67] *Novitii utantur postillis instar corticum, quos tandem abiiciant postquam ipsi nature didicerunt.*

[68] *Servilis enim ingenii est, duci malle quam ire.*

our days, Augustine is a far higher authority. In *De doctrina christiana* book IV, chapter 29 he says:

> There are, indeed, some men who have a good delivery, but cannot compose anything to deliver. Now, if such men take what has been written with wisdom and eloquence by others, **and commit it to memory, and deliver it to the people,** they cannot be blamed, supposing them to do it without deception].[69]

Whoever uses a sermon collection faithfully also will learn from it how to speak freely, whenever office and call, opportunity and time urge him to do so. And whoever does it wisely will learn more in this way than he would unlearn.

When we talk about using sermon collections, of course it should be understood that the pastor should not just **read** someone else's work. A congregation also should learn to be able to listen to readings for its own blessing. The so-called reading funerals and reading prayer hours could then bring a rich blessing. One also should train the congregation to listen to readings; therefore one ought to learn to read correctly, just as if one spoke. However, with **certain kinds** of reading, especially the liturgical ones, this would **not** work. However, free speech does speak in a special way, from heart to heart. Truth forces itself from one soul into another with strange power. But if a pastor on his own has worked through a sermon collection, received it himself and reworked it inwardly; if what he has received flows from his mouth freely, from the heart powerfully, there is no difference in tone and effect between a sermon from a postil and one's own. And a pastor who acts honestly and openly in this regard will have more peace and a deeper contentment while preaching.

V. To Whom Does the Preacher Speak?

In recent times this simple, easily-answered question has been answered in an unnatural and perverted way, especially by men who were spiritually minded. They say that one should look more above oneself to the Lord, rather than to the congregation. The intention of this claim was to preserve the pastor from passion, to let the pastor keep a clear conscience, and to put him into the holy presence of God while preaching. Certainly that is a good intention, but as it is stated, it can be misunderstood to a great extent.

During prayer, one may have the **intention** of influencing the **congregation** to keep God and all the good that one asks for in focus, even while

---

[69] *Sunt sane quidam, qui bene pronunciare possunt, quid autem pronuncient, excogitare non possunt. Quod si ab aliis sumant eloquenter sapienterque conscriptum,* ***memoriaeque commendent atque ad populum proferant,*** *si eam personam gerunt, non improbe faciunt.* [Editor's note: Loehe omits the final word about the motive of deception. The text is from *NPNF1* 2:596]

speaking to God in the name of the congregation or also in one's own name. Thus, with the best intentions, one perverts the prayer and gives it a wrong direction and effect.

With a perversion that follows directly [from the above], one may want to turn the meaning of the sermon away from the congregation, into and above oneself. But in preaching one **must** address the congregation in the name of God. Doing this [looking up], one has robbed two parts of the service of the right goal. The intention of the preacher during the sermon is no other, must be no other, than to lead the congregation through the Word to salvation, to strengthen and establish it. A preacher must want this with all seriousness and fulfill it with all strength. Therefore it cannot be otherwise; he must seriously turn **to the congregation,** come into that inner, secret relationship that grabs the souls in a magic rapport, but is divinely beautiful and pure. He must take hold of the souls with the Word, keep them, and guide them. With all this there can be a mighty sighing toward God for a gracious success—that is how great the secret of the inner life is. The soul of the preacher can and should be lifted up, enlightened, and carried, full of devotion and moved toward heaven by the Spirit of the Lord. But with all celebrating in God, and all being lifted up to God, nevertheless the direction of the preacher is first toward the **congregation.** It is a sort of cherubic life; one is filled with God, and for that very reason full of power and might of speech directed to the outside, toward the congregation. Rest and effect are together, but the effect comes out and appears, while the rest is enthroned in the profound quietness of the soul.

W. PRONUNCIATION

Speaking deals with a) weakness and strength of the voice, b) slowness and speed, c) delivery, d) the pulpit tone. It is easier to make rules for all these things than to keep them, since each preacher is too dependent on his own individuality. Nobody can learn to speak according to rules. Everybody talks before he knows any rules and uses the rules only as a corrective for his faults and deficiencies.

As to **strength or weakness of the voice**: Some are given a smaller measure of physical strength than they need. A weak voice is bad luck for a preacher. It should keep him away from being called as a preacher from the start because his entire calling would be a failure if people do not understand him. It would take many other gifts of speaking, a rich and solid content of the sermon, and great personal dignity in order for the listeners to get used to the soft and weak voice of the preacher and make up with their quiet attention where he is lacking in penetrating strength.

Those gifted with a strong voice have to consider the size of the room and the number of listeners in order to gauge the necessary vocal effort. I repeat: Consider not only the space, but also the attendance, since a full church requires a louder voice than an empty one, if one wants to be understood by everyone. If one knows what loudness is required by the space and the number of listeners, one should stick to it, without neglecting the natural variations of strength and weakness that are required by the subject and the circumstances. A different measure of voice is appropriate for teaching than for warning, punishing, encouraging, comforting, or mourning.

A medium measure of voice is simply medium. One goes up or down according to need. When the Lord commands: "Proclaim to my people their transgression, and Israel its sin," He introduces this exhortation with the words: "Lift up your voice like a trumpet." This certainly indicates that the same measure of voice is not to be used under all circumstances. Under no circumstances should a preacher go above the measure of voice that is given to him. He should not shout until he screams or becomes hoarse. That would just bring the deserved reproach of being measureless and present a hindrance for the office without giving the comfort of the word: "The zeal for your house has consumed me." Even less should the preacher try to cover up his lack of thoughts by greatly raising his voice. "Much ado about nothing"[70] is not going to be forgiven because one might be inclined to forgive the [bleating] if [the sheep had] much wool.

As with vocal effort, likewise one must also consider the **slowness and speed of speaking.** It is unbearable to listen to someone speak always in the same tempo, be it always slow or always fast.[71] A change that is appropriate to the matter is desirable in preaching. Start slowly and warm up with the congregation. Let the flight of thoughts speed up once the congregation has been warmed up and their attention grasped. If needed, let the wings beat slower again, just as one will speak louder or softer according to the subject. This will recommend itself and comes by itself to the preacher for whom the sermon is a part of his life. Especially with a periodic way of speaking, a greater dexterity of speaking, not to mention speed, would further the clarity of comprehension; with this kind of speech a slower presentation will support the memory less. Otherwise, in general, the admonition given by the ancients **not to talk too fast** will be completely in order and very practical.

If the rule concerning measure of voice and of time just mentioned is used simply as a corrective, one would be guilty of sinning against a sermon if one were to expect the preachers to use the rules of **delivery** with any other intention or measure. There is no question that one should present every matter appropriately and purposefully. No doubt, this is aided also by the study of proper speech, of the tone, the voice and its modulation, and of gesture. However, it seems to be improper for spiritual speech to **want** to speak

---

[70] The important point in the proverb *viel Geschrei und wenig Wolle* (much shouting and little wool) is the inordinate level of shouting. A sheep bleats loudly when shorn, yet one sheep produces only a small amount of wool.

[71] Loehe used *Ton* (tone) in the sentence when he probably meant *Takt* or *Tempo*.

according to rules, although it would be completely in order to eliminate mistakes with the help of existing rules. There is such a thing as the art of spiritual speaking, but as far as it follows outward rules and pronunciation, it is like the Ten Commandments. More of them forbid than command.

A great malady of preachers is the so-called **pulpit tone.** It is a product not only of the organ of speech, but also of the great content that is being presented, also the way the heart of the preacher relates to it.[72] A pulpit tone is almost unavoidable, and it is better than a conversational tone in which one should not talk in the pulpit, because there is a tremendous difference between public speaking (ὁμιλεῖν) and conversation. The eternal wisdom and truth is no subject for mere conversation, least of all in the pulpit. But as true as that is, it is still the duty of every preacher to fight against an improper pulpit tone, against its monotony as well as the frequently tremendous changes between heights and depths. One should exhort trusted friends to be merciful, and, by open criticism, help to do away with this defacing of the divine Word.

But an ugly pulpit tone will be prevented most effectively if the preacher realizes for each sermon what he must do; if he remembers that he has to deliver a divine charge to the congregation, address them in the name of God, and talk with them for the salvation of their souls. The less preaching becomes a habit and the less the preacher just "pushes out" his presentations one after another—then they will become less affected. The more he remains conscious of his calling and his task, the more appropriate and simple, right and natural they will be. Just like that bush that did not burn in the fire, nor was consumed, but stood transfigured, thus the fire of the office must not make the natural way of speaking something extraordinary, but transfigure it. When he officiates, the language of a preacher must appear in the brightest light that he is capable of producing without seeking it.

X. GESTICULATION

Melanchthon wants to say nothing about **gesticulation.**[73] New customs and habits have been formed that are different than the rules of the heathen. Indeed it may be best to say little about gesticulation. If the ancients claim

---

[72] [Loehe:] But often it comes from simple imitation. A student or candidate hears a preacher whom he likes. He imitates him and becomes used to it, so that it becomes his second nature. Later he no longer can do otherwise than what he has become used to. As often as he preaches, he stops being himself and plays the role of his idol and puts on a different nature. Sad fate for many.—And how often even the content gradually becomes just a role and a masque, so that the seriousness of life stops precisely where it ought to be, with the Holy Office.

[73] [Loehe:] Against this see Bahrdt's *Rhetorik für geistliche Redner*, 1778 [*Rhetoric for Spiritual Speakers*]. It is distinguished only through the teaching of action. Two-thirds of the book deals with action.

that it is not proper to lift the hand higher than eye level, one will well recognize in that rule a borderline of the beautiful for a quiet speech. But who would be so bold as to make this a rule for all occasions, for every part of the speech, for every speaker and for every subject? No one would feel comfortable with saying that this rule applies its measure equally in all cases, in every venue of speech, for every speaker, and for every circumstance. Everyone has his own way that is appropriate for him, if not for others. One has to let him have it, as long as he does not go beyond his own measure and thereby becomes conspicuous, possibly distracts attention, makes it difficult to keep it, and hinders the purpose of his speech. An honest friend can do here what no system of rules can do, even if there existed a really thorough one, although it cannot be denied that true friends with the courage to talk a friend out of an ugly superficiality, a mere bagatelle, are hard to find. Often the whole world knows about the bad habit of a preacher; only he does not. He can grow old and die with it, and yet not find out what he would have understood, hated, and put away, had he been told in time.

Y. Announcements

Everybody knows that after the proclamation of the divine Word and after the "Amen" is said, the preacher still has to announce from the pulpit all things that pertain to the outward leading of the congregation. That includes donations and gifts, school conferences, administrative meetings for the poor or the church, etc. Engaged couples are proclaimed, special services announced, etc.

All this does not require any special preparation and it is not hard to compose it, since one can use well-ordered and traditional words and expressions. It is just a matter of writing down and announcing everything exactly and true to form. In addition to these mere formal things, there are still others that usually are listed among the announcements: Coming festivals are announced; people are exhorted for acts of mercy in this or that case; a collection is announced; days for confession and Communion are ordered; special events with the proper warnings and admonitions are announced, etc.

Such announcements of the more noble kind stir up common attention, a deep calm prevails, the sleepers awake, no one misses anything, and one can be sure that a successful announcement is noticed not only by the entire assembly but also will be carried to the homes. Altogether there is no publication that is as highly regarded as a church announcement. The longer one occupies the office, the more one is impressed by this, and the more one has to learn that in these church announcements one possesses a remarkable means of influencing the congregation. Therefore one will be more and more inclined to use special diligence with the announcements and to prepare them with great care. But as soon as one has arrived at this point, one also realizes that the announcements belong in the realm of **homiletics,** the area of speeches for specific occasions (*Kasualreden*). Even if it is called a speech for a specific occasion, no one will get the idea that an announcement has to be a complete speech. On the other hand, everybody will realize that a successful announcement will reflect the form of a speech, and that it is good to remember this when preparing it.

Let us think of a young preacher who reads these lines and decides to have this experience. In trying, it will not take long for him to experience the usefulness and the blessing of church announcements. He will practice and love it more and more. Perhaps the same thing will happen to him as it did to the writer of these lines. When he was young, he thought little of announcements. His little notebook for announcements was small and was used only as a memory aid. But now that he is old, he often stays at his desk for hours in order to prepare his announcements, enters them diligently in a sizeable book, and when he walks to the church with the book under his arm, he is happy like a hunter who is sure of a specially selected arrow. Sometimes, when he realizes during the sermon that his speech does not hit home, he comforts himself by thinking that there are still the announcements. He saves time, energy and strength for the announcements, and he realizes that he often has made up for some lack in his sermon through some announcements.

In books for the instruction of pastors there is no mention of announcements; one will seek it in vain. That is why the present author really felt good when he found a section that deals with the same subject in Zwickenpflug's *Grundzügen einer Pastoral im Geiste Christi und seiner heiligen Kirche* (Regensburg 1844), pp. 213–21 [*Basic Pastoral Instruction in the Spirit of Christ and His Holy Church*].[74] The section is headed: "Concerning special memorials that a shepherd of souls may bring at various times of the year." By special memorials he means approximately what we called announcements of a more noble kind above. Even if Zwickenpflug's words are not always fitting for us Protestants, nevertheless the following communications will be of value for those who do want to occupy themselves with this subject.

In the beginning Zwickenpflug says: "The memorials are or should be for each a word at the proper time. If well applied, they are at times more effective than common sermons, admonitions, and catechetical instruction." Then follow some rules for the composing of memorials:

I. The pastor must prepare himself well for the memorials he wants to present. He must think what he has to say, and how. This requires a special talent.

[74] Kaspar Zwickenpflug (d. 1860) was a prominent Roman Catholic theologian. He was head of the seminary in Regensburg and advisor to the bishop. A prolific author, he helped to revive and enliven practical theology. His name is misprinted in the German.

II. He must support his memorials with good reasons, but not with threats or maligning. He should do it by quoting a passage or example from Holy Scripture, explain it, and make it into a useful application.

III. He should not be long-winded in his memorials and not make them too long.

IV. All his memorials have to be especially seasoned with the salt of wisdom. That means to be serious and well-meaning, emphatic and tender, honest and trusting, that they will be followed.

V. If the memorials did not have the hoped-for effect, he has to repeat them and express his sadness over it. But if they have brought fruit, he has to express his satisfaction.

After these rules Zwickenpflug exhorts young pastors never to talk about harm and evil, and not to bring memorials that are not public knowledge; but to talk about public nuisances and harm that must be resisted, yet here especially to be careful and well prepared, and never to do it in the presence of people who do not belong to the congregation. Of course this latter point may not be achievable in some congregation. Besides this, one might question his position that memorials should never be mentioned concerning small things, but only concerning those that are of great importance for salvation. Sometimes even something small is worthy to be brought into the light of remembrance, because the small is often like the seed from which something great grows, etc.

As for the time, Zwickenpflug is right when he warns not to present memorials too often. He is also right with his admonition to choose the right time for each memorial. Some memorials can be repeated several times in one year; others should not come more than once. He also thinks that sometimes a memorial could be presented instead of a sermon, speech, or catechetical instruction. One could bring it before or after the service, before or after a simple presentation.

After these common instructions Zwickenpflug presents guidelines for memorials during the Advent season, and in general for feasts of the Church Year, also for the beginning of festive seasons, in very brief but instructive words. He also presents memorials for harvest and seed-time, for winter, for accidents and sorrow, hail and killing frost, infectious disease, sudden death, fire, public nuisance, fights within a congregation, leaving of a soul shepherd, or beginning of a new office bearer. As brief as these instructions are, nevertheless they can motivate a young pastor to nurture memorials. We want to give a very brief example:

The memorial for the workers in the field during springtime should have this content: The field workers should not give up their morning and evening prayer. In the morning, and several times during the day, they should "sanctify all their work by awakening a good opinion." While walking out to the field, while working, and on the way home, they should sing spiritual songs. From time to time they should remember the last things, they should not infringe on someone else's property, not do any harm, not curse or swear, patiently bear bad weather, the burden of work, the ill humor of their co-workers, etc. The shepherds also are being exhorted at the beginning of springtime to occupy themselves with some decent work while guarding the flocks, warned not to guard together with people of the opposite sex; if they cannot attend the services, they should read the catechism during that time and sing spiritual songs, go sometimes to the Sacrament and to church, and such.

Everybody may have his own thoughts concerning such announcements and memorials. But the author would have punished himself if he would not have said as much in this new edition of his book as he has said. His experience has deeply convinced him that announcement of memorials are worthy of consideration, of diligence and care, exactly because they are followed by so much blessing.

Chapter Two

CATECHESIS

A. WHAT IS CATECHESIS?

"Catechesis means an instruction whose echo or sound resounds in the ears of the listener,"[1] says Deyling, and at the same time he shows how the word is used by the Greek. Therefore the word really indicates an "oral instruction, a teaching from mouth to ear, unless one would rather say from mouth to mouth. For the latter description would also express what the common perception of catechetical instruction today is: A teaching of Christian doctrine, which is passed on in conversations from mouth to mouth. The word does occur in the Septuagint and in the New Testament: Genesis 18:19; Exodus 12:20; Deuteronomy 6:2; Luke 1:4; 1 Corinthians 3:2; Hebrews 5:12–14; 6:11; and Acts 18:25. These passages may be reduced to the meaning mentioned above. Originally there was no difference if the instruction was given as a lecture or as a dialogue. The word *catechetical* is used for both kinds of presentation; both kinds are known in the ancient world. We have a short explanation of the faith[2] under the name of St. Basil, which is entirely in the form of question and answer.[3] Likewise there are running lectures of St. Cyril of Jerusalem under the name catechesis, and in the middle of the homilies of St. Chrysostom one can find a "catechesis for those about to be enlightened."[4] In *On the Catechizing of the Uninstructed* chapter 13, Augustine wishes that the catechist **use questions to be convinced of whether or not he was understood.** So **he combines both elements of lecture and dia-**

---

[1] Κατήχησις *talem indicat institutionem, cuius echo sive sonus aures audientis personat.*

[2] ἔκθεσις πίστεως ἐν συντόμῳ.

[3] Basil of Caesarea ("the Great," 329/30–79) was bishop of Caesarea Mazaca in Cappadocia. He supported Nicene Christianity over against the Arians and Apollinarians. He gave much aid to the poor and helped to establish communal monasticism in the Eastern Church.

[4] κατήχησις πρὸς τοὺς μέλλοντας φωτίζεσθαι.

logue, thus recognizing both as catechetical elements. Indeed, this was also the case later, especially in the Lutheran Church. One only has to compare, e.g., the widespread excellent catechism sermons of the Brandenburg Church Order and the **instructions** for their use, and one will become convinced that our fathers took the combination of both elements for granted. This is a very **natural** combination. Christian instruction is not based on inborn concepts or commonly acknowledged principles. Nobody can develop a Christian doctrine from ideas like those in the manner of Socrates found in Xenophon's *Memorabilia*.[5] In the field of Christian teaching there cannot be a "Socratism" in the sense of developing something out of what is innate and known to all the world. In Christian catechesis one first must communicate what one wants to pass on to the pupil in conversation, [with the goal that the instructor is] convinced that [the pupil] has understood it. Anyone who wants to try it will be convinced through his own experiences that **communicating** the **content** of Christian doctrine in the manner of a conversation is slow, useless, and fruitlessly wastes away both time and strength.[6] Therefore catechetical instruction must combine both elements. It cannot do otherwise, and therefore even today there must be catechetical speeches as well as catechetical conversations. The former indicate the content and measure of what has to be learned, while the latter shows how one can bring the content close to the hearers and students. If catechetics is the science of catechetical instruction, it has to deal with the **catechetical speech** as well as with the **catechetical conversation,** for it has to present content, measure, and form of instruction.

Of course one could say that these days the catechetical speech is used seldom. But the reason for this is finally that one no longer teaches much orally. For several reasons of different value, instead of an oral address one hands the students printed instruction that determines content and measure (i.e., the catechism, which itself means instruction, by metonymy a book of instructions). This is a surrogate for oral instruction that should precede the catechetical conversation. That is the way it is, but it should not be so, because if it is the right kind, oral instruction can never be replaced by writing or printing. Therefore, even though the students have the printed catechism

---

[5] Socrates (470/469–399 BC) was an Athenian philosopher known only through the works of his pupils Plato and Xenophon. Through the *Dialogues* of Plato (428/427–348/347 BC), founder of the Academy and of much classical Hellenistic thought, Socrates became known for a pedagogical method of questioning ascribed to him. With Aristotle (384–322 BC), also a great philosopher and tutor of Alexander the Great, Plato and Aristotle form the core of Western philosophy.

[6] [Loehe:] There are also *articuli mixti,* not only *articuli puri.* From those one can always profit with a Socratic or catechetical method. Even with the *articuli puri,* once the doctrinal statement (*Satz*) is given, much light and knowledge can be developed unexpectedly through question and answer, and this through the activity of the teacher and the sincere participation of the student.

before them, the teacher nevertheless should first **present every subject in lively speech, then let it be read, then ask questions**. This would result in the uniting of three different teaching moments and would lead so much more surely to the goal.

Against the claim that lecture-style teaching during catechetical instruction is necessary, one cannot just point out that most catechisms are written in dialogue form. No catechism has the form of a catechetical dialogue, and should not have it. But the right form of the catechism is that of an examination, of giving an account, of confessing the faith. This form is indeed related to dialogue. Yet even this form can be done away with since it is clear that there are enough catechisms that are edited in continuing paragraphs that pose no questions. That leaves even less reason for the printed catechism to do away with continuing instruction, the oral, introductory and preparing word of the teacher. But whether the catechism has been written in the form of question and answer or in paragraphs, above all else it has to serve to pass on the right catechetical measure to both teachers and learners.

B. CONTENT OF CATECHESIS

The purpose of catechetical instruction is teaching. Thus, everything that can be taught is also a fitting subject of catechetical instruction. Yet the wide field of catechetical possibilities that results from this situation also has its limits. One has to keep in mind that a catechist cannot bring everything that one could possibly teach, but only what the **Church** has taken care to make a part of catechetical instruction. Such material has become the recognized content of catechesis over the course and experience preferably of many centuries. For example, one could teach about the inner, hidden life of a Christian. At times the teacher may enter the field of spiritual experience and it would be a blessing. There are certain experiences that every Christian has and must have. But who would make the general claim based on the notion that catechesis has to find its material especially lying on the fields and among the often marvelously labyrinthine walks of internal experiences? Catechesis has to do with what is certain, what is clear and simple in God's Word, what is necessary for salvation. The special depths, distances, and heights of Christian knowledge and experience should be excluded from catechetical instruction because those who are being instructed are of a **young age** and first need a foundation. It is the elementary doctrine of Christ,[7] not the mature fullness (ἡ τελειότης), the foundation (θεμέλιον) of which Hebrews 6:1–2 writes, which the teacher has to present and to impress.[8] The differences

---

[7] ὁ τῆς ἀρχῆς τοῦ Χριστοῦ λόγος.

[8] [Loehe:] One could say that this strange passage contains the principal parts of the **apostolic catechism.** It is very interesting to compare it with Luther's Small Catechism. It does show a certain relationship with the latter. The passage reads, "Therefore let us leave the elementary doctrine of Christ and go on to maturity, not laying again a foundation of

that one has seen at times between **children's instruction** (*Kinderlehre*) and **general Christian instruction** (*Christenlehre*) by no means contradict this. *Christenlehre* indeed considers especially the adult Christians assembled, but its special emphasis is directed toward the children. And even if this were not so, how seldom is it that one can proceed further with adults than with children? How often is the opposite true, that the adults in their knowledge have sunk down to a lower level than that of the children and are in need of the simplest repetition? The old gentleman was not alone when he answered a question of the catechist with the words: "When I was the age of these children, I knew everything. Now I no longer know anything." His name could be legion. Therefore the content of catechetical instruction will remain basically the same under all circumstances.

Thus **Bible history** and the **Catechism** have to be mentioned as the main subject of general catechetical instruction and should be distinguished from **special** instruction. Even if some pastors add special subjects for their confirmands, they usually do not deviate much from the usual topics. The characteristic difference of special instruction deals more with some special intention and relationship. It should not be that way, as we shall see below, but unfortunately that is the case.

One may find it questionable to include **sacred history** in the realm of catechesis. But for the most part, Christian doctrine is nothing other than a pure abstraction of history, whether of the great salvific works of God or of just history itself. Apart from history, no one can learn Christian doctrine. If one had to do without one of the two, either doctrine or history, then one would lose less if doctrine were absent than if history were gone, which itself provides the content of doctrine and is itself instructive.*

C. Measure of Catechetical Content

Presently, catechesis deals not only with Christian knowledge in general, but also with knowledge necessary for salvation that must be offered to the youth. That very fact is something authoritative. But to find the right measure in such way of thinking is nothing small. Rather, it is a test of great catechetical wisdom. Even if one knows that one must teach biblical history and the catechism, this is as good as nothing unless one knows the right measure of doctrine. One does not know what to give if one does not know at all times how much to apportion from the wealth of the whole. The manly virtue of prudence (σωφροσύνη) basically consists in being aware of the right measure and keeping it.[9] This goes for all professions, but especially for the teacher of catechetical instruction.

If one speaks of catechetical measure, this means two things: 1) **the measure of the entire instruction,** and 2) **that of the individual lesson.** One could sum up both by asking: What should be accomplished with the **whole** [**course of study**], and what is to be done **in each**

---

repentance from dead works and of faith toward God, and of instruction about washings, the laying on of hands, the resurrection of the dead, and eternal judgment." [Διὸ ἀφέντες τὸν τῆς ἀρχῆς τοῦ Χριστοῦ λόγον ἐπὶ τὴν τελειότητα φερώμεθα, μὴ πάλιν θεμέλιον καταβαλλόμενοι μετανοίας ἀπὸ νεκρῶν ἔργων, καὶ πίστεως ἐπὶ θεόν, βαπτισμῶν διδαχὴν ἐπιθέσεώς τε χειρῶν, ἀναστάσεώς τε νεκρῶν καὶ κρίματος αἰωνίου.]

* Loehe took this to the point of having biblical interpretation and thus doctrine evolve with history. See not only *Vier Bücher von der Kirche* by Franz Delitzsch (Dresden: Naumann, 1847), but also Matthew C. Harrison, ed., *At Home in the House of My Fathers* (St. Louis: Concordia, 2011), 114–17.

[9] Few languages outside of Greek have one word that encapsulates "excellence of character and soundness of mind." Many words in Latin and English approximate it.

individual period of instruction if one wants to be sure to fulfill the entire measure [i.e., goals and content of the curriculum]?[10] Generally and also regarding individual lessons, one should not decide on the largest measure [of difficulty], neither on the smallest, but on something in the middle. This middle measure [of difficulty] again will tend more toward the lesser one because the average students (*mittleren Köpfe*) are usually the majority in the world and the teacher who has to decide on the measure [of difficulty] for the pupils often is seduced to view the average group as sub-average[, thereby setting his idea of "average" too high].[11] As a result, the majority of average students becomes depressed by all kinds of circumstances and thus is hindered from developing existing gifts. The measure of the middle must be a small measure [of quantity or difficulty]. If there has to be a mistake, let it rather be that of making the measure too small than too great. A smaller measure that one is sure to reach ought to be valued more and create a deeper and more fruitful impression than a greater measure. Achieving the latter one becomes unsure, one gets excited, and one feels under pressure.[12]

As for the **special application of these principles,** one can find a way that is much more traveled in the case of teaching the catechism than when it comes to teaching Bible history. The small Lutheran catechism (*der kleine lutherische Katechismus*) and its method that is taught in the introduction, which is based on keeping the right measure, recommends itself more and more to the catechist as his experience increases.[13] The introduction shows the lessons in general, i.e., the courses, how one is to progress from memoriz-

---

[10] In this section we see considerable use of "measure" (*Maß*). Loehe uses the word to mean the extent of the content itself, the extent of its difficulty, the extent of students who conform to groups able to understand things at a given difficulty, and the degree to which one is likely to strive.

[11] Loehe simply leaves this part out and proceeds to the conclusion.

[12] [Loehe:] When I worked on the first part of my *Hausbuch* (1845), I felt that I had given a small measure [of quantity or difficulty] to the knowledge given in the "questions and answers concerning the six principal parts." Since then, 20 years later, I do not find it small any more, but rather large, and I am satisfied with a smaller achievement. In our schools as they are—at least in the rural schools—one cannot go low enough. But I have also had the experience through the years that even a small part of Christian knowledge surpasses all the wisdom of the world. The Holy Spirit only has to bless what little a child has learned and this will grow, enlighten, strengthen, and sanctify to the astonishment of those who may witness this. What is small in the Christian faith?

[13] This is one place, among others, where Loehe wants to reach out to other Protestants in his use of "the small Lutheran catechism" instead of "Luther's *Small Catechism*" (*der Kleine Katechismus Luthers*). One can ponder if Luther would have considered his catechism to be merely "Lutheran." Questions remain about the ancient and modern, Protestant and Roman Catholic authors used by Loehe. How does this or that commendable aspect fit together with the rest without sacrificing something? If certain concepts bring other ideas and presuppositions with them, how is that resolved in detail? Is Loehe bringing in unstated principles and presuppositions to sort out conflicts among times, denominations, and the like?

ing the words to catechetical understanding, and how to lead back from the catechetical words to Holy Scripture. One could find even the small lessons divided in principal parts and subdivisions, although one has to use greater care with the more detailed instruction, leading to understanding, and the scriptural foundation.

The little children's book from Nuremberg, which certainly can no longer be used in its form, nevertheless could give some guidance for the length of individual lessons. At least the length of the single lessons is **short** enough in the little book. In the books with biblical passages, the measure is usually too small and not clearly defined, yet the spiritual bread in them should be cut clean and thin. There should be a hint even for the smallest part. Without much thinking, one could arrive at the same point if one could decide what would be the right **middle** measure and choose a **smaller** one. If this is reached, it is easy to do more. But it is not so easy to help when one notices that the task is too great.

Concerning **biblical history** one has less advice than with the catechism. [One might advise] first to tell stories from the history in order to teach history later on, i.e., the connection of the stories. That is a good exhortation, but too vague for the practice. The stories have to be selected in such a way that it will be easy to show the historical connection and to attach the proper historical instruction later on. Indeed, every presentation of individual stories depends on the proper historical instruction, so much so that one has to ask: **Even when instructing younger children, why not have also a very brief survey of the historical process, including some numbers, in addition to the presentation of stories?** Why not basically present history in the stories, even for the very young?[14] There exist innumerable helpful publications. Who does not know the biblical histories from Calw, Basel, Zahn, and Buchrucker? But one still seems to lack a textbook that is simple, brief, and easy. It would be more of a rule and general guide. The content, courses, and lessons in Holy Scripture or a biblical history book, both for teachers and pupils, would teach certain steps that lead to the goal. So far there is none that would have found general recognition.

---

[14] [Loehe:] What was posted above as a question has long stopped being a question for the author. In the meantime he gained the necessary experience (between the first and second edition of this writing eight years have passed) that taught him that the short survey of the kingdom of God can be comprehended by a young child and is as **attractive and moving as the story of Joseph or David.** It is easy to step up from a survey to insight. Also, memorizing a small amount of numbers, which is simply necessary, is a principle of order and clarity even for the childish spirit. And how easy it is here to achieve what is necessary! How lively each story becomes for the child when she is put in the order of the survey of the history of the kingdom of God by using the ruling memory numbers. Whoever tries it will soon get this insight and confidence and will give his students "stories from the history," i.e., in the context of the great whole.—Stories **from history,** or history in the stories!

As an example, and because of its general measure, the following might deserve a recommendation: *Kirchengeschichte des Alten und Neuen Testaments, zum Gebrauch für Schulen und Konfirmandenstunden* [*Church History of the Old and New Testament, for Use in Schools and Confirmation Classes*], by Friedrich Dümichen. Breslau by Trewendt.[15]

D. PREPARING FOR CATECHESIS

With any kind of teaching it is most important that the teacher should be master of his subject. But this is impossible without preparation, indeed preparation for any lesson, any subject. The teacher has to know what he has to give and accomplish in every hour. On this, and on his ability to do it, is based all his calmness, sureness, ease, and liveliness of his behavior while teaching.

In general the preparation is made much easier through existing and newly introduced catechisms. One does not have to invent the contents. But when it happens at times that one has to teach about certain subjects, or give free catechetical instruction, then here applies everything we said above concerning preparation for the sermon in praise of dialectics. Here also one has to find and prepare a subject, an introduction, a partition, and a peroration. The only difference between preparing for catechetical instruction and for a sermon is that one does not need to consider the rhetorical element and outside of an exact disposition one does not need any details. Catechetical instruction depends so much on the **children** that are to be taught, on their gifts and their good will, that it is simply impossible to decide in advance how to deal with individual questions.

One can hardly say that catechetical instruction has a greater effect than the sermon, or that it would be a greater gift to teach than to preach. On the contrary, one must assign the greater blessing and the **higher** talent to the sermon. Indeed, a richer and more manifold gift is required for the latter. But there is a gift, though necessary for both, that can be missed more easily with the preacher than with the teacher, namely, **dialectics**. A preacher can cover up his lack in this regard or make up for it with great diligence in preparation. But the teacher, who often has to change direction in his thoughts because of questions and answers, needs a great facility and swiftness in treating concepts and sentences, if he wants to stick to his disposition and the general course of instruction and lead to the determined goal. And for this there is no other preparation besides continuing diligence in dialectical training and the constant joy over dialectical exercise in general. If the lessons follow a guideline, a preparation still will always be necessary, namely, the one that exist in exact knowledge and living penetration of the entire guide-

[15] Friedrich Dümichen (fl. 1850s) was a pastor and author of catechetical materials who served in Herrndorf near [Gross-]Glogau (Silesia), now Głogów, Poland.

line and of every lesson that applies, according to the teacher's trend of thought. It is certain that with time the preparation will become easier. Sometimes it can be limited to just checking the guideline and the course of instruction. It may take just minutes. Still, one has to hold on to one thing, namely, never to omit the **necessary** preparation, be it long or short.

There is one **danger,** both for catechetical and homiletic preparation. Namely, the preparation is often undertaken with some sort of **scholarly** interest, not in the interest of the purpose of the sermon or of the instruction. Through the [scholarly interest] one arrives at a richer knowledge, a deeper understanding, and more complete satisfaction. Then, in a self-satisfied way while teaching, one unpacks much wisdom that does not serve the purpose, or one expects things from the students that one should never expect. Things happen to the teachers on their level as happen to university professors. The latter, steeped in their own continuing learning, often forget that they are not to train theologians as they are, but pastors. Thus at times a catechist acts as if he were not forming Christians, but pastors. Therefore in preparation one ought never to forget the purpose of preparation, namely, to make oneself able to give the child **what is necessary, in the way that is easiest to comprehend, is lasting, and brings blessings.**[16]

Since we have lifted up one danger, we must not forget **another one.** That consists in being exactly faithful **to a pre-written lesson,** the old humdrum way (*Schlendrian*) of a hireling, **dead monotony**. Whoever knows and wills what he should do will also be guarded by God so that he does not get stuck in this danger.

The most important gift and formation of the catechist is also dialectics, namely, in contrast to the homilist and liturgist. It is well known how little or nothing of formal logic and dialectics is practiced in our schools and universities, how little dialectical training the ministerial candidates bring to their office. But is also known that the way our schoolteachers are taught gives them a much smaller dialectical education. The formal training to become a catechist therefore is lacking for the young teacher no less, but just as much or even more than it is lacking for the candidate for the ministry. Through the candidate's kind of learning and his grammatical and linguistic training he is led, almost subconsciously, to greater dialectical activity. From this one can conclude how much there is to the oft-repeated claim that a teacher in general is a better catechist than a pastor. The only thing that can be stated with this claim is that necessity teaches one to swim. Due to their profession,

---

[16] Here Loehe could have found just cause to criticize the LCMS system of education. Ludwig Fürbringer (*Eighty Eventful Years*, 1944; *Persons and Events*, 1947) and William Dallmann (*My Life*, 1945) both indicate that teachers could get caught up in their areas of expertise or perhaps assume that pupils might be able to make a greater extent of application at a certain point than was generally the case. Reactions ranged from brotherly urging to frustrated exclamations.

teachers feel this necessity more often than pastors, and therefore have a greater motivation to acquire some catechetical form.

E. The Form of Catechesis

In Section A we have already pointed to the combination of the lecture and the dialogue elements in catechetical instruction. This combination perhaps could be done most simply and naturally in the following way:

Just as the sermon has an introduction, catechetical instruction also has a longer or shorter homiletic introduction that leads to the theme. This needs to be named, even if one is not catechizing according to proper themes, but according to lessons and guidelines or to the catechism itself.

After the introduction it will be good to present the entire content of the lesson or catechesis in a short, clear, not homiletic but dialectical summary. The students will pay attention to the short presentation because they know that a catechesis will follow and will enlarge on its content.

Once one has presented the content of the lesson to be learned, it might also be very useful to have the lesson read from the guideline, if one has a guideline to follow.

Then one should let questions follow that explain, enlighten, and examine, always keeping the eye on the goal, namely, that the lesson has to be **learned.**

If this goal has been reached, one can sum up the content of the catechesis once more, and in the peroration lift up the value of what has been learned, and encourage pupils to execute and practice what has been learned. This is good, even if such things have been mentioned during the catechesis already and even if it may appear as a repetition.

What has just been mentioned may appear to some like making things harder through some clever tricks. However, what does it matter in the end? One does not catechize in order to catechize. The last intention cannot be to prove one's mastery in the catechetical art and form. This is what should happen: Through catechizing the purpose of salutary knowledge should be achieved, that one would learn for salvation. For this the above-mentioned form does serve, yet one should not stick to it pedantically, but again under the rule: Usefulness is the greatest rule of all.[17] Here also one cannot avoid pointing to the excellent catechism sermons[18] of the *Brandenburg Church*

[17] *Summa utilitas omnis regula.*

[18] [Loehe:] But as other sermons of that time, even they do not want to be homiletic masterpieces in their simplicity. They only deserve our praise as catechetical presentations in view of the short lessons they contain. Title: *Katechismus oder Kinderpredigt* [*Catechism, or Children's Sermon*]. Printed by Johann Petreus, 1533. Foreword: "This catechism of children's sermons was not written for the sake of pastors or preachers; for it is well-known that most of them have enough Christian wisdom, praise God, that they could handle such teaching themselves in a good and useful way. But it has been composed and

Order, which can be taken as a pattern for introductory catechetical introductions, even though they would be too long for our purposes despite their brevity. But the Brandenburg sermons do not take a printed catechism for granted, as do our catechetical introductory speeches; they themselves take the place of the catechism.

F. The Dialogical Form

The dialogical form serves; it does not rule, as we have seen. If one asks now what should be the original image and goal for which one has to wrestle in dialogue form of catechesis, it is **mutual free conversation.** A catechist has achieved the most not only when he has brought his catechumens to comprehend and maintain a question and answer dialogue, but also when they start asking their own questions, making them part of the teaching discussion. The twelve-year-old Christ in the temple shows the perfect form of a proper catechumen and the right catechesis. If such an interest has been gained, so that the students themselves get into the matter, join the conversation, and ask questions, the catechesis becomes easy, fruitful, and a blessed joy. The art disappears and is transfigured into the sacred nature of God-pleasing conversation. But of course, only very few teachers and fewer students arrive at this goal. Many a teacher is foolish and tasteless enough to consider the tender plant of growing mastery in life and freer participation by the students as something unbecoming, instead directing the students to questions and answers, as practiced in the school.

With this goal in mind, but also realizing the sad condition of most confirmands and students, which is our starting point, first of all we have to ask and clarify how we can shape the dialogical from of the catechesis.

---

put together out of great necessity, just for the sake of the young children. Daily experience shows that whoever wants to teach children should not give them too much at one time. But what he does give them he should present often and thoroughly, always in the same way and with the same words. For if one tells them now this, now that, now with these, now with other words, they not only will remember nothing, they also become more awkward and less able to learn than they were before. . . . And since there was the concern that not every pastor or preacher should take on the trouble to put the catechism into such a form that one could teach it the same way all the time, and it was not necessary to bother everyone with this kind of work, also that everywhere it should be done the same way, which prevents much annoyance with the common people—this work will serve them, so that the children may understand and keep the beginning of Christian teaching so much easier. For if this happens, they not only will understand all other teaching better, but also will become fine, pious, Christians, capable and wise people for all kinds of good professions and offices. They will also gladly assist and help father and mother, pastor and preacher, and all Christian government. May God give His grace for this." Cf. Loehe's *Erinnerungen aus der Reformationsgeschichte von Franken* [*Remembrances from the History of the Reformation of Franconia*]. Nuremberg 1847, p. 131.

If one should give a catechetical presentation and then catechize about it, the questions would first have to be examining questions. They would be followed by questions concerning the understanding, and at the end again examining questions. But if one has to teach according to a catechism or a guideline, after reading and reciting the proper lesson corresponding questions of construction and exegesis will begin and, depending on how things go, questions concerning understanding and questions of examination will finish. Of course one could also refer to the exegetical and examination questions as questions of examination. Yet they are not always that kind, rather, they often open up the understanding for the student.

Here one cannot refrain from remarking that in the end all catechetical questions, in fact all questions in general are included in construction questions, and that learning **sentence construction** and **style** can be very useful for the catechetical training of the catechist. With little children one always has to begin all catechesis with simple construction questions. This is a safe way to approach comprehension and understanding of the subject and lays a foundation for all other questions. If in doing so one turns to the child and always lets her[19] see the intention to introduce her to understanding of what has been read, and to memorizing, she might become trusting and finally ask herself questions. There follows the right catechetical relationship, the common effort of teacher and pupil to bring the latter to the knowledge of truth.

With catechesis of biblical history, in addition to examining there is still another exercise that is very fruitful, namely, **letting what was read be retold.** Not only does this promote formal education—both the oral and the written expression of thoughts is regulated and practiced—but also, what one retells impresses itself even deeper into the soul. But one will have to give up the idea of making all children retell. Experience teaches that some individuals who can excellently absorb and retain things show a lack of talent precisely by being incapable of repeating in connected sentences what has taken a hold of them inwardly and what moves them. Of course this also means that many who otherwise have wonderful natural gifts are unable to put the thoughts down in writing in an orderly fashion.

Often it has been emphasized, with Luther, that one should strive for a **standing form** of questions and answers, and entire generations should grow up using this. Of course this does not mean a senseless drill, which would enable the child to hear the familiar sound of the question and give the familiar, though not understood answer. Nor does it mean that all questions should always recur in the same way. That would be possible, but it would also be the most mind-killing undertaking one could imagine. However, the church terminology has to be kept in all cases, also the same established word

[19] German *Kind* is neuter, a child of like *kind* as its forebears. English avoids referring to people as "it," therefore we use the masculine or feminine pronoun variously—to avoid the bad grammar of "them" and the awkward "he or she."

for the same leading thought or for the catechism. This will expedite the unity of knowledge for the generation one has to educate. But given the one content and keeping the one terminology, a catechetical talk should be able to spread out in great variety and freedom. For it is the goal and fulfillment of catechetical achievement to open up the most detailed, easy to understand conversation about what is fixated.

If one wants to achieve this, one has to permit and even encourage at least the rural children to talk as they are able, be it High German or **dialect.**[20] At times it may even serve a purpose and be necessary that the teacher also come down in conversation and use the [Alemannic] dialect, as one can hear in Württemberg and in Switzerland. The dialect itself is not something ignoble. It only becomes that if it is made the language of peasants. Instead, the educated classes should practice it, and by their use preserve it from excesses, which it often can get in the mouth of uncouth and ill-advised people. It becomes common through a common meaning and mouth. In the mouth of educated people it becomes dearly familiar and beautiful. That is enough reason for not needing to be ashamed of the dialect. A teacher should permit it and practice it himself, especially if it serves to introduce the youth to the understanding of holy doctrine. And it certainly does this when the child who is just unable to speak High German or refuses to do it because he is wrongly ashamed, can in this way be coaxed into talking.[21]

At the end of this paragraph there is still this perhaps superfluous remark: Only infrequently should one ask questions that can be answered only with *yes* or *no*. Of course, at times *yes* and *no* are not small matters either, and therefore it should be left to the catechist in such a case, i.e., in the right case, to ask for a *yes* or *no*. However, everybody knows or can easily learn what is disapproved when one opposes the constant repetition of *yes* and *no*.

---

[20] High German spreads out across the highlands of southern Germany from Basel, Munich, and Salzburg to around Mainz, then east to Meissen (and formerly, Breslau). Low German extends throughout the lowlands from Bremen, Hamburg, Kiel, and Rostock to the same Mainz-Meissen line. Frisian clusters about Emden and elsewhere in the north. It sounds most like Old English, then Low German, then High German. Dialects include not only those of the old "tribal duchies," such as Alemannic in the southwest, Bairic and Frankish in the southeast, Upper Saxon, Lower Saxon, Rhenish, Hessian, and so on; they also belong to the long legacy of people who have lived, worked, loved, and died in the same place for over a thousand years, who shaped their villages and let them shape their words. "High German" can be as much an imposed linguistic convention as it is a native tongue.

[21] One might see this advice apply to linguistic subcultures and multicultural settings in the modern U.S. Yet one still should exercise caution here.

G. SHOULD CATECHESIS BE DONE FROM THE PULPIT OR WALKING ABOUT?

If the ideal of a catechesis is the lively conversation of two, or the decent conversation of a community of saints about the wonderful things of the kingdom of God, there can be no doubt that one should walk around in the congregation of children or catechumens. This makes a mutual relationship much easier and more natural. It is also easy for the catechist to be both calm and excited in this way, depending on what is needed. How strange would it be to have a conversation, a talk from the pulpit, unless one is used to hear that such things exist here and there from youth on. The pulpit is not meant for entertainment, rather, for the sermon. Catechesis, on the other hand, requires the nearness of the teacher.—Of course, the way children are, the pulpit gives a standpoint from where one can have an overview of all and it is easier to keep quiet and order. While walking around, mischief can happen behind one's back. That is an accidental advantage and disadvantage, which cannot raise suspicion against the natural form of walking about, and yet often enough, especially in small churches, that (disadvantage) can lead to a victory [of the pulpit] over the ambulating way of teaching.

H. CONFIRMATION CLASS

In the older Lutheran Church one often had a very simple confirmation. When the superintendent traveled around his diocese to conduct the examinations during Lent, he was presented with children who were going to receive their first Communion. He would examine them in the minimum measure of catechetical knowledge, and if they passed the examination, he would pray while laying his hands on them and then declare them to be mature enough for their first Communion.

With this custom the ancient wisdom was kept, not to let the pastor pronounce the final judgment concerning the maturity of his catechumens, but to put the examination and confirmation into the hands of the official Church government. But one thing was completely pushed into the background, namely the renewal and confirmation of the baptismal covenant, the confirmation proper. The official act of the superintendent only referred to the qualification for Communion. With this lack, confirmation was not honored or valued, and could not be so. Of course more recently the opposite happens in many places, causing great harm. The Sacrament is put far behind the celebration of confirmation. It seems that here and there, confirmation is a much greater festival than the time when the child comes for the first time to the table of the grace of Jesus. The right thing to do would be to give to each act **its own** proper dignity. That means absolutely to give the first place to the Holy Meal.

One should conduct confirmation instruction based also on this standpoint. This instruction is nothing but preparation for confirmation and first Communion. Because this is so, it would be wrong to consider it as religious instruction in general. A general religious instruction should be taken for granted before confirmation class, if the latter is to have and keep its proper character. However, there are only very few congregations where one could take the previous instruction and the corresponding level of knowledge for granted. But in this place, speaking of confirmation instruction, we **cannot** pay attention to this lack.

However, even if the children have received a sufficient amount of previous training, so that a proper confirmation instruction can be given, one cannot do without a certain completeness that deals with the entire Christian doctrine. During confirmation class the entire doctrine will be repeated to a large extent, but in a special way, **for a special purpose, and relating to special subjects.** The special subjects of confirmation instruction, based on its double importance, are the **Sacraments, Baptism, and Communion,** and what leads from the one to the other: **confirmation and Absolution.** Therefore by its very name confirmation instruction is sacramental and the course of instruction could be something like this:

1. What is Baptism?
2. Baptism of children.
3. Duties of sponsors and how to thank them.
4. Order of Baptism.
5. Emergency Baptism and **instruction** for it.

---

6. What is confirmation in general?
7. What is the baptismal covenant that is to be renewed and confirmed?
8. The special renouncing during confirmation.
9. The *Credo* of confirmation.
10. The true Church, in relation to the seventh confirmation question, which asks to be faithful to it.
11. Admission to and true value of confirmation.
12. Order of confirmation.

---

13. Absolution. Why Absolution before confirmation?
14. Confession. Instruction for the various kinds.
15. The holy discipline of brotherly love, based on Matthew 18.

16. The place of confession before confirmation, also order and form of confession and Absolution.

---

17. Institution of Holy Communion.
18. Holy Communion. Confessional differences.
19. Dignity and self-examination.
20. Communion fellowship.
21. Order of Communion.
22. The doctrine of the Sacrament, also appreciation of the seven sacraments of other churches.[22]
23. Prayer and its blessed practice.

If one takes up confirmation instruction in this proper form and limitation[23] and takes for granted a previous general religious instruction, one can understand why, in former years, one dedicated only a few hours to confirmation instruction. A six-week instruction, as introduced into Franconia by Margrave Georg Friedrich of Ansbach (1557–1603), is completely sufficient to reach the goal mentioned above, especially if taught daily. It may not even be good to drag out an instruction that is so strictly defined.

The confirmation instruction is by nature something festive, given on the threshold of Communion fellowship, rich in expectation. For this very reason the congregation expects it to be something especially uplifting and stimulating. But how would it be possible to keep the festive relationship to the coming sacred acts firm and fresh throughout a whole year, or even half a year? Here the right measure is necessary in order not to miss out on the purpose.

---

[22] [Loehe:] No. 22 could be put at the beginning of the entire instruction concerning the Sacraments. [Editor's note: Loehe means Greek Orthodox and Roman Catholic churches. The *Book of Concord* disqualifies penance, holy orders, marriage, confirmation, and unction, leaving Absolution and ordination in restricted senses. Loehe's "appreciation" appears to be in tension with Apology XIII (VII).]

[23] [Loehe:] Pastors who understand this matter should be an example for their colleagues. With a written preparation of the confirmation instruction they should show them **what** one should give—and if it is possible to put this in writing—**how** to give it.

In 1860 the author of these pages tried to explain "the Sacramental part of confirmation instruction" according to the sequence given above. See *Wilhelm Löhes Traktate für die Seelsorge VI. Der sakramentalische Teil des Konfirmandenunterrichts. Zur Repetition für Konfirmierte*. Nuremberg, U. E. Sebald 1860. That very much unfinished attempt is just now (1868) experiencing a new edition. It has found manifold recognition, which in its condition it did not deserve. Even in its new edition it is and remains a poor attempt to execute a correct thought, namely, that confirmation instruction should be separated from the remaining religious instruction and should be treated as an introduction to life in the Church and the Sacraments.

It is not our opinion that the pastor, who is to give a brief confirmation instruction, should thereby be excused from the preceding general instruction just to lighten his workload. He can and should instruct the children from their youth on, but in such a way that he would keep the right difference between general religious instruction and confirmation instruction, not getting them mixed up, but leaving to the latter its own solemnity and dignity.

Finally, the nature of confirmation class has the result that those **in the lower class (*Präparanden*) still belong in the general instruction** and can only be **auditors** in confirmation class, while those in the upper class (*Repetenten*) will **listen** and repeat. But this does not mean that those two classes should be eliminated. To celebrate before and after is very good here. And those who can have it and use it are well off.

Chapter Three

Liturgics

A. Sacred Times

Humans live in time and space; therefore worship life, which liturgics deals with, also has to be considered according to **time** and **space**, as well as the **kind** and **manner** that it possesses in itself. Therefore let us speak first about the **time for worship,** then about the **space for the service**, and finally about the life of **worship** itself.

As for the time for worship, we have to speak of the day, the week and the year. The Lord of our time, our days, our weeks, and our years is the crucified Christ who is risen and sits at the right hand of the Father. On Good Friday the Lord died. What could be more natural than to live through the following day completely in remembrance of the preceding day? That remained for Christianity. Each day passes in remembrance of the suffering of Jesus. The course of His suffering and dying rules daily worship.

And just as the day of the death of our Lord rules all our days, thus His great week gives meaning, measure, and goal for our **weeks**. The Sunday that started his suffering is outshined by the resurrection Sunday. But every Sunday has now become for us a brother of Easter Day. **Wednesday**, with the openly-declared decision of the betrayal; **Thursday**, with the institution of the holy meal; **Friday**, with the story of the suffering and dying; **Saturday**, with Jesus' rest in the tomb—these **all** imprint the liturgical character on our Wednesdays, Thursdays, Fridays, and Saturdays. And just as every **day** passes in remembrance of the suffering of Jesus, thus every **week** passes in remembrance of His last week until the day of resurrection.

And just as every day is a repetition of Good Friday, every week that of Jesus' last week, thus the **year** repeats the whole life of Jesus in celebration. We start the time of waiting in Advent. From Christmas to Septuagesima we see Him being born, grow into mature manhood, and start work in his office.

From Septuagesima to the vigil of Easter we celebrate His suffering.[1] Then follow the celebration of His resurrection, His forty Easter days, His ascension, the pouring out of His Holy Spirit, and during the rest of the year, the remembrance of the building and the life of his holy Church. Thus we live all days, weeks and the entire year for our Lord Jesus.

And indeed, we always celebrate the remembrance of the suffering and the resurrection in the **same** way. At **eleven** a.m. all the bells in the land ring out to remember the hot noon hour when Jesus hung on the cross, surrounded by night.[2] Somber celebration of His suffering in repentance for sins and in praise of His most holy merit fills the soul of the Christian. At **three** p.m., during the daily office, one remembers His death and prays for a good death. Every week, on Wednesday and Friday, one remembers Jesus' suffering with repentance, and every Sunday His resurrection with joy. And during the year the forty, even seventy day time of remembering Jesus' suffering is a time of repentance, fasting and prayer; fifty days after Easter is a high time of rejoicing.—We see that the history of Jesus, Jesus Himself, is our life. The Church year, the week, and the day simply are there to remember Jesus, and whoever lives in the Church year lives in Jesus' suffering and in his entire life.

However we cannot hide the fact that the Church year still has a double meaning. At least it did have it, and indeed should still have it, even if it has been lost among us Protestants. All at once, every calendar with many names that are added to each day, which could easily be supplemented and augmented, shows that the entire year is full of remembrances of the **saints**.[3] Just as the stars accompany the course of the sun, thus the manifold remembrance of pious conquerors accompanies the remembrance of the life, suffering, and dying of Jesus. And every saint reflects in his life, suffering and death the life and the fulfillment of his Lord. From Luther's writings and that of others, and from the rich calendar literature it can be shown that the Lutheran Church never was against this thought. Beginning with Luther, upon whose encouragement and with whose introduction Georg Major edited the improved *Vitae Patrum*,[4] to the most recent times, there are many writings

---

[1] The historic lectionary has one or two Sundays after Christmas, then the Epiphany season thereafter until Transfiguration, then Septuagesima, Sexagesima, and Quinquagesima (Estomihi) before Ash Wednesday.

[2] [Loehe:] Thus we should understand the ringing of the bells at eleven a.m., because it has become the generally accepted opinion that Jesus Christ was not crucified at eleven a.m., as the ancients believed, but at nine a.m.

[3] [Loehe:] See the "*Calendarium sanctorum oder die Zeugenwolke des neuen Testamentes*" in *Haus-, Schul- und Kirchenbuch* by W. Loehe. Part II 1859, p. 115ff.

[4] [Loehe:] Lives of the Fathers, for the Use of the Ministers of the Word, Improved As Far As it Could Be Done, by Doctor Georg Major. With a Preface of Dr. Martin Luther, Wittenberg 1562 [*Vitae patrum, in usum ministrorum verbi, quoad eius fieri potuit repurgatae. Per D. Georgium Majorem. Cum praefatione D. Doctoris Mart. Luth. Witebergae 1562*].

that celebrate the deaths of the saints of God, imitating the Lord of whom it is written that the memory and the death of His saints are precious to Him.[5]

Besides this, the Church formerly also celebrated the **natural course of the year**, its progress from seedtime to harvest, from summer to winter, from frost to heat and again to frost, with its Ember (*Quatember*) times of fasting. In more recent times it still celebrated Harvest Home, New Year's Eve, etc.[6]

Every calendar reflects this threefold annual celebration according to the course of Nature, the life of Jesus, and the history of His saints. Sun, moon and stars show in it their course, but walk reverently around Jesus and His saints, whose remembrance and celebration grant to the natural year and its times and days sacred meaning and importance, worth and life. Therefore one cannot easily find a book that could make a total impression of how all of history, the great clock of time, and the starlit heaven are subject to the Lord and his Church, as does the calendar. Of course one has to omit all embellishments and superstitions, of which older and newer calendars are full, just to please the people that have been spoiled with superstitions.

---

[5] [Loehe:] The literature of the Protestant churches concerning the suffering and dying of the martyrs has increased a lot during the few years since the first edition of this book appeared. A reference to Piper's *Calendar* and Fliedner's *Book of Martyrs* should be sufficient to help you find a whole series of similar literary works. But there are portrayals of martyr stories that will not be fruitful or blessed for the examples of the martyrs. Yet it is certain that besides the Holy Scriptures, which are incomparable, no other reading matter is as moving and blessed as the stories of the passion of the martyrs. The entire flood of Christian entertaining and romantic literature is flowing past us here. But the stories of the heroes of Jesus will remain and have their effect to the end. The examples of heroic faith during the Middle Ages will also have a refreshing and strengthening effect for those who know and appreciate the different times and circumstances. [Editor's note: The LCMS also produced a book of martyrs, namely, *Die Märthyrer der evangelisch-lutherischen Kirche* 2 vols. (St. Louis: Niedner, 1854 and 1856) by C. J. Hermann Fick (1822–85). The research, however, was a bit spotty, e.g., Caspar Tauber (d. 1524) was not a Lutheran, as one might believe in *Märthyrer* 1:1–5, but an Anabaptist. Additionally, the LCMS lectionary and agenda printed in 1902 had lectionary readings for apostles' and saints' days (113–34) that were absent by the 1922 agenda. Ceremony was the norm when the LCMS began (see *Law and Gospel: How to Read and Apply the Bible*, 184). By the 1920s nonconformist American Protestantism changed that former richness into a thin anti-Roman gruel. See also Kenneth W. Wieting, *The Blessings of Weekly Communion* (St. Louis: Concordia, 2006).]

[6] German *Quatember* comes from *quattuor anni tempora*, the four seasons of the year. English *Ember* may come from German or more likely from Anglo-Saxon *ymb-ryne*, a circuit. Ember weeks fall between the third and fourth Sundays of Advent, the first and second Sundays of Lent, Pentecost and Trinity Sunday, and the liturgical week beginning on the Sunday after Holy Cross Day (September 14). Ember days themselves fall on Wednesday, Friday, and Saturday of those weeks. Roman Catholic priests traditionally are ordained on those days.

B. ORIGIN OF THE MAIN FESTIVALS OF THE YEAR

The Church Year is a whole, but not something invented or fabricated; it is no timid human system. Here and there, there is missing a certain roundness, an even, harmonic development, as simply pointing to the long row of Sundays after Trinity after the festive half-year can show. But what is lacking in roundness of the year is made up by the beautiful celebrating of the ordinary **day** and the ordinary **week**. Their quiet glory also has its perfect right and its sweet blessing. For if every day were a festival and if there would be a system of feasts that would make every day a festival, even though it were the most manifold and different feast, in the end no day would be a festival. The extraordinary would become common, ordinary, and for that very reason it would be deprived of its specialty and uniqueness. But if the whole year is not rounded off, there are at least two smaller entities within the year that rule the year just like sun and moon; they standing in the Church sky and dominate the year. We mean the really great festive time of the year from Septuagesima to Trinity and the Christmas season from Advent to Epiphany with its postlude during the Epiphany Sundays.

It was quite natural that, from the beginning, above everything else the Lord lived and accomplished, the memory of **His suffering and His resurrection was lifted up**. Our entire salvation depended on the suffering, dying, rising and glorification of the One who had become man. Here the tree of life is blooming and bringing fruit for us. The second festive season, the one of Christmas, become more meaningful and more serious only with and after the big doctrinal controversies that were fought concerning God and humanity, the natures and the person of the Lord. Once the divine truth concerning these extremely important points had gained the upper hand, after tremendous fights, the Church could not express the newly-won and more thoroughly-known faith, and the great certainty of Christ, the Immanuel, any better in churchly celebration than through the festival of His birth. Before the whole world it knelt down at the crib of the Child Jesus; for He is God and man in one person.

In the beginning one celebrated the great week[7] among the weeks as one would celebrate Friday among the days, but soon one extended the celebrat-

[7] This refers to Passion Week (old form *Charwoche*). The German tradition celebrated the Sunday of the Passion (*Charsonntag*), likewise *Charmontag*, *Chardienstag*, and *Charmittwoch*. "Herb Thursday" (*Gründonnerstag*) comes from missionaries to the Germans substituting the pagan custom of eating the first greens of the season with the bitter herbs of the Passover and Jesus' mandate in the New Passover. Then came *Charfreitag* and *Charsamstag*. Only English and German use the old Germanic *Easter / Ostern*. Most Christians refer to a variant of *Pascha*, from Greek πασχεῖν, to suffer. "Palm Sunday" arose in England out of the medieval passion plays that opposed the false doctrine of the Lollards regarding the Eucharist.

ing of the suffering much further—to forty days.[8] For one had to count approximately forty hours for the time from the death of Christ to His resurrection. For each hour one should give one day of the year as a remembrance! The Lord Himself had fasted forty days and forty nights, also Moses and Elijah. Thus forty had become a sacred number. From ancient times onward, the time to remember the suffering of Jesus also lasted forty days. But since every Sunday was a brother of Easter Day, which was dedicated to the remembrance of the resurrection, full of joy, it could not count during the forty somber days when one remembered Jesus' suffering. Therefore these Sundays had to be exempted from remembering the suffering. They were points of joy in the midst of the days of sadness (although the joy appeared dampened because of its proximity to mourning). The forty days, the *Quadragesima*, had to be counted back to the Wednesday before Invocavit, Ash Wednesday. With these days began the *Quadragesima*.

In the Orient, where one did not fast on Saturdays as in the Occident, one observed the Old Testament Sabbath with joy like a brother of the New Testament Sabbath. One also exempted Thursday from fasting, the day of the institution of the Holy Meal. Therefore one had to extend the forty days of fasting before Easter even farther back than in the Occident. Thus a *Quinquagesima, Sexagesima* and *Septuagesima* developed from the ancient *Quadragesima*, so that the time of remembering the suffering began ten weeks before Easter.

Even in the Occident one went along with this, to celebrate not only the *Quadragesima*, but to begin a certain kind of celebrating already with Septuagesima Sunday. One liked to think of the seventy years of the Babylonian Exile and accepted the somber, sad celebration like an exile from joy, like a time of testing and castigation, which nevertheless one longed for to end, looking for the beautiful Easter Day. Completely corresponding to this view of the fasting time is the character of Laetare Sunday. It is in the middle of the *Quadragesima* and has a joyful character. After a half-completed chastisement it appears as a joyful resting place that looks toward the near end of sadness, while the other Sundays of the fasting time still smell like a garden of absinthe in the midst of which their joys are blooming.

Even though it still was a day of fasting, the vigil of Easter already was full of joy and also the baptismal day for the catechumens. One already was close to the open gate of joy, the free mountaintop of joy. One forgot the ongoing chastisement, in view of the joy that started after midnight with the Hallelujah. There followed a *Quinquagesima* of joy. Every day was a Sunday. One went from joy to joy, until the year reverted to its normal course again with Pentecost, later Trinity. The forty days before Easter and the fifty days after Easter together present a wonderful system of celebrating. In its bright splendor it was so well-known by the whole world that the Church fathers in

---

[8] Thus the Greek name for Lent, the "Great Forty Days" (*Μεγάλη Τεσσαρακοστή*).

their writings challenged the heathen to show something of that kind in any of their heathen cults.

Just like before the great joyful season of Easter, there was also a time of preparation before Christmas. It was an image of the four hundred years before Christ appeared. Just like the time of preparation before Easter it was celebrated with serious examination of one's own heart, with fasting, praying and giving of alms. And just as Easter was followed by the *Pentekoste*, the birth of Jesus was followed by the season of Epiphany, a joyful season that was not of the same water as Pentecost, and yet a season of joy.[9]

Beautifully and somberly the **ember** (***Quatember***) celebration was folded into the time of the greatest holidays. In December one celebrated on the *Quatember* of the so-called **tenth month** the feast of the completed harvest with repentance, fasting, praying, and alms. That meant in addition to the seriousness of the time of waiting for Christ there was also the seriousness of harvest fasting. At the beginning of the *Quadragesima*, in the *Quatember* that came on **Wednesday before Reminiscere Sunday**, one looked forward to the coming year, and joined the hope of a harvest with repentance, fasting, praying, and alms. And once **Pentecost was past**, while the year stood there in perfect splendor, yet the end of the joyful season invited serious examination of one's behavior, there came again, as also later in **September**, a *Quatember* fasting. Four great days of fasting, repentance, and prayer returned every year at designated times and invited reflection.

It could seem surprising that one designated the time of harvest and the annual progress of nature as time for **serious repentance**, just like the time of the Passion. Yet if we rightfully see the suffering of Christ as the reason for our joy, then the ancient thought to observe the cause of our joys with repentance is tender, faithful, and intimate. One suffered during the time of suffering by repenting for one's sins, which had brought such great suffering to Christ, in order to rejoice on Easter and Pentecost from the bottom of one's heart. In celebration, one clung to the words: "He was handed over to death for our trespasses and was raised for our justification." In this manner one added the proper suffering to the punishment for sin, and heartfelt joy for the justification of the resurrection. And if we celebrate the harvest with hymns of praise, and with thanksgiving, the ancient times certainly knew no less how to receive the divine goodness in the best way, with abstinence and repentance, and giving thanks with alms and collections.[10]

---

[9] One might consider that Advent is the result of the Greek Church's old penitential season from St. Martin's Mass to Christmas encountering the joyful four weeks before Christmas celebrated in Rome. One gets four reflective, yet hopeful weeks.

[10] [Loehe:] Compare the beautiful sermons of Leo the Great: *Of Collections and Alms, about the Fast of the Tenth Month and Alms, etc. Works of Leo the Great, the First Roman Bishop of This Name, etc.* Antwerp, by Philipp Nutius 1583, p. 11ff, 18ff. [*de Collectis et Eleemosynis, de Jeiunio decimi mensis et eleemosynis, etc., etc. Opera D. Leonis Magni, Romani Pontificis, eius nominis primi, etc., etc. Antverpiae, apud Philippum Nutium. 1583.*]

C. THE LECTIONARIES OF THE ANCIENTS

Again and again the Holy Scriptures were read in the assemblies of Christians. At least in the Occident this was done in this way: One did not read the sacred books continuously, word for word, but one used selected lessons. This can be traced back to the most ancient times and is expressed especially in many lectionaries that have continued to exist. These lectionaries are remarkable not only because one can see from them what one used to read in church, but also because one can see from them what festivals were celebrated. From the selected lectionaries one can conclude the meaning of why they were chosen, also on what **thoughts the festivities were based.**

But the ancients had different lessons. There are **hourly lessons** and **mass lessons.** The former extended across the whole year and provided the opportunity to read through the greatest part of Holy Scripture in one year, according to a beautiful order that was fitted to the Church year. They differ from the mass lessons because they have not been taken arbitrarily from this or that biblical book, depending on need and judgment, but a certain sequence of the books was kept in their selection. In the Occident they represent the principle of reading entire books, the cursory reading of the Bible, though in excerpts, or selectively. The mass lessons are not distributed over all the days, as are the hourly lessons, but only for the celebrated days. Therefore we have to recognize that the days for which there are mass lessons are festive days. And here it becomes especially apparent how carefully the lessons were selected for the celebration of the *Septuagesima*, the Advent season, and the *Quatember* days. Therefore one gains the certainty of the greatness of the celebration of the times mentioned from the riches of the lessons. In general, one cannot get a better concept of the Church year of the ancients, the remnants of which are still a part of our Church life, than from the lectionaries.

From them one also has formed the judgment mentioned above concerning the lesser roundness of the Church year as a whole, but also concerning the *Quadragesima* and the Pentecost *Quinquagesima* as jewel and crown of the year. From *Septuagesima* until Pentecost, not only the hourly but also the mass lessons fit together beautifully. One trend and thought goes through all of them. But from them one also can see that the festive thoughts of the ancients are not always the same as what we tend to keep for these festive times. The thoughts concerning the feast times and *Quatember* times, which we just hinted at, are based e.g., completely on the lectionaries, even though they are also confirmed and proven by other historical circumstances.

For the modern age, which has not been able to create a lectionary of any value simply because it wanted to create it by reflection, one can only recommend the study of the ancient lectionaries and the ancient Church year. But in those very products of the ancient world one would have to realize where at times the ancient Church year would permit a different understanding than the one we are used to. But with them one would also learn to admire the reason and wisdom of the ancients, and be so much happier to join them, since one does not possess the strength and wisdom to create something better or even equal.[11]

D. Sacred Space

As certain as the ordering of the time is most meaningful for the liturgy, it is also certain that a proper furnishing and ordering of the space is of great importance for the same purpose. A Christian can pray everywhere and lead a spiritual life. One also cannot imagine a place so ugly that it could not turn into a Bethel through an exuberant spirit. The services that were conducted by the ancients in caves prove that richly. One cannot deny that the location and its nature can present a hindrance to human devotion, and yet, on the other hand, these can further such devotion to a certain extent. We lead our spiritual life in space and time. Our body takes part in this as an inseparable companion of the soul. Corporeality and space cannot be put in contrast to service in the Spirit and in Truth. On the contrary, wherever the spirit is able, it will also form the corporeal and the spacious surroundings and furnishings so that they correspond to the spiritual purpose of worshiping.

This is also seen in the most ancient time. It is not recognized by those who get spiritualism and abstraction mixed up with simplicity. It was precisely the simplicity of the total church life that taught the ancients to furnish their church space worthy of its purpose. Therefore, wherever the persecution rested during the early days, the altar and the house of God were decorated, and that to such an extent that today it would be called luxury, just as Judas declared the nard of the anointing woman as refuse and waste.

However, it is not our intention here to speak of building a church in general or of the outside of a church building. We simply want to keep an eye on the liturgical space, the interior of a church building. Just as the ancients left the outer wall undecorated, we also do without the exterior, without despising it, or thinking of it as unimportant.

Now the main question is this: What is the first and most important place in a Lutheran church: The altar or the pulpit? It is easy to answer this question. In a Lutheran service it is not the sermon but Holy Communion that is the greatest celebration. The sermon itself leads to the holy meal as to the most intimate, mysterious union of Christians with their Christ. But the goal of the entire Divine Service also sanctifies the place where it is completed, elevating it to first place in a Christian house of God. Therefore the altar is and remains the most important place, also for building a Lutheran church and for the furnishings of our places of worship. The entire sacred space has

---

[11] [Loehe:] For an attempt of restoration see W. Loehe's *Haus-, Schul- und Kirchenbuch für Christen des lutherischen Bekenntnisses.* 2 vols. Stuttgart: Bertelsmann, 1859, pp. 141–58.

to be in relation to it. For this very reason the arrangement of the ancient houses of God should by and large become proper for the Lutheran Church as well.

Subconsciously, but recognizably, the ancient furnishings of worship locales is based on those of the Tent of Meeting [the Tabernacle], or the temple of Solomon. In front of the sanctuary there stood the altar for the burnt offerings, an image of Golgotha, which is put ahead of the entire temple worship. From the altar the priest is led to the wash basin, which cleanses hands and feet, and thus is an image of Baptism and its aftereffect in the Absolution, through which we are endowed with the power of Jesus' sacrifice. Only the one who has been washed can proceed from the outer court to the sanctuary; only a person who is baptized and standing in the grace of forgiveness can enter to the service of the New Testament. In the sanctuary there stands the lamp stand, which symbolizes the Word of God; the showbreads, images of our thank offerings and love offerings, also of the bread that we bring to the Lord for his Sacrament; and the altar of incense on the threshold of the holiest of holies, which reminds us of the great sacrifice of prayer, of thanksgiving, and praise.

In the holiest of holies there is the ark with the atoning cover made of pure gold covering the Law, which the cherubim gaze at and venerate, together with the vessel (*Gelte*), and Aaron's blossoming staff. All this is an image of eternal life, also of the sacred meal where the one dwelling in the clouds comes to us, He who is our reconciliation and whose wonderful union with humanity cherubim and all angels desire to see.

Completely corresponding to this, the churches of the New Testament have an outer court with the antitype of the wash basin, the baptismal font, which stands on the threshold between the outer court and the sanctuary. In the sanctuary the priestly congregation moves and is enlightened by the Word of God, according to the image of the lamp stand. There it also practices its worshipful prayers, gives thanks and praise, and brings showbread and sacrifice to its Lord. And in the holiest of holies stands the altar, from which it receives much more than it can give, where it celebrates its sacrificial means, and meets its Christ for a most intimate fellowship. In front of the altar is the place of highest revelation and union, and that is the difference between the Old and the New Testament.[12] From this results the threefold division of any Christian church. The altar explains the holiest of holies of the Church militant. But the pulpit stands either at a proper place in the nave of the church, or at the threshold of the chancel.

The natural place of those who serve at the altar is close to it. It makes no difference whether the shepherd and bishop of his congregation, while offici-

[12] Such revelation would not be direct, but indirect, mediated by an interpretation of Scripture as understood by the *Book of Concord*. Loehe's more dynamic model of exegesis in the community could possibly change the meaning of *revelation*.

ating, is turned to the [liturgical] east, or is facing [liturgical] west, standing behind the altar. Either way there is a beautiful meaning. But it does matter and it is liturgically required that the entire congregation face east toward the altar, so that all the chairs and pews should be directed toward the altar. This means that it is also best if the pulpit is placed in the east of the nave.[13]

The choir, together with the cantor, should probably best be placed in front of the singing congregation, on the threshold of the chancel or in the nave, perhaps also in the so-called *Vierung* (the cross between the main nave and the transepts). But due to the size of the organ, the choir could not very well be placed there. It belongs to the opposite end of the nave, above the outer court. One has also found it practical that the choir would gather next to the organ. That way everything that would lead the congregational singing would sound from above.[14]

The entire establishment of the service points to the necessity for the altar to be above the nave, so that the whole congregation can be eyewitness to what is happening at the altar. However, Protestants will not be interested in having the altar too high, because they do not permit a mass sacrifice or the worshiping of the host. Nor do they want to indicate a separation of the sacramental space from the priestly congregation.

The pews should have comfortable kneelers, since kneeling is a churchly gesture, and certainly a position that is most favorable to devotion, unless it is disturbed through pain and knee discomfort. Therefore a support for the arms of the kneeling person is necessary.

Balconies are an old custom. However, the ancient Church was right in finding it more proper to send the women to the balconies rather than the men.[15]

It is good if the worship space is not too small. Narrowness contradicts liturgical thought, which expresses its differences and intervals also through a certain separation in space. Neither does a church that is too small invite devotion—especially if it is crowded with bench after bench all the way to the altar steps, as is the custom among Protestants. But especially for the liturgist it is more comfortable if he does not have the congregation too close. It is strange but true that one feels more intimately connected to the congregation if it is physically somewhat more distant than if it is too close. Understood,

[13] The cardinal directions within a church have no direct relationship to its external orientation. The narthex is in the west, forming an axis with the choir, chancel, altar, and apse in the east. Between narthex and chancel is the nave. The pulpit should be located at liturgical north and lectern at south, both near the choir or chancel.

[14] Loehe admires the historic architecture of many churches, yet he is flexible and sensitive to practical developments in Protestant church architecture.

[15] These were still the days when men in church sat segregated from women and children. That very segregation helped confirmation to be seen as a *rite de passage* where a boy would join the ranks of the men.

there are no dogmatic reasons for this, only psychological ones, but they do count. Of course there is no doubt that the discomfort has to be overcome if its cause cannot be removed.

E. SACRED VESSELS

Under this title I would like to combine the immoveable as well as the moveable equipment in our churches, since we have no all-inclusive term for the things that serve our worship purposes. Therefore I refer here to the baptismal font (*Taufstein*), the pulpit and the altar, the baptismal basin (*Taufbecken*) and cans, chalice and ciborium, together with the linens and covers that are used for both. I not only put them together because of their common purpose to serve the Christian worship, but also because I feel coerced to express the same judgment in regard to them. At least that applies to the more modern ones and to the understanding that their users have of them.

I find it all very poor and below all expectation. We take great care of anything else that is dear and beloved to us, sparing no cost and expense. Even a poor person becomes very resourceful when it comes to decorating and honoring the graves of his own, etc. And without any doubt, what is given to us in our churches is the greatest and best that can be given to us in the whole world. In Baptism and in the Word we receive the Spirit with all its powers, and in the Sacrament of the Altar the body and blood of the Lord. Therefore we ought to honor and decorate the places where we receive these heavenly gifts, and also the vessels in which we receive them.

We decorate the graves in which the dead bodies of our fathers are resting. But the places and vessels from which we receive heavenly goods we treat as if we would follow completely different conclusions and thoughts in their regard. Whoever wants to convince himself of this just has to wander through the churches in his vicinity. Let him look at baptismal fonts, at pulpits and altars, ask to see the sacred vessels and altar hangings, and he will be surprised how poor all that is, and what contrast one can see between the purpose and the appearance of the sacred vessels. But if here and there the opposite should be found, and the inherited love of the congregations for their churches should show itself in a certain display, or even some kind of wastefulness, then the poverty and shabbiness, the tastelessness and ugliness, despite riches, will be even more noticeable, more glaring and offensive.

Every Protestant is confident that he can judge the interior of Roman churches, and considers it his inherited right to be allowed to express his opinion. But he finds it quite tolerable if his own church suffers deficiencies, which for an unprejudiced person may be just as offensive, or even more so, than a tastelessly overloaded Roman church. Where does all this come from? One could mention this and a few other things, if not from a boundless ignorance, one almost could say crudeness, of the pastors and the entire Protestant clergy. I do not want to blame the congregations. With honorable exceptions everything in their churches seems good enough to them. But how long ago is it that the pastors themselves considered it part of their care and worthy of their zeal [to consider] what the sacred vessels in their churches looked like?

One can certainly call it a new stirring of life in our Church, that at least here and there one can see signs of discontent and some effort. But even where this effort shows itself, does it have light before it? Do the pastors really know of what quality the sacred vessels ought to be? Even apart from the beauty, the practice alone makes it necessary not to let everything go as it might. Whoever is even in the least interested in how to officiate comfortably and efficiently should be forced to consider certain requirements in the condition of the vessels. But if a servant of the Church is not only concerned that everything should be practical, but also dignified and beautiful, and if he really loves his office and the holy sacraments, and is disturbed by everything that is tasteless, undignified and poor among the vessels and the furnishings of his church, he must have the urge and desire to change and improve things.

Not only his perception of what is beautiful, but also his very piety must protest against any substandard, undignified or even tasteless vessels. And if a Protestant pastor feels this way in his heart, what is he going to do? Since he has not learned anything about all this, and therefore understands nothing, he will let his self-conceit and caprice be his teacher. Perhaps he even trusts his wife to have tactfulness and taste, so he asks for her advice, even though she of course knows even less than he does. Or he asks his sacristan, or he feels his way in a fog, since he does not even know of any source for knowledge from which he could draw. Everywhere one can find the fruits of such ignorance and lack of counsel and can point them out, if one is willing to do that.

The Roman Church, which by no means is without resources, but possesses in its churchly books enough stored up instructions and lessons, nevertheless has had no less a period of decay in this regard than the Protestant one. In general it also has not yet found its way back, but the reaction toward something better has started within it, and with its rich sources it is easier for it to recuperate, while the Protestant Church has hardly any sources, and the church orders of the Reformation are so poor that one can hardly find anything in them and the contemporary literature about the furnishings of the churches and their vessels. Even the few studies that have been made during the first centuries after the Reformation have been lost and forgotten, not even to mention whether their value was great or small. Later came the miserable time when one no thought of such things any longer. Therefore the same thing happens to us here as when it comes to the church building. Not too long ago one struggled with the question of whether or not the Protestant church should be different from the Roman one. Should not the pulpit be for us just as important as the altar is for the Romans? It is almost a miracle that one recognized so quickly that for us Lutherans the highest and most important thing in conducting church is the Sacrament, and in a church building it is the altar, no less than in a Roman church. Thus we have to condescend in God's name to return to the writings of the ancient Church and its traditions concerning the church vessels, and learn what is practical and beautiful from the experience of the centuries. Only everything has to be studied with a reformatory mindset, and we have to let go of anything that contradicts the dogma of the churches of the Reformation.

We want to give an example. The Roman baptismal font (*Taufstein*) has to be a real stone (*Stein*), because the Roman Church consecrates the water in it only once a year and keeps it there for use throughout the year. For this reason the Roman baptismal font has a lower lid that can be locked, and indeed from Baptism to Baptism it is locked carefully, and the key is kept by the parish priest himself.

The baptismal font of the Lutheran Church is totally different. Since it follows the principle that the consecration of the elements is effective only for the duration of each sacramental act, from the start the church rejected the consecration of the baptismal water for a longer time. In drastic contradiction to its own practice during Holy Communion, it completely gave up the consecration of the baptismal water and no longer consecrates it.

Most pastors would never get the idea that the water should be consecrated, just as bread and wine are consecrated during the Sacrament of the Altar. As is well known, only men like Höfling have recently pointed the Church in the right direction.[16] This principle of the Lutheran Church, and the practice derived from it, has made the Protestant baptismal font into something totally different. Since one only needs the amount of water necessary to sprinkle one single child, one does not need a stone. It can be wood, or no font at all; one can baptize on any table. Therefore some baptismal tables actually exist, which are more comfortable for the wrapping and unwrapping of the children (in places where the children are unwrapped for Baptism). But one does not need a table at all; it is enough just to have a baptismal basin. This takes the place of the font and the table, and if the sacristan would hold it under [the child] and the pastor himself would handle the pitcher, it would be so much easier to just throw the water out after the Bap-

---

[16] Johann W. F. Höfling (1802–53) was pastor in Nuremberg (1827) and Erlangen professor (1833–52), as well as member of the Bavarian high consistory (1852). He specialized in liturgics and helped found the *Zeitschrift für Protestantismus und Kirche*. In his influential *Grundsätze evangelisch-lutherischer Kirchenverfassung* (1850), Höfling established a delegation theory (*Übertragungstheorie*), whereby the rights of the general priesthood of believers are delegated to the clergy. He was influential in shaping the 1853 revision of the Bavarian *Agende*.

tism.[17] The old custom with the font has been lost anyway, and such a Protestant custom would be more practical.

Of course with a Roman font one also uses a baptismal basin in order to catch the water that one has baptized with, since it was drawn from the font. But after it is used should not be poured back into the consecrated water. With us the use of the baptismal basin is not to prevent anything; it has only a practical purpose, since one does not want to let the water fall on the ground. Even so, in the end it might happen that afterwards the sacristan might pour out those few drops of baptismal water on the church floor or outside the church door. [In doing so] He would not have that much decency or feeling to treat the element after the Sacrament with respect, since it was used for the best [thing] ever possible.

From this one can see how very different a Protestant baptismal font is from a Roman one, and has to be different. Nevertheless, the mere churchly taste and the correct practice of Holy Baptism, as well as the pedagogy of the Church, will never agree with the poor system of a baptismal basin. It will demand a baptistery for every church, a place that is symbolically chosen at the entrance of the church, enclosed and provided with an elevated or recessed baptismal font. But as soon as one has arrived at this demand, one will learn the best and most beautiful possible from the entire building of the Roman baptismal font, after omitting the lower lid and the lock. One will let go of the miserable contradiction of a wooden baptismal font, provide it with the ancient piscina under its base, baptize in the Protestant way above the baptismal font, and let the water run off through the pipe in the font, most appropriately into the piscina.[18] (This will eliminate any misuse, any superstitious use of the baptismal water, any lack of reverence by an uncouth sacristan). One will be able to install the [stone] cover of the font in the old way, with full or lesser embellishment, with or without pulleys, for the enjoyment of the congregation and the glorification of the Sacrament.

With this example I meant to show what I understand by a reformatory study of the old liturgical vessels. It is almost the same with all vessels and with all Protestant altar hangings, beginning with the altar, the ciborium, and the chalice. One should make it the duty of every young pastor, especially during this time of rampant ignorance and coarseness, to study the sacred vessels and to make his own contribution, so that the ancient wisdom, decorum, and beauty, purified and cleansed, would also enter our churches and gain a place there. Old pastors do not even know how to have an altar hang-

---

[17] Loehe does not recommend just throwing out the water without due reverence shown to the material of a sacramental act. He explains this below.

[18] A *piscina* (Latin for fish pond) is a basin connected to a drain (*sacrarium*) that runs directly to the earth. It is meant for the reverent disposal of water from ablutions, baptismal rites, and washing the sacred vessels after Communion.

ing made, or what a chalice should be like and how one should hold it, etc. That shame should be taken away from our church and its servants

One could say that the leaders of the Church should give out rules. But the leaders are usually old men who come from the times of ignorance. This matter could not be spoiled in a worse way as when their subjective opinions would be foisted upon the congregations in the form of orders, before daylight rose in the Church for these things. Thanks be to God, there are beautiful beginnings here and there, which could quickly be suppressed by the hand of the powerful. In recent times one has had enough experiences of what can happen if what is good and necessary is to be introduced in the form of orders and commandments. One can spare oneself the bitter experience of what would happen if one would command what is proper and beautiful, even if one knew it and understood it. In the area of the Church, one ought to honor what is done voluntarily in order to awaken and to educate. But one should not demand obedience for a command. Since we have come to the point where the Holy Spirit has awoken the feeling for what is proper and beautiful in the Church in regard to vessels and altar hangings, He will continue to help, and the only thing a church government should do would be only [to mount] a modest defense against what is obviously wrong.

Perhaps the place to refer young pastors is to the altar studies of Laib and Schwarz,[19] which are almost reformatory in themselves. From all the altar formations of the time of the service of saints and relics they lead to the beautiful simplicity of the holy *Mensa*, the table of Jesus.

And by the way, here one should have a whole book, instead of a single paragraph that is written as a stimulus, an *Instructio pastoralis liturgica.*

F. THE PARTS OF THE SERVICE

Of the first congregations it is said: "They devoted themselves to the apostles' teaching and fellowship, to the breaking of bread and the prayers."[20] Some have challenged the fact that fellowship meant the sharing of the alms of the church, or that the breaking of the bread meant the Sacrament of the Altar, without being able to find a better explanation and without being able to claim that the linguistic use of the ancient world was on their side.

---

[19] [Loehe:] *Studien über die Geschichte des christlichen Altars* [*Studies of the History of the Christian Altar*] by Friedrich Laib and Franz Joseph Schwarz, Stuttgart. Rümelin, 1857. Both Laib and Schwarz (1821–85) were leading members of the Rottenburg Diocesan Association for Christian Art. Schwarz also authored three other books on biblical exegesis. The result was the increased use of the ancient table or *mensa* as the altar in Roman Catholicism, widespread after Vatican II. Yet some Protestants, influenced by High Church Anglicanism, had migrated toward the baroque Roman Catholic high altar over the same span of time.

[20] ἦσαν δὲ προσκαρτεροῦντες τῇ διδαχῇ τῶν ἀποστόλων καὶ τῇ κοινωνίᾳ, τῇ κλάσει τοῦ ἄρτου καὶ ταῖς προσευχαῖς.

But even if the understanding of this verse, which we confess, would not be correct; if one could not admit that in this verse the parts of the divine worship are mentioned; one nevertheless could not deny the fact that apostolic teaching, churchly giving of alms, Sacrament, and prayer are the main parts of worship life. They are the ones that make Sunday to be Sunday, and make the great assembly of the congregation what it is.

But besides the great assembly, the *communio*, one can think about whole other services wherein one of the four parts may have preference over the others. There are preaching services, where prayer and songs are secondary. There are prayer assemblies, where the sermon and the teaching of the apostles, Communion, and other things are secondary. One could even imagine get-togethers for the sake of alms, where all the other parts of worship life are in the background. One should not criticize the separation and the lifting up of individual parts. Yet none of these are complete, and it is clear that no part can do **completely** without the others.

This applies especially to three of the parts. Who can assemble together for any business concerning worship without praying, for example? What worship assembly could be without the Word of God? Devotion and Word of God cannot be separated from any worship assembly. As far as it is natural and possible to separate the parts mentioned, one may do so if there is a good reason for it, as has been said. But they should also be combined, and that happens in the *communio*, as also was mentioned.

Worship life appears there in its completeness. The congregation receives through the word and deed of the Lord (Sacrament) and gives through word and deed (fellowship, *κοινωνία*), and the meeting of God, the Lord, and His congregation in most solemn earnestness of the high point of life.[21] In the *communio* there is not just the sound of words, not a celebrating of all works. On the contrary, the highest and best works of deepest peace are being practiced. The matter is almost too great and too high to use the name, but nevertheless we will have the courage to express it in this way: Here is highest poetry, and whatever epic, lyric, and dramatic poetry can make and shape out of the stuff of an ordinary human life, it cannot touch the combination of all the most sacred life[-giving] blossoms and fruits in the *communio*. No wonder, if in the ordering of the four parts of the *communio* the highest work of art that ever came from human hands is displayed. Here is the nature of a life that is supernatural, and next to the highest simplicity one finds here a wonderfully rich splendor, which is worth being pulled out from

[21] Here Loehe refers to the liturgical prayer and outward concern of the Church as a part of its *κοινωνία* in Christ. The latter forms the basis for the former. Yet it will become clear that Loehe realizes the controversial nature of his theology of sacrifice (only hinted at so far). He knows that he has been labeled as a Romanist and believes that he still has a position founded on the Pauline epistles.

its hidden chambers, especially the ancient liturgies of the Orient, to be looked at and to be enjoyed.

G. THE ANCIENT *COMMUNIO* AND THE LITURGY OF THE ANCIENTS IN GENERAL IN RELATION TO OUR TIME

When it comes to liturgy, the Lutheran Church acted in a truly reformatory way. It did not overlook or throw away what was beautiful [as a reaction to] the disgusting and spiritless way in which the Romans lowered [the liturgy] in the sixteenth century to [mere] undignified formalities and formal service. [Lutherans] kept the beautiful, which the Romans also had kept to a large extent. Even if Luther, in his 1526 "*Deutsche Messe*," went beyond the limit of reformatory procedure concerning the liturgy and went a different way from the truly reformatory one he had walked on in 1523, his example was not so decisive that one would have always followed him. At least in many of the territorial churches one refrained from throwing away anything that could contain a blessing.

However, a liturgical study and an insight into the development of the great liturgical whole of ancient times was still lacking, even among old Lutherans, that even then would have prevented the eliminating of many faultless and splendid inherited parts of the ancient times. I for my part cannot find that a Lutheran principle was used in the Lutheran agendas, except a negative dogmatic one.

Later some situations occurred that necessarily impoverished the Lutheran Church in liturgical matters. The Latin hymns disappeared, and with them the Gregorian chant, since one could not manage to create German texts for the ancient notes because the German language had sunk down so low. In the place of Gregorian chant there came the spiritual folk-song, the **so-called** choral, and the liturgical strength of the Church retreated into it. As time went on, one had to lose the understanding of the old order of worship, which was the main thing in the old liturgies. Therefore one could be could be glad to lose one piece after another of what one did not understand. Finally the unavoidable point came: the remnant of the old time was perceived to be bothersome; one could tolerate only the simplest combination of the four principal parts of the service and found them beautiful. One cannot but say that before long, Reformed emptiness and poverty seemed to be the goal that the Lutheran liturgy tried to achieve.

A reaction against this could not fail to come. Here and there someone started to take a look at the Lutheran liturgies. Right from the start the fullness and organization found in **them** appeared to them to be beautiful, straight from paradise, and highly poetical in comparison with the poverty that had become the rule, with its old humdrum way, which became even more unbearable than the old humdrum way of the ancient richness.

But if one spoke warmly in favor of the good of the old time, one's contemporaries found even the love of old Lutheran agendas to be Romanizing, and one would hardly believe that the fullness and organization of the service could be Lutheran. The ignorance and unfamiliarity of one's own poverty makes one impudent and shameless enough to insult those as Roman who knew more of ancient Lutheranism and showed a warm love for what they knew. If even the love for that is truly Lutheran was so badly misunderstood, how could one escape malicious gossip if one were to find and praise liturgical orders or products from the oldest time, even with the Romans. One would openly disapprove of Roman corruption of the ancient liturgy, but regret that some of it had become antiquated, which even today could serve devotion wonderfully, if only it would be used again with joy and devotion. Openly-shown love and admiration of the ancient liturgies was not the least, but the most important reason—or better unreason—why so many faithful Lutherans were maligned as Roman, who nevertheless with all seriousness clung to the results of the Lutheran Reformation. Of course one overlooked the fact that these maligned men admired the ancient oriental liturgies even more than the Roman ones. It did not occur to those people that one could accuse the same men for the same reason of their inclination toward the oriental Church—in fact to its sects—since the oldest liturgies have been preserved by the sects.[22]

At present, times have changed. At least there are ever-increasing circles where people have taken the side of the old Lutheran liturgy. They even started to inflict ordered liturgies on the unprepared congregations, in part newly collected from old pieces. The same men who at first awoke the sense for liturgy now had to do the opposite and stand warning at the road of the new liturgical progress. It is true; people will eventually get used to liturgical forms if they are constantly being presented with them every Sunday, and they finally will accept them as something unavoidable, yet nothing is gained this way.[23]

What good is it to get used to something that one neither understands nor appreciates? If the American congregations in Frankenmuth, Frankenhilf, Frankenlust, etc., accepted and practiced joyfully the liturgy of Loehe's *Agende*, this is easy to understand in the context of the churchly education of their members. They have a certain measure of love and understanding for

---

[22] [Loehe:] See *Liturgiarum orentalium collectio opera et studio Eusebii Renandotii Parisini. Editio secunda correctior.* [*Collected Works and Studies of Oriental Liturgies by Eusèbe Renaudot the Parisian. Second improved edition*] *2 tomi.* Frankfurt a/Main 1847. [Editor's note: Renaudot (1646–1720) was a French theologian and orientalist. Loehe shows here that he has no plans of backing down from his detractors.]

[23] The LCMS learned this lesson the hard way through the divisive experiences created by the heavy-handed adoption of *Lutheran Worship* and its emergence from work with the ILCW and the search for organic American Lutheran union. *Lutheran Service Book* has fared much better as a unifying liturgical focal point.

the liturgy that preserves them from disgust and sloppiness. With other congregations, who do not have the same liturgical prerequisites, one has to go slow, not forcing anything, but working through understanding and conviction. One can learn such wisdom well from Article 28 of the Augsburg Confession. Of course one must first keep in view a sure, total goal, and proceed on a path that leads first of all to good order and a simple service. Later one can develop the more complete décor and beauty without any trouble.

But by far the most important task is to teach the congregations the beautiful variety of the **common prayer,** and to practice it with them. A congregation that enjoys the bidding prayer—praise and thanksgiving for all people—is a truly liturgical congregation even if its services do not have any of the ancient glory of the liturgy, nor practice it. Whoever would have brought his congregation to this level would also have overcome the essential lack of present-day congregations, who only want to listen and be stimulated internally but do not want themselves to be active, and therefore do not want to pray themselves. Prayer is automatically followed by the psalm, the hymn, the *Credo*, etc. There is a greater mental and spiritual progress from praying to singing than from singing to praying because singing, through the beauty of sound, often detracts more from the meaning of the song than it leads into it. After the prayer one could start teaching about *κοινωνία*. It certainly would be good to teach the congregations from the epistles of Paul about the sacrifice of alms in the Church and to win them over, to guide them to a pure practice of the same, far from works-righteousness.

Regarding the celebration of the Holy Supper, even today's congregations are bringing enough understanding and reverence to it. Experience shows that even those who quickly smell Romanism in the rest of the service will put up with a richer development of sacred forms and sacred content in this holy action.

H. DAILY WORSHIP

In his *Hausagende* Dieffenbach lets daily worship proceed according to forms that have been borrowed from the *communio*.[24] If he would have appreciated the Lutheran morning and evening services and their connection with the ancient hourly services, doubtlessly he would have left the proper forms to the *communio*. For the main service he would have rather drawn from the Lutheran Matins and Vespers, although the main service does not necessarily have to follow them because it needs no churchly form and has no proper right.

---

[24] Georg Christian Dieffenbach (1822–1901) was a German poet and theologian whose devotional, homiletic, and liturgical works were very popular. His children's poems remain popular today.

Of course things are different if one is able to introduce daily main services in the congregation. For this intention the Matins and Vespers of the old Lutheran Church can give enough hints. When the teaching of the merit of works, including that of prayer, was dropped, eager participation in the service also sank right at the beginning of the Reformation. In many Church orders Matins and Vespers appear purely as a service of the school. For that reason there are special provisions in case adults show up for Matins or Vespers. In that case the lessons should also be read in German, while otherwise they are recited only in Latin.

Whether one would have better luck today introducing daily services remains dubious. Here and there, as an exception, a greater participation may be found. In general one could hardly speak of much luck. If the idea of **sacrifice** would be recognized and practiced more, there would be a greater and more powerful motivation to pray together, even though this thought is so high that one cannot hope that the multitude could cling to it. Because of inborn laziness it would always stumble into work righteousness, and pervert the very best. What is truly spiritual just is not for the masses.

A completely different question is whether for this reason one should do without the daily services altogether, namely where one was just about to introduce them. Even if they are not generally accepted, one might find a certain measure of acceptance, and they would open the possibility of devotion for many. An ambitions pastor might perhaps be able to form liturgical groups. They would get together, not just to practice liturgical singing, but also for serious prayer. Through them the participation and skill for liturgy could be roused and kept within the congregation. There certainly is no reason to omit something good just because it is omitted in general. On the contrary, what is good has to keep and enjoy the right of free participation within the congregation, and therefore free associations have to have their justification within the congregation. If this is true in general, then liturgical societies also should be permitted and acknowledged. The daily services could become gathering points for them, even though it should not become a bylaw that every member would have to attend every daily service. Without any sanguine hopes, this should be only one more means to awaken sympathy for the daily service. This should be free and earnest, without any hard coercion. Besides that, it might be easiest to guide the school toward daily service, just like during the time of the Reformation, even though one cannot trust the school any more than any other human bunch that they would never turn prayer and hymns into screaming and sing-song. What the monks did with the daily offices, one can expect no less from students during daily worship.

As for the order of the daily service, one has to be just as careful as with the *communio,* due to of the riches available. Here also there exists a simple introductory form that one can choose so much more unhesitatingly, since even in the old daily services there is no ruling connecting thought, as with the *communio*.[25]

I. Lack of Symbolism in General, and of Symbolic Action in Particular

The liturgy of the Lutheran Church is not totally bare of symbolic action. But in general, especially with benedictions, one refers so much to the sole use of speech that benedictions say very little on their own, nor are they very attractive. This can best be demonstrated with the example of a Protestant dedication of a church cemetery. The consecrator stands in his place, talks, and prays from there; everything he does happens through the word. If only there were, e.g., a singing procession, as is done at funerals, or even better, a singing procession that walks around the place or the building, outside or inside, whose singing would be interrupted in prominent places by the prayer of the consecrator. Such a consecration could be far more appropriate and could be recognized more easily in its proper meaning. It is not our intention further to enlarge on this subject, but it may be an impulse for thought: Especially in former times the Lutheran Church had much symbolism that disappeared more and more. We remember, e.g., the baptismal gown (*Westerhemd*) in Baptism. But of course superstition clings all the more easily to the most innocent ceremony, the more appropriate and the more meaningful the intention is.

J. So-called Liturgical Principles in the Lutheran Church

Freedom and love are called the principles of liturgy in the Lutheran Church. Freedom works variety; love prevents variety from becoming too multicolored. It is very easy to misinterpret the principle of freedom. When Luther praises freedom, he only means to oppose the coercion of human teaching and to guard the rights of the conscience that Christ has liberated so that we would no longer be servants of people. But by no means is he of the opinion that any liturgical caprice should have praise and honor under the name of Christian liberty. Even for things that are permitted and merely human there are rules and measures that one must not transgress, despise, or

---

[25] [Loehe:] Cf. Loehe's *Agende für christliche Gemeinden des lutherischen Bekenntnisses*, Part I (Nördlingen 1853), p. 69, the instruction concerning Matins and Vespers and the various orders of their four parts (psalm, lesson, hymn, prayer). Thinking about the old matins and vespers, one can feel our great sin, that we completely omitted the psalms, and the great, heavy sin of omission that, though we enjoy better light again, we do nothing to bring the psalms back to public use. It would be better to do without all our hymnbooks than to miss the psalms.

mistreat unpunished. Every area of human life and knowledge can be built on or planted in the right or wrong way. It is not Luther's opinion that it does not matter in what forms one would serve God. He only wants to assert the lack of a divine commandment, a positive, legal pressure. Therefore one can keep the freedom of liturgical forms and yet strive for the best and most beautiful, worthy of God and his Church. One can even pray for thoughts and ceremonies, for forms that promote devotion the most.

K. Liturgical Presentation

There are homiletic, catechetical, and liturgical presentations. The easiest—and easiest to promote and to keep—is the catechetical because, if it is in dialogue form, is closest to life. But if it is in lecture form it will follow the most definite road through the intention of teaching.

Between those forms stands homiletic presentation because, although related to a common speech, according to its content it moves so much in the *genus dicendi grande* that a pulpit tone easily, almost naturally, sneaks in. The sacred speech could and should progress completely in the natural individuality of the speaker, but of course in sanctified naturalness. This exactly makes the homiletic presentation more difficult than the catechetical one.

But without doubt liturgical presentation is the most difficult. It is difficult whether one sings or speaks. An old man says one should sing the collects and lessons because for the liturgy individuality should not be emphasized; no subjective stress should be permitted. Therefore one ought to sing, so that each one can put in his own tone. In order to achieve this, one makes every liturgical song into a pure recitative these days, and one trains the young pastors in this. There are some young people who sound off without spirit at the altars. Neither is the congregation served with this, nor is God honored. Despite the fact that subjectivity has to step back, the liturgical son nevertheless is capable of special emphasis. For there is a kind of emphasis that comes from the relationship of the congregation toward God, and the liturgist at the altar in his spiritual preparation somehow must untangle himself from his own mood and feeling, and look for the tone that is common to all, and should be common. To find this chanting and speaking tone is impossible for a non-spiritual person. Nor is it possible, I believe, for one who does not bear in himself the task and the knowledge that he is the voice of the congregation before God.

At a time when Protestants also would sing and speak at their altars according to tradition, when every young pastor could daily hear what a traditional liturgical tone is, one still had much more truly liturgical singing and presentation than now, when one has to find his way into it first through study and reflection. It may sound almost offensive to the ears of the young clergy, but in the end there is some truth to the saying: How to sing liturgically, one could learn best from Roman priests educated in the church.

However, here we only have to deal with singing at the altar, because it shares a principle with speaking at the altar: Subjectivity, subjective feeling, and [similar] emphasis have to be avoided. In order to be able to read correctly at the altar, one must be in the situation that one must read at the altar. The school of liturgical speech starts only after years of study, when life in the parish begins. A newly ordained servant of Jesus and His congregation then has to learn in humility and devotion what he ought to do, namely, to speak to God, not for the sake of his own devotion, but in the name of the congregation, and to present the *ipsissima verba* of God and his apostles to the people, so that they recognize the voice of the Good Shepherd and learn to understand it.

If this calling rules a liturgist, it will be easiest for a pastor who serves with him and next to him, to tell him the mistakes and where he lacks. Speaking with such a one about the success or failure of his performance will educate his feelers, so that more and more he will comprehend what a churchly liturgical presentation is. But whether there is success in this or not, the capability and skill will soon decrease again and disappear, unless the liturgist will faithfully remain in spiritual preparation for the liturgical service, and in his own devotion before and during the same. Whoever wants to pray and read in spirit and in truth, in the name of the congregation, needs above all subjective piety and spiritual practice. Whoever is not serious about his own devotion and preparation for the liturgical service will learn the least the great art of holy servants of God: to read and emphasize correctly at the altar. Whoever omits to prepare himself will soon be just a laborer at the altar, whom the Spirit will remind in his heart: "Take away from me the noise of your songs; I will not listen to the melody of your harps."

Chapter Four

Pastoral Care

A. Our Understanding of *Seelsorge*

No word seems to be easier than the word *Seelsorge* (pastoral care).[1] It is the care of the pastor for the souls of the flock entrusted to him. But this care means not only the inner thinking and reflecting of a soul-caring man for the best outcome of his parishioners, but also the actions derived from this. In the final analysis one can include everything a pastor has to do. Every sermon and address, every catechesis, every prayer service, also administering Communion; all of these are to be considered pastoral care. Yet, in a special sense, one understands it still as something else. Whoever has preached, catechized, given Communion, baptized, etc., usually does not call all this pastoral care. One considers pastoral care in a special sense to be the efforts of the pastor and the sharing of the divine Word as that relates to the pastoral conditions of the congregation.

But not every condition of a soul is called pastoral, only those to which a person comes on the way of the order of salvation, in view of the guidance of the Word and the Sacraments. Everyone who is called by the Spirit reacts toward the divine call and the divine guidance in his own way and brings his own special hindrances. One must guide a person in such a way that the hindrances are lifted and the soul is led, as simply and securely as possible, to the common goal of the divine calling. Whatever the pastor does in this sense and with this intention, is called pastoral care in its special meaning.

There is such a thing as pastoral guidance **for the whole congregation,** but also **for individual members.** Idiosyncrasies and hindrances make individual members different than one other. One can talk about pastoral conditions of whole congregations, but also about pastoral conditions of individual

[1] German *sorgen* means to care for, worry about, or sorrow over. *Seelsorger* means precisely beings a curate of souls, a committed caregiver who cares for, worries about, and sorrows over those souls in his care.

Christians. For example, there are congregations where cursing, or drinking, or stealing have become rampant, and these commonly ruling sins give the whole congregation a special reputation. A ruling sin is like the top of a mountain by which the whole mountain first receives its special form.

If a pastor takes over the leadership of a congregation, at best he can find out about its pastoral condition from others who told him. This communication can only sharpen his view, but he must not treat the congregation from the start according to it. It is his duty first to act without prejudice, and only start a special treatment once he has recognized the physiognomy of the congregation by his own experience. Only from his own acquaintance with the pastoral condition of the congregation can he discover his pastoral goals. These goals are different for different congregations, therefore no pastor can simply follow another one in the leadership of his people. But that is not to say that different goals are totally exclusive, or that there could be no other common goals beyond the immediate goals for the congregation, and finally the highest one, common to all.

If, for example, the pastoral circumstances of a congregation are conditioned especially by avarice and an earthly mind, the next goal of pastoral guidance certainly must be to guide them toward mercy and mildness. However, once this near goal has been reached, one that is farther and higher certainly will show itself. The congregation could become merciful and still keep the lust for pleasure, which perhaps it already had before, with all its saving, scraping and avarice. A pastor then should work toward a higher perfection of the congregation, by guiding it with all patience toward renunciation and self-denial, toward a life that is disciplined for the sake of prayer. One could say that a pastor who can so easily err when guessing the pastoral condition of the congregation, thereby establishing false goals, should not set any goals, but simply do whatever is the next thing that comes along. There may also be pastors who simply have no other choice than to do whatever comes along, without any proper goal. But in general one cannot advise anyone to choose this path.

Go slow in forming a judgment concerning the pastoral conditions of your congregation and in establishing a pastoral goal. You should be very concerned rightly to recognize both condition and goal. Until you have a sure knowledge, you may do whatever is at hand, according to your best knowledge and conscience. But once you are certain about the condition of the congregation and your next pastoral goal, a great strength will come from this, and your knowledge will be like a belt around your loins, enabling you to take firm steps.

It is quite similar with pastoral guidance for the individual. Here also you should not be hasty in making a judgment. Do not affirm it too quickly. The one who is ready quickly with word and judgment is neither the best nor the wisest. The pastoral condition of the individual is not easier, but more difficult to establish than that of a whole congregation. You will never get to the point where you can have a firm judgment about everybody. Human conditions are not always the same and what you know about them will change. That has to change, just like the conditions themselves. There are many individuals and it is a tremendous job for one person to know so many individuals correctly and set the right pastoral goal for each one. Since these are true, if one were satisfied with the least that one can do, it would be more forgivable if one would despair of the great and manifold task of caring for the individual than for the whole congregation. Nevertheless, pastoral care for the individual becomes valuable only if it is based on the recognition of the pastoral condition and goal, even though they may often change. And even if every pastoral counselor in modesty has to give up the idea of being able to guide and lead **every** individual from a secure central point, nevertheless it should be a constant challenge for him to serve as many as possible, even though he would wish to be able to serve everybody.

If the pastor sets a high goal for himself, it will not only be a challenge for him, but also a cause for humility. For a man who so often has to be right in his office, this is less a punishment than a reward for his endeavor.

B. PASTORAL AND MENTAL CONDITIONS

A pastor was called to a deathly sick farmer in his parish in order to give him the Sacrament. He was very careful in what he said in the presence of his attentive sacristan, because he was not sure how bad the sickness and its effect was. With the exception of a few words, which one could have interpreted as being nasty against the pastor, the sick person talked the way one would wish a dying one to talk. His pastoral condition seemed to be one of a repentant sinner, hungry for mercy. Pastor and sacristan agreed that one could give him the Sacrament, and so he received it. The next day the brother of the sick person came and asked, in the name of the latter, for a repeat visit by the pastor: The patient did not remember a thing about having received the Sacrament yesterday. But he now was especially upset, because his family had told him that he had given the pastor a nasty answer, and now he wanted to ask him for forgiveness. While the pastor had been of the opinion that he had treated the patient carefully and had recognized his pastoral condition correctly, it now turned out that he had not even been accountable, and that his mental condition had been taken for a pastoral one.

One can read similar things in the first part of de Valenti's *Medicina Clerica*, p. 273ff.[2] A woman [delirious] in [puerperal fever] who had a milk

[2] Ernst Josef Gustav de Valenti (1794–1871) was the son of an Italian instructor at Jena. De Valenti earned a PhD in 1818 and thereafter was permitted to practice medicine. In Sulza an apparently inept rationalist pastor accused him and some friends of being "mystics" and holding unauthorized conventicles in 1822. Much of this history is revealed in *Medicina Clerica oder Handbuch der Pastoral-Medizin für Seelsorger, Pädagogen und Aertzte; nebst einer Diätetik für Geistliche* (Leipzig: Köhler, 1831). De Valenti moved near

disorder [made requests concerning] her funeral in such a vain way that it was hard to understand. [She directed] the dress she wanted to wear in the coffin, who should get her other dresses, etc. When a Christian surgeon talked to her disapprovingly, she started to repent. An apparently thorough repentance followed, along with a faithful reaching out for Christ the Lord, according to the order of salvation. But what really did happen? When the danger was over, she remembered nothing, neither of her vanity about her clothes, nor of her conversion, and she was as healthy as before her sickness. What had appeared as the changing circumstances of a person from vanity to repentance had been just the game of a delirious soul. The existing mental conditions were so similar to pastoral conditions that one could be fooled. How much was pastoral care in vain in both cases? It would have been much better just to pray for the dying farmer and the young mother. But of course, in both cases—and certainly in the case of the farmer—one could not do anything else than what been done.

So we see that mental conditions often look deceptively similar to pastoral ones. Once this has been recognized, one will stand at sickbeds much more reserved and poor. One is so much more eager to establish a firm foundation of salvation while people are healthy.

If mental and pastoral conditions would get mixed up only in the case of sickness, pastoral care for the sick would be reduced to something of modest value. Yet everybody, including most pastors, considers it to be highly valuable. Even that is something very sensitive. However, mental conditions get mixed up with pastoral ones even among the healthy, much more than one would think. That means in general it has become very difficult for the pastor to recognize the pastoral condition correctly and to set a pastoral goal accordingly. Mental conditions often are independent of the spirit of the person, which is the sole object of pastoral care. Often there are physical reasons. They are like dust, whirled up by the wagon of the spirit. They make a monkey of the person who wants to evaluate himself and much more of another one who needs an unprejudiced judgment about his neighbor.

This observation, which constantly presses upon a person, urges the pastor to apply the following apostolic word especially to himself: "Be slow to speak, slow to anger." This makes clear the difficulty of private *Seelsorge* and justifies the wish that pastors should also occupy themselves with the study of mental conditions.

C. Mutual Influence of Body and Soul

The highest a person can achieve is the independence of his spirit from the influences of body and soul. [This is] the highest, but of course [it is] also

Düsseldorf and became a prolific author. The case mentioned by Loehe occurs on pp. 279–90 in *Medicina Clerica.*

the most difficult, reached in only the rarest cases. Independence of the spirit from these influences and free, willing, and faithful dependence of the spirit on the divine Word and will has to be the ultimate goal of educating oneself and of all education and pastoral care through others. If that goal cannot be reached completely by anyone, nevertheless, one should strive after it. One also can strive after it successfully step by step, for which we have many proofs from the lives of the saints.[3]

The freedom of the mutual effect between body and soul is something totally different than the freedom of the spirit from physical and mental influences, and vice versa. This mutual effect comes from God. Human misery does not consist in the fact that there is such a mutual effect, but in the fact that the spirit does not calmly stand above it. Constantly, especially the mental, but sometimes even the physical gets mixed up with the intellectual and the spiritual. If the spirit had its complete freedom from the mental and physical, it would also have full power over both. It could also work the way it should in the areas of emotions and the life of the soul. For the spirit, with its thinking and willing, should have the most decisive influence upon the soul, indeed also of the body.

If the spirit would be influenced by the Word of God, then soul and body would be directed equally by the spirit and the divine Word, and the total person would be walking on the road to perfection. At least according to the beginning, that person would then correspond to his glorious condition, which is going to be given to him as an eternal heritage in the resurrection of the just. For in those blessed times spirit, soul, and body will live in perfect harmony, and the spirit will be king over body and soul.[4]

But in order to prepare the way for this freedom and the rule of the spirit, and in order to cut off the mixing of the mental with the intellectual and spiritual, one should endeavor to get to know this mutual effect. As far as it has been recognized, one can attempt to make it subject to the spirit and to free the spirit from its influence. In this opinion, already decades ago, the author of these lines turned to an authority whose judgment deserves recognition, both from the standpoint of the physician as from that of the practical

---

[3] Loehe takes a tripartite view of the human nature (the others being bipartite and monist). The Old Testament Hebrew terms for flesh, living being, and spirit did not have a greater differentiation until the translation of the LXX incorporated words from Platonism. The New Testament includes σάρξ (body), ψυχή (soul), and πνεῦμα (spirit) as major terms. The Apollinarian and Pelagian heresies caused a backlash against trichotomy. Augustine and John Calvin both held to dichotomist views. Trichotomy tended to be the majority view in the early Church.

[4] It appears that Loehe stands closer to AC II and SA III.I than, e.g., the Roman Catholic position summarized in *Catechism of the Catholic Church*, 2nd edition (Washington: United States Catholic Conference, 1997), 13–18. Yet at times Loehe speaks in a manner that is broader than Lutheran, especially at those points where he may see the *Book of Concord* as lacking. Some terms might need greater definition.

theologian. He asked for an answer to the following question: Would it not be good if future pastors would have at least a minimum of medical training, so that they could recognize the existing physical sicknesses and know in advance the mental effects and what they can expect.

However, the answer was not what was expected. The pastor should simply fulfill the duties of his office, according to the best of his knowledge and his conscience, without worrying about the sickness of his parishioner. For an example the questioner was referred to **Oemler** in his well-known writings.[5] The questioner had known Oemler for a long time, and whatever one could praise concerning the treatment and pastoral care of this man had long been recognized and also used. But the questioner did not know how the reference to Oemler would answer his question. This was no answer for him, even though he himself had counseled young pastors who liked to dabble in medicine in the same way, warning them that they should strive for simplicity in the office. At the time of his question he had long ago given up to occupy himself with medicine, even though as a vicar, working in a large congregation, he was very successful giving out homeopathic advice and medicine while consulting a well-known doctor.[6]

All he wanted to do was to safeguard himself and other office bearers from the illusions of mental conditions at sickbeds. Therefore he turned to other medical authorities, but noticed very soon that doctors in general had very little knowledge of mental effects on physical sicknesses, so it was no wonder that he could not get the desired advice. After some time he got to know the book by **Albert Mathias Vering,** *Über die Wechselwirkung zwischen Seele und Körper in Menschen*, Leipzig 1817 [*About the Mutual Effect between Soul and Body in Humans*]. This finally gave him what he wanted. And even though one could not expect from a doctor of those days what one could not expect fifty years later—namely the acknowledgment and use of the greatest mental means, the divine Word and Sacrament—nevertheless the seriousness of the well-meaning man was refreshing. With all the arbitrariness and subjectivity of his mental advice there was still so much modesty and occasional respect for religion, which he acknowledged.

The significance of the mutual effect of body and soul for the pastoral care of the sick seemed to him so great that, based on what he had learned from Vering, he not only gave detailed instructions to the deaconess students

---

[5] Christian Wilhelm Oemler (1728–1802) was an influential theologian and educator, a church leader in Jena, and an opponent the naturalistic religion of Carl Friedrich Bahrdt. Oemler's works on pastoral theology were quite thorough and he was a leader in the fields of casuistry and pastoral medicine.

[6] In this section Loehe refers to himself in the third person in order to explain how he developed his position. Perhaps de Valenti was the physician, given that echoes of *Medicina Clerica* appear in these pages. Both the young Vicar Loehe and a young de Valenti had been accused of holding conventicles and had to defend themselves against aggressive, rationalist church politics.

in Neuendettelsau, but also dictated [those instructions]. During these lessons he tried to make up for what Vering lacked. He set pastoral medicine from the Word of God in the place of rationalistic-subjective and mental means. Thus came about the dictation that was printed as an appendix in the first edition of this book (p. 195ff.): "About the influence of physical ailments upon the mental condition of the sick, also about the use of spiritual means for the lifting of danger for the soul, originating from this." For myself, the occupation with this dictation became a great blessing for my pastoral care. I was guided especially toward modesty while applying the divine Word. Eight years have passed since the printing of that dictation, and since it was time now to bring out a new edition of *Evangelical Pastor II*, the question had to be asked if, and in what form, this dictation should be added to the new edition.

I therefore asked a trusted scientific doctor to test the dictation from his standpoint, and was given the answer that Vering's standpoint was no longer up to the present level of medicine. This judgment was made believable by the use of examples, and this influenced the decision not to reprint the dictation, especially since it is still available in print. Like the whole *Evangelical Pastor*, it was printed in 1858 at S. G. Liesching in Stuttgart (now C. Bertelsmann in Gütersloh). But at the same time, the author (W. Loehe) decided he would recommend as earnestly and emphatically as possible the study of the mutual influence between body and soul for pastors in the new edition of the second part of *Evangelical Pastor*. He would incorporate some examples from the dictation mentioned above in a proper place within this second edition.[7] This should slam the door on the opinion that the author of *Evangelical Pastor* had given up his high esteem for the pastoral significance of the mutual influence of body and soul. On the contrary, experience has made this mutual effect of body and soul for him so much greater and more important. The proven deficiencies of Vering's medicinal standpoint were not able to lessen his joy over Vering's book. On the contrary, now as always he would like to recommend its study to his young colleagues and to encourage them to compare the mental means in this book with those we have in the Word of God.

The doctor friend, who had been consulted because of the new printing of the appendix for the second part of this book, recommended a new book to the author: *Die psychischen Zustände, ihre organische Vermittelung und ihre Wirkung in Erzeugung körperlicher Krankheiten* [*Mental Conditions, Their Organic Mediation, and Their Effect in Causing Physical Illnesses*] by Doctor Ottomar Domrich, professor of medicine, published by Friedrich Maunke in Jena, 1849.[8] This highly interesting book, which certainly is worth

---

[7] [Loehe:] See § 63. [Editor's note: This is chapter 5, section D.]

[8] Ottomar Domrich (1819–1907) was a physician and educator. His medical dissertation was on the esophagus. He was active in educational reform.

being read by pastors who know the importance of the subject, carries the stamp of present-day science. It does not read like the simple, sober book of the older doctor Vering, but it does treat thoroughly the same subject in a more modern way.

One could say that Domrich's book deals with the influence of mental conditions on the body, while the pastoral counselor has to be mainly concerned about knowing the influence of physical conditions on the soul, so that he can separate the mental conditions from the pastoral ones. However, if I have a staff, I can hold it on either end, yet the staff will remain the same. It is exactly that way with the subject of the mutual influence of body and soul, and in general one can easily translate Domrich's book [about mental influence on the body] into the related subject of the influence of the body on the soul. But as it happens to a man of science so easily and so often that instead of faithful **observation** he **draws conclusions from principles,** it may have happened to the excellent scholar here. One has to use his work for the purpose of pastoral care with reason and in different ways. Judging from the scientific worth of the book, when it comes to practice, its author is less competent than others.

Oh, if only the coming generation of pastors would recognize how important it is for [pastoral] practice to know the mutual influence of body and soul! And may God soon give to his Church some powerful pastors who through medical studies would be able to serve their colleagues through public instruction!

What simple person would not admit that the demand of today's doctors to lead the discussion concerning mental life may not be modest but at least justified? The pure rationalism of today's psychiatry, even if formed scientifically, does not recommend itself any more than any other kind of rationalism to people whose source of knowledge is the divine Word, even for the mental conditions of people. It always teaches more certain steps than the results of a discipline, psychiatry, which is still wrestling with basic conditions. But on the other hand, how insufferable also is the arrogance of young pastors who do not know their own pastoral conditions, let alone those of other people, and now start talking about mental conditions and mental maladies as if they knew everything! How are they going to know anything? The education of our young pastors is really not able to achieve anything in this area.

Thus these young men start in their office and talk about mental condition like the blind would talk about color, and the deaf about sound. One should be quiet about what one does not understand, at least until one has learned and experienced something. But in the area we are talking about, one should encourage all young pastors to learn and to make experiences. Nobody, not even a doctor, has as much calling to practice psychiatry as those who care for souls (*Seelsorger*). In the divine Word they have the richest treasure of the best mental means, which stand far above the uncertain rationalistic advice of unchristian, perhaps even materialistic-minded doctors. But studying is necessary; experience is needed. In order to achieve something on the fallow ground of Christian and churchly psychiatry, first of all one must know that one is nothing, and not be ashamed to use serious diligence and strive forward.

D. General Medical Knowledge of the Pastor

In old textbooks for pastoral theology, even in church orders, the study of medicine is not only recommended for pastors, but there is even permission to practice a certain amount of medicine. Formerly, when there were not as many doctors as today, especially in the country a person was very helpless in sickness and had to be happy to ask his pastor for advice instead of all manner of quacks and charlatans. Therefore, for example, Andreas Hartmann—not the pastoral teacher who is renowned even today—but the author of a small but excellent pastoral instruction for rural pastors, writes:[9]

> To this end (namely to disentangle guilt from suffering) some medical knowledge and a frequent occupation with medicine and surgery, if it is available, may well serve a minister. For I believe that a minister would gain a huge advantage in making a sick person recognize his sin if he understands the causes of illnesses based on both natural and supernatural principles.[10]

The *Cynosura wuertembergica* of 1658 says the same thing concerning the medical studies of pastors:

> Along with doing their job, they may also read *medicinam* and use it for their own benefit and that of good friends and neighbors. But they should not profit from it publicly, nor seek to establish a practice without the permission of licensed country doctors.

Despite the fact that our conditions have changed so drastically, and one can easily find medical advice everywhere, nevertheless everyone who knows something about the area of activity of a country pastor even now will approve of the good Andreas Hartmann and the Württemberg *Cynosura* for the same old reasons.

We are very courageous when we say that no one is more suitable for a medical practice in the country than the pastor, provided that he has been trained for this and is a licensed doctor. He would be the cheapest and most

---

[9] [Loehe:] *An Unprejudiced—Simple—and Well-Meaning Sketch of How a Village Pastor May Guide the Congregation Entrusted to Him in an Edifying Way, to the Acclamation, Honor, and Praise of Jesus Christ, the Arch-shepherd of Our Souls, and to Be of Profit and Service in the Fear of the Lord for the Righteous Under-Shepherds; Written Previously, but Now Published by Magister Andreas Hartmann, Serving in the Territory of the Most Serene Duke of Württemberg, Pastor at Truchtelfingen* (Ulm: Georg Wilhelm Kühns, 1710).

[10] *causas morborum ex principiis tum naturalibus, tum supernaturalibus.*

available doctor of his congregation, and on top of that [he would be] the most faithful, since his divine main calling would give him the sacred reasons for counseling his poor people. However, under our present circumstances one cannot even talk about this. The professions have been separated. And as long as this is so, one cannot give better advice to a pastor, even if he had studied medicine and was able to practice it, than completely abstaining from practicing medicine or giving medical advice. And that goes not only for practicing allopathic, but also homeopathic medicine.

It is the proper thing for a pastor neither to interfere skillfully, nor to bungle, and not to get mixed up with the doctors. The professional has the responsibility and the word. Do not stick your nose into something that is not your business. As long as no way can be found to combine the pastor and the doctor in person under public approval, one should keep the separation of the two professions even more strictly. One should seek love and friendship of the doctors by way of renouncing all medical talk and work.

E. Means of Pastoral Care

Everything can influence a person, whether it is good or bad, right or perverted. Whoever does not pull causes delay[11]—this is a sentence from the experience of the pedagogues. This also goes for the care of souls. Whoever has the profession of pastoral care will have an effect, no matter if it be the right or the wrong one. Much depends on the right means. The right means for pastoral care have already been named and treated: Sermon, catechesis, and liturgy; in short: God's Word and the holy sacraments. But one would be limiting pastoral care too much if one would stop with the public and common use of these means, if one would be done as soon as one has preached, catechized, [celebrated] the liturgy, and administered the Sacrament. To the common and public use of the Word one must add the special and extraordinary, which is summed under the name of private pastoral care (*Privatseelsorge*). On the other hand, it would be great foolishness to make the extraordinary into something ordinary, ignoring the fact that sermon, catechesis and liturgy, and God's Word and Sacrament do the best in pastoral care. Private care of souls is something extraordinary, and with all its blessing it belongs only to the ones for whom the great means of common pastoral care have worked.

For unconverted people there is no **other** pastoral care outside of sermon and catechesis. One often feels this at the sickbeds of the godless. One can feel it, one really ought to preach—even to a single person. One ought to catechize and teach, even if only for one old man. There is no pastoral condition except unbelief, no pastoral means except the common Word of God. As soon as one wants to do and say more and different things than what one

[11] *Wer nicht zieht, verzieht.*

should do and say to the godless in general, one feels poor and miserable and depressed. The great general means of pastoral care must have done their work before one can deal with special circumstances of the soul.

Often one puts the private care of the soul into the **power of human persuasion.** A young pastor got the idea that he was lacking the popular, easy to understand language of pastoral care when he did not get very far with his reasons in order to make his farmers give up their gross sins. So he took along the schoolteacher on his pastoral visits, who knew the language of the people very well and could talk it. And behold, with his help he brought the people to the point that they would do what he wanted them to do. However, he was fooling himself. The people had been persuaded with reasons of temporal advantage, with honor and a peaceful life, but they were not converted nor any better. The old Adam was derailed from the way of gross sins by the teacher, but no new man **emerged there,** let alone any turning toward the good. Precisely because they were blind and dead, because they had not yet come to any spiritual life or understanding, they did not understand the young pastor, even when he spoke clearly and simply, and they were unable to understand him. They were lacking the blessing of the preached Word; therefore there was no care of souls for them.

This example shows clearly what the right means of pastoral care are, and what the false ones are. Even Demosthenes and Cicero have worked great things with the multitude and among them, but the people remained as they were. Even heathen could work, but not morally, not for eternity. One cannot call what they accomplished care of souls. Human reasons and human wisdom do not help, not with the sermon, not in private care of souls. God's Word is the only means for the care of souls. God's Word alone penetrates.

Of course it is understood that no pastor should be accused of a crime for letting human reasons under the divine Word also to work on his parishioners. He cannot do otherwise. But he has to know that he can truly succeed in caring for the soul only if God's Word found a resonance in human hearts, when it works its own tutelage (παιδεία) on the human soul. There the principle for the pastor has to be: "Whoever speaks must do so as one speaking the very words of God. *Loquator eloquia dei.*"

F. Methodology of Pastoral Care

No one can find other means for the effectiveness of a pastor besides those given and mentioned above. But one could finally get the idea that the means are not penetrating enough, unless they are used in **some special** way. That means that one can take refuge with one-sidedness in order to achieve in general something worth mentioning. That is a method like wanting to work with the point of the knife, because the cutting edge does not help.

Spener saw the dead way of listening to a sermon, which had taken over everywhere. So he used special meetings in order to go over the sermon again,[12] and behold—it helped—for a while. The human participation was stirred in a special way for the Word of God through this special arrangement. The Word of God received more attention than during a public sermon; it penetrated and worked in an unusual way. However the remedy lost its effectiveness once it stopped being something unusual. Indeed, some strange evils attached themselves to the Methodist use.[13] In the same way a Methodist assembly can make an impression on the person who is not used to it so that he offers less resistance to the Word, and therefore it helps him. It can also happen that a camp meeting will benefit **many** people. Such a one-sided Methodism might even work **for quite a long time**—but in a human way. Even Christ, the Wonderful, might catch fish for a while under the tumult and excitement of human powers. However, once this no longer happens innocently, once it is **promoted,** and once the extraordinary becomes ordinary, **the blessing stops.** In all these things there is an inner moral measure known to the Lord. In our foolishness we transgress it a thousand times, but He no longer forgives this transgression once one has arrived at the insight that enough is enough, according to His mind.

The same goes for the application of the divine Word that we call private care for the soul (*Privatseelsorge*). If one reads a [book on] Lutheran pastoral theology, the rubric of private pastoral care may be missing altogether. According to these authors the rubrics are sparse, and the duties of a preacher and pastor are few. On the other hand, if one reads a Gottfried Arnold, a Baxter—Oh, what duties, what responsibility, what unbearable pain, so that one would to exclaim a thousand times with Chrysostom: It is a wonder that the priest might be saved![14] But do Arnold, Baxter, etc., know new means of pastoral care? Did formerly-hidden treasures open themselves to them? No,

---

[12] [Loehe:] Spener's sermon on the Sixth Sunday after Trinity 1669 had an influence like perhaps no other since Peter's first sermon in Jerusalem. It introduced the great work which Spener had been entrusted with by God. [Editor's note: Philipp Jakob Spener (1635–1705) was known as the "father of pietism." He was influenced by Johann Arndt, Lewis Bayly, Jean de Labadie, and Theophil Großgebauer. Main points were Bible study groups, increased lay roles, emphasis on faith in action, avoidance of controversies, educated and pious clergy, and focus of preaching on developing faith in believers. He helped found the university at Halle in 1694, and was accused of 264 theological errors by the University of Wittenberg in 1695, a controversy that lasted to his death.]

[13] Although Methodism had an episcopal polity that grew out of its source in the Church of England, that was only down to the level of the congregation. Within the congregation were various cell groups led by laity who determined what sort of people could join the congregation. Attendance of Bible classes in cell groups was mandatory, as was a conversion experience. This set up a tension between the pastor and the Bible class leaders. Resolution often came when heterodox Bible class leaders took their groups out of the congregation and formed their own churches. In this fashion the Holiness Movement was born.

[14] *Mirum, si sacerdos salvetur!*

but what the ancients have, they have only in a special way, only in a specially spiritualizing application. What is self-understood is lifted up; what happens once in a while, is emphasized beyond measure. In their simplicity the old teachers of pastoral theology knew how to put the spiritual weapons for safe guidance into the hand of the beginner and encourage him to use them, and to trust the good Spirit to give strength, endurance, and gradual experience. These others just give a very detailed description of the work and the responsibility of a pastor (*Seelsorger*), which can frighten a person. This legalistic way humbles deeply, but it takes away courage and joy. Methodology enforced with the best intention has the opposite effect. It cripples because the achievements seem impossible.

The simple rule is this: Use the old means in the old way and remain in teaching, learning, experience, struggle, and prayer, so that you may mature as a pastor. There are a hundred and a thousand ways in which you can get close to your parishioners, but do not overdo it in any way, with no means, with no gift. Do your own thing in simplicity. Prayerfully use the ancient means in every way that is indicated, and let God worry about the outcome. You may make house calls or not, make sick calls if called, or sometimes when not called. You may do this and that, or not do it, whichever way you consider best after considering all circumstances before God. But do not let anything become a fetter or a burden of conscience for you. **Avoid any kind of methodology.**

G. DIVIDING THE DIVINE WORD

The preacher already has to take care that he **divides** the Word of God rightly. The Word is Law and Gospel. It is useful for teaching, for reproof, for correction, and for training in righteousness.[15] That means to be careful not to preach Law when one ought to preach Gospel, not to teach when one ought to punish, not to punish when one ought to teach. But it is even more important in private care for souls (*Privatseelsorge*) to divide the Word of God. Just like a doctor first gets to know the sick person and his sickness before he prescribes medication and makes the medication fit the sickness, a pastor should search for the condition of the person and his level in the order of salvation, and will adjust the divine medication exactly to the condition of the pastoral condition. When the pastor deals with a private person, he is completely a doctor. Here it is not a matter of prescribing food, or what to wear, but medicine, the spiritual diet of the sick person, etc. Therefore a pastor has to get to know the different steps of the Christian life, its sicknesses and weaknesses, and for each the medicine from the Word of God. Just like a pharmacist puts things he needs into many different glasses and containers, and with a skillful hand extracts this and that—the pastor, the soul physician,

[15] Here Loehe and Walther are in agreement.

does much the same. For this the study of such books [on pastoral care] and of authors who possessed pastoral wisdom is useful, but not enough. One becomes a good pastoral care giver (*Seelsorger*) only through experience. One should never forget this. But especially one ought not to forget that private pastoral care (*Privatseelsorge*) is a **cure for the soul** and the private pastoral caregiver is the **soul physician.** Private pastoral care can never be something permanent; it cannot be continued with every parishioner, just as one cannot get the medicine mixed up with food, the doctor with the chef, or the pharmacist with the cook.

Once one clearly has recognized the condition of his sick person, **one should lead him to the point where he himself can recognize it.** This is necessary with the cure of souls, not as much with the cure of the body. If the sick person realizes his evil, one should show him the right medicine, that part of the divine Word that makes up for his lack and heals his sickness. One should help him by teaching, reproving, encouraging, educating toward the use of the means, and taking a hold of them, toward patience and endurance while using them, and one should stay with him until help has come.

In any case, one should always go with clear words and plain thoughts. For man was made this way, that in the beginning, before the fall, the life given to him also had its light and brought light with it. But now all life is given through the light and the warmth that radiates from the Light. Every thought from the Word of God has its blessing and practices it all the mightier, the clearer it is given. Only based on certain verses and truths can reproof, comfort, encouragement, etc., be given. Let no one be blinded by an opposite procedure.

Should there be obstacles in the way of the prescribed medicine, then one has to be led here also to a clear recognition of the same. By the power of the divine light, whatever hinders the soul from getting well has to be removed. Here also light drives away the night, and out of the light shines the warmth that melts the ice of the soul. Every advance in the good, every retreat to the bad, is caused by light, truth, thoughts, and through the Word of God.

H. CASUISTRY

Some people recently did not want to know anything about casuistry because the step from common knowledge and recognition of the truth to the special is easy, and the anointing [ordination] teaches many things. However, on the one hand is it not apparent that the anointing, which teaches many things, is proven in the casuistry. On the other hand, despite the anointing that we have, many a weak spirit—perhaps also some that fancy themselves rich and great—do not know how to counsel and help themselves in a case that might come along.

Even if the Jesuits gave casuistry a bad name, they could do it only to **their own** casuistry, while casuistry by itself has to remain valuable for all those who know how weak we are, and how we therefore are in need of counsel and direction by those who through God's anointing could see clearly and serenely. Far from considering casuistry as something superfluous, it can be most helpful to the young pastor, and he can **learn** it. If he studies it correctly, it will make him **modest and humble** because there is a limitless ocean of different cases. And often there are two cases that look alike, and yet have to be interpreted differently. In former days of the Lutheran Church nobody thought about casuistry as disdainfully as many do today.

In his *Isagoge historico-theologica ad theologiam universam singulasque eius partes, novis supplementis aucta* [*Historical-Theological Introduction to the Whole of Theology and Its Individual Parts, Augmented with New Supplements*] (Leipzig 1730, p. 638) Dr. Johann Franz Buddeus complains about the unjust accusations of the Romans that Protestants did not know **what is allowed or not.**[16] [Buddeus writes that] Didacus (Diego) de Bezal says:

> In England, Holland and Germany there are some of the richest merchants of the Lutheran confession, who not only were without a clue, but also did not know anyone whom they could consult about what was right in matters of public contracts or of restitution. The study of morals was totally neglected.

Such accusations either were based on ignorance or came from insolence. Johann Joachim Zentgraf in his introduction to his *Summa iuris divini* did deal with merit.[17] Buddeus admits that on our side there are no such thick tomes about morals and casuistry as with the Romans, but still, there is no lack of pertinent writings. On the contrary, one could mention a significant number. He then divides those writings into properly **casuistic** ones, then those that explain the **Decalogue,** and finally **theological considerations.** Then he does not list the entire literature that belongs here, but at least he lists the main writings down to his time. Since one has to take it for granted that this would be of use to many a young pastor, we permit ourselves to list the most important works quoted by Buddeus and others. Since, as a rule, these books are not very much in demand, they are not very expensive either. Whoever is willing can acquire them at a modest cost if he just looks for them when going through catalogues of used books. We immediately bring here a list:[18]

---

[16] Johann Franz Buddeus (Budde, 1667–1729) was a Lutheran pastor and dominant theologian who was a professor in Halle (1693–1705) and Jena (1705–29). He saw the danger of the Cartesians and Spinozists, writing against their rationalism.

[17] Johann Joachim Zentgraf (1643–1707) was a German Lutheran theologian in Strassburg, where he was professor from 1695 to his death.

[18] Some names in the list have been corrected without comment.

1. The famous Wittenberg theologian Friedrich **Balduin** lectured from 1622 to 1626 on cases that concern the conscience. After his death in 1628, and a number of times after that, four of his books about cases of conscience (*de casibus conscientiae*) appeared. The work did not get the last revision from Balduin himself, and therefore is not as worthy as his other writings. But the Wittenberg theologians recognized the necessity of such a work.
2. The Giessen theologian (later in Coburg) **Kaspar Finck** followed Balduin. In 1631, the year of his death, he published *Sylloge quaestionum illustrium theologicarum, theoreticarum, maximam vero partum practicarum et quotidianarum ex assidua bibliorum, orthodoxorum patrum sinceriorum theologorum, iure consultorum, etc. lectione, experientia propria, etc. rotunde decisarum.* The work has three sections, the last of which came to light in 1632 after the death of the author.[19]
3. In 1632 the Reval pastor **Ludwig Dunte** published in Lübeck: *Decisiones mille et sex casuum conscientiae e diversis theologorum scriptis collectae, contractae et in brevitatem redactae, et iuxta ordinem locorum theologicorum positae.* This work found approval because of its compendious nature and was often printed.
4. The Coburg theologian **Andreas Kessler** wrote in German a *theologia casuum conscientiae, hodierno cumprimis tempori accomodatorum,* which his successor Johann Christoph Selde had printed in 1658 in Wittenberg. The book is in some respects a supplement to the preceding and contains a harvest of cases that had been overlooked in other similar writings.[20]
5. **Georg König** published in 1654: *Casus conscientiae, qui in sex capitibus doctrinae catechetizae, una cum tabula oeconomica subinde solent occurrere, erudite et fideliter decisae.* In 1676 his son Matthäus König published a new edition completed from the manuscript of his father.[21]

---

[19] Kaspar Finck (1578–1631) emerged from poverty to become a professor of physics, metaphysics, logic, and rhetoric. Later he became a professor of theology. He was a prolific author.

[20] Andreas Kessler (Kesler, 1595–1643) was an educator, preacher, and church leader. He died of a heart attack while preaching. He received a doctorate from Jena in 1627 and wrote extensively against the Socinians, early Unitarians.

[21] Georg König (1590–1654) studied under prominent theologians like Hutter and Balduin. He remained an orthodox Lutheran, yet he also cultivated relationships with theologians who were considered heterodox, including Johannes Crell, Martin Ruarus, and Georg Calixtus.

6. From the same author appeared after his death in 1665: *Heptas casuum conscientiae miscellorum.*

7. **Arnold Mengering** published several writings from the field of the theology of conscience in the German language: *Erneuerter evangelischer Gewissenswecker* 1645. *Erneuerte evangelische Gewissensruhe* 1647. *Geistesrüge und Sündenregister nach dem Katechismus Luthers* 1652. *Evangelisches Gewissensrecht* 1661.[22]

8. **Johann Konrad Dannhauer** surpasses his predecessors mentioned thus far. His *Collegium decalogicum* appeared first in 1639, but in 1669 it was edited, much improved and augmented by Balthasar Bebel under the title *Deuteronomium Dannhauerianum.* His *Theologia casualis,* edited in 1706 by Johann Friedrich Mayer in Greifswald, is nothing but the first draft of Dannhauer's *Liber conscientiae apertus,* or *Theologiae conscientiariae tomi duo.*[23]

9. Even before Dannhauer, **Johann Schmid** in Strassburg published his *Collegium casuum conscientiae* (1634 and 1635) and also wrote *conciones conscientariae* in 1645.[24]

10. Especially to be recommended for our younger pastors should be a short but comprehensive book in duodecimo.[25] The author is **Andreas Prückner** of Schweinfurt. The title: *Manuale mille quaestionum illustrium theologicarum, praecipue practicarum, decem centuriis inclusarum et succincte quidem, nervose tamen ex praecipuis theologis decisarum.* It appeared 1679 at Nuremberg, with notes of the Jena theologian Philipp Müller. If only there would be at present a pastor with enough theoretical and practical education who could write a *Prucknerus redivivus* for the needs of our present time! That would be a precious gift for the future generation of young pastors.[26]

11. Opposite of the Prückner book stands the *Theologia casualis* of **Johann Adam Osiander,** *in qua quaestiones, dubia et casus consci-*

---

[22] Arnold Mengering (1596–1647) was a proponent of Lutheran orthodoxy during the Thirty Years War, in which he suffered direct persecution. Most of his works arise from his experiences as a pastor and instructor.

[23] Johann Konrad Dannhauer (Conrad, 1603–66) was a Lutheran orthodox professor in Strassburg who opposed Calixtus. His disciples included Fecht and Spener, and his symbolic-allegorical method of interpretation helped to facilitate pietism.

[24] Johann Schmid (Johannes, 1594–1658) was an orthodox Lutheran theologian and educator, but he was influenced by the Puritans and proto-pietist Johann Arndt (1555–1621); He in turn influenced Spener.

[25] A printed sheet folded twelve times to yield 24 pages in a sewn gathering.

[26] Andreas Prückner was born in 1610 and flourished 1663–73. He wrote numerous biblical commentaries as well as works on ethics and polemics. Philipp Müller (1640–1713) was a professor at Jena and church leader in Magdeburg.

entiae circa credenda et agenda enucleantur. It appeared in Tübingen 1660 to 1662 in six parts. The same man wrote other pamphlets in which he presented what things are *iuris divini.*[27]

12. A book written in German appeared in 1692 in both Frankfurt and Leipzig: **Samuel Schelwig,** *Cynosura conscientiae sive perspicua et scripturae sacrae congrua multorum, maximam partem singularium nec e trivio petitorum item quorundam nondum satis enucleatorum casuum conscientiae decisio.* (**Leitstern des Gewissens,** Stettin 1692.)[28]

13. At the end of Buddeus' list of books that belong here, there is **Friedemann Bechmann,** *Theologia conscientiaris, seu tractatus de casibus conscientiae.* Jena 1705.[29]

14. **Dr. Johann Nikolaus Misler,** *Opus novum quaestionum practico-theologiarum sive casuum conscientiae.* Frankfurt 1676. This book should not be overlooked. Besides the Prückner duodecimo volume it can be used very comfortably, even though it has 668 pages in small folio.[30]

15. One could also recommend for special use, especially in our time when there is so much confusion concerning the Lord's Supper, his **August Pfeiffer's** *Informatorium conscientiae eucharisticum, complecteus triginta quaestiones in administratione sacrae coenae piis mystis adprime utiles.* 1687. But this same Pfeiffer also edited a school of conscience (*Gewissensschule*) in 1717.[31]

16. Buddeus himself answered in 1717 the well known book: *Gotthold's Manuale casuisticum.*

---

[27] Johann Adam Osiander (1622–97) was the great-grandson of Andreas Osiander, the fourth generation of church workers in his family. He was a tenured professor of theology at his alma mater in Tübingen from 1660 to his death, serving as chancellor, rector, and in other roles. He was a prominent theologian of New Testament Greek and argued against Cartesianism and unionism.

[28] Samuel Schelwig (1643–1715) bore the same name as his father. He was a professor and educator, described as a vehement supporter of Lutheran orthodoxy against pietism and Spener. He was a professor in Danzig from 1685 to his death.

[29] Friedemann Bechmann (1628–1703) was a theologian and philosopher at Jena.

[30] Johann Nikolaus Misler (1614–83) studied at Marburg and was a professor in Giessen. He wrote four books in addition to the *Opus novum* above.

[31] August Pfeiffer (1640–98) was a theologian, orientalist, and church leader. He served several parishes, then became Professor of Hebrew at Leipzig (1684–89). He then was called to be the *Superintendent* of Lübeck until his death. He was a strong proponent of Lutheran orthodoxy and an influence on Johann Sebastian Bach. His *Hermeneutica sacra* (*Thesaurus hermeneuticus*) was influential in the early LCMS.

The Reformed Church also has its casuistry authors. Among them, the works of Johann Heinrich Altstedt, William Ames, Hall, Perkins, Taylor, and Hoorenbek are not to be confused with the products of the Lutheran Church.[32] One must note that in books, even in Lutheran ones, the answers to the questions that are being asked are not always guaranteed. It can happen that in a good confessional book one can find the answer of a theologian of a totally different confession because one could not find the answer of an orthodox one. Of course such answers serve no other purpose than to make one think. In fact, the highest praise that one can give the entire casuistry of the Lutheran Church is to recommend that it should be studied.

The same thing applies here as, for example, to the definitions of the great scholar Melanchthon. One cannot simply repeat them or subscribe to them, but they can lead to thinking and the attempt to produce something better. The entire casuistry of the Lutheran Church needs a new and unprejudiced re-working related to Scripture. But it would be worth it, even for the sake of the great blessing it could bring. It should be melted down once more, and be re-worked again by the theologians of the future, so that it would be beneficial at any given time.

It is obvious why Buddeus includes the explanations of the **Decalogue** with the proper casuistry, as was mentioned above: "Those look mostly to divine jurisprudence who illustrate the Decalogue, or the sum of divine justice, with their own comments."[33] They too, just like the casuistries, have to do with divine jurisprudence. Dannhauer and Dorsch are celebrated names on this field of endeavor.[34]

It is also obvious why Buddeus adds here the collections of theological judgments and counsels. They could simply be included in the proper place among the books of casuistry. The following books belong here:

1. The *Novem Consiliorum Theologicorum Decas* of the Württemberg theologian **Felix Bidembach,** published in cooperation with his

---

[32] William Ames (1576–1633) was a Puritan educated at Cambridge. He attended the Synod of Dordrecht (1618–19) as a Calvinist observer. He served in the Netherlands as pastor and professor, but died before moving to New England. Loehe may refer to Joseph Hall (1574–1656) who wrote *Meditations and Vows* (1605) and *Characters of Virtues and Vices* (1608). He was an observer at Dordrecht on behalf of James I. William Perkins (1558–1602) was a Fellow of Christ College, Cambridge and a Puritan voice in the Church of England. John Taylor (1694–1761) was an English dissenting preacher and Hebrew scholar. Loehe may refer to Reformed theologian Johannes Hoornbeek (1617–66), writer of polemics and works on mission. References to Altstedt remain obscure.

[33] *Ad iurisprudentiam divinam vel maxime spectant, qui decalogum seu summam iuris divini commentationibus suis illustrarunt.*

[34] Johann Dorsch (Dorsche, 1597–1659) was an educator and professor at Rostock who studied with some of the greatest theological minds of his time. He was a leading voice in orthodox polemics that defended the Formula of Concord. He also defended the orthodoxy of Johann Arndt, thereby influencing Spener.

brother Johann Moritz in 1608. Moritz edited the ninth edition after the death of his brother, and in 1614 he followed it with a tenth in Frankfurt.[35]

2. Abraham Calov, Johannes Meisner, Johann Andreas Quenstedt and Johann Deutschmann published the *Consilia theologica Wittenbergensia* in 1664 in Frankfurt/Main.[36]
3. The Hamburg theologian **Georg Dedeken** undertook to edit a *Thesaurus consiliorum et decisionum* in three folio volumes. Johann Ernst Gerhard of Jena enriched and completed the work, but died before the printing was completed, so that Christian Grübel published it in Jena in 1671, enlarged with an appendix.[37]

If one would finally add here the noble and pious **Philipp Jakob Spener** among the theologians of casuistry, because of his numerous deliberations known in the Church, one would think that one would have done away with the opinion that the Lutheran Church always shied away from casuistry, perhaps even hated it. Perhaps it was because tasteless people inflicted very impractical questions, just for the sake of a dialectics exercise, into this field of sheer practice. Of course pastoral care does not just deal with solving casuistic questions. It has much more to do. It works primarily on the will and it rules the heart. But it is also true that one cannot do without casuistry. If it is indispensible, it will also be useful and worth a renewed effort.

I. TRUST

I can receive God's Word from any mouth, God's Sacrament from any hand, as long as it is pure, whether I trust the pastor, the preacher, the serv-

[35] Misprinted as *Decades* in Loehe's original. Felix Bidembach Sr. (1564–1612) was an educator and church leader. He died suddenly of a stroke. His brother Johann Moritz Bidembach (1565–1624) was a parish pastor.

[36] Johannes Meisner (1615–81) was a professor in Wittenberg who took an irenic stance based on the difference between fundamental and non-fundamental doctrines, for which he was excoriated by Abraham Calov. Johann Andreas Quenstedt (1617–88) succeeded Meisner and was the last great practitioner in the high age of Lutheran orthodoxy. Johann Deutschmann (Johannes, 1625–1705) succeeded both Meisner and Quenstedt at Wittenberg. He was Calov's son-in-law and held a position quite close to Calov. He was criticized both during and after his lifetime, having become something of a stereotype for "dead orthodoxy" and its failings.

[37] Loehe mistakenly uses Johann. Georg Dedeken (1564–1628) was the well-educated pastor of the Catharinenkirche in Hamburg whose specialty was casuistry. He also edited the works of his friend, the renowned Philipp Nicolai. Johann Ernst Gerhard Sr. (1621–68) followed his father as a theology professor in Jena. He published some of his father's literary remains, as well as an introductory *Isagoge* to the *Loci Theologici*, an *Epitome* to the *Confessio Catholica*, and a harmony of near-eastern languages. Christian Grübel (1642–1715) published several exegetical and philosophical works.

ant, or not. But I cannot choose a soul physician, and even less a pastor (*Seelsorger*) whom I do not trust, just as I would not choose a medical doctor in whom I have no confidence. One can even say that for the care of people who are spiritually ill, trust is even more necessary than in the case of bodily sickness. How could I entrust the troubles of my soul to someone unwise, dishonest or unfaithful? And if someone were wise, honest and faithful, but I did not know or recognize it, would that help me? Could I believe and trust? This is so simple and natural that one cannot understand how a pastor could **demand** trust when [anyone can see] that he is not trustworthy. Even based on plain reason, where is modesty easier than in matters of trust? But of course, pastors are also human and human things can happen to them. They should humbly recognize their weakness and sin and let themselves be healed, instead of demanding trust and gaining it through means that have to cause more mistrust with the better parishioners instead of creating trust.

If a pastor has trust, it will only be increased through **sincerity** and **holy discipline.** One wishes from a pastor that he takes things seriously. No comfort will comfort, coming from the lips of a man who takes everything easy. But because trust can reconcile a person with what could really be frightening, the one who possesses trust also has a high responsibility. Based on trust you can lead in the right direction, or **lead astray**! Everybody has to give an account for those that trust their pastoral counsel.

May the merciful God help us through Jesus Christ. Amen.

J. CONFESSING

Exactly thirty years ago the author of this book wrote a little pamphlet under the title: *Einfältiger Beichtunterricht für Christen evangelisch-lutherischen Bekenntnisses* [*A Simple Instruction for Confession for Christians of the Evangelical Lutheran Faith*] (Nuremberg: J. Ph. Raw, 1836). The intention was to awaken a new love and desire for confession, especially private confession, among people he had contact with. In the meantime the pamphlet has been forgotten, but at that time it served to such an extent that when he became pastor in Neuendettelsau a year later, the people there thought for sure that they all would have to confess privately again. The first person he met in the street was an old mentally-impaired man, and the first words he said were: "I can make my confession." However, the new pastor was not willing to reintroduce private confession with the speed of a storm wind. It took no less than six years, during which time he used every opportunity to praise private confession and its blessings.

In the spring of the year 1843 he received an official communication from the Church government, which he had to announce. It permitted the use of private confession where it was desired. This gave him the occasion to invite those who desired private confession to do so on the following Saturday. He guessed that the few people who previously had asked for private confession would show up. But something quite different happened. The next Saturday the church was filled with private penitents. This first time already, quite unexpectedly, he had an enormous amount of work with confession. The first who entered the sacristy was at that time the oldest man of the congregation. The second, also one of the oldest, was a council member of an affiliated church, a man you could not fool with, one of the most difficult characters in the congregation. Seeing these men gave the pastor the idea that his announcement may have been misunderstood, as if private confession should now be forcefully introduced, and he had to defend himself against this understanding. But the first one who had entered replied that he had always longed for private confession, for he had practiced it in his youth already. The second one, a tall and strong man, beat his chest and said: "I understood you alright, but I want to, I want to." That sounded like a *mea culpa, mea culpa,* coming deep from his chest.

From that day on, all of a sudden, private confession was ruling, and there were times when about a hundred were confessing privately, and only one asked for a common confession, which then, of course, again turned into a sort of private confession. It took a while until the disruptive part of the congregation, of which there were not many, recovered to the extent that they all agreed to always come together on the same days for a public confession. So these disagreeable people came together to public confession and assured everyone, the longer the louder, how much more beautiful and touching public confession was than private confession, already because of the address that was given there. But now public confession almost became something shameful, as if it were the assembly of the disruptive, resisting the pastoral leadership of the congregation. This also could not be tolerated.

In the beginning of the year 1848 the chapel R. became incorporated with the Neuendettelsau parish. This became a big benefit for the new parishioners. Formerly they had to walk a long way to their parish. Now they went at most half an hour to Neuendettelsau on a level road. When confession was administered for the first time in this chapel, right away the entire congregation came for private confession. Whoever did not know how to make confession and was incapable to confess from the heart, nevertheless they came for private confession and asked the pastor to help him to the best of his ability. This total participation in private confession was supposed to be a kind of thanks for the pastor of Dettelsau[38] who had faithfully helped

[38] The name *Neuendettelsau* has three parts: *neu+en, new* plus the adjectival ending; *Dettels*, belonging to the Dettel family; *Au*[*e*], a water meadow. This means a place was called Dettel's Meadow (*Dettelsau*), and then it was enlarged, reordered, or rebuilt into New Dettel's Meadow (*Neuendettelsau*). Sometimes Germans will drop additions to their town names like new, old, upper, lower, and the like when speaking among the locals. Loehe is emphasizing that he is "talking like a local."

with their incorporation. They were convinced that he would be very pleased if they all came to private confession.

But what had been achieved? Private confession had been introduced, and it seemed that even the recalcitrant could be led along the common way through some clever effort. However, this had not been the intention, and the pastor was not pleased with this exclusive rule of private confession. His pastoral goal had been completely different. He wanted to lead the congregation to a more frequent participation in the Sacrament of the Altar. He did what he could in order to destroy the old humdrum way of attending Communion twice or four times a year. His long-term goal in leading the congregation was to have Communion every Sunday, and to have the congregation participate—not by force of habit or because it was a traditional Communion Sunday—but because it was a heartfelt need. But if one would keep private confession for all communicants, even with more frequent Communion, this would have become an insurmountable hindrance for the real pastoral goal.

If such a farmer, instead of taking Communion twice a year, would go twenty times, or even just twelve times a year, what should he then confess? Of course he does not lack sins, but there is a lack of the necessary education on how to renounce them. He also lacks the education to recognize the change of his sinful conditions, let alone the change of his sinful deeds and words, in the midst of the monotony of his life. The least he should do in confession is babbling and lying, so where should he find his material? That brings up the danger of just using a formal confession to help with the problem. The old humdrum way, which he wanted to eliminate, comes back with a vengeance. On top of it, to listen to all these formal confessions becomes an unbearable burden for the pastor. He also will see that there is nothing for the future but the certainty that the entire institute of private confession will die out under the next successor. After all, private confession died out some time ago in the entire Protestant Church for the same reason, and public confession was forced upon pastors and congregations as an anchor of rescue.[39]

One had to strive to make **possible** the goal of more frequent participation. Private confession in the Protestant Church is based on totally different views and reasons than in the Roman Church. The Protestant person is not obligated to wrestle for a complete confession. Therefore the institute of con-

[39] Followers of Loehe and others who held to a high view of the ministry in eastern districts of the LCMS promoted an ecclesiology where private confession was the unalterable rule and pastors were instructed to make their laity follow that rule. In western districts of the LCMS the situation was shaped by the misuse of private confession by Martin Stephan Sr. for sexual misconduct. The Saxons almost exclusively used public confession and made that part and parcel of lay rights. These differing views divided and polarized the LCMS for 40 years. Yet from Loehe's own words, it does appear that some who were influenced by Loehe may have been less evangelical than Loehe himself. See also Walther, *Law and Gospel: How to Read and Apply the Bible*, p. 474, "Absolution, Lutheran history of."

fession in our Church can never become the **general,** powerful means of education that it had become in the Middle Ages. And even for the Roman Church a completely different time has come. Our Catechism does not demand that all sins are confessed, but only those that one knows **and feels** in his heart, and even those not just for the sake of Absolution. Absolution includes not only those sins that are unknown to the confessor, but also those that are not recognized by the penitent. Not confession itself, no matter how great a blessing it can be, but repentance, or rather the soul's readiness to repent, is the indispensable requirement of the Protestant Church for a true communicant.

There is a Church order, based on the Augsburg Confession, that no one should go to the Sacrament without having been examined, having confessed, and having been absolved. Even though this order is nothing but human work, and according to Protestant teaching could be done away with, nevertheless one ought to be happy that this order exists, so that no one throws himself at Communion without preparation. One ought to hang on to this order as long as possible, at least for the masses, even though it is nothing but foolishness and an act of violence to make it apply to all and sundry without distinction. But if it is kept, one must make it possible and not demand something that is not appropriate.

The first congregations went to the Sacrament daily. It was taken for granted that they would daily and forever be willing to repent. But should they all, each of them, have confessed, or would they even have been able to do so? If private confession should happen before each Communion, one can predict a less frequent attendance, or Communion itself must become less frequent, and thus the **principle** has to be abandoned. Therefore, whoever wants to achieve a very frequent attendance at Communion cannot demand private confession from the masses of the congregation as an indispensible requirement. One has to exchange it with other forms of confession and lead the congregation to the point where they can confess in different ways. Only one should not "let fall" the especially important and blessed private confession—to use the words of the Augsburg Confession. If this has been achieved, the old humdrum way has been overpowered as much as possible, willingness to repentance has been promoted as much as possible, and the congregation has been prepared for a dignified participation in the Sacrament as much as possible.

It is obvious that by no means could the pastor be happy with what he had achieved in his congregation. Private confession had been introduced. But the right spirit and the right measure were lacking, and the next pastoral goal had been reached in such a way that it became a hindrance for the more remote and higher goal. That made necessary the task of establishing a standard. Through instruction [the pastor would] bring the congregation to the point where they would appreciate private confession in **its relationship to public confession.**

This task was extremely difficult. The confessional admonitions were the principle means to shed light on the subject. Though they were an introduction to public confession, they were also heard by those who had already been absolved privately. The following was what the people were supposed to understand and what was meant to become part of the life of the congregation:

> Private confession is good and wholesome; it should never have been discontinued. It should be reintroduced everywhere, and it is a high necessity for the Church. But public confession also has its right. It has always been practiced in some form, even during the times when private confession was quite common, even if it was not in the form of a preparation for Communion as commonly used now.
>
> If private confession alone is used all the time, experience shows that it becomes an unbearable routine.—One has to use both, according to the **changing needs** of the souls, so that one can be used to prevent the other from becoming habit and routine. Each penitent, before registering for Communion, should think which kind of confession would be the best for this time.

One should think that this matter was not that hard to understand. Yet in reality, as already mentioned, this goal was extremely difficult to reach, and actually it was never quite reached. The people from the chapel mentioned above had taken the shortest time to get used to private confession. They had to be cured first, so to speak. But they were not sufficiently [spiritually] alive and willing to take on an additional duty besides the one for dutiful self-examination before each Communion, required by God and the Church. They were now also to come to an agreement in their conscience as to which kind of confession they should choose. Because they were too lazy to absorb so much religious commotion in themselves, they tried to create a conflict between the double goals of the pastor. Before, all had confessed only publicly. Now the majority confesses privately. That one was not right, now this one is not right either. What should one do? One simply turns again toward public confession. It is much more comfortable than private confession, and under certain circumstances—namely if the pastor is a good speaker—it also **can be** more pleasant and enjoyable. That shows how little the pastor succeeded in leading his own to a better goal.[40]

While matters were hovering in this stage, the pastor fell sick and for a long time was unable to continue his former activity as confessor. For quite a

[40] Here Loehe refers to the fact that public confession and Absolution is itself a service with a confessional address or sermon. Only in the twentieth century did public confession and Absolution threaten to turn into an unfortunately *pro forma* brief segment of the hymnal at the beginning of the Divine Service.

while there was only public confession. When this period was over, one had to build completely anew. The chapel had its own days for confession and Communion. The majority of its members had sunk back to the sole use of public confession during the sickness of the pastor. The parochial places are divided among members who already used public confession previously and those who mostly use private confession. In the main parish there is greater understanding. There are those who even now go to public confession, as formerly. But there is also much private confession, and there are not a few who observe a laudable change between both kinds of confession. One cannot really say that the pastoral goal has been reached, but at least one can assume that one is closer to it. That means that there are **more** members now who know the difference between both kinds of confession and use both of them wisely.

A congregation that would be aware of these differences and would act accordingly would not only be motivated in a Christian way, it would also have reached a high level of churchly life. But if it is already a great rarity for a congregation to accept a Christian **motivation,** it happens even more seldom that one can find a truly confessing and communing congregation. It remains a question whether there is any pastor who has the great fortune to serve such a congregation. That would be something very different, and on a much higher level, than to have a congregation that somehow got used to and became familiar with private confession, as do Roman Catholics. One probably has to give up the hope of ever reaching such a pastoral goal. Nevertheless it is worth every effort and truthfully, it already means a good deal to have reached just any level on this way. In the face of failure a diligent worker can at least find comfort in the thought that God's way is always the narrow one, and there are only few that walk on it. The pastor who has been mentioned so far through much experience has gained the conviction that a general goal for congregational leadership cannot be reached. It can only be striven for if one resigns the hope of complete success. Nevertheless it can be held up as a pastoral goal for the **better individual parishioners,** and as a goal for self-education, which is worth all striving and is dripping with blessing. The free use of all kinds of confession, depending on the need of the soul, is a wonderful step of Christian and churchly education.

K. Different Kinds of Private Confession

One should be able to say that most of the presently-living people of the Protestant confession are poor penitents, namely, if one can call only someone a good penitent who knows how to rightly use private confession and does so. The use of private confession requires that one has been educated in it, trained in honesty in general, and honesty toward the confessor in particular. But there is no such training among us, and all of us will have to admit that neither **have** we been educated in this way ourselves, nor **did** we train our children in such a way that honesty toward the confessor would be a goal. We grew up without ever getting the idea to reproach ourselves for being silent concerning our sins.

That is the reason why, for many of us, it is exceedingly difficult to open our heart and to confess privately; and we are really embarrassed once we try to go to private confession. If the first time was a failure, one is through with private confession for the rest of one's life. In fact, from that very hour one might perhaps malign private confession, even though one had an experience that could teach one that he does not understand anything of this matter and is completely incompetent to form a judgment concerning it. Nevertheless one does judge, and spoils not only for oneself, but also for others the desire and taste for the most precious growth that has grown freely on the ground of God's Church. It is a cause for high lament that things happen this way, and that in consequence it is extremely difficult to bring private confession into the Church again, but it is not hard to understand this.

One also has to say that at present there are very few pastors who know anything about private confession [or even] confess privately themselves. Never in their life have they been in a situation where they would make a private confession, not to mention that they would introduce others to private confession or be able to educate them in this. Thus it is quite natural to say: as the king, thus the people (*qualis rex, talis grex*). And yet private confession is something so excellent and such a requirement for the inner life that in all places and with all confessions at least surrogates arise, as soon as there is a Christian life. On the way of salvation one just cannot do without guidance, without having to pay dearly for the lack of it. "Brothers, what should we do?" Since the days of the apostles, this question goes from mouth to mouth among those who have been overtaken by the Holy Spirit. Therefore, without doubt, it is very necessary that within the Lutheran Church one would consider whether one should deal with private confession directly, instead of just with surrogates, and whether one should deal with it with the due diligence it deserves.

The most modest form of private confession is **the formula.** It is also most widely used where one is striving for something better. Nevertheless, it also can be used. Its relationship to true private confession is like that of a primer to a reading book, if only one knows how to use it. With the low educational level of most country folk it can happen that a poor soul cannot even recite a formula, but will instead recite something memorized to thank a sponsor. One could call that a big shame for private confession. But something like this presents an opportunity for a teaching moment. Whoever speaks the thanks for a sponsor instead of the formula for confession can learn at this occasion how to tell the difference between the thanks and the confessional formula. He will go home wiser than when he came. He also will justify the judgment of a confessor, namely, that in the end the worst private confession is still more useful than a common public confession. During the latter the people often sleep through the Absolution, together with the admonition.

The most modest formula of confession is a tablet of repentance and instruction. From it a penitent can be instructed with very little expenditure of time and strength about what he needs for eternity. One cannot teach a poor soul about its great need as summarily and yet as clearly and plainly as in the confessing formula. It cannot be presented in any other way, and it has the great advantage that one can speak to the heart of the penitent through his own words, for he indeed does recite the formula. How much one can add to the confessional formula, in what wide circle one can use it, is proven by the so-called books of Absolution of the Lutheran Church, even though they have to be called just a token of the **declining** pastoral activity of the Lutheran Church in the confessional. Therefore one should not be satisfied with confessing by formula, but on the other hand should not despise it, or be so disgusted with it that one would rather throw it away. Basically that would be no different than to throw the baby away with the bath water. A pastor should just be intent on patiently teaching his elementary Christians the ABC, the primer of the confessional formula, and not spare himself any trouble. He will find a blessing. At least he will not find any more attentive students and listeners than in the confessional, nor will he find hearts more ready and willing to receive what he has to say.

Of course the confessional formula is not the highest level of confession, even though it can often serve even the most advanced Christian Many who received the highest blessing from the free exercise of private confession will finally return to the use of the formula with a calmed soul. Between the two conditions of elementary Christianity and a sanctified soul that makes regular progress in peace there are in-between circumstances for which the formula is completely insufficient. In that case a free expression of the soul has to be demanded, and it will happen almost by itself. If the soul has been touched in its essence, as were the listeners of the first sermon in Jerusalem, it will also start speaking. Confessions of awakened souls are done with their own words, shyness and embarrassment fall away, and sheer necessity teaches to confess and to pray, be it in dialect form or whichever way will work. If such a time happens, a somewhat able confessor will know how to use it. He will meet the poor soul, clarify its desire, and lead it to the point where it finally will solemnly pronounce its needs and find in the Absolution the greatest calm and strength. From now on it will give itself joyfully and eagerly to the best school under heaven, also the best education and self-education, namely, the school and education of private confession.

L. The Work of a Confessor During Private Confession

I stand in my place and wait for the penitents. One after another they come up in order to confess and to receive not only Absolution but also any kind of advice or another good word that can bring light, strength, or comfort. Whenever this happens I know and feel it that my most serious hour of the week has come, and that I am facing my most difficult task. I stare at the door and wait for the one who is entering. As soon as I see him, the form of his soul is before me. Even before he starts talking, I already ask myself what I can say to him. I search and I study more than I would if I had opened books and had looked for wisdom there. Once the penitent starts talking and revealing what is in his soul, I am completely an ear. I am totally concentrated on not letting anything get lost or unobserved. But I cannot but search for what I have to say. I know that right now I am like a flower about to break out of the bud, and should give form and odor. By my salvation, I am dead serious, knowing that I may and should give, but not take.

And this, my inner condition, repeats itself as of as a new penitent appears. I have to enter as many special lives as there are penitents. Nothing in my eyes is more difficult than this: Burdened with my own pastoral condition, I yet have to make other peoples' condition my own, so that I live in them and speak from them for their healing. I stand still; no foot, no hand is moving. But if this has gone on for several hours, I cannot do it anymore. I feel that it is getting too much for me. I am tired and would like to rest from these journeys of my soul into a strange life. For a while I would like to have nothing to do with anything except myself, no, not even with myself. I just want to rest, away from everything and everybody.

I often listen and speak with increasing joy, I somehow feel that living water is flowing from me, that there is blessing from above, and that I am serving in the house of my Lord. **And yet**, it does not work for any length of time. I know of no other **labor** like that of **private confession** that makes a person so tired, if not from misery, then at least from joy. Body and soul, nerves and thoughts feel their limits. Therefore I would advise anyone who is serious about hearing confession not to overdo it, but divide it and plan it. It is a great benefit for the penitents themselves if the confessor is wide awake and strong, both to listen and to speak. But he cannot be that if he has to listen to too many in a row and has to give advice. The last one will feel it, they receive nothing. Therefore, do not put too much trust in your strength.

Of course if everybody only uses a formula for confession, and you in turn also use only a formula when you lay on your hands and give Absolution, this also can become objectionable for you in the end. But you will not get to know the labor I am talking about, as well as getting tired, which I know. One gets used to the work of hand and mouth.

M. NECESSARY WISDOM OF A CONFESSOR

Even the effort of soul, nerves, and body is great if one seriously wants to hear confession. Even the wanting, seeking, and making an effort is difficult. But if only one would be able to do what one wants and should do—would find what one is seeking, and if the effort would reach its goal! But no contemplating will help the one who knows nothing and can do nothing. No phrases will help here, and the little powder that one brings along from his own poor experience is soon shot. One gets hungry for advice and instruction. No student notebooks will help. The school has no advice for matters that are highest in the office. But perhaps something: The writer of this no longer has any notebooks from school, but he heard something in his youth that he wrote down, black on white, and carried it home, and now in his old age often is able to use. It is a lecture on pastoral theology and catechesis, read by the blessed court preacher Strauss in Berlin. Fellow students did not like it. But he wrote it down, because it promised him blessing and usefulness for the office.

But even this often was not palatable for his life as a pastor. There just are no Protestant books from which a pastor could receive the desired blessing—especially if it comes to the care of souls (*Seelsorge*) of the highest order, the pastoral care in the confessional, unless one takes refuge in the *theologia conscientiaria,* namely casuistry. There is hardly anything more needed for a confessor than casuistic studies.

I do not want to repeat myself. But I want to exhort [the reader] to commit the most honest theft one can think of—namely to rob from the Roman pastoral writings and instructions for confession. Here are multitudes of treasures that are easy to unearth. The great Thomas Aquinas has left us a little booklet from which everybody can convince himself that there still is a lot to learn from the Middle Ages, especially in matters of pastoral care and confession. There are many such books. How much we can learn from [Jean] Charlier Gerson, and how much we can take from his writings! But for the time being, I only **want** to refer to Thomas of Aquinas. The little book I mentioned is titled: *Confessionale seu libellus peroptimus beati Thomae de Aquino de modo confitendi et de puritate conscientiae, cuilibet confessor et confiteri volenti perutilis et necessarius* [*Confessionale, That Is, a Most Thoroughly Useful Little Book by St. Thomas Aquinas Concerning the Manner of Confessing and the Purity of the Conscience; Very Useful and Necessary for One Wishing to Make Confession to Any Confessor*]. May there soon be people, even among us, who know how to use such writings and to prepare them for others. Similar things apply to other writings that belong to the Roman Catholic Church. As much as is useless in them, there is much that can be used. The ***Regula aurea confessionariorum*** [*The Golden Rule of Confessionaries*] or *Instructiones saluberrimae Caroli Borromaei* [*The Beneficial Instructions of Carlo Borromeo*] weigh heavier for the purpose of confessors than many a pastoral library.[41]

[41] Thomas Aquinas (of Aquino, 1225–74) was the greatest medieval theologian after Augustine of Hippo. He used Aristotelian philosophy in a manner that shaped much of European thought either as an affirmation or as an opposing reaction. Known for *Summa*

Whoever says [things like] this can be wrongly understood; his words can be misinterpreted. But in the long run one will not have to fear being called a heretic because truth will remain what it is. In short: We do need study and instruction for the confessional office.

N. DANGER FOR CONFESSORS

Whoever finds trust as a confessor and gets to know the power of private confession will also meet a danger—namely the danger of **immodesty.** There is no power on earth to equal the one of the confessor over willing souls. From the confessional all natural conditions can be blessed—by Protestants no less than by the Romans. But from the confessional all natural conditions can also be undermined and exploded. And that can happen with people who never planned it that way, and would not want to be accused of it, even if it is true. The confessor is like a farmer who directs water to the farthest corners of his garden and who, happy in his strength and knowledge, does everything in order to accomplish his goal. Thus the confessor directs the water of the divine Word into the most specific areas of life. Happy with his success, he then can strive with full knowledge to become lord over all conditions. He can succeed, and often has succeeded, to unseat father and mother, man and wife, to stir up one against the other and cause a riot, to destroy family peace and to light a fire that Christ did not want to have burning.

Young pastors just starting to feel their power often let themselves be enticed to look into everything, talk about everything, and thus rule over the people. But may Christ preserve His poor servants from this. In addition to all their troubles and sins they do not need to desire becoming lords and rulers in all areas of life, or actually be that. Sacred modesty and reticence is necessary for confessors. Even as a confessor you should not interfere in any condition that is none of your business.

A true confessor does not want to know everything or talk about everything. He will strive to conduct his confessional office in such a way that he does not burden anyone, that he keeps himself distant from every condition of life, having only a need-to-know basis, and for that very reason he exercises an innocent influence on all his penitents and their conditions. He waits to see what is coming and then fulfills his office as if he did not do anything.

There is such a behavior that makes it possible to be the best friend of a family, and yet keep one's distance. May God free His own from the folly that assumes that the confessor should be the friend and comrade of all his penitents. May God teach us to know this and keep our distance.

---

theologica and *Summa contra gentiles*, he also wrote on ethics and philosophy. Carlo Borromeo (1538–84) was a cardinal and archbishop of Milan. He was a leading figure in the Counter-Reformation who fought corruption, yet who suppressed Protestantism and sanctioned witch trials and burnings.

O. THE CONFESSIONAL SECRET

Where could you find a confessor who has not been accused from time to time, even by his best penitents, that he violated the confessional secret? Naturally! Every confession belongs to some area of common sins. So if the pastor mentions common sins during or outside of confession, some imagine that he is talking about conditions that he could know only from hearing confession.

Pious me will learn to suffer this also, together with suspicion and hatred originating from it. In addition to this, many penitents have the bad habit of telling their circumstances to the pastor in confession, but then telling them to their friends in good confidence. If something then comes to light they do not mistrust their friends, although they would have reason to do so. Rather, [they mistrust] their confessor, who perhaps even has the gift and the grace to forget the confession and for that very reason he does not betray a single syllable. If the confessors are unfortunate enough to come under suspicion of gossiping, sometimes no assurance or proof will help, but aversion and ill will remain insurmountable.

These and similar experiences excuse—or at times even demand—the decision to observe absolute silence, just as the Romans do, and to hide **even those** words or omissions of the penitents that do not even belong to confession, and cannot belong to them. Oh confession! How many misuse it to communicate things that have nothing to do with the confession of sins! How many misuse it to lie, to slander and [commit] every kind of wickedness! How many lie intentionally, either to fool the confessor or to achieve other evil intentions! Confession often is a quagmire of sin and egotism, a playground for all passions. A confessor has to secure himself and **study** silence and forgetfulness, and learn not only to be silent, but also deaf.

The position of a confessor is so unique that he cannot even make use of a judgment concerning his penitent that he formed based on the confession. He must not know what he knows. It is not falsehood, but highest honesty to give a judgment in confession, and one outside of confession, and to refuse to let the one influence the other.

How unclear are our thoughts in this area of life, how perverse our behavior! We **cannot** help being unclear; we have such bloody little **confessional experience.** How long will it take until we know again what the confessional secret is, and what it is not, and until confessors and penitents learn what kind of **mutual** duties they take on and have! And how long will it take until one takes the trouble to **think,** and to create living conditions for the noblest institute of the Church, private confession, which it cannot do without.

Chapter Five

Pastoral Care of the Sick

A. Its Value in General

People who form their judgment concerning the value of pastoral care for the sick often overestimate its value [if they do not draw] from daily experience but are used to talking about it from prejudice or impressions. But those who daily stand at sickbeds and practice the Holy Office often have the opposite temptation, namely, to consider its value to be too little when they talk about it.

The truth remains that pastoral care for the sick **seldom** has conspicuous results. Most of our parishioners are elementary Christians. They are content with a minimum of spiritual life. They have never searched for their inner trouble and spiritual needs and they are also too uncouth and uneducated, too unfeeling and careless to let themselves be driven toward self-examination. Even when they are healthy one cannot find an entrance to their souls, and when they get sick it is even harder. Of course there are times when sickness benefits and teaches one to listen to the Word, as do other trials. But usually, instead of bringing the benefits of conversion and awakening from the lazy, dull sleep of sin, it only brings obstacles. Therefore the pastor has good reason to preach: "Do not save your repentance for the time of sickness."

I repeat: The word and the wisdom of the pastor have a hard time finding their way to the soul in a healthy body. How much more [is that so] in a sick body! And the souls of sick rural people are especially hard to find. The lack of a broad education makes all pastoral work difficult, just like a bad road makes it hard to go ahead. Oh, pastoral care of the sick has so little success, or none, and it is so hard to understand, so hard! There are so-called humiliations and disappointments! It is hopeless to walk among the sick and to have no other satisfaction for having spent the precious time in the service of the sick, that to know that one did the right things and practiced love. So put down your sanguine hopes from the start, and do not hope **much** from your visits, either for yourself or for the sick. You will get used to the visits, together with the look of death, and the **people** themselves are slow to open the door of their heart.

It is true what Sailer (*Pastorale* III, p. 6) says: "To stay with a dying person is much more instructive than to watch the sun come up, as much as this is to be recommended, or rather does not need any recommendation."[1] But just do not take it as something too great or too high. Rather take your care of the sick very seriously, and do not be surprised, when you recognize your impotence and powerlessness nowhere as much as especially by the beds of the sick and dying. He is wisest who expects very little. He then is so much more thankful for every little success. And if sick calls now seem of little value to you, because you achieve so little, follow the wise and good Sailer so much more gladly when he says in the above quoted place, p. 14: "Never visit a sick person, unless you have implored the Father of life with daring and strong confidence for the **rare gift** always **to find the way into the heart of a fellow man in need of comfort, and to lead the sinner away from any other path to God.**" Without God's very special blessing you will accomplish very little and sick calls will be a heavy burden for you, unless you bear it out of pure compassion and the desire to show love, and therefore you return again and again to the sickbeds.

B. Special Purpose of Pastoral Care for the Sick

Pastoral care is meant for all Christians, the **sick** as well as the **healthy.** Since the sick do not have a different way to heaven than the healthy, and all have to go the Christian way of salvation, and since there are no other means of grace for the sick than for the well, pastoral care for the sick and the healthy is basically one and the same. The pastor has to get to know the sick person and his pastoral condition, has to select the right means for salvation and furtherance on the way to life, and has to apply them wisely and faithfully.

And yet there is a difference between spiritual care for the sick and the special care for the healthy. The pastor not only has to lead the sick person on the way to salvation, and support and keep him on the same to the end; but he is also required to know the **specific obstacles** that every sickness confronts a person with on the way to eternal life. For example, dropsy in the stomach or the skin not only makes the sick person quiet and resigned; it also makes him **dull** at times. Suffering from tuberculosis in the lymph nodes (scrofula) often makes children who have it **stubborn, quarrelsome, moody,**

---

[1] Johann Michael Sailer (1751–1832) was a professor of theology and Bishop of Regensburg. He placed strong emphasis on education and piety and he reached out not only to fellow Roman Catholics but also many Protestants as an opponent of the Enlightenment. His promotion of prayer had an influence felt throughout Germany.

cunning, and bossy. Patients with tuberculosis in the lungs often cling to life as to the highest good, etc.

A pastor is not only required to know the general pastoral condition of the person and to improve it. He is not only supposed to lead the impenitent to repentance, the penitent to the peace of God, the believer to the diligence of sanctification, etc., but he should **watch for the mental and moral influences of sicknesses and through the divine Word that works miracles he should overcome the discords of the sick person's soul and threatening temptations and sins.** The person with dropsy should be brought out of the danger of dullness to a serene, lively interest in the wellbeing of his own soul and that of others; the scrofulous child should be made peaceful and full of energy against his temptations; the consumptive should find courage in dying and learn to look forward to death. But if anything is to be achieved, this special part of caring for the sick requires knowledge, the gift of observing, detailed experience, and great skill. Whoever just took a whiff in this profession will soon notice, what an invitation to modesty and humility is coming his way.

C. CONCERNING TEMPTATION AND POSSESSION

One can divide temptations into three different classes:[2]

1. Physical,
2. Spiritual, and
3. Mixed.

Temptations of the first and second group are seldom; the most frequent are those of the third group. If one speaks of physical temptations, one understands temptations of a demonic kind. These are influences of Satan upon the physical condition, be it through unnatural wellbeing or sickness. One understands especially under physical temptations the demonic deceases.

Among spiritual temptations there are the exaggerated and disorderly influences of certain thoughts, desires, and feelings upon the entire condition of the person, be they thoughts, desires, and feelings coming from people or from demons.

One calls a temptation mixed if it originates from one part of the person, either body or soul, and pulls the second part into its realm and power.[3] A

---

[2] Here instead of *Versuchung* we see *Anfechtung*, which can mean temptation, but more in an involuntary sense. Luther often writes of undergoing a difficult trial or being pursued to one's physical and mental limits by satanic malice. God tempts no one but He allows such trials and temptations according to His permissive will.

[3] Although Loehe clearly used a tripartite anthropology earlier, now he focuses on the division of body and soul. Perhaps that can be a question applied to this book in a broad sense. Is Loehe being consistent in his mixing of traditions and sources? How strongly

temptation of this kind need not only develop from a temptation of the first group. Any kind of physical condition of a person, willed by God, can also become the cause for the temptation of his soul.

The **signs** of **physical** temptation are not easy to recognize. Our fathers used to think that there was a demonic-physical temptation if no medical means would work. But this sign in itself is unreliable because it may have been possible that the right medication had not been found. Nothing more than a mere probability can be found this way. The Romans use their exorcisms not only against real possession but also against witchcraft, which is counted among demonic temptations. They assume that there is witchcraft if the evil becomes even more powerful after an exorcism.[4]

However, since not only the devil is a liar, but human nature also is full of deceit, hypocrisy, and dissembling, the use of exorcism alone does not present a certain sign for the existence of witchcraft or demonic temptation, even if we have no objections to it. Therefore one has to give up looking for certain signs and content oneself with the greater or lesser possibility.

The purely **spiritual** temptations are easier to recognize, as long as one does not attempt to find out the source of the temptation, only that it exists. To determine the latter is the most important thing. A spiritual temptation is based either on a false thought, or a false desire or feeling: I am tempted either through thoughts, desires, or feelings. If a person is otherwise reasonable, but despite good gifts and usual sobriety he entertains a thought that is recognizably false and is inclined to follow it in his life, he is tempted, no matter where his temptation comes from. If someone in general has a good purpose and a pure desire, but in a single case cannot get rid of an indecent desire and is tempted to give in to it, he stands in temptation, no matter where it comes from. If someone has some kind of feeling for which there is no reason, which is being resisted by existing reasons, yet he feels the inclination to give in to the feeling, he is in temptation, no matter where it comes from.

---

should one press Loehe on his terms? Is he willing to use terms only insofar as they meet a specific purpose?

[4] The witch craze emerged from the recovery of hermetic literature in the Renaissance, the Great Plague in the mid-fourteenth century, and the growing fascination with both eschatology and phantasmagoria. The exchange of smallpox from the Old World and syphilis from the New World after 1492 only increased epidemics and mortality. Especially women, but also men often were the unjustified targets of fear, brutality, and superstition that had neither theological nor scientific merit. Pope Innocent VIII issued the bull *Summis desiderantes* on 5 December 1484 at the instigation of German inquisitor Heinrich Krämer, the author of the 1486 *Malleus maleficarum*. There followed Jean Bodin's *De la démonologie des sociers* (1580), Nicholas Rémy's *Daemonolatreia* (1595), the *Demonologie* of King James (1597), and an encyclopedia of witchcraft by the Jesuit Martin del Rio (1600). The last witch burnings occurred in the eighteenth century.

If a spiritual temptation, no matter of what kind, influences the physical condition, I may perhaps doubt for a while whether this is the case, or whether it is likelier that a physical condition influences the soul. Yet the mixing of the spiritual with the physical will not make recognizing the existing temptation more difficult, but easier.

One can give hope for **freedom from the burden of temptation** to anyone who is tempted, inasmuch as the very word *Anfechtung* does not indicate the highest degree of suffering, but basically only the beginning of suffering. However, one will do well to place hope itself into the realm of uncertainty and make it dependent in part on the will of God and in part on the behavior of the tempted one. It is plain that God does not want to free everybody, not even his apostle Paul, from temptation that he has permitted. It is also clear that resistant and clumsy behavior of the sick can dull the efficiency of all means. In regard to demonic temptations in particular, one will do well to apply with great emphasis the instruction that one has to give to the tempted person in general about the treatment of his temptation and its importance for his eternal salvation. Demonic temptations, the physical as well as the spiritual ones, are accidental burdens even though they are heavy. One can fully apply to them the verse: **For those who love God, all things have to work together for the best** (Romans 8[:28], Luther).

By explaining this view to the sick person, above all things one must take away the overestimation of his burden [from the ill person], which is the basis for healing and recovery from such evils. Therefore one will have to say and impress upon the tempted one approximately the following:

> Your sickness in itself is not an incurable evil. Therefore you have hope for improvement.
>
> But it is possible that a continuing condition of suffering will bring you the greatest blessing and give greater honor to God. In this case healing is not desirable. You can also put up an obstacle against healing and make it impossible by mistrusting your counselors and pastors, or by disobeying their instructions. In this case you bear the just punishment for your behavior. Above all things you need to give yourself into the hand of the Lord, to have patience if your suffering lasts longer. And if you should get to the point where St. Paul was, to let God be powerful in your weakness, you would be a spectacle for the angels and a joy for God, since He is glorified more when weak Christians bear evil cheerfully than if the evil itself is lifted. You also would be helped as much in the former case as in the latter, because one that is heavily burdened will receive equal help by increasing patience or by lessening the burden.

In this way one correctly limits the hope for getting well and has already prepared, even begun, the help.

As far as the treatment of the persons under trial is concerned, the first thing always has to be to enlighten the patient about his condition and to serve him with the truth. Just like the physician loses the confidence of his patients if he serves them with lies, the soul physician (*Seelenarzt*) who keeps his tempted persons or mental patients in doubt about himself deserves no trust. There can and will be exceptions, but in general one has to say that with tempted persons and the mentally ill one should appeal to what is still there of sound reason by presenting the full truth. Full truth also includes hope or hopelessness, as has been said above. But the truth has to be presented to the sick person calmly and with confidence on the one hand, and with meekness on the other hand. But one must not feign calm and confidence before one has it. One cannot hide from the patient the fact that one has no opinion concerning his suffering as long as one does not have any opinion. The experienced one will not consider it a disadvantage to appear ignorant and inexperienced; he will be so much less disappointed. Only the vain person will always want to play the wise man.

Once it is recognized that there is physical demonic temptation, this is the right means against it:

1. The instruction that was already given for preparation concerning the importance of demonic temptations, which leads to contempt and disdain of the same.
2. The often-repeated and continuing prayer against temptation.
3. Whether or not to perform exorcism—that will remain a question in the Lutheran Church.

Some mental treatment in a different way is possible. If one could succeed to inspire the patient for a great cause or a great truth, he would be raised above his suffering and the power of the good can become so great in him that the demon **gives up** his vain attempt to bring a child of God to fall.

When it comes to spiritual temptations we first have to deal with the class of people whose temptations either consist of false thoughts or in the wrong application of correct thoughts. In both cases the first and most necessary thing to do is to tell the tempted one the full truth about it, as soon as one knows about his condition. [One must] completely contradict his wrong thoughts and come up with the necessary proofs against them. One must not continue to bring new proofs but keep repeating clearly and simply the ones that have been established. But since a tempted person is also about to become a mental patient, one seldom has to deal with his reason and wrong imaginations by themselves. One often must [deal] with his will, or rather ill will. The sick person often does not want to be healed, but gives in to his inner pull and clings to the thoughts that plague him. Therefore one has to deal not only with teaching, but also with punishment, encouragement, and education.

This various application of one and the same truth has to be continued until the victory is won. It takes wisdom and reflection for the application of each individual step, but also great and continued patience. The longer the temptation has lasted, the more time is needed to overcome it. Therefore one cannot expect a fast progress. It is possible that a complete change of surroundings would be very beneficial if the soul physician (*Seelenarzt*) has the authority to order this. If one has to seek the temptation in some great desire, one should not think that the temptation came from a single thought that is the cause of all desire. If it is, the temptation belongs into the first class. With temptation of desire one understands nothing but an inverse measure of the [desire]. For example, a person can come into great spiritual torment (*Seelennot*) either through lack of love or through an excessive measure of love for another person. When treating a person thus tempted, as always one has to be completely truthful. If, for example, there is not enough love, one must not lose the confidence of the tempted person by assuring him that he has enough love but that he just does not recognize it. However, if the sick person [really does] get enough love and just does not recognize it, one should not refrain from communicating this to him, even at the risk of losing his confidence. He can always find it again. The entire treatment has to be based on absolute truthfulness. If there is an overabundance of desire, the treatment is easier than for the lack of it because a contradiction is easier. On the other hand, one often has to wait a long time until the tempted heart lets the divine Word make up for what it lacks. In all cases the divine Word remains the chief means. The change of circumstances and conditions remain useful secondary means.

Under mixed temptations one understands mainly those whose origin is either in the body or in the spirit. But because of the mutual influence between body and soul, they also take hold of the other part of the entire being and pull it into the suffering.[5] It does not make any difference whether they are demonic temptations or whether they can be explained in a natural way. Once the suffering appears, just as the doctor, or pastor, or nurse has to have a clear understanding about what [sort of] evil he is facing, he also has to try to find out whether the temptation of his patient is simple or mixed, and whether it started in the body or in the soul. However, with the obvious and continuing mutual effect between body and soul, some success will happen if the next effort of the soul physician is applied toward the part in which the evil originated. In fact, one should not want to work one-sidedly at all, first with the body and then with the soul, or vice versa. Yet it would be a blessing if from the beginning one could attack that part of the human nature where the temptation originated. From what has been said so far, even if there is no

[5] Again we have no clear explanation of the interaction between body and soul, and how that relates to spirit. Loehe is drawing on his experiences perhaps, but more casuistically than formalistically.

clarity in a particular case concerning the origin of the evil, even the attack on the part that has been dragged along by the other can be blessed. Anyway, it will be proper for a nurse if she first treats the mixed temptation as a simple one and provides the soul with the kind of medicine that it needs. One should treat the unclear, mixed temptation as a simple one. But if one has arrived at this point, the further effect is already indicated in what has been said before.

Because the two subjects are related, we now talk about the condition of **being possessed.** From what has been said before, it is clear than one must not confuse demonic sicknesses and temptations with being possessed. Many demoniacs whom the Lord healed in the Gospel were not possessed; they only had demonic sicknesses.[6] Nor do we talk here about those of whom it is said that they are possessed in their soul; [we talk] simply about those in whose body one or several demons have started to dwell. That means the person is physically possessed; the body has become a home of the devil or of a demon. As to the effect of being possessed, this also can be very different. One can imagine that a man is possessed without the indwelling demon even giving a sign of its presence. One could think about possessed people where others do not know that they are possessed, nor do [the possessed ones] know it themselves. Yet on the other hand, there are enough effects and signs of possession. But they are very manifold, and precisely due to their great variety they are uncertain. Signs can occur [that aid] in the recognition of the possessed person. For example, a possessed one knows things that no person can know in a natural way. To this also belong the foreign languages that possessed people speak.

But possession can also show itself in a tremendous stimulation of lust or of the will. [This happens] especially in being pulled and greatly inclined toward evil or something disgusting and unnatural, so that the person does things he would never do under other circumstances.[7] Possession also shows itself in a strong and unnatural excitement of feelings. Especially feelings of fear signal the beginning of an evil condition. The signs of possession are not merely spiritual but also physical. They show themselves, e.g., in unnatural movements of the inner and outer members of the body, in unnatural strength, dexterity, and quickness of the body and its members. But all these signs in themselves, especially if they are sporadic, are deceptive. On the one hand, the human ability of spirit and emotions is an unsearchable ocean; on the other hand, mental illnesses that have nothing to do with possession frequently also have quite unexplainable and striking effects on the body.

---

[6] Here it would have been helpful if Loehe had provided concrete, specific examples based on clear exegesis.

[7] One could imagine some of the more violent and depraved expressions of homosexual and heterosexual fetishes in this category. Violent video games, pornography, and other stimuli may well have demonic components.

Therefore one must be slow with the explanation that there are signs of possession in this or that person. Part of the bodily signs of possession is also the circumstance, presented in many recent examples, that things and materials that are impossible for the human body to produce, e.g., broken glass, nails, needles, etc., come out of the mouth or other members, and all those who see it feel the greatest astonishment and embarrassment.[8]

As for the beginnings of possession, Satan often is lured through physical circumstances and especially approaches those who have not learned about the Cross or did not know how to apply this teaching. Whoever knows how to bear his cross—as Christ the Lord not only teaches but also grants—is a wonder of God in this world; the temptation of the devil bounces off him.

The ancient teachers say that possession occurs through personal entry of the devil into the body of a person, either through the mouth or another member of the body. According to their witness, and also many examples, all kinds of things precede the act of entering, which the doctors call "hallucinations." Especially at night, the tempted one sees changing forms, animal-like but also human, which come closer, scare him, entice him, and often frighten him in the worst way. He hears things that others sometimes hear, sometimes not. He feels incomprehensible pains in his body and has experiences that can only puzzle others. Finally he gets to the point that he either gets tired of the whole thing or no longer resists and in prayer and faith. Perhaps after another difficult night, he says that everything is different; the devil moved into him. Whether the unusual mental experiences that preceded the entering are real hallucinations or something essential, and whether the entering really happens when a tempted person talks about it; that is a different matter. In any case, the report of the experienced ones from all time periods indicates that possession begins in this way.

As for the treatment of the possessed, there are two ways: The [first is the] regular one of teaching and pastoral care. [The second is] the extraordinary one of exorcism. The most thorough help probably happens in the first way The possessed one, or the one seeming to be possessed, must receive detailed instruction about his own condition, and one should by no means separate the instruction from applying it to the case in which the possessed one finds himself. Light comes through this practical instruction into the depressed soul, which then learns to understand itself and to oppose the burden of its oppressor.

But instruction must be given not only concerning the nature of the evil but also concerning the importance and unimportance (*Wichtigkeit und Unwichtigkeit*) [of the matter] for the guidance of the soul toward eternal life. Every possessed person overestimates the burden and difficulty of his suffer-

[8] Some of this may have its origin in illnesses like pica or in hormonal imbalances that can occur, e.g., with pregnancy. One is driven into the necessity of having to investigate each case, for which the charisma of discerning spirits may be necessary.

ing and does not like to agree with the true statement that possession is like any other kind of suffering. It is a temporary evil that does not hinder the development of the soul for eternity; it may even advance it. Once the possessed one learns this truth and takes up his heavy cross patiently because of this, his condition contributes more to the glory of God as if he had been liberated from it quickly and suddenly.[9]

If the possessed one is an unconverted person, it is even more necessary to guide him on the way of repentance and faith in the strength of his suffering. If Christ becomes his righteousness, he will also be able to become his freedom and his health, and in the midst of suffering his joy will increase. This pastoral way, which of course does not end with the instruction, but must be accompanied with a strengthening of the will, is the noblest and the most blessed. Once the house is full of light and life, which formerly was full of darkness and twilight, it will no longer be comfortable for its hellish inhabitant and he may leave it without the loathsome and onerous demonstrations that accompany the second way [exorcism].

Even with the first way there should be fasting and prayer, which the very mouth of the Lord orders for the healing of the sufferer.[10] But this must happen especially in the second way, both from the side of the sufferer and from the pastor or exorcist. If someone should doubt the legitimacy of the second way, one can easily assure him with the words and actions of Jesus that his way also has its full justification in the kingdom of God. But if someone walks on it, there may indeed be gifts and people with a heroic faith and a wonderful power of prayer that quickly bring this matter to an end. But it could also be that months and years will pass with this treatment, that there will be apparent healings and real relapses, as well as real healings and apparent relapses. No evil will be so full of deception and disappointment, deceit, and discouragement as this one. For this very reason one must attend to this matter with great devotion and patience, and continue with earnest prayer, or also with exorcism, in addition to instruction and pastoral care.

The old Church orders, e.g., the one from Pomerania, contain formulas whose use should make it clear whether a person is truly possessed or not. The Pomeranian formula seems to be worth more, but it does not offer complete satisfaction. Those who deal with this evil in the orthodox (*rechtgläubige*) Church can pass on much wisdom to the following generation. The Pomeranian formula does not contain an instruction for exorcism, not even the prayer for possessed people common in the Lutheran Church. Time must

---

[9] Yet what is truly the crux in this matter? The Fritschels and others in the Iowa Synod, which Loehe helped to create, tended to promote ethics as the proof of baptismal grace in their *intuitu fidei* arguments for election. Grace got lip service while ethics was key. Is Loehe making cross-bearing a similar key here?

[10] Matthew 17:21 is not attested in the earliest and best Greek manuscripts.

bring maturity and insight and give clarity to the spirits before the missing pieces in this matter can be found.

If one can go neither the first nor the second route, one may simply resort to praying for the possessed person and being faithful in doing so.[11]

D. HYPOCHONDRIA AND HYSTERIA[12]

Even though one says that the first illness [hypochondria] is to be ascribed to the male, the second [hysteria] to the female, it cannot be denied that both are related, and without doubt they deserve the greatest attention because the patients that suffer from them are without number.[13] The point of origin of the suffering is the vegetative system of the organism.[14] But here it does not have a firm and limited seat. It changes its location more easily and more often than any other physical suffering. Being first tied to the process of inner breathing,[15] it can appear anywhere in the body where this happens. Therefore while dwelling the lung it can take on the form of a lung ailment. It can wander from the windpipe into the muscular substance of the throat, into the alimentary canal, into the upper region of the kidneys, into the brain, and into the voluntarily moving muscles. At times it can appear as a sickly affection of the alimentary canal, at times as hallucinations or convulsions and spasms. But once a really permanent affliction, a change from the truly normal formation of the parts and their mixture has been formed in any of these organs, its wandering effect has been halted and the special manifestations of this sickness disappear.

With the sufferings that we are contemplating here, especially the mutual exchange with the outer world is slowed down and interrupted. That means that the organic substance loses the kind of tension that enables it to have contact with life-giving air. Every healthy, strong activity of the spirit and of life, every joyful mood promotes interior breathing. Every ongoing inactivity in which there is no real rest because no true labor preceded it: the busy idleness of many life-styles and estates and a joyless mood—these inhibit its progress. One must also point to the quality of food. Some of it furnishes the combustible element which, penetrated by the power of life, sustains breathing, easier and richer, while other food does it in a harder and sparser way.

---

[11] [Loehe:] The following section has been incorporated into the paper of the author concerning mental diseases, which can be found in the first volume of Vilmar's pastoral-theological papers, p. 172.

[12] [Loehe:] From the appendix of the first edition of Loehe's book, p. 229ff.

[13] This falls far short of the modern knowledge of the endocrine system.

[14] This is clearly a term that has no present medical currency.

[15] [Loehe:] Concerning the inner breathing, see Dr. G. H. Schubert's *Die Krankheiten und Störungen der menschlichen Seele* [*The Illnesses and Disturbances of the Human Soul*]. Stuttgart and Tübingen 1845, pp. 11, 12, §5; 132, §18. See also concerning "Hypochondria and Hysteria."

Those workers who earn their living only through a mechanical movement while constantly sitting, perhaps with their hands, and have no change in their work that would increase their attention, are especially inclined toward hypochondria. This goes, e.g., for weavers, tailors, copyists, and many government workers. It also goes for people who, in the overabundance of earthly good have only learned to enjoy but not to produce and work. With them often there is no individual activity.[16]

Since the inner breathing is promoted by a joyful disposition of the mood, but this disposition often is based on an accustomed contentment and satisfaction, which the soul finds in the enjoyments and influences of the accustomed surroundings, the hypochondriac suffering often comes from homesickness, from an unfulfilled longing for a dear habit, now interrupted, for a lost possession.

At times hypochondriac suffering happens because of a relaxation that usually follows a great and joyful exertion of organic activity. The person who first felt like being lifted up to heaven because of inner activity now feels a lack of inner breathing and falls into a deep depression and sadness, just because the excitement is over.

All such conditions and influences of life that cause hypochondria in men give to women even more reasons for hysteria. The manner of living and the occupation of a large part of women are similar to that of the men mentioned above. The helplessness and lonely position of the unmarried or unhappily married women, the natural weakness of the gender, causes much more often and easier inhibitions of powerful movements of life and suppression of a joyful mood, than is the case with men.[17] But the efficacy of the vital energy of the woman, according to her natural disposition is directed more toward a becoming and moving in the vegetative region of the organism, rather than in the mental one. Therefore, with the female sex the manifestations of hypochondriac suffering start and develop mainly in the vegetative region of the organism, mostly in that part that is the most essential for its natural disposition. And thus the hypochondria of the woman becomes basically hysteria, which is inclined more toward cramps and convulsions, while the hypochondria of the stronger sex is free of this suffering, but often shows itself in strange imaginations and temporary entanglements in the upper sphere of mental perceptions and imaginations.[18]

The independent vital activity, on which the healthy progress of inner breathing depends, is stimulated and kept with the man especially through

[16] We now consider cholesterol, circulation, vitamins, diet, exercise, and pollution.

[17] Much natural weakness of the gender was addressed with the development of antibiotics, which made surviving the puerprium much more likely and which led to women generally outliving their "stronger" husbands.

[18] Thus we observe the pseudoscientific basis for the former assertion that menstrual cramps were all in a woman's head. Modern research has disproven this.

mental elements, with the woman mainly through physical ones, for example, through relaxation of the organism after frequent pregnancies and long nursing of the children, or by passing from a very active way of living to a sedentary one. Therefore hysteria often changes to a deep derangement of individual organs of the vegetative region, and consumption ends the hysterical life and suffering, while with a man the change to melancholia and madness is more common.[19]

The individual indications of hysteria point to the reason for it being the slowing down of **inner breathing.** Often the outward breathing, the source of the inner one, is suddenly restrained. Anxiety and oppression rise to convulsions, consciously or unconsciously. The members grow stiff and cold. In general hysterical women constantly complain about being cold. They have icy cold feet and dry skin until suddenly a flying heat comes and with it often shortness of breath and oppression of the chest. A strange change of moods is also connected with these sudden transitions. For hours the patient is happy without any cause and laughs constantly until, again without any reason, she cries and is anxious. All other indications of the sickness are connected with the slowing down of breathing. Hysterical people have little need to drink. Thus there comes an appetite like a ravenous hunger, which soon is stilled with just a few bites. The abdomen swells tremendously but soon collapses again. Choking attacks the alimentary canal, and especially the throat. This, together with the feeling as if a round ball was stuck in the throat, is a characteristic sign of the sickness. Sometimes the hysteric person is overcome by a sudden terrible headache. She does not know how to get hold of herself. Then along comes a friend or an interesting subject, a strange event—all of a sudden the headache is gone.

Things are different with a hypochondriac man. Once his time of work, his business day is over, he sinks back into contemplation of his physical condition. His body is his world. With sickly tension and anxious care he watches all changes in his body. In each of them he imagines dangers of an approaching evil, even of death, which he fears, because he lacks courage to live or to die. He also suffers digestive problems, hiccups, irregular eliminations, lack of appetite, and sees strange images, even though he knows that they are hallucinations (Tasso). With those hallucinations of the depressed hypochondriac there is the serious danger for the weaker patient that they will overpower the will and energy of the sick person and become the center around which the whole of life turns.

The hallucinations of women seem to have a more plastic effect, and often are related to a strange movement of the hollow muscle of the digestive canal. A mouse has crept through the open mouth into the stomach, a living

---

[19] Here we have a very antiquated understanding of tuberculosis, completely devoid of the knowledge of bacteria. When women began to live longer, they also began to suffer dementia like their male counterparts.

frog, a toad, an orange-speckled toad (*Unke*), a water salamander; a snake is in their intestines, they feel it; the cold body of the animal rubs against their stomach; they can feel the feet. Now they feel the bites and one hears sounds like from a frog or a toad. Where the animal is crawling, the body is elevated, and everything is so deceiving that even others start worrying, and yet the animals are only gasses.

The suffering of hypochondria and hysteria, if it increases and if a strong will does not take courage and seriously opposes it, will effect a sickly changed influence, not only on the perceptions and feelings, but also on the attitude of a person. The soul of a hypochondriac eventually will tend toward selfishness, which will disturb his relationship to the outer world to a high degree. His participation is weakened in anything that is not him; the participation of others in him always seems to him too little. The forceful, happy movements of the healthy aggravate him, even make him bitter. He becomes suspicious, probably also hateful toward others, or at least he becomes one-sided in love and in hatred, loves the one passionately and hates the other just as passionately. And because love and hatred are not based on a reasonable recognition, or on a reasonable will, neither love nor hatred will be lasting, but they are changing and wandering, just like the conditions of the sickness itself. Too bad if in such cases there is also a lack of spiritual discipline, which would come by itself with a higher education.

At times the suffering causes the sick person to despair about himself. In many cases this does not take the form of a humble knowledge of oneself, but can exist together with the most arrogant self-elevation. That is if the sick person is looking for the reason for his failure and the frustration of his selfish wishes not in himself, but outside of himself. The conditions of hypochondria and hysteria are very close to that of melancholy. The sick person sometimes becomes so tired of life that death attracts him as powerfully as the voluptuary is attracted by sensual pleasure. At times this is indeed followed by suicide. Another high point of the sickness, namely somnambulism, cannot be concealed here. Somnambulates often carry in their suffering the punishment for their laziness and their ill will against the cure for their soul that is offered to them.

When the doctors prescribe physical means according to what is mentioned above, they should be especially concerned of repairing and lifting the inner breathing. Therefore the doctors advise ocean air, ocean baths, and travel to the sea because the air at the sea is much more compressed than on the heights and contains a much greater amount of air for life. The same is true for cold air; therefore patients of this kind often are better in cold weather than when it is warm. But on the other hand the doctors also recommend the air in the mountains. It may not contain as much substance as the compressed air at the sea, but does influence the process of breathing because of a special kind of tension.[20]

But mental help is more necessary than medical help for the sick. Self-help must be aroused again, and for this a stimulation of the will is needed. Sometimes this succeeds in another way, but the surest one is through complete honesty and truthfulness concerning one's life, and through the call of the Gospel to a complete conversion. One should teach the sick person the causes and the kind of his sickness. One should point out to him that the strange feelings that plague him do have their basis in physical evils, but do not point to evils that would be very important or dangerous. One should show him that the painful sufferings of the soul that he has to bear are part of the sickness. If one is fortunate enough to bring the sick one this far, so that he calmly thinks about his situation, much is already gained. One should also show the sick one especially the great power of the will and the necessity of a reaction against the oppressing feelings, and one should seek to educate his will toward the good and toward obedience. With all this, it will be completely appropriate to teach to understand the individual consequences of the sickness as what they are. One should listen patiently to the complaints of the sick person. The insight that—for the moment—there is no danger from evil should not tempt one to treat the subject in a frivolous, negligent, or even laughing way. With sympathy one should show the sick person in every single case the true reason for his suffering. But one should guard against bringing the sick one into the company of other hypochondriacs or hysterics, since it is well known that even healthy people can be infected by the hysteric evil. One should also keep him from reading medical books. Every day his sick fantasy would only take a new anxiety and a different sickness from them. On the other hand it would be quite right to move his thoughts away from his imagined suffering and terrifying images, and gradually get him used to activity and work.

Very often the sick person is helped by a change in his situation, especially if the seed of the sickness was in the present situation. The hysterical girl often gets well through a marriage. The person who became a hypochondriac as a result of an economical misfortune improves by being transferred to a worry-free situation. All in all, a thorough change of situation is an excellent antidote against this sickness. But without doubt the most excellent remedy is when the worldly person is brought into a different relationship with God. The one stuck in the delusion of repentance is brought to the peace of reconciliation. The one who despaired because of a lack of progress in his faith is brought to an excellent progress in sanctification. Unstoppable progress is the best antidote against all mental diseases.

---

[20] Then again, the mountains and the sea have much less pollution than do, e.g., the industrialized Ruhr valley and the coal fields of Saxony. Today we know why *Stickfluss* (asthma) was a cause for high infant mortality in these places.

E. A VENERABLE SCHEMA FOR SICK CARE

From Felix Bidembach's *Manuale Ministrorum Ecclesiae*, Tübingen, 1603, p. 642.

- In pastoral care of the sick there are three considerations, namely:
  - Beginning, what can be done in such a way so as to show to a sick person
    - 1. The occasion for our visit. Why a minister should be present, in particular
      - If not summoned, then this will show
        - Excluding that one might not be Christian, the principles of the Office, by which the pastor is allowed to come near, admonish, comfort, etc. the sick person.
      - If summoned by the sick person then he either
        - Lets the sick person initiate.
        - He starts making the point.
        - Note: The beginning of the dialogue can be done best according to God's will (Matt. 10:30).
    - 2. The cause of all disease, namely, sin. And that either in
      - General: if nothing else, the patient has or admits that he needs the minister.
      - Particular: Perhaps if a serious wrong has been committed by the sick person.
    - 3. The remedy for sin: repentance, of which consists
      - Recognizing one's sin
      - Contrition for sin
      - Confession of sin.
      - FAITH in Christ.
      - The intent to change one's life, the longer that the use of this light be granted.
  - Middle, to which pertain these:
    - Absolution. The confession of deeds.
    - Communication of the Lord's Supper. The acts of grace.
    - Explanation of the use of the Supper. Consolation, etc.
  - End, which is varied, according to the assessment of the sick person even at the time of our entry. Here pertain:
    - 1. Exhortations toward
      - Patience, especially if the illness be
        - Grave
        - *or*
        - Chronic.
      - Meeting death cheerfully, for there one shall see God.
    - 2. Consolations for dealing with temptation, indeed concerning
      - Admission of sin, etc.,
      - Predestination, etc.,
      - Final perseverance,
      - And likewise various other trials that are considered to arise from these three headings.
    - 3. Final means of support that are of aid at the time of death and are the most effective.
      - Comfort to move the soul
      - prayers on behalf of either
        - His own death
        - *or*
        - the death of others

Appendix C

A Short Treatise on How to Preach Aright and How to Expound and Apply the Sacred Text.

By Dr. Andreas Adam Hochstetter, Theologian at Tübingen

Third edition, edited by Christoph Friedrich Sartorius,
doctor and professor of sacred theology.

Printed 1. 1701; 2. Göttingen 1741; 3. Tübingen 1767; 4. Gütersloh 1876

Translated with annotations by Joshua J. Hayes

* * *

Preface to the First Edition

You have here, dear reader, a short treatise on the right way to craft sermons. I would have preferred it to have been published by the author himself and embellished in his presence, but a sense of modesty prevented him. For eight years he kept it in his personal files until, finally, he reluctantly allowed it to be printed for the Church at large at the request of several people who had become acquainted with its clarity in teaching. It was all written sincerely and for the edification of its readers, so that none of us doubts the fruit such a work as this will produce. May God cause a booklet soon to follow this one on how to catechize aright. Farewell in the Lord Jesus, and pray to God that He may help His Church, which is afflicted and rent into factions, and be ever present with His aid.

New Preface

This treatise was first published anonymously in 1701. As so often happens with small booklets, even to a great and well-known one, it was almost consigned to oblivion, but the sainted Dr. Jakob Wilhelm Feuerlein thought it had merit. He took care to have it republished in 1741 at Göttingen and used it as a guide with his students for explaining precepts for preaching. It seemed good to reprint it so that our [theologians] may have a guide to follow in homiletics. If they want a fuller treatment, along with this book they will take up with advantage an equally approved mentor, the sainted Dr. Johann Christian Klemm's *Centuria paragraphorum regulas, cautelas, et monita homiletica complectentium.* His long awaited *Centuria,* first published in 1744, is conveniently being reproduced this month, which we feel is clearly a good omen. As concerns the present book, we have made no changes from how it was first published except that a mistake was corrected, the titles of cited books have been printed in full, the paragraphs have been more conveniently divided by numbers, and an overview has been added at the end to make the book easier to use. Those who become familiar with this treatise will certainly want in earnest another book on how to catechize aright, as we do. But it is not clear to us, at any rate, that such a book has ever been published. All the more reason is it to be hoped that our theologians will diligently ponder this outstanding book. May they gain great salutary benefit from both the remaining admonishments and advice, as well as from the spiritual insight sprinkled in the precepts throughout and in the opening and final two paragraphs. Tübingen. 4 May 1767.

* * *

Iesu iuva

How to Preach [Aright]

§ 1

Although not only the ancients and those at rest in the Lord but also modern theologians who have distinguished themselves in the orthodox Church have developed all of homiletics with such effort that there seems to be no need for a new primer on it, it still seemed only right to yield to the wishes of friends and to produce something in the fear of the Lord on a subject as useful as it is necessary, which could promote their further good and more easily prepare their spirits for the holy office in the Church. May God grant success! It is with devout invocation of Him that we undertake this subject, which will be sketched out in several short paragraphs.

§ 2

Let the **material** [*materia*] for the sermon be nothing but the biblical text, suitably adapted for the congregation lest there be too many or too few words. [The text] is usually and conveniently divided into the fixed or predetermined and the chosen, appointed by the preacher's free choice.

§ 3

There are two general things that one who is going to preach should especially observe above all.

One is natural knowledge, so to speak, of the text (§ 4).

The second, however, is artistry (§ 19), which surrounds the text itself for the purpose of exposition and explanation.

§ 4

The very **nature of the sacred text** may be discovered from these five things: first, the subject matter must be investigated; then one must proceed to genus and species; there must be an inquiry into arguments; finally, the theme must be decided from these (§§ 5, 6, 9, 10, 12).

§ 5

The **subject matters** in the text are:

1. The articles of the Christian faith, or dogmas set forth in the Word of God for belief.
2. The conduct of the Christian, whether virtuous or depraved.
3. The afflictions that befall us on the way to heaven. You will never read anything in the Scriptures that cannot, nay should not, be ascribed to one of these three categories.

§ 6.

This becomes clear if we recall a little more deeply the **genera** of speaking, which sacred orators draw from 2 Timothy 3:16 and Romans 15:4. Although five of them are enumerated, they do not handle more subject matters than we just listed above.

1. The teaching genus [*genus didascalicum*] defines and inculcates articles of the faith, whether matters of historical fact (James 2:19) or of faith and salvation. The refuting genus [*genus elenchticum*] defends these and refutes contrary teachings.
2. The training genus [*genus paedeuticum*] involves behaviors, commending and encouraging them if they are good, censuring and discouraging them if they are bad. If the latter have gained acceptance among the hearers, the correcting genus [*genus epanarthoticum*] rebukes them more vehemently.
3. The comforting genus [*genus paracleticum*] gives comfort in the face of afflictions and ills.

§ 7

Now, we gladly embrace these genera of speaking, because it is surely better to follow the Holy Spirit's lead, especially in sacred matters, than to bind the sayings of God to the inventions of men. Indeed, we keep to those ancient three words of Irenaeus: "Nothing apart from Scripture." There are some who feel that in these matters the uses and applications should be sought rather than the genera themselves, but they can easily be satisfied if we distinguish the form of teaching, reproof, training, correction, and encouragement situated in the text from a doctrinal, refuting, etc. deduction that flows from the text. Right now our discussion is about the former, then later we will learn about the uses.

§ 8

However, we are not unaware that the genera of speaking of the secular rhetoricians are commonly observed by some in crafting sacred orations. Not [only] Hunnius[1] did this, but also Lucas Osiander in the very elegant book *De ratione concionandi*, which he published in 1582. Still, more than once does he suggest that sermons can be adapted to those genera, but without superstition. Also, since the forth genus of cases, the judicial, is too difficult and obscure, he advocates that students relate those controversies they find in sacred matters to the teaching genus. Nor, he says, can those precepts always be conveniently and beneficially applied to matters of theology.

§ 9

Species are nothing but the various ways the genera are expressed or determined.

In the teaching genus, for example, the species are: all narrations, testimonies, assertions, demonstrations, descriptions, etc.

In the rebuking genus: accusations, defenses, complaints, disputes, denials.

In the training genus: praise, persuasion, dissuasion, encouragement, discouragement.

In the correcting genus: imprecations, threats, discouragement.

In the comforting genus: sympathy, laments, encouragement, promises of God's help, recalling affliction. Hence, you could also apply prayers to this genus.

§ 10

Next follow the **arguments**[2] through which the text is drawn out. Here the preacher must accurately grasp what the text teaches, approves, clarifies or amplifies. To this number, teachers have limited the kinds of arguments to the so-called

1. Explaining, that is, the circumstances as comprised by the common line: "Who, what, where, with what help, why, how, when?" Among these stand out:

    a. Who?, or the subject (or rather, the subject's circumstances to which the situation in the text seems most appropriately fitted or to require fitting)

---

[1] *Methodus concionandi*, p. 8.

[2] On arguments, the above recommended Johann Christoph Klemm has a lengthy discussion in *Centuria Regg. Homilett.*, §§ 38ff.

   b. What?, or the object

   c. How?, that is, an action's form. This can usually be discerned from antecedents and concomitants.

2. Proving, that is, intervening propositions that confirm statements asserted in the text and destroy the reverse.
3. Clarifying (I also include Amplifying). These make the theme clearer whether by comparison, maxim, or example. Moreover, these are either in the text itself or situated outside the text and procured from elsewhere. Of these, note well that one should preferably heed those situated in the text and then those brought in (and of these, those that are closer to the text).

§ 11

If you keep these things diligently, you will detect what is most suitable for creating commonplaces and collections, and you will more easily progress in something that is as arduous as it is controverted.

§ 12

Finally, one must also give thought to the **theme**,[3] which can be either simple or compound. It is commonly called simple when, because it asks nothing, no answer to it can be given in the positive or the negative. The compound, however, is that which has a question in itself and can be either affirmed or denied.

In short, if we are judging the matter correctly, themes are compound in every genus except the teaching genus since everything has something to be refuted, or persuaded or dissuaded, or more vehemently censured. Only the teaching genus has [both] some compound themes (the articles of the faith to be proved) and some simple, which serve to explain the nature of things that must be believed.

§ 13

The **means** for fruitfully accomplishing everything mentioned above are **analyses**:

§ 14

1. Grammatical analysis, which is chief in unpacking the emphases of words and expressions in the source. With this purpose it also examines parallelisms of words as well as of things. As much as possible it does not even omit minor parts of speech, seeing as very often it not only elucidates con-

[3] Translator's note: The theme is "the question itself proposed by the speaker for consideration," Johann Micraelius, *Lexicon Philosophicum Terminorum Philosophis Usitatorum* (Wolfenbüttel: Höpfnerus, 1661), col. 1338.

junctions ("also," "and," etc.) but also lays open the meaning if one pays good attention. On this see especially Glassius, *Philologia Sacra* (bk. 4, tract. 1ff.); also Martin Geier brilliantly leads the way with his own example in his learned commentaries on Psalms, Proverbs, Ecclesiastes, and Daniel.

§ 15

2. Logical analysis, which discerns the connection or disjunction of individual words and also periods. From this it argues and draws conclusions and progresses in this way until it perceives the natural proposition (which is having all the members of the text accurately analyzed) under its components of species and object. If, however, the text is fairly long, it can be broken down into several statements for the sake of this analysis. Regarding context, which here must be accounted for the most, read Glassius, "De Scripturae sensu eruendo tractatus," in *Philologia Sacra*, bk. 2, p. m. 351 (new ed., p. 492). Also consult the outstanding exegete Sebastian Schmidt throughout his commentaries, but especially in *Paraphrasi Evangelii S. Johannis*. This, above all his other works, should be commended to our theologians.

§ 16

3. Rhetorical analysis, which unwraps tropes and figures in the sacred text. On these consult Glassius, *Rhetorica Sacra.*

§ 17

At this point one must also think about moving the passions, because, as Augustine[4] said: "It is not only the sacred orator's duty to teach, but also to persuade and move hearts." See Fr. Johann Benedict Carpzov, *Hodegeticum*, membr. 50, aphor. 9, where he commented on the arguments to arouse disgust of sin, love of virtue, and hope and trust in God.

§ 18

On this point the following will also be serviceable: what the very learned Edward Reynolds wrote in English *On the Passions*; and in French, Le Pere Senault's very beautiful treatise *Des Passions de l' Ame.* Also Abbas Brettevillanus in *Eloquentia Cathedraria et Forensi* (Paris: 1689). Above all, he very eloquently explores the remedies of the passions. Johann Joachim Zentgraf, the phoenix of the German moralists, once improved this material in *Collegio Theologiae Moralis*. Also on this subject, Spener provided something remarkable, which you will only find in his *Die Lebens-Pflichten*. See also blessed Gerhard's *Schola Pietatis* and his homilies, *passim*. Dannhauer has good advice (*Hermeneutica Sacra*). He says that the homilist, as interpreter, should be very conscious of the writer's mood and imitate him as

[4] *De doctrina Christiana*, bk. 4, ch. 11 and 17.

much as possible. Dr. Seligmann of Leipzig should also be admirably commended, to whom I freely and happily admit I owe much.

§ 19

We called the second thing that one who is going to preach should observe, **artistry**. This has to do first with method (§ 20), the series of parts (§ 23), invention (§ 46), and ornamentation (§ 47).

§ 20

Method is twofold (we have kept the distinction that some today attack): Analytic and Synthetic. The analytic [method's] role, as the word suggests, is to ἀναλύειν, that is, to break down the text into its parts, to explain the force of words and expressions, and then to tie in the teachings that flow from there. On the other hand, the synthetic [method] draws out a commonplace from the text and confirms and amplifies it with arguments situated in [the text] (and these chiefly) and those situated outside [the text].

§ 21

This is the general and most common division of method, and others have shown that the fourfold division into periphrastic, dogmatic, articulated, and thematic does not contradict it. For, the so-called periphrastic, dogmatic, and articulated can be ascribed to the analytic method, while the thematic is seemingly the same as what others call the synthetic method.

§ 22

Moreover, this distinction between analytic and synthetic method should be derived from arrangement and proposition, for it is either the same as the text's [method] and thus analytic, or it is textual deduction, or synthetic. Pliny's words apply here: "I think that **order** is the one thing from which most of the whole speech's clarity, grace, and delightfulness usually comes."

§ 23

Among **the parts of a sermon**, the first that stands out is the **opening** [*exordium*]. (It's pointless here to discuss prefaces, for they are not used everywhere and usually make for a disagreeable sermon while very rarely gaining an eager and ready ear.) It serves as a sort of gateway and entrance to the oration and should fit with the argument of the text and the scope. Above all, brevity and clarity merit commendation in an opening. Long openings usually tire the hearer the less attentively to hear the rest, though skilled allusions should not be shunned when necessity calls for such a thing.

§ 24

Openings can be taken:

1. From the subject itself or praise of the subject we are treating. Or it may proceed
2. From a general assertion to something more specific, a hypothesis, whether regarding actions, promises, or threats. For example, if in our proposition[5] we are going to discuss Paul's captivity, we might speak in the opening about the discomforts and misery of captives in general.
3. Likewise, from antecedent to result. For example, if our speech is on the Redeemer's kindness, then we can begin with our antecedent wretchedness, in other words, a pathetic description.
4. Or from examples or contrasts, things that are related, contrary, or independent. Take the twenty-second Sunday after Trinity, for example. If the proposition is that men, being slaves of God, must be called to give account, then the opening could be taken from the related contrast that God is our Lord.
5. Or even from the circumstance of place—for example, the dedication of temples[6]—or of time—for example, on festival days and anniversary celebrations of a benefit from God (Deuteronomy 4:9–10)—or of persons. Be advised, however, that in sacred sermons, goodwill is not suitably enough gained from the part of the speaker just as it is very often not possible to gain it from the part of the hearers without raising suspicions of flattery, though you might find one or two exceptions. For example, if a pastor regains his health, he could begin with Philippians 2:27.
6. Or from coherence of the text. When a continuous biblical text is being expounded, some replace the opening with a repetition of the main things that are in the earlier part of the text. This summary (ἀνακεφαλαίωις) should be brief lest the preacher give the appearance of laziness. The speaker needs wisdom in this matter, to be sure, and he will strive mightily to always bring new vigor in the opening like little flames that affect people's inward being so that the hearers' hearts may be the more ardently raised to God.

[5] Translator's note: The proposition, or "setting forth," is the portion of a speech where one begins to speak on the topics he promises to address; see Micraelius, *Lexicon Philosophicum*, col. 1151.

[6] Translator's note: "Temples," that is, church buildings where God dwells with His people in Word and Sacrament.

There are those who derive openings from an abrupt succession, which at times is irreproachable. (See Nicolas Caussinus, *De eloquentia sacra et civili*, VI, 7, pp. 242, 251.)

§ 25

Furthermore, there are about three parts to an opening:

1. The introductory proposition (πρότασις). Sometimes the main proposition itself is elegantly contained here.
2. Ἔκθεσις, a sort of brief explanation made by a comparison, saying, or example.
3. There is the departure or transition to the proposition. Without omitting an account of the text, this should flow quickly from the opening. Johann Olearius, [*Oratoria ecclesiastica*], listed seven parts of an opening, but needlessly so.

§ 26

The second part of a sacred oration—the Archimedean point, so to speak, on which the whole sermon can be turned and arranged—is the **proposition**. This will be in accordance with the difference of method, be it analytic or synthetic.

§ 27

The analytic posits the aim of the text by the arguments of what will be said. It's nothing else than (as Carpzov defines it) pointing out the very argument of the text in brief and clear words. For example, if you wanted to make your proposition from the Gospel for Trinity 21, then the aim of that [pericope]—the healing of the nobleman's son—could be adduced in place of the proposition too.

§ 28

A synthetic proposition, however, is one that posits a commonplace drawn out from the text. So, using the same Gospel [for Trinity 21] for example, you could make the synthetic proposition: "faith tried in the cross." An opening from 1 Peter 1:7 would fit especially well here. Incidentally, it must be noted that it is sometimes elegant to state the proposition in the opening phrases. If this cannot be done nicely, then one should at least keep in mind that [the proposition] will be the more welcome the closer it is to the opening thought. Hence, it easily becomes clear that we cannot give our assent to some learned men who have said that a commonplace cannot be mentioned in the opening, for that is the function of a synthetic proposition. Indeed, one must distinguish between a commonplace, which can be proposed, and its use, which cannot.

§ 29

The next and third part of a sermon is the **division** [*partitio*]. This is nothing other than dividing the proposition into those things that it immediately contains. Now, the sacred orator should not neglect this so that the hearer may very clearly understand what to expect about the given proposition, what it is, and to what in particular he should relate everything he is going to hear. Here belongs blessed Hunnius's advice [*Methodus concionandi*, p. 12]: "The division should be so arranged that it encapsulates the whole text without omitting even the smallest bit of the text that is not contained within some part that has been mentioned here."

We will just mention *homoioptoton*[7] and *homoioteleuton*[8] (in which some seek nearly all beauty, but how wisely?). And let the cultivator of homiletics take notice that propositions are explained and divided by almost all the commonplace arguments: through opposites, causes, effects and side-effects, circumstances, parts—both essential and integral—from utility, necessity, etc., through entire propositions, and other ways mentioned elsewhere.

§ 30

The **prayer** [*votum*] is a sort of appendix to the proposition and division where one asks for God's help fruitfully to accomplish this sacred task. Although prayers are poured out before beginning, usually from 2 Corinthians 13:[14], and continued by the Lord's Prayer, it is still a fitting plan to add yet a third group of prayers, since God's house is a house of prayer and the task being performed by the one praying and also the hearer is utterly heavenly and divine—the most important by far. Therefore, we justly disapprove of the habit of some who omit such pleas and prayers (which, I recall, was done by even a famous preacher) out of a misguided zeal for brevity; but surely some other things, perhaps less useful, could have been omitted or at least abridged rather than the prayers, which our Savior commanded to be poured out continually (ἀδιαλείπτως).

§ 31

The fourth and most chief part of a sacred oration is the **treatment** [*tractatio*] (which secular rhetoricians call the "confirmation"). It is nothing other than a fair explanation of the argument proposed and it consists of two parts: **exposition** (§ 32) and **application** (§ 34).

---

[7] Translator's note: Repeating words that have similar case endings.

[8] Translator's note: Similarity of endings of adjacent or grouped words.

§ 32

In rightly constructing the exposition, one will observe the three analyses given in § 13ff. Now, this should by no means be solely about the words but, if you want to undertake this fruitfully, the contents of the text analytically.

1. First, one should consider, order, and divide [the text] into its particular parts (this is the second division [Carpzov, *Membr.*, 2, aph. 3, § 1] and rightly orders all the parts of the text among themselves), that is, by showing what is the aim, the occasion, the circumstance of place or time. For example, if [the exposition] considers the time of writing of the Epistles (on this see C. H. Sandhagen, *Harmonia*) it will never be praised enough: what is its subject, its suitableness.
2. Then, one should move to a study of the way the text speaks and explain the kind of speaking and the emphasis of words and phrases. Next, if there is disagreement among interpreters, only that interpretation should be mentioned in the sermon, which, based on the context and diligent study of what precedes and follows (here I am referring also to the reliability of the best manuscripts), you perceive aims most of all at the present aim of the Holy Spirit. And since doubts tend to arise sometimes in the minds of the hearers from the false interpretations of adversaries and seemingly contradictory passages, these should be removed wisely, and it should be briefly shown how even the everyman can give a sound answer to them and how the text can and should be reconciled with this or that doubt. From these, then, will arise a true paraphrase (which must be accurately distinguished from metaphrase; such is the doctors' rule about Luther: he did paraphrase, not metaphrase).[9] Among former scholars, Erasmus of Rotterdam gave a most brilliant example of [paraphrase] in *Paraphrasis N. T.*; from more recent scholars, see Sebastian Schmidt, also Johann Adamus Osiander, chancellor at Tübingen, in an unpublished manuscript. Hochstetter, his executor, mentioned this work with high praise and, I hope, will not allow its publication to be put off.

§ 33

One should not overlook here what we said in § 10 about the three kinds of arguments. These should ever be at hand so that what has been said may be amplified and illustrated through sayings, comparisons, examples, and, wherever suitable, by the inclusion of morals. This is where digressions should belong, which we mention in passing. Finally, although in § 20 we said that in the synthetic method a commonplace is treated, one should still

---

[9] Translator's note: Metaphrase is translating or explaining word-for-word in a hyper literal fashion, whereas paraphrase goes phrase by phrase.

note that an exposition of the text obtains in that method just as much as in the analytical. For, though the analytical is more given to exegesis, [in the synthetic method] the exposition itself should still show the basis for one's deduction, because in the synthetic a commonplace or deduction was proposed from the text. Otherwise, we might seem to have spoken beyond the text. Commonplaces should arise from the text like branches and rely upon the text as their foundation, lest in reverse order the plow go before the ox.

§ 34

The second requisite part of the treatment is the **application** of that which has just been explained from the text according to commonplaces (§ 35; the position of this is not prescribed but free) and logical inferences (and among these in particular [§ 36] observations) and then through the five uses or at least those that especially flow from the text (§ 37). Note well: [the use should be] suitably adapted to the hearers.

§ 35

Commonplaces should be drawn out from the text, not brought into it. Thus, let the hearer understand that we are setting forth only what is divine dogma, as Peter teaches: "He who speaks in church, as one who speaks oracles of God" (1 Peter 4:11). For "faith comes from the Word of God," says Paul (Romans 10:17). Moreover, not every deduction from a commonplace or logical inference that could be said needs to be said (this is usually the cause of sermons that are, if not long, at least inapt and annoying to the hearer), but those that especially and naturally follow from the very heart of the text. Neither should quantity but rather gravity of arguments be considered. Let it suffice to mention one or two of them and illustrate them with a quote, comparison, or example.

§ 36

It is called observation when after expositing the text you draw out more deduction from the circumstances and parts of the text and set them forth for consideration by the hearers. This way of handling [the text] is truly elegant and helpful, but it is still more difficult and especially more common to those who are naturally prolific. We will offer and consider as examples in practice what Carpzov mentioned (*Memb.* 2, aph. 7) about how to mix and blend the exposition of a text together with its application, though nothing can be fixed for certain about this (as he himself admits) nor (I might add) should such a thing be attempted except by practiced theologians.

§ 37

Therefore, having given due consideration to these things, one should move on to use. He should apply that which is formally contained in the sacred text or drawn out from it through a doctrinal commonplace or observations to the consciences of the present hearers. He should also note how the orthodox teaching of our Church is thereby confirmed, how opposing [teachings] can be refuted, virtues commended, vices censured, and finally how the afflicted and weak can be raised up.

§ 38

The first use is the teaching use, where a doctrine of the faith or moral teaching proposed in a commonplace or in observations is applied to the present hearers and commended and inculcated for their pious and devout consideration, so that they may be instructed about performing their duty on this matter. Such is the case (to clarify this with an example) when the sermon is about an article of the faith, and they nicely apprehend God's revealed truth, which sounds forth in our Church even now. Here one could advantageously appeal to the Augsburg Confession, the Creeds, and especially our catechism.

§ 39

The second use is the refuting use, which refutes contrary teaching. In this use, the preacher should be very careful not to attribute to an adversary what he did not claim. Hence, if the issue is with the Papists, it is not useless to appeal (briefly though) to the public teaching of the Roman Church as set forth in the Council of Trent, the Roman catechism, or in Canisius's catechism, which is more generally had in hand. Some people certainly think it seems better not to mention outdated and antiquated heresies. It is prudent not to warn when no warnings are needed, for there are many more evils from contemporary enemies threatening the Church than for us to be anxious about unnecessary and practically outdated ones. How one should proceed circumspectly with this use in a persecuted church was taught by the reverend leaders of [the University of] Strasburg, especially Isaak Faust. He, while the Jesuits Johann Dex of France and P. Baumgartner of Bavaria were shouting and raging most harshly, chose to calmly dismantle their objections rather than return the shouting.

§ 40

Next comes the correcting use, which censures sins that militate against the text or a teaching set forth from it. To usefully undertake this:

1. The sins that especially beset the present hearers must be exposed, and one should appeal to their consciences, as to whether or not most have been disobeying the Word that has been preached[10] so far, since, as for the rest, those who preach it have not omitted any of it at all. (See Jeremiah 25:3; Hosea 11:7; Acts 20:26.)

---

[10] Translator's note: Read *praedicato* instead of *praedicatio*.

2. The severity of such sins and how unfit it is for a Christian to indulge in them must be shown; especially seek proofs from the text.
3. Finally, the threat should be added such as, for example, Leviticus 30:14ff.[11]

Above all, the correction must be free from an overly harsh spirit so that the hearers may know that we have undertaken these correctives only out of love for them and the desire to promote their welfare. To this end, one might also advantageously employ figures, for example, entreating renunciation [*detestatio*]—where the speaker asks "for the love of God," "by the wounds of the Lord Jesus," "for thought of one's salvation"—omission [*praeteritio*], apostrophe, etc. (On these see *Praxis*.)

§ 41

The fourth use is the guiding or admonishing use, where from the text or a teaching drawn from it the hearers are admonished of their duty so that they may cease from what is evil and pursue what is good with all their heart's might (Hebrews 12:14). But a bare admonition is not enough. The following must also be added:

1. Arguments or incentives to rouse the hearers effectually to show obedience. These come from necessity, virtue, utility, beauty.
2. One must also show what it means to follow so that we can more happily and easily progress in the pursuit of piety. Sometimes it's productive to encourage remembering admonishments by a certain and almost daily reminder [*symbolo*]. We shall clarify this by the splendid examples Theodorus Dassovius once showed us.
3. Last, preachers usually employ certain figures of speech in this use, though perhaps without realizing it, such as apostrophe, candor [*licentia*],[12] repetition [*epizeuxis*], exclamation, amplification [*expolitio*], summarizing [*epiphonema*], epistrophe,[13] climax [*incrementum*], anaphora, reasoning [*aetiologia*], etc.

§ 42

Finally, the fifth use is the encouraging or comforting use, which answers to the bodily and spiritual ills that typically oppress the faithful in this life. To rightly undertake this:

[11] Translator's note: There is no Leviticus 30. Perhaps Leviticus 19:14ff.

[12] Translator's note: Especially when one asks permission or forgiveness of the audience to speak frankly.

[13] Translator's note: Ending sentences or phrases with the same word(s).

1. It can be fitting first to describe the anguish and magnify its circumstances, especially if it arises from spiritual affliction. Indeed, experience shows that it is not very helpful for the afflicted if [the preacher] immediately negates every reason for their suffering.
2. The grounds for consolation should be sought from the text, but if they cannot be procured from there, then they must be derived elsewhere from the sources of Israel's river.[14] The comforts must be placed in opposition to the calamities, and some are in the habit of making them memorable by one or two tokens.
3. Sacred speakers often use figures as well, such as apostrophe, etc. Contrary, almost, to one's expectation, this happens among all the best preachers and without any affectation. For in these things one's care should hardly be seen at all, and "to avoid artistry is the highest art," says Quintilian (*Instit. Orat.*), where he discusses concealing one's artistry.[15] "The appearance of artistry and cunning diminishes the speaker's credibility and removes his authority" (Cicero, *De inventione*, bk. 1). "The affected speech loses grace. Excessively rhetoricizing in sacred matters befits the preacher as a boy's clothes, patched together from many colors, befits the serious, venerable, grey-haired speaker" (Lucas Osiander, *De ratione concionandi*, p. 71).

§ 43

The conclusion remains, the fifth and final portion of a sacred oration. Rhetoricians usually divide it into two parts, the review [*enumeratio*] and the admonition, both of which find their place in the conclusion.

§ 44

1. The review, according to Cicero, "is that through which the things said in various places are gathered into one place and viewed together for the sake of remembering them. This causes the hearer to recall them to memory and at the same time believe there is nothing else he should need." Cicero, the greatest of orators, continues: "Moreover, this is given as a general rule for the review, that from each part of the argument, since the whole cannot be restated, one should select that which will have the most impact and mention each as briefly as possible so that the memory, not the speech, seems to be renewed" (*De inventione*, bk. 1, ch. 52).

---

[14] Translator's note: That is, Scripture.

[15] *Institutio Oratoria*, bk. 4, ch. 1.

§ 45

2. Following the review is added a serious and weighty admonition to rouse the hearers so that they take to heart what has been said and apply its precept to the ways of their life.

Sometimes, however, the review of parts is omitted (though it is most helpful) and this latter part of the conclusion is immediately given, whereby the hearers' spirits are struck by the manifest gravity and necessity of the matter and are given a sting, so to speak.

§ 46

Invention and the right way to arrange [*disponendi*] the text should also be mentioned now, but Carpzov has already said more than enough on this. Moreover, it is for others to judge whether variation can be useful for the arrangement of a given text if it has been extended even to a hundred. But I do at least advise that the use of concordances to find arrangements should not be spurned. With these, if you want to unpack a word in the text that stands out from the rest, you will hardly ever lack something for the sermon opening and a way to adorn the proposition supplied from the natural form. Nevertheless, be careful that the text does not seem to have to be adapted to the opening, since the opening should be adapted to the text.

§ 47

Regarding embellishment, there is no reason for the studious reader of sacred Scripture to be anxious, for [Scripture] itself teaches every genus with arguments that embellish. Still, I am presupposing an awareness of rhetorical figures and experience with the three ways (mentioned above [§§ 14–16]) to resolve [questions].

Appendix

§ 48

As an appendix, authors on sacred oratory usually give a study on elocution, memorization, delivery [*pronunciatio*], and finally, the way to write sermons. We will discuss these briefly.

§ 49

First, preachers differ greatly regarding the **character of one's speaking**, or **elocution**. For there are some (as blessed Hunnius studiously observed[16] and day-to-day experience teaches) who delight in a grand, almost princely kind of speaking, while others, from a sort of levity, act more like buffoons than preachers. Some use irksome tautology, repeating the same thing over and over again with barely changed wording, heaping together many syno-

---

[16] *Meth. conc.*, p. 31.

nyms that have no particular nuance. These all clearly do not understand what kind of speaking is appropriate in church. Indeed, those who have an affectation for excessive elegance in their speaking usually preach without fruit, since the people cannot understand them. They clearly forget the apostle's word in 1 Corinthians 2:1: "Not with lofty speech or wisdom."

§ 50

They deserve equal, nay, greater censure who employ scurrilous speech in the church and expose themselves and their sermons to the hearers' contempt, completely unaware of how they should rightly comport themselves in the house of the living God (1 Timothy 3:15). Finally, they have more words than ideas who revel in excessively copious speech and who fail to reach the primary objective of the sermon, which is edification.

§ 51

Therefore, the best kind of speaking is used by those who preach in clear and simple language that can be understood by the learned and unlearned alike. This is the way of speaking our Savior employed as He so comprehended the greatest of matters, even the mysteries of the kingdom of heaven, in parables drawn from the average use of things in a familiar way without pomp and glory. His parables are not difficult if you learn what "the kingdom of God" means (see Sandhagenius, *Harmoniam*, and that of Usserius[17]). Following this [kind of speaking], the apostle of the Gentiles declares of himself that his preaching among the Corinthians was not founded on words persuasive to human wisdom but by a show of the Spirit and power (1 Corinthians 2:13), "lest the cross of Christ become empty" (1 Corinthians 1:17; 2:4).

§ 52

Therefore, they are chiefly to be praised who have so diligently read the sacred writings that they can express most things they want to say using words and phrases from Scripture that are also known to the hearers. Though this should not be taken to mean that the speaker is not free to speak his thoughts in his own words; for the sermon should be shaped according to the meaning of Scripture, not its syllables.

Blessed Luther's style is praised above all by the most influential theologians, as is Balduin's (whom Carpzov recommended as a wonderful example in his time to his hearers, *Hodegeticum*, membr. I, aphor. XI) and also blessed Johann Ardnt's in *Postilla* and *Psalterio*, which is clearly beyond compare.

---

[17] *Harmonia Evangelica, wie solche in Iacobi Usserii Bibliothek gefunden, cum praef. b. Franckii*. Hall, 1699, 8vo.

§ 53

The second thing usually treated in the appendix is **memorization.** You see, because sermons today are not usually read from the page (as is customary among the English) but recited from memory to the people, there is surely a need for the service of the memory so that we may be able to remember things reliably and suitably express them to the people.

§ 54

Nothing helps and strengthens the memory better than if we correctly capture the actual structure of the sermon in our mind; if the arrangement of parts has been well ordered and the texture, so to speak, is skillfully put together; and if we thoroughly grasp the arguments we assigned to each part, whether they explain, prove, or amplify. In this way it will surely happen that, having devoutly invoked the eternal Godhead, our preacher will not have anything to complain about when it comes to his memory.

§ 55

This concludes my discussion on the surest and most prominent memory aid. Whoever so desires may urge the conception of images. I see that Daniel Georg Morhofius does this (*Polyhist.*, bk. 2, c. 6, pp. 364–65). We leave this free here for everyone to decide. The author of *Commentarium Rhetoricorum ad Herrennium* (bk. 3, chs. 16–17) recommends [using] places and thinks that images should be placed in them.[18] But one cannot have such an artificial place when he must preach two, three, or even more times per week. In reciting a speech from memory, some use certain letters and words sparingly as signs and markers (see Morhofius, *loc. cit.*, p. 376).

§ 56

The third item in the appendix is **delivery** [*pronunciatio*]. For though the hearers must attentively listen to and obey the Word of God however it is recited to them, delivery still carries great importance, that it be pleasing and appropriate so that they may hear the preacher gladly and without annoyance. For though the voice cannot be faked, rather one must use the one God gave him, we can still suitably regulate it and partially improve it. This will happen easier if we kindly ask our loved ones to advise us freely about defects in our delivery and if we honestly get rid of or fix what they have suggested.

§ 57

Moreover, Cicero lamented in his day that everyone thought it was hardly possible to write clearly about the voice and gesture, since these things

---

[18] Translator's note: The author of this ancient work, once thought to be Cicero, describes the common practice of memorizing a speech by associating its parts with memorable places and images, such as rooms in a house and their contents.

relate to our senses. After he gave precepts about delivery, he concluded thus: "I am not unaware of how great a task I have undertaken in having made an attempt to describe the motions of the body with words representing sounds in writings. I did not believe it was possible to write about these things suitably enough, and if it were possible, I would not think that what I have done will prove useless, because it was my intention here to advise what is needed. The rest we will leave to practice" (*Ad Herenn.*, bk. 3, chs. 11, 15).

§ 58

The first and most important thing Cicero (ibid., ch. 12) teaches is this: "It's helpful for vocal endurance to start with a subdued voice. What is more disagreeable than shouting in the opening of a speech? Pauses strengthen the voice, at the same time making thoughts more elegant by dividing them up and giving hearers time to think."

Therefore, in starting a sermon one should use a subdued tone, which may then be raised somewhat in the middle of the speech according to the nature of the subject matters, yet without ever being raised beyond one's ability.

§ 59

The preacher should also apply this wisdom so that he employs a moderated speech when he is simply teaching; but when he vehemently reproves or exhorts, he should exert his voice greater, adapted to the matters at hand. In brief, flee all affectation. The unnatural and foreign is truly unpleasant, but a natural delivery (unless faulty) is the most pleasing of all, to which should be added moderation in countenance and the dignity befitting a theologian who remembers that he is not acting on his own behalf but God's.

§ 60

Therefore, the delivery should not be dull nor the sermon recited in monotone. Diversity of subject matters demands variety in vocal inflection. No one syllable of a word should be so stressed that the rest are barely expressed or not heard distinctly enough. The final syllables of a sentence should not be neglected so that we seem to swallow them. Rather, let these be understandable. Finally, no letter that does not belong at the beginning should be put there "a-n, n-a-dass, 'dass." These blemishes have been thoroughly documented by Lucas Osiander (pp. 84–85). We said that the voice should be natural, and it is especially in this that skillful delivery consists, if we flee artificiality in the voice. And thus the voice should not be shouting, the delivery neither too hurried nor too slow and sluggish. Commas should not be confused so that poor timing ruins the context.

§ 61

Lastly, on gestures, Osiander has long since judged: "Just as all gestures are not simply rejected, so also moderation is required. For it is the tongue, not the hands or fingers, that must do the speaking. Actors should not be imitated on this, nor even the ancient, secular orators who dealt with civil cases, not theological ones before the people."

§ 62

It remains for us to touch briefly on **the way to write sermons.** Clearly the zeal and effort of those who write down their whole sermons verbatim and recite them nearly word for word is worthy of all praise and admiration. For thus it is not easy for something potentially offensive to the hearers to slip by improvidently.

§ 63

But since this way of speaking can become difficult as one ages and his pile of work grows, blessed Lucas Osiander the elder, and Aegidius Hunnius, those brightest of authorities, think it preferable for the preacher to learn how to express with premeditation those things whose arguments and gist he has in his memory so that, as he is speaking, he may select the words and phrases that are needed to convey his mind's thought and that suit the context.

§ 64

Nevertheless, let our theologians, even those who still enjoy the use of a good memory, bear in mind that it is more purposeful to take up this labor for the sake of the Church and diligently commit to memory what they have first expressed in writing. Therefore, they should surely be chastised most severely who, unnecessarily relying on the quality of their natural eloquence, blather on extemporaneously about whatever rolls off the tongue. In something so needful and serious that concerns the glory of God—the hearers' eternal salvation—they unashamedly act and speak with negligence before God, the Church, and the holy angels. One day they will have to give a grave account to the Chief of pastors for their open impiety and intolerable carelessness.

§ 65

Contrariwise, if the preacher approaches speaking with forethought, he will be able to speak more from the heart and persuade all the more. Thus he will confirm his faith before God and the Church, and by his diligence stir up the gift of God that is in him. Then finally he will sense a further increase in God's grace, and having finished his course well, he will receive from the

Lord Christ's hand the enduring crown of life. To Him be honor and glory forever and ever.

* * *

These, then, seemed to be the admonishments that had to be given here about the due formation of the sacred orator. Even as I proposed them in the fear of the Lord and with the sole intent of building up the Church God redeemed by His own blood, so I openly trust that in the Lord this labor will not prove vain. I again earnestly pray God almighty that He will shape and send workers into His harvest, and mercifully grant a heavenly increase and every kind of blessing as our pastors do the watering. Amen.

* * *

An Overview of What Will Be Considered in This Treatise on How to Preach

A. The internal structure of an oration.
- I. The material of the sacred oration (§ 2)
- II. It's due formation (§ 3), for which are required
  - 1) An understanding of the nature of the sacred text (§ 4)
    - A. Which is discerned from these five things
      - a) Subject matter (§ 5)
      - b) The genera of speaking (§§ 6–8)
      - c) Species (§ 9)
      - d) Arguments (§§ 10–11)
      - e) Theme (§ 12)
    - B. Reached by the help of analysis (§ 13)
      - a) Grammatical (§ 14)
      - b) Logical (§ 15)
      - c) Rhetorical (§§ 16–18)
  - 2) Artistry (§ 19)
    - A. Which involves method, which is
      - a) Analytic
      - b) Synthetic (§§ 20–22)
    - B. Reached by the help of analysis (§ 13)
      - a) The opening, of which the following are listed
        - i. Its requirements (§ 23)
        - ii. Its sources (§ 24)
        - iii. Its parts (§ 25)
      - b) The proposition (§ 26), which is

i. Analytical (§ 27)
ii. Synthetic (§ 28)
c) Division (§ 29), and its appendix, the prayer (§ 30)
d) The treatment itself (§ 31), which consists of
i. Exposition (§§ 32–33)
ii. Application (§ 34)
1. To commonplaces (§ 35)
2. To observations or deductions (§ 36)
3. To uses (§ 37), which are
a. Teaching (§ 38)
b. Rebuking (§ 39)
c. Correcting (§ 40)
d. Guiding (§ 41)
e. Encouraging (§ 42)
e) The conclusion (§ 43), which has two parts
i. Review (§ 44)
ii. Admonition (§ 45)
C. Invention (§ 46)
D. Embellishment (§ 47)
B. The outward appearance of the oration, which is a discussion on (§ 48)
I. Elocution or the character of one's speaking (§ 49), the requirements of which are
1) Some negative, lest one err
A. Either in excess (§ 49)
B. Or in defect (§ 50)
2) Others positive (§§ 51–52)
II. Memorization
1) Its necessity (§ 53)
2) Helps (§§ 54–55)
III. Delivery (§§ 56–60) and gestures (§ 61)
IV. The way to write sermons (§ 62)

Scripture Index

Old Testament

John

Acts

Romans

1 Corinthians

9780758650276.